Re...Pedagogy for a Digital Age

Through a critical discussion of the issues surrounding the design, sharing and reuse of learning activities, the second edition of *Rethinking Pedagogy for a Digital Age* examines a wide range of perspectives on effectively designing and delivering learning activities to ensure that future development is pedagogically sound, learner-focused, and accessible. This powerful book:

- examines the reality of design in practice
- analyses design within complex systems
- discusses the influence of open resources on design
- includes design principles for mobile learning
- explores practitioner development in course teams
- presents scenarios for design for learning in an uncertain future

Illustrated by case studies from across disciplines and supported by a helpful appendix of tools and resources for researchers, practitioners and teachers, the second edition of *Rethinking Pedagogy for a Digital Age* is an essential guide to designing for 21st Century learning.

Helen Beetham is an independent e-learning researcher and writer, and has worked as a consultant in the UK Higher Education sector since 2001.

Rhona Sharpe is Head of the Oxford Centre for Staff and Learning Development at Oxford Brookes University, UK and a Higher Education Academy National Teaching Fellow.

Rethinking Pedagogy for a Digital Age

Designing for 21st Century Learning

Second Edition

Edited by Helen Beetham and Rhona Sharpe

Routledge
Taylor & Francis Group

NEW YORK AND LONDON

First published 2007
This edition published 2013
by Routledge
711 Third Avenue, New York, NY 10017

Simultaneously published in the UK
by Routledge
2 Park Square, Milton Park, Abingdon, Oxon OX14 4RN

Routledge is an imprint of the Taylor & Francis Group, an informa business

Library of Congress Cataloging in Publication Data
Rethinking pedagogy for a digital age : designing for 21st century learning /
edited by Helen Beetham and Rhona Sharpe. — Second edition.
  pages cm
  Includes bibliographical references and index.
  ISBN 978-0-415-53996-8 (hardback) — ISBN 978-0-415-53997-5 () —
  ISBN 978-0-203-07895-2 () 1. Computer-assisted instruction—
  Curricula—Planning. I. Beetham, Helen, 1967–
  LB1028.5.R44 2013   371.33'4—dc23
  2012034251

ISBN: 978–0–415–53996–8 (hbk)
ISBN: 978–0–415–53997–5 (pbk)
ISBN: 978–0–203–07895–2 (ebk)

Typeset in Times New Roman and Gill Sans
by Bookcraft Ltd, Stroud, Gloucestershire

Printed and bound in the United States of America
by Edwards Brothers, Inc.

Contents

Illustrations

Figures

Tables

Boxes

Contributors

Shirley Agostinho is a Senior Lecturer in educational technology in the Faculty of Education at the University of Wollongong, Australia. Shirley's research interest in learning design began more than ten years ago when she was project manager for one of the first large-scale Australian higher education projects that developed innovative reusable learning designs. Since then she completed a post-doctoral fellowship that examined how learning objects could be integrated with learning designs when developing online learning environments and has worked on a number of projects investigating how the learning design concept can be used to support teachers with their design thinking.

Helen Beetham is an independent consultant, researcher and author in the field of e-learning, with particular expertise in UK higher education. Since 2004 she has played a leading role in the JISC e-learning programme, advising on programmes in curriculum design, learning literacies, open educational resources, and learners' experiences of e-learning. She is an experienced workshop leader and a regular speaker at conferences in the UK and abroad. She has also co-edited *Rethinking Learning for the Digital Age* (Routledge 2010) with Rhona Sharpe and Sara de Freitas. She was a member of the expert panel for the DCSF-funded Beyond Current Horizons programme.

Sue Bennett is an Associate Professor in the University of Wollongong's Faculty of Education, Australia. Sue's work investigates how people engage with technology in their everyday lives and in educational settings. Her aim is to develop a more holistic understanding of people's technology practices to inform research, practice and policy. She has been researching design thinking and learning design since 1999.

Lucila Carvalho is a Postdoctoral Research Associate in the CoCo Research Centre at the University of Sydney, Australia. Her PhD research investigated the sociology of learning in/about design, and ways of practically implementing sociological principles into e-learning design. She has studied and carried out research in Australia, New Zealand, the UK and Brazil. She has presented her work at various international conferences in the fields of education, sociology, systemic functional linguistics, design and software engineering. Her most recent research has been published in *Design Studies* and she is co-editor (with Peter Goodyear) of the forthcoming book *The Architecture of Productive Learning Networks*.

Gráinne Conole is Professor of Learning Innovation and Director of the Beyond Distance Research Alliance at the University of Leicester, UK. She was previously Professor of E-Learning in the Institute of Educational Technology at the Open University, UK. Her research interests include the use, integration and evaluation of information and communication technologies and e-learning and the impact of technologies on organizational change. Two of her current areas of interest are how learning design can help in creating more engaging learning activities and on open educational resources research.

James Dalziel is Professor of Learning Technology and Director of the Macquarie E-Learning Centre of Excellence (MELCOE) at Macquarie University in Sydney, Australia. James leads the development of LAMS (the Learning Activity Management System), including roles as a Director of the LAMS Foundation and LAMS International Pty Ltd.

Sara de Freitas is Director of Research and Professor of Virtual Environments at Coventry University, UK, with responsibility for applied research, teaching and learning and business development. Sara was responsible for setting up the Serious Games Institute, a hybrid model of research, business and study, the first institute of its kind. She holds 23 research and development projects and publishes widely in the areas of: pedagogy and e-learning; change management and strategy development for implementing e-learning systems and serious games and virtual worlds for supporting training and learning.

Rachel Helen Ellaway PhD is the Assistant Dean for Curriculum and Planning, Director of Simulation and an Associate Professor for Education Informatics at the Northern Ontario School of Medicine in Canada. She was previously Director of eLearning for Medicine and Veterinary Medicine at the University of Edinburgh. Widely published in the field of medical education, her academic work concentrates on online learning, simulation and the use of new technologies for teaching and assessment in and around health professional education. Her work in developing and implementing profession-focused educational systems was recognized in the award of a Queen's Anniversary Prize for Higher and Further Education to the University of Edinburgh in 2005.

Peter Goodyear is Professor of Education, Australian Laureate Fellow and Co-Director of the CoCo Research Centre at the University of Sydney, Australia. He has been carrying out research in the field of learning and technology since the early 1980s and has published seven books and almost 100 journal articles and book chapters. His most recent co-authored book was for Routledge, *Students' Experiences of E-learning in Higher Education: The ecology of sustainable innovation*, with Rob Ellis, 2010. His research has taken place in the UK, mainland Europe and Australia and has been funded by the Australian Research Council, the UK Economic & Social Research Council, UK Government, industry and the European Commission.

Derek Harding began by teaching modern history, social science and politics and in the early 1990s began using computers to support his teaching. He directed the TLTP-funded Courseware for History Implementation Consortium project and has been involved with the Association for History and Computing for many years. A member of the History Advisory Panel for the History, Classics and Archaeology Subject Centre, he was a Learning and Teaching Consultant at the University of Teesside, UK.

Barry Harper is an Emeritus Professor of Education at the University of Wollongong in Australia. He has extensive experience in the design, development, implementation and evaluation of technology-mediated and online learning materials. His research focuses on the design, development, implementation, theory and evaluation of technology-supported learning environments with a recent emphasis on learning design. His research has been supported by a wide range of funding bodies.

John G. Hedberg is Millennium Innovations Chair in ICT and Education, and Director of the Macquarie ICT Innovations Centre at Macquarie University, Sydney, Australia. He has been Professor of Learning Sciences and Technologies at Nanyang Technological University in Singapore where he directed several research projects exploring the role of technologies in engaging students in mathematics, science, history and geography classrooms. He is also the Editor-in-chief of Educational Media International and President of the International Council for Educational Media.

Bruce Ingraham was a Teaching Fellow at the University of Teesside, UK. With more than 30 years of experience in higher education, he began his career as a literary semiotician. For the past 15 years he has specialized in the semiotics of multimedia and in the production of online learning resources. His research interests included the impact of multimedia on the conduct of scholarly discourse and the role of e-books in higher education

Christopher R. Jones is a Professor at Liverpool John Moores University, UK. His research focuses on the utilization of the metaphor of networks in the understanding of learning in higher education. Chris has a longstanding interest in collaborative and cooperative methods for teaching and learning. Chris has led a number of research projects and was the principal investigator for a UK Research Council funded project "The Net Generation encountering e-learning at university" until March 2010. Chris has published more than 70 journal articles, book chapters and refereed conference papers connected to his research. He is the joint editor of two books in the area of advanced learning technology: *Networked Learning: Perspectives and Issues* published by Springer in 2002 and an edited collection with Lone Dirckinck-Holmfeld and Berner Lindström (2009) *Analysing Networked Learning Practices in Higher Education and Continuing Professional Development*, Sense Publishers, BV.

Jennifer Jones is a PhD candidate in the Faculty of Education at the University of Wollongong, Australia. Jennifer's PhD investigates how university teachers can be supported to design a unit of work using a learning design.

Agnes Kukulska-Hulme is Professor of Learning Technology and Communication, and Associate Director of the Open University's Institute of Educational Technology, UK. She has been researching mobile learning since 2001 and co-authored the first handbook in this emerging field in 2005. Her recent work has focused on the role of mobile technologies in social inclusion and lifelong learning, with particular emphasis on informal mobile language learning. She is also active in academic staff development. She is the President of the International Association for Mobile Learning.

Diana Laurillard is Professor of Learning with Digital Technologies at the London Knowledge Lab, Institute of Education, University of London. She was previously Head of the e-Learning Strategy Unit at the UK Government's Department for Education and Skills and, prior to that, held two terms of office as Pro-Vice-Chancellor for Learning Technologies and Teaching at the Open University.

Dean Lockwood (DPhil, York) is a Senior Lecturer in Media Theory in the School of Media, University of Lincoln, UK. He teaches undergraduate and postgraduate courses, and researches and publishes, in the areas of visual, auditory and digital culture. He has a special interest in the application of Deleuzian assemblage theory and affect theory. He is the author, with Rob Coley, of *Cloud Time* (Zero, 2012), which deals with the culture and politics of cloud computing.

Lori Lockyer is the Vincent Fairfax Family Foundation Chair in Teacher Education and Head of School of Education at Macquarie University in Sydney, Australia. Lori's research focuses on the how technologies facilitate teaching and learning in K–12, higher and professional education. For more than 10 years she has been involved in a number of projects that investigate the development, use and issues associated with learning design.

Patrick McAndrew is Professor of Open Education in the Institute of Educational Technology at the Open University, UK, where he teaches and researches on ways to support learning online. His interests include the way in which openness can be an agent for change in the ways that people learn, software systems to support the use of learning design and methods for the research and evaluation of open content.

Liz Masterman is a senior researcher with the Learning Technologies Group at the University of Oxford. She has conducted research into design for learning since 2004, and has also led research into the learner experience of e-learning for both JISC and the University of Oxford, and into the impact of open educational resources in UK universities. Liz has an interest in the integration of cognitive and sociocultural approaches in the design and evaluation of learning technologies

Terry Mayes is an Emeritus Professor at Glasgow Caledonian University, UK. He has a long experience as researcher, author and practitioner in the pedagogical aspects of learning technology in which area he has collaborated in many research projects. Recently he has acted in a variety of advisory roles for the higher education sector.

Martin Oliver is a Reader in ICT in Education at the London Knowledge Lab, a research centre of the Institute of Education, University of London. His research focuses on the use of technology in higher education, with a focus on theory, methodology and students' digital literacies. He is currently president of the Association for Learning Technology.

Ron Oliver is the Deputy Vice-Chancellor (Teaching, Learning and International) and Vice-President at Edith Cowan University, Australia. He has wide experience in the design, development, implementation and evaluation of technology-mediated and online learning materials. He uses technology extensively in his own teaching and his ideas and activities are all grounded in practical applications. Ron has won a number of awards for his innovative teaching and research including the inaugural Australian Award for University Teaching for the use of multimedia in university teaching.

Chris Pegler is a Senior Lecturer in the Institute of Educational Technology at the Open University, UK, where she develops and leads online courses within the MA in Online and Distance Education and researches reuse of online open resources. She founded the ORIOLE (Open Resources: Influence on Learners and Educators) project within OLNet http://www.olnet.org/ and was Academic Director of the national Support Centre for Open Resources in Education (SCORE). As a UK National Teaching Fellow her approach to online learning design is informed by more than two decades managing distance and e-learning, supplemented by experience as both online tutor and student. She has particular interest in supporting fellow practitioners. Chris is co-editor (with Professor Allison Littlejohn) of the Routledge book series Connecting with eLearning, within which she co-authored *Preparing for Blended eLearning* and *The Educational Potential of ePortfolios.*

Rhona Sharpe is Head of the Oxford Centre for Staff and Learning Development at Oxford Brookes University, UK. She was the project director of the support and synthesis project for the JISC Learner Experiences of E-Learning programme and has conducted reviews of e-learning literature and practice for the JISC and Higher Education Academy. She was previously an editor for *Research in Learning Technology*, is a founder member of ELESIG – a special interest group for those investigating and evaluating learners' experiences of e-learning – and a UK Higher Education Academy National Teaching Fellow.

John Traxler is Professor of Mobile Learning, probably the world's first, and Director of the Learning Lab at the University of Wolverhampton, UK. He is a Founding Director of the International Association for Mobile Learning, Associate Editor of the *International Journal of Mobile and Blended Learning* and of *Interactive Learning Environments*. He is on the Research Board of the Association of Learning Technology, the Editorial Board of *Research in Learning Technology* and *IT in International Development*. He was Conference Chair of mLearn2008, the world's biggest and oldest mobile learning research conference. He has guest edited three special editions devoted to mobile learning including *Distance Education* and an African edition of the *International Journal of Mobile and Blended Learning*. John has co-written a guide to mobile learning in developing countries for the Commonwealth of Learning and is co-editor of the definitive book, *Mobile Learning: A handbook for educators and trainers*, with Professor Agnes Kukulska-Hulme. They are now working on a second book, *Mobile Learning: The next generation*, due to be published in 2013. He has written 30 book chapters on mobile learning.

Sandra Wills from the University of Wollongong, Australia, has authored more than two hundred publications and educational products spanning 30 years and attracted $12 million in grants. Elected Fellow of the Australian Computing Society (1991) and Fellow of the Australian Council for Computers in Education (2002), she has also received an International Federation for Information Processing Silver Core Award (1995), Education Innovation Award (1990) and ACS Lecturer of the Year Award (1980).

Joss Winn is a Senior Lecturer in the Centre for Educational Research and Development, University of Lincoln, UK. He coordinates the work of LNCD, a cross-university group interested in technology for education and manages a number of research and development projects supported through external funding. His research interests include hacker culture within academia and hacking as a new type of craft that is learned. Joss currently teaches on the Level Three module in Online Journalism with colleagues from the School of Journalism.

Foreword to the Second Edition

Do we need to rethink pedagogy again? Does technology innovation imply the continual renewal of what we mean by pedagogy?

There is some continuity of thinking within education. No one has yet shown that we need to change our understanding of how students learn. There have been some wild statements from opinion-formers about technology revolutionizing how students will learn in the 21st century, but the research-based fundamentals of what it takes to learn have not been challenged. The theoretical concepts and approaches still call on Dewey, Vygotsky, Bruner, Papert, Lave and Wenger, with no challenge to our fundamental understanding of what it takes to learn in formal education. Pedagogy is still seen as guiding the learner to learn. The emphasis is still on pedagogy leading the use of technology, rather than adapting to what technology offers.

However, pedagogy has a close relationship with the technologies of learning, and inevitably the scope and style of pedagogy change as the technology changes. The multiplicity of learning technologies, beyond the classroom and away from the teacher, opens up new territories for education. Digital technologies trigger a different kind of relationship between the teacher, the learners, and what is being learned. Yes, we do need to keep rethinking the style and scope of pedagogy as the digital age continues to throw up new technology-driven challenges.

The focus has shifted in recent years from the individual teacher designing a module or session to include teams designing whole courses. There is a greater sense that, with learner access to the burgeoning resources on the web, and with their increasing digital skills, we should remodel education so that learners can take control of their own learning. Certainly, the research literature and the national 'e-learning' policies and strategies of the past few years are full of the promise of the 'self-directed' and 'independent' learning that now become possible. The past few decades of educational thinking have maintained an unchallenged drive to more active forms of student learning – collaborative, experiential, inquiry-based, problem-based approaches citing theories of constructionism, social constructivism and situated learning. The initial manifestation of the web allowed little more than the acquisition learning that was familiar from books and lectures, and did little to address the active learning sought by educators. With the development of opportunities for user-generated input to digital repositories, crowd-sourcing and social media, the web has at last begun to enable these active forms of learning.

At the same time, the Open Educational Resources movement has turned the web into a universal educational library of lecture materials and well-produced educational resources, available to all. This is a significant shift for education because it provides access to educational materials to anyone who has Internet access. It is a wonderful democratization of access to resources. But it is not the same as access to education. And learning technologists have to keep alive the vision for what technology-enhanced learning could be.

We have to contribute to the policy debates about learning technologies, because opinion-formers outside the field easily overplay the capabilities of technology. At the time of the first edition, learning technologists were insisting that there was more to online learning than lectures on the web, and we should be looking to the active forms of learning that could be offered. Since then, we have had the explosion of social media to connect learners to each other, there are more opportunities for user-generated content, and yet now there are even more lectures on the web. The wider expectation is therefore that 'self-directed' and 'independent' learning have indeed become possible but online access to opportunities for inquiry, discussion, production, collaboration and acquisition is not itself education. It does enable informal, self-directed, independent learning activities, just as public libraries and public houses have always done – which is wonderful, but it is not education.

This is what the contributors to this book help to clarify. Our digital native students may be able to use technologies, but that does not mean they can learn from them. Being able to read and write never meant you could therefore learn from books. Learners need teachers. As learners we cannot know what it is possible to know, or how to make that journey to what we want to become. We need guidance. Pedagogy is about guiding learning, rather than leaving you to finding your own way. Pedagogy puts the onus on teacher to guide the learner's journey to a particular and productive end. We may prefer to find our own way. Good. There have always been libraries and friends and experiences to enable us to do that, now supplemented with digital resources and Internet friends and virtual experiences. Informal learning continues with ever better opportunities. Education does something different from what we can do for ourselves. As learners going to education we have higher ambitions – for this we need teachers because that learning journey is as hard as it ever was.

This is why, throughout these chapters, there are references to the centrality of the role of the teacher, and to the complexity of designing for learning. The complex architecture of activities learners engage in as they tackle new ideas and high-level skills shows the difficulty of the teaching task. The field is beginning to recognize that teachers need to help each other discover how best to organize the mix of learning technologies in support of learning.

Equally important is the role of students in helping teachers discover how best to develop the new pedagogies. The exploration of a greater equality of control over the design of learning could be a significant shift for pedagogy. It is a powerful idea that the teacher can learn about teaching from their exchanges with students. Technology gives teachers much better access to how students discuss and debate in an online forum, to data analytics that describe how they progress through a sequence of learning activities, what they produce in a collaborative wiki, how they reflect on their learning journey in their e-portfolio. If, as teachers, we use technology to elicit and make use of this extensive information to remodel our teaching that will be a new task to fit into the teacher's repertoire. It is an exciting prospect, but requires a major rethink of how to manage teacher time to optimize pedagogy.

There is another important source of information about teaching: students themselves. The design for learning field is exploring new ways of representing pedagogy, so that teachers can articulate and exchange their designs. These new forms of digital representation, available in design pattern libraries on the web, can also be available to students, to annotate. It is a much richer and better-targeted form of evaluation than the termly questionnaire, or the feedback sheet. It also raises the prospect of another kind of information explosion for the teacher to handle. Again, this is part of rethinking pedagogy in the face of technology opportunity.

Innovation in digital technology will continue, with teachers being warned that they will revolutionize education, as they have been told repeatedly over the past few decades. Clearly it does not happen easily. There are many actors taking responsibility for what happens in the education community, from ministers to agencies to institutions to employers to families, and in the midst of it all are the teacher and learner trying to accomplish a difficult journey. Digital technologies have many different roles to play in helping us achieve our ambitions for education. One fundamental question is how best to use them to support the teacher and learner in their journey. We will continually be rethinking pedagogy as we explore the answers.

Diana Laurillard, London Knowledge Lab,
Institute of Education, UK

Foreword to the First Edition

Education is in an interesting transitional phase between its 'ICT-free' past and its 'ICT-aware' future. That it is in such a transition is a fairly safe claim. Over the centuries prior to digital technology, education evolved into a system that used paper technology in a variety of highly sophisticated ways to fulfil its mission to develop and accredit knowledge and skills. Its future must certainly be one in which it extends this capacity to a sophisticated use of digital technology. Like every modern enterprise, education is currently learning and adapting to the opportunities afforded by information and communication technologies, albeit slowly. Learning technologists make it their business to accelerate the process because the learning cycles of the education system are long, while those of its immediate environment – youth culture, employment demands, scientific knowledge – are short, and changing ever more rapidly.

Leaders in the education system know that it derives its support from the communities that recognize its value, but have been slow to realize that this increasingly depends on how well it exploits the transformational potential of digital technology. All our educational ambitions for the post-compulsory sector are challenging: personalized learning, higher attainment standards, wider participation and improved retention in further and higher education, closer relationships between education and the workplace, lifelong learning, a more highly skilled workforce for our knowledge economy. We do not lack ambition. Achieving these ambitions, or even significant progress towards them, would have enormous value for the communities served by education. Every one of them requires the improved quality and economies of scale that proper use of technology will confer. Yet so many of our institutional and organizational strategies for education consign digital technology to the merely incremental tasks involved in improving our current systems supporting education, not to the transformational task of changing them.

What are we doing? In teaching and learning currently, we tend to use technology to support traditional modes of teaching – improving the quality of lecture presentations using interactive whiteboards, making lecture notes readable in PowerPoint and available online, extending the library by providing access to digital resources and libraries, recreating face-to-face tutorial discussions asynchronously online – all of them good, incremental improvements in quality and flexibility, but nowhere near being transformational.

What might we be doing? Let's look at it through the lens of the learner, and embrace all those vaulting ambitions in considering how they could combine to transform the educational experience of one individual. How can a young person who has always hated study, who believes further education is not for them, with few skills and low self esteem be persuaded to achieve their learning potential? The ambitions are right – their combined effect would certainly be to bring motivation, opportunity and support to that young person. But look at what it takes to achieve that: the processes of teaching and learning have to engage their attention so that they enjoy study; the knowledge and skills they need must link to their interests so they are motivated to study; they need constant personalized support and encouragement at the pace and level to keep them engaged; the content and process of learning must be compatible with their social culture; they need to be able to see the long-term value in the hard work of study – every teacher with a vocation to teach wants to provide all this, but in a non-elitist system this level of personalization cannot be offered for every student. The promise of new technology is that it can, for every one of those learner needs. It is an engaging and highly responsive medium; it can gather content according to interest; it can respond to individual needs of pace and level; it fits with the style and forms of youth culture; it can link the classroom to the workplace and in doing so enables teachers to provide much more of what only they can do for their students. Wherever we find an impossible challenge to inclusive educational provision, there is usually a way in which digital technology could make a significant difference.

But we focus the majority of technology provision on what we already understand – information systems, data gathering, communication processes, presentation – rather than using it to tackle the really difficult problems presented by our ambitions for universal and effective education. Imaginative use of digital technologies could be transformational for teaching and learning, taking us well beyond the incremental value of more accessible lecture presentations. The problem is that transformation is more about the human and organizational aspects of teaching and learning than it is about the use of technology. We have the ambition. We have the technology. What is missing is what connects the two. If education leaders were fully engaged with this, it would be strategy, and we would have a top-down change process. If practitioners were fully engaged it would be experimental innovation, and we would have a bottom-up change process. Better to have both, but too many educational institutions still lack serious leadership engagement with the innovative application of digital technologies. In any case, innovation in the pedagogical aspects of teaching and learning should be coming from the academic community. That is the focus here.

In this book, learning technologists from the UK and further afield pool their ideas around one way of accelerating the exploitation of digital technology: bringing its creative use within the capability of the individual teaching professional. By setting out to explore the design of learning activities in educational contexts already rich in electronic and mobile technologies, the authors show us what a technology-aware future for education would be like.

When our education system is making sophisticated use of e-learning it will pervade everything we do, just as paper technology does. Lecturers will count it as part of their professional responsibility to 'design for learning', using a variety of forms of digital technology. We will have discarded the idea that the problem of pedagogic innovation can be left to the commercial suppliers, and instead see their role as being the provision of the tools and environments that lecturers can use in all the creative, innovative and scholarly ways they currently use paper technologies. We don't expect the publishers to write the textbooks, we shouldn't expect them to create the educational software for us either. The authors collaborating on this book are providing the means for this to be possible, researching and developing the forms of learning activity, the tools for pedagogic design, the environments for collaborative practice, the conceptual frameworks, all of which will contribute to building the bridges between what digital technologies make possible, and what our educational ambitions require.

Diana Laurillard, London Knowledge Lab,
Institute of Education, UK

Acknowledgements

The editors and authors would like to acknowledge the support of the UK Joint Information Systems Committee (JISC) in the creation of this book. The JISC funded the original work on which many chapters in the book are based. In particular, the following chapters were developed from research originally funded by the JISC: Chapter 1 (Mayes and de Freitas), Chapter 2 (Beetham), Chapter 4 (Masterman), Chapter 5 (Conole), Chapter 8 (McAndrew and Goodyear), Chapter 10 (Sharpe and Oliver), Chapter 16 (Kukulska-Hulme and Traxler). In addition, the JISC supported the collaborative writing process for the final Chapter 17.

The material presented in this book has in many cases been developed in consultation with expert practitioners, through the meetings of the JISC Learning and Teaching Practice Experts Group, and programmes of JISC and Higher Education Academy workshops in 2004–5 (Planning and Evaluating Effective Practice) and 2011–12 (Developing Digital Literacies). For example in Chapter 2 some of the content of the original chapter was developed in collaboration with educational innovators who were invited to share aspects of their practice during these workshops. In Chapter 17, the themes were created through consultation with the JISC Learning and Teaching Practice Experts Group. We are deeply indebted to those practitioners.

Abbreviations

AI	artificial intelligence
AIM	access and identity management system
ANT	Actor Network Theory
API	Application Programming Interfaces
AUTC	Australian University Teaching Committee
BYOD	bring your own device
CAD	computer-aided design
CADMOS	Courseware Development Methodology for Open instructional Systems
CC	Creative Commons
CERD	Centre for Educational Research and Development
CETL	Centre for Excellence in Teaching and Learning
CHIC	Courseware for History Implementation Consortium
CLFP	Collaborative Learning Flow Pattern
CMC	computer-mediated communication
CMS	courseware management system
CPD	continuing and professional development
CSCL	computer supported collaborative learning
EML	Educational Modelling Language
FAQ	frequently asked question
FDTK	Fund for the Development of Teaching and Learning
GPS	global positioning system
ICT	information and communication technology
IEEE	Institute of Electrical and Electronic Engineers
IMS	originally Instructional Management System(s): now usually refers to IMS Global Learning Consortium and its interoperability standards and specifications
IMSLD	IMS Learning Design
IP	informant practitioner
IPR	intellectual property rights
ISD	instructional systems design
IT	information technology

JISC	Joint Information Systems Committee
LAA	learning activity authoring
LAMS	Learning Activity Management System
LD	Learning Design
LDVS	Learning Design Visual Sequence
LMS	learning management system
LOM	Learning Object Metadata
LOR	Learning Object Repository
MIT	Massachusetts Institute of Technology
MOOC	massive open online course
OCSLD	Oxford Centre for Staff and Learning Development
OEP	open educational practices
OER	open educational resources
OOC	open online course
OSID	Open Service Interface Definition
PAT	Pattern Analysis Template
PBL	problem-based learning
PCK	pedagogical content knowledge
PLE	personalized learning environment
REAP	Re-Engineering Assessment Practices
RLO	reusable learning object
SCORM	Shareable Courseware Object Reference Model
SIG	special interest group
SLM	structured learning module
STEM	science, engineering, technology and mathematics
TESEP	Transforming and Enhancing the Student Experience through Pedagogy
TLTP	Teaching and Learning Technology Programme
TPCK	technological pedagogical content knowledge
UML	Unified Modelling Language
URL	universal resource locator
VLE	virtual learning environment
X-Delia	eXcellence in Decision-making through Enhanced Learning in Immersive Applications
XML	Extensible Markup Language

An Introduction to Rethinking Pedagogy

Helen Beetham and Rhona Sharpe

In her foreword, Laurillard encourages us to build bridges between the technologies we have at our disposal and the ambitions we have to transform post-compulsory education. Throughout this book we argue that this can be achieved by a reconsideration of the pedagogical practices that underpin education. As learning contexts are increasingly rich in electronic and mobile technologies, so research into e-learning has more to offer the mainstream of educational practice. The chapters collected here offer a critical discussion of the issues surrounding the design, sharing and reuse of learning activities, and offer tools that practitioners can apply to their own concerns and contexts. The aim is to bring the insights of learning design into the educational process, and to extend the repertoire of tools and techniques in everyday use.

What is pedagogy?

The term 'pedagogy' is not without its critics, particularly in the field of post-compulsory education from which many of the ideas and practices of this book originate. Malcolm Knowles, for example (1990), notes that the term derives from the ancient Greek word *paidagogos*, meaning the slave who led children to school, and argues that this makes it inappropriate for the years beyond school in which learners gain in self-direction and self-reliance. Others have found the usual definition of pedagogy as the 'art or science of teaching' at odds with their preferred emphasis on the activity of learning. In a truly learner-centred environment, they suggest, teaching should not be the focus of concern.

These debates and difficulties are, in fact, one reason why we have chosen to foreground the term 'pedagogy' in this book. First, despite its etymological connection with children (*paidia*), contemporary use of the term has lost its exclusive reference to childhood while retaining the original sense of leading or guiding to learn. We observe that the need for guidance is not confined to childhood, and that even the most self-directed of adult learners can benefit from the support of others. At a time when learning is increasingly seen as a lifelong project, it makes sense that the associated 'art or science' of guidance should extend its scope into adulthood. And as – in the West at least – the boundaries

are becoming blurred between school and college, formal and informal education, learning *for* work and learning *at* work, it also makes sense to consider the
continuities across different contexts of learning. How people learn, and how
they can best be guided to learn, are no longer concerns that belong behind
school gates.

Second, the word 'pedagogy' embraces an essential dialogue between
teaching and learning. This is particularly significant in a context of educational
discourse in which the two terms have come to be used in tension and even
in opposition to one another. In extreme cases, the term 'teaching' is seen as
denying the active nature of learning and individuals' unique capacities to learn
(see for example the review by Alexander 2002). How are we to make sense of
this apparent contradiction?

In the last century, a series of educational thinkers in the West sought to rein-
state 'learning' as the central concern of pedagogy, arguing that undue emphasis
had been placed on the content of what was taught, and that this had led to rigid
and unhelpful habits of instruction. These trends in pedagogical thinking are
discussed in more detail in Chapter 1. Taken together they amount to a new
emphasis on the individual capacities and needs of learners. Learners are no
longer seen as passive recipients of knowledge and skills but as active participants in the learning process. Fields such as psychology and cognitive science
have contributed to our understanding of how this process takes place, and how
it can differ from one learner to another. Social scientists have demonstrated
the impact that social and cultural contexts have on people's engagement with
learning. Rightly, there is excitement about these advances and eagerness to
ensure that they are set at the heart of educational practice.

One of the ways in which this revolution has been acknowledged is in the
privileging of the term 'learning' over 'teaching' in educational discourse.
Throughout this book, we use the term 'pedagogy' in the original sense of guid-
ance-to-learn: learning in the context of teaching, and teaching that has learning
as its goal. We believe that guiding others to learn is a unique, skilful, creative
and demanding human activity that deserves scholarship in its own right. We
will not be afraid to use the term 'teaching' as well as 'learning' in this volume,
recognizing that education concerns not only how people learn 'naturally' from
their environment but also the social interactions that support learning, and the
institutions and practices that have grown up around them. In fact, the essential
dialogue between these two activities is at the heart of what we mean by 'pedagogy', and helps us to reclaim the idea of teaching from negative associations
with dominant, unresponsive, or even repressive forms of instruction.

It will be seen from this discussion that there is a further complexity to the
term 'pedagogy'. As well as referring to the activities of learning and teaching,
it is also used to describe how we think and talk about, plan and structure those
activities when we are not actually engaged in them. From the time of Plato
at least, thinkers have proposed specific theories of – as well as methods for –
education. Pedagogy, then, involves ways of knowing as well as ways of doing.

Like other applied disciplines, it is centrally concerned with how we understand practice (the 'evidence base' for theory), and how we apply that theoretical understanding *in* practice once again.

Ironically, the establishment of education as a field of study in its own right has helped to divide these two elements, so that within the same institution there may be professionals 'doing' teaching and professionals researching, thinking and writing about teaching who never have contact with one another. Educational developers, following the example of Schön (1987), have established the ideal of *reflective practice* as one means of reconnecting the two aspects of the discipline. Practitioners are encouraged to continuously evaluate the impact of their own pedagogical approaches and choices on their learners. At the same time, educational researchers and thinkers have used the term *scholarship of teaching* to describe the body of theory they have developed and the ways in which it can be applied (Trigwell *et al.* 2000). Rightly, the techniques used by reflective practitioners and by scholars focused on the pragmatics of teaching – such as evaluative methodologies, conceptual toolkits, and model teaching approaches – often resemble one another quite closely. In using the term 'pedagogy' we are therefore initiating a dialogue between theory and practice, as well as between learning and teaching, which draws consciously on these traditions.

If we are serious about this dialogue, we must acknowledge that pedagogy needs to be 're-done' at the same time as it needs to be 're-thought'. Throughout this book we have tried to keep theoretical arguments and real-life examples of practice in alignment with one another. Many creative and innovative teachers have been involved in providing ideas for this book so that our theories can be rooted in the practical business of guiding learners to learn. Our understanding is that neither of these two activities – the doing or the thinking – makes sense in isolation from the other.

The digital age

If the last century did so much to reinvent the art or science of teaching, why does pedagogy need to be re-thought again just now? This is a particularly urgent question in relation to the new digital technologies, because teachers who are excited about these technologies are often accused of using them regardless of whether or not they are pedagogically effective, and even in ignorance of the long tradition of pedagogical evidence and thought. The argument that technology should be at the service of effective learning experiences is one with which all the authors in this book would concur. However, we would take issue with the idea that there is nothing particularly new for educators to consider as digital technologies enter the frame.

Papyrus and paper, chalk and print, overhead projectors, educational toys and television, even the basic technologies of writing were innovations once. The networked digital computer, and its more recent mobile and wireless counterparts are just the latest outcomes of human ingenuity that we have at our disposal. It is true that none of these technologies has changed human beings' fundamental capacities to learn, if learning is understood in purely cognitivist terms. But they have profoundly changed how ideas and practices are communicated, and what it means to be a knowledgeable or capable person. While this book will situate discussions about the new technologies for learning firmly within established educational discourse, we also contend that these technologies represent a paradigm shift with specific and multiple impacts on the nature of knowledge in society, and therefore on the nature of learning. The final chapter looks in more detail at this paradigm shift and considers what it means to design for learning in a period of radical and uncertain change.

In rethinking pedagogy for an age of digital information and communication, then, we are not trying to define some new aspect or area of the discipline: we are trying to re-articulate the entire discipline in this new context. The danger of 'business as usual' with digital enhancements – when they are proven effective – is that we reproduce existing practices rather than appreciating where digital technologies have the potential to disrupt norms, challenge assumptions, innovate disciplines and professions, and usher in completely new forms of learning activity.

So how do digital technologies constitute a new context for learning and teaching? The technical advances are relatively easy to identify. The latest figures for access to the Internet in the UK are that 77 per cent of households have Internet access, but the modes of access are changing with 45 per cent of users having accessed the Internet from a mobile phone. For the 16–24-year-old group, social networking is the main online activity (Office for National Statistics 2011). Personal web pages, blogs, podcasts and wikis are democratizing the creation of information; social software is allowing participation in online communities that define and share the information they need for themselves. Individuals have access to processing power in personal applications that even five years ago would have been confined to specialist institutions. Personal mobile and wireless devices are increasingly integrated with the global computer network, to provide seamless, location-independent access to information services. Chapters 14 and 16 deal with some of these technologies in terms of their specific impacts on, and benefits for, learning.

But what of the social and cultural changes that have accompanied these technical developments? The phrase 'information age' was coined by Manuel Castells (1996) to describe a period in which the movement of information through networks would overtake the circulation of goods as the primary source of value in society. Some of the social and cultural reorganization that he predicted can already be traced in the ways that the contexts of education are changing.

Epistemologically, for example, what counts as useful knowledge is increasingly biased towards what can be represented in digital form. Many scientific and research enterprises now depend on data being shared in the almost instantaneous fashion enabled by the Internet. Vast libraries have been digitized, and there are movements to ensure that governmental and publicly funded scientific data are openly available online. Open educational resources of the highest quality can be accessed – for the cost of getting online – by people who will never see the inside of a university. Academic institutions have a central role to play in these developments and in the debates over personal data and copyright that increasingly shape our digital information landscape. However, less thought has been given to the knowledge that is forgotten or lost in the process of digitization: practical skills, know-how that is deeply embedded in the context of use, and other tacit knowledge associated with habits of practice (Dreyfus and Dreyfus 1986). Ironically, it may be exactly this kind of knowledge that is drawn on by effective teachers, and by effective learners too, in their most transformational work.

What are the educational goals in a world where the knowledge and skills that were once valued are changing (Facer 2011)? The nature of work in Western societies has altered beyond recognition, and learning institutions have changed their offering in response. As more and more jobs demand advanced levels of ICT use, graduate employability has been refigured as the acquisition of capabilities – new forms of literacy and numeracy, adaptability, problem solving, communication – rather than the mastery of a stable body of knowledge (Barrie 2007). And as the job market demands ever more flexibility and currency, post-compulsory education has been reorganized around a model of constant updating of competence – lifelong learning or continuous professional development.

Technology has also had a profound impact on educational organizations themselves. Schools and colleges are networked in a way that cuts across traditional institutional sectoral, and even national boundaries: if not yet completely 'borderless', the walls of the classroom are increasingly see-through. Learners are more mobile between institutions than could have been imagined before standardized credit, e-portfolios and personal learning records – all of which require digital technology to be implemented at scale. As learners have more choice about when and how – and whether – they participate in formal education, they are also interacting with educational institutions in a way that is increasingly mediated through digital systems. They probably use a public website to find out about courses of study, apply and enrol online, contact tutors by email, access course information and resources through a managed learning environment, take examinations and receive grades via a computer-based assessment system. Colleges increasingly see the need to present study opportunities in transparent and open ways if they are to attract students and meet their expectations once enrolled (McGill 2011).

The wholly virtual learning experience is still a minority choice, and most such courses are provided by specialist institutions such as the Open Universities of the UK and the Netherlands, or Phoenix University in the US. Institutions of this kind are now competing with more traditional universities and colleges for market share, and this is having an impact on the way that all educational institutions relate to their learners, and to potential learners in their communities. For example, the UK Open University has made much of course content openly available and is encouraging everyone to engage in some small way with its knowledge, whether through watching a television documentary, ordering a poster, downloading a podcast, browsing course materials, discussing them with other learners, participating in a massive open online course, or finally, signing up for a fully online course (Bean 2012). This represents both a marketing strategy and a public expression of the institution's mission and values.

Finally, learners themselves are changing. Most young people in Western societies make routine use of the Internet and email, text messaging and social software, file sharing sites, cloud services and mobile devices. Their familiarity with these new forms of exchange is carried over into their learning. Beyond whatever engagement with technology is required by their institution or course of study, learners use the communication and information tools they have to hand to help manage their learning. Indeed some curriculum transformation projects have found that more progress can be made by allowing students to choose their own technologies (McGill 2011).

Some of the habits of mind associated with personal and social technologies are regarded by teachers as unhelpful, particularly the often uncritical attitude to Internet-based information, and the cut-and-paste mentality of a generation raised on editing tools rather than pen and paper. There have been worrying findings that such behaviours are persisting even until doctoral studies (British Library 2012). The brevity of chat and text pose a challenge to traditional standards of spelling and grammar, and there is no doubt that the use of personal technologies creates new inequalities among learners. Teachers should be free to respond critically, as well as creatively, to these new technologies, but they cannot afford to ignore them if they want to engage with their learners.

This is not a book about social change – many others have covered this terrain – but it does take change within and beyond the educational organization as essential background for understanding the new pressures on learning and teaching. Against the argument that new technologies make 'no significant difference' (Russell 2001), we contend that learning is a set of personal and interpersonal activities, deeply rooted in specific social and cultural contexts. When those contexts change, how people learn changes also. We do not intend by this argument to suggest that educational practice is determined by technology *per se*. The developments outlined in this section were not pre-destined when the first two computers were networked by Thomas Merrill and Lawrence G. Roberts in 1965. Such events may dictate that our society and its relationship with knowledge will change, but not what form or direction those changes will take. Otherwise there would be little point in a book such as this one, in which we lay out some of the alternative possibilities over which we, as human actors, have decisions to make. Understood as a social and cultural phenomenon, technology cannot but influence the ways in which people learn, and therefore what makes for effective learning and effective pedagogy.

The idea of 'effectiveness' in this discussion should alert us to the fact that pedagogy and technology also involve issues of value. Just as the impact of technology is changing how knowledge is valued in our society, so it is also changing how we value different kinds of learning and achievement, and different models of the learning organization. Some values, such as the values of the marketplace and the values of the traditional academic institution, are brought into conflict by the effects of technology. Though different contributors to this book have different perspectives on these debates, we will be explicit about the alternatives wherever we find conflicts over value arising.

Design for learning

If 'pedagogy' helps to locate this book within a tradition of thinking about learning and teaching, 'design' helps to identify what is different and new about the ideas we are proposing. Why is 'design' a good term around which to reclaim the scholarship of teaching, and to rethink pedagogy for the digital age?

First, like pedagogy, design is a term that bridges theory and practice. It encompasses both a principled approach and a set of contextualized practices that are constantly adapting to circumstances. In other words it is a form of praxis, both in the widely used sense of iterative, reflexive professional learning (e.g. Kolb 1984) and in the more radical sense of developing a critical awareness in action, in order to bring about transformation (e.g. Freire 1996).

Second, 'design' is a highly valued activity in the new digital economy, and a discipline – or capability within other disciplines – of increasing importance as more of our significant interactions take place via designed spaces or interfaces. In the academic world, we have already touched on the impact that new information technologies have had on what counts as valuable knowledge. This change has been variously characterized by commentators as a 'postmodern turn' (e.g. Hassan 1988) or as a shift from 'mode 1 to mode 2' knowledge (Gibbons *et al.* 1994). In either case, knowledge comes to be seen as provisional, contextualized, culturally specific, constructed or designed rather than discovered. This shift is not without its critics, particularly from within the natural sciences and other 'enlightenment' disciplines of the academy. It can seem at odds with the academic values of disinterested, independent investigation. Nevertheless, even within these disciplines, knowledge is understood to have specific uses and users, and the ways in which it is communicated to those users have become an essential aspect of what is known. Design has therefore become a valued activity in many academic disciplines as well as in graduate professions.

Third, quality assurance of courses and professionalization of teaching have meant an increasingly formal approach to course design. 'Designs' in the form of lesson plans, validation documents and course handbooks are routinely produced as evidence for quality enhancement or personal/professional review. Although it takes different forms in different states, the desire of national governments to establish the 'return on investment' available from higher and further education has added to the pressure to standardize representation of educational design processes and their outcomes.

So design is both a significant aspect of professional practice in education and a powerful metaphor for the approach teachers take to the learning of others. As in other areas of professional practice, the process of design in education involves:

- *Investigation*: Who are my users and what do they need? What principles and theories are relevant?
- *Application*: How should these principles be applied in this case?
- *Representation or modelling*: What solution will best meet users' needs? How can this be communicated to developers and/or directly to users?
- *Iteration*: How does the design stand up to the demands of development? How useful is it in practice? What changes are needed?

Teaching has always involved 'design' in these senses, though it has also always recognized the process of learning as emergent – valuing the capacity of teachers to respond in the moment – and performative – valuing what teachers can accomplish with their voice and physical presence. With the use of digital technologies, new elements of the learning situation ask to be planned or designed for in advance. Teachers continue to be responsive and to give engaging performances, but sometimes these interactions with learners may be via digital media either live or asynchronously. An interesting and unforeseen consequence of the greater reliance on technologies in education has been that aspects of pedagogic practice become more visible and so more available for reflection, revision and review.

'Design for learning' is a phrase we have coined for the process by which teachers – and others involved in the support of learning – arrive at a plan or structure or designed artefact for a learning situation or setting. The situation may be as small as a single task, or as large as a degree course. In a learning situation, any of the following may be designed with a specific pedagogic intention: learning resources and materials; the learning environment; tools and equipment; learning activities; the learning programme or curriculum. In this book we are mainly concerned with the design of learning activities and curricula. For practitioners, who are rarely involved in the design of the materials and environments they are offered as pedagogically useful, the crucial questions are: how can I choose from, use, adapt and integrate the materials available to me to provide a coherent experience for my learners? Our aim is to focus on design as a holistic process based around the learning activity, in which designed elements such as materials and environments must also be taken into account.

When we talk about design for learning we are viewing design as an intentional and systematic, but also a creative approach to the encounter of learners with subject matter and task requirements. In reality learners and learning situations are unpredictable: as teachers, we encourage learners to engage in dialogue with us, to respond individually to learning opportunities, and to take increasing responsibility for their own learning. The use of digital technologies does not alter this fundamental contract. We acknowledge, then, that learning can never be wholly designed, only designed *for*, from principled intentions but with an awareness of the contingent nature of learning as it actually takes place. This contingency demands constant dialogue with learners, recognizing that effective designs will evolve only through cycles of practice, evaluation and reflection. Also in this book, 'learning designs' will be used to mean representations of the design process and its outcomes, allowing for aspects of design to be shared.

In using the term 'design for learning' we are conscious that 'Learning Design' is a discipline in its own right, with its own specific protocols and modelling language (Jochems *et al.* 2004; Lockyer *et al.* 2008). Historically, Learning Design has emerged from instructional design, but with a focus on learning activity as the central concern of the design process. The theoretical scope of Learning Design, and particularly its goal of providing a generalized means for describing and sharing learning activities, is clearly relevant to our project. All the authors of this volume would like to see pedagogical ideas discussed in ways that are meaningful across different settings. However, pursuit of this aim has uncovered many challenges, some of which are discussed in chapters by Masterman, Conole, McAndrew and Goodyear, and Ellaway. Some general principles can certainly be offered, but it is an open question whether general designs or patterns exist that make sense across a wide range of different learning contexts. Individual contributors to this book have different views on this question.

Reading this book

As we have outlined, a number of approaches – theoretical, practical and research-led – are relevant to effective design for learning. Part I of this book, Principles and practices of designing, outlines our current understanding of how people learn and of how planned, purposeful activities can help them to learn more effectively. Chapter 1 looks in detail at the principles and theories that are relevant to pedagogic design, while Chapter 2 suggests how these might be applied to the design of specific learning activities. Broader considerations for the design of complex learning environments are dealt with in Chapter 3. Moving on from theory to practice, Chapter 4 presents evidence that how practitioners actually design for learning may be a much less rational – and more responsive – process than design protocols allow. A number of design tools and environments are explored in Chapter 5, while the challenge of representing and sharing real designs for learning is addressed in different ways by the authors of Chapters 6 to 9.

Specific contexts are given more detailed consideration in Part II, Designing for learning in context. Starting with the practice of design which takes place in course teams (Chapter 10), we go on to discuss specific disciplinary aspects of design, recognizing not only that there are many differences in pedagogical cultures between the subject areas (see for example Meyer and Land 2005), but that the discipline of educational design itself has different faces and draws on different traditions. We also include consideration of institutional cultures (Chapter 13) and the specific technical advances in mobile and wireless computing (Chapter 16), not simply to illustrate general points made in the first half but as an intrinsic part of our exploration of what 'design for learning' means. The final chapter looks towards an uncertain future and asks how we design for resilience and adaptability.

Each chapter opens with a brief introduction from us, the editors, to help guide your reading. Part III provides a range of conceptual tools that we hope you will find useful in your own communities and contexts of working.

References

Alexander, R.J. (2002) 'Dichotomous pedagogies and the promise of comparative research', paper presented at the American Educational Research Association Annual Conference, New Orleans, April 2002.

Barrie, S.C. (2007) 'A conceptual framework for the teaching and learning of generic graduate attributes', *Studies in Higher Education*, 32 (4): 439–58.

Bean, M. (2012) 'Great expectations: not a choice, a reality', Keynote to the Higher Education Academy conference, Manchester, July 2012.

British Library/JISC (2012) Researchers of tomorrow: the research behaviours of Generation Y doctoral students. British Library and JISC. Online. Available at http://www.jisc.ac.uk/media/documents/publications/reports/2012/Researchers-of-Tomorrow.pdf (accessed 18 July 2012).

Castells, M. (1996) *The Rise of the Network Society, The Information Age: Economy, society and culture*, Oxford: Blackwell.

Dreyfus, H.L. and Dreyfus, S.E. (1986) *Mind over Machine: The power of human intuition and expertise in the age of the machine*, Oxford: Basil Blackwell.

Facer, K. (2011) *Learning Futures: Education, technology and social change*, London and New York: Routledge.

Freire, P. (1996) *Pedagogy of the Oppressed*, (trans. Ramos, M.B.) London: Penguin.

Gibbons, M., Limoges, C., Nowotny, H., Schwartzman, S., Scott, P. and Trow, M. (1994) *The New Production of Knowledge*, London: Sage.

Hassan, I. (1988) *The Postmodern Turn: Essays in postmodern theory and culture*, Ohio: Ohio State UP.

Jochems, W., van Merrienboer, J. and Koper, R. (2004) *Integrated e-Learning: Implications for pedagogy, technology and organization*, London: Taylor and Francis.

Knowles, M.S. (1990) *The Adult Learner: A neglected species* (4th edition), Houston: Gulf Publishing.

Kolb, D.A. (1984) *Experiential Learning: Experience as the source of learning and development*, Englewood Cliffs, NJ: Prentice-Hall.

Lockyer, L., Bennett, S., Agostinho, S. and Harper, B. (eds) (2008) *Handbook of Research on Learning Design and Learning Objects: Issues, applications and technologies*, Hershey, PA: IGI Publishing.

Office for National Statistics (2011) Internet Access – Households and Individuals. Online. Available at http://www.ons.gov.uk/ons/dcp171778_227158.pdf (accessed 9 July 2012).

McGill, L. (2011) *Curriculum Innovation: Pragmatic approaches to transforming learning and teaching through technologies*, Bristol: JISC.

Meyer, J.H.F. and Land, R. (2005) 'Threshold concepts and troublesome knowledge: considerations and a conceptual framework for teaching and learning', *Higher Education*, 49 (3): 373–88.

Russell, T.L. (2001) No Significant Difference Phenomenon: A Comparative Research Annotated Bibliography on Technology for Distance Education, International Distance Education Certification Center. Online. Available at http://www.nosignificantdifference.org/about.asp (accessed 31 July 2012).

Schön, D.A. (1987) *Educating the Reflective Practitioner*, San Francisco: Jossey-Bass.

Trigwell, K., Martin, E., Benjamin, J. and Prosser, M. (2000) 'Scholarship of teaching: A model', *Higher Education Research and Development*, 19: 155–68.

Part I

Principles and Practices
of Designing

In the Introduction we argued for a view of design as praxis, that is both theoretically informed and based on the lived experience of practitioners. In this first part of the book we explore some of the principles that inform design for learning, and some of the approaches that have been adopted to understanding, representing and sharing the practices of real-world teaching staff in their different settings. All but one of the chapters that appeared in the first edition have been significantly revised, and three new chapters are included.

At first sight this is something of a paradox: surely the fundamentals of learning and teaching have not changed radically in half a decade? In response, Masterson (Chapter 4) reminds us that design is both the application of 'systematic principles and methods' and 'a creative activity that cannot be fully reduced to standard steps' (Winograd 1996: xx, xxii). While the systematic principles have changed little, the methods available to learners and teachers have evolved, and new approaches have proliferated. Learners' independent access to networked technologies has allowed an intermixing of personal, social and academic practices which has made learning both more accessible and more unpredictable, and has led to creative new hybridizations.

One promise of learning design foregrounded in our first edition was that the computational facilitation or capture of the design process would lead directly to the production of 'runnable' or ready-to-use learning experiences. At the very least it was hoped that it could short-cut many of the administrative aspects of curriculum design and delivery: building reading lists, generating evidence for course selection by students or for review by external accreditors, creating course documentation, building module shells for a virtual learning environment. This aspiration has not been forgotten – the learning design tools explored by Conole in Chapter 5 continue to be investigated for the efficiencies they might offer in organizational processes as well as for the enhancements they might bring to individual designs – but it remains elusive. And the search for general design models has largely been overtaken by the promise of representing and sharing practice more effectively among teaching staff. Indeed, the empirical research reported in Chapters 4 and 7 indicates that staff tend to use designs as sources of teaching ideas rather than as reusable instances of a learning activity, and to see the integration of technology into their teaching as a long-term project, based on their own confidence and expertise, rather than a problem to be solved on a case-by-case basis.

As a corollary to this, we have seen less production of self-contained, professionally designed artefacts (reusable learning objects) than we might have predicted, and the rise instead of ad hoc, community-based and ready-to-hand ways of sharing materials relevant to learning. Recording and uploading lectures, for example, is now routine and technically trivial. Community repositories are proving more sustainable than design projects that insist on a common format and standard presentation for materials. Our first edition focus on individual teachers and the decisions they make in task design has given way to a focus on curriculum teams and the design of whole-course offerings. This is both a necessary corrective – design is after all a collaborative and culturally invested activity – and a response to contemporary economic and political pressures, which require institutions to improve their design processes and outcomes across the board.

Design for learning – as Chapters 1 to 3 assert in different ways – is task or course design plus attention paid to features of the material and social setting. Like the earlier innovations of writing and printing, digital technologies change what qualifies as socially useful knowledge, as well as providing material means for knowledge (re)production. Educational systems are responding on a macro scale to these changes. Yet some of the more profound shifts we have noted are at the micro level of learning activities, where, for example, digital technologies are blurring the boundaries between public and private, crossing formal and informal practices, and shifting the ground for learners as they negotiate multiple identities in hybrid spaces.

Part I maps how established principles of design for learning have fared in these new circumstances, and what new practices are emerging. In Chapter 1, Mayes and de Freitas review the available theories about how people learn and conclude that no new class of theories is required to describe learning in a digital setting. Drawing on Activity Theory and Actor Network Theory respectively, the authors of Chapters 2 (Beetham) and 3 (Goodyear and Carvalho, new in this edition) describe the systems of human and non-human actors that are involved in a learning activity, while Oliver *et al.* (Chapter 6) show a similar design model being applied to a national teaching enhancement project. Chapters 4 (Masterman) and 7 (Agostinho *et al.*, new in this edition) summarize empirical research into how practitioners go about designing learning tasks and environments, and consider what this tells us about the representation and sharing of practice. Meanwhile, Chapter 5 (Conole) investigates a variety of tools developed to support design for learning, while Chapter 8 (McAndrew and Goodyear) explores different forms of representation. In Chapter 9, new in this edition, Pegler outlines how open educational resources (OER) have evolved as a practical, distributed and accessible approach to the sharing of materials, with teachers and learners benefiting in different ways. Barriers to sharing have apparently come down without the help of design principles and patterns, as educational assets circulate freely alongside celebrity videos and sensational infographics. However, a principled approach to design continues to be prized by educators and sought after by institutions, even if those principles are being played out in new forms.

Reference

Winograd, T. (ed.) (1996) *Bringing Design to Software*, New York: ACM Press.

Chapter 1

Technology-Enhanced Learning
The Role of Theory

Terry Mayes and Sara de Freitas

EDITORS' INTRODUCTION

Mayes and de Freitas argue that design decisions need to be based on clear theoretical principles. While there is consensus on many theoretical issues in pedagogy, the authors identify three broadly different perspectives on learning and three sets of pedagogic priorities that arise from them. They go on to suggest that each of these perspectives is incomplete, and that a principled approach to e-learning requires an understanding of all three as distinct viewpoints on the learning process.

Introduction

It is arguable that there is no need for a theory of technology-enhanced learning. Technology can play an important role in the achievement of learning outcomes but it seems unnecessary to explain this enhancement with a special account of learning. Rather, the challenge is to describe how the technology allows underlying processes common to all learning to function effectively. A theory of the enhancement would need to demonstrate on what new learning principles the added value of the technology was operating. Where, for example, the technology allows remote learners to interact with each other and with the representations of the subject matter in a way that could simply not be achieved for those learners without it then we may have a genuine example of added value. However, in this example the role of the technology may be primarily to get remote learners into a position to learn as favourably as though they were campus-based, rather than offering a new learning method. In such a case the enhancement is an educational one, though the underlying learning theory explains both campus-based and distance learning with the same theoretical constructs.

New paradigms for achieving learning outcomes with technology do not need new theories. For example, a peer-to-peer learner-matching tool or a task-based training game will not need a new account of learning, even though it may have enormous educational value if it can be exploited through an infrastructure which integrated its use with quality assurance methods.

We will argue below that in the powerful new learning opportunities that are being facilitated in a substantively new way through the Internet, we are beginning to witness a new model of education, rather than a new model of learning.

The need for theory

Biggs (1999) describes the task of good pedagogical design as one of ensuring that there are absolutely no inconsistencies between the curriculum we teach, the teaching methods we use, the learning environment we choose, and the assessment procedures we adopt. To achieve complete consistency, we need to examine very carefully what assumptions we are making at each stage and to align those. Thus, we need to start with carefully defined intended learning outcomes, we then need to choose learning and teaching activities that stand a good chance of allowing the students to achieve that learning, then we need to design assessment tasks that will genuinely test whether the outcomes have been reached. This process is easy to state, but very hard to achieve in an informed way. Biggs' book is largely about how the task of making the design decisions can be made more straightforward by adopting the assumptions of a constructivist pedagogical approach, where the focus is always on what the learner is actually doing: placing the learning activities at the heart of the process. Thus, Biggs uses the term 'constructive alignment' to indicate that, in his view, the guiding assumptions about learning should be based on constructivist theory. The relevant point is that the alignment process cannot proceed without first examining the underlying assumptions about learning, and then adopting teaching methods that align with those assumptions.

The main purpose of this chapter, then, is to outline the theoretical underpinning of technology-enhanced learning, and to argue that, to be comprehensive, its design must consider three fundamental perspectives, each of which leads to a particular view of what matters in pedagogy. The intention is to show how technology-enhanced learning can be approached in a principled way, which means uncovering the implicit assumptions about pedagogy, and then asking the right questions. We thus try to place technology-enhanced learning models within the design framework described above. But the crucial step is the one Biggs made when he adopted a constructivist approach to ground the design decisions: there must be guidance on how to judge whether the learning and teaching processes adopted will really achieve the intended learning outcomes. For good pedagogical design, there is simply no escaping the need to adopt a theory of learning, and to understand how the pedagogy that is suggested by the theory follows naturally from its assumptions about what is important. Even when defining a learning outcome there are implicit assumptions about what is important. Is the learning to demonstrate smooth performance – applying a clinical procedure, say? Or is it to demonstrate the deep understanding of a principle – so that it can be explained clearly to someone else? Or is it being able to make appropriate judgements in a difficult social situation? Each of these intended outcomes would require a different kind of theoretical perspective and a different pedagogical approach.

Learning theory and pedagogical design

There are distinct traditions in educational theory that derive from different perspectives about the nature of learning itself (de Freitas and Jameson 2012). Although learning theory is often presented as though there is a large set of competing accounts for the same phenomena, it is more accurate to think of theory as a set of quite compatible explanations for a large range of different phenomena. In fact it is probably true to say that never before has there been such agreement about the psychological fundamentals (Jonassen and Land 2000). Here, we follow the approach of Greeno *et al.* (1996) in identifying three clusters or broad perspectives, which make fundamentally different assumptions about what is being explained.

The associationist perspective

The associationist approach models learning as the gradual building of patterns of associations and skill components. Learning occurs through the process of connecting the elementary mental or behavioural units, through sequences of activity followed by feedback of some kind. This view encompasses the research traditions of associationism, behaviourism and connectionism (neural networks).

The associationist view of feedback as automatically reinforcing a connection, rather than as providing information, encouraged the behaviourists to regard learning as a process that occurs without the need for conscious awareness. In contrast, the Gestalt tradition, also originating in the early part of the 20th century, emphasized the essential role of thinking and problem solving in learning. The tension between these two fundamental views of the nature of learning has dominated learning theory ever since (for a modern review, see Shanks 2010). It is not the case, though, that associationist theory can explain only simple learning, a point emphasized by the apparently high-level processes that emerge in machine-based neural network or parallel distributed processing models (Thomas and McClelland 2008).

Associationist theory requires knowledge or skill to be analysed as specific associations, expressed as behavioural objectives. This kind of analysis was developed by Gagné (1985) into an elaborate system of instructional task analysis of discriminations, classifications and response sequences. Learning tasks are arranged in sequences based on their relative complexity according to a task analysis, with simpler components as prerequisites for more complex tasks.

The basic principle of this approach, known as Instructional Systems Design (ISD), is that competence in advanced and complex tasks is built step by step from simpler units of knowledge or skill, finally adding coordination to the whole structure. So ISD consists of the following stages:

- analyse the domain into a hierarchy of small units;
- sequence the units so that a combination of units is not taught until its component units are grasped individually;
- design an instructional approach for each unit in the sequence.

Analysis of complex tasks into Gagné's learning hierarchies – the decomposition hypothesis – involves the assumption that knowledge and skill need to be taught from the bottom up. This assumption has been the subject of long controversy (e.g. Resnick and Resnick 1991), but is still prevalent in training, and underpins the kind of e-learning often found in industry. Combining this approach with immediate feedback, and with the individualizing of instruction through allowing multiple paths to successful performance, where each student is provided with the next problem contingent on their response to the previous one, brings us to programmed instruction. This approach, ideally suited to automation through simple technology, came to be widely discredited along with the excesses of 'behavioural modification' in a crude application of behaviourist theory to education. However, it is worth underlining the point made by, for example, Wilson and Myers (2000), that although behaviourism has often been dismissed as not a serious theoretical basis for education, and mistakenly often regarded as a teaching-centred model of learning, this view is seriously wide of the mark. Behaviourism applied to human learning emphasized active learning-by-doing with immediate feedback on success, the careful analysis of learning outcomes, and above all with the alignment of learning objectives, instructional strategies and methods used to assess learning outcomes. Many of the methods with the label 'constructivist' – constituting the currently accepted consensus on pedagogy among educational developers – are indistinguishable from those derived from the associationist tradition.

The cognitive perspective

As part of a general shift in theoretical positioning in psychology starting in the 1960s, learning, as well as perception, thinking, language and reasoning, became seen as the output of an individual's attention, memory and concept formation processes. This approach provided a basis for analysing concepts and procedures of subject matter curricula in terms of information structures, and gave rise to new approaches to pedagogy.

Within this broad perspective, certain sub-areas of cognitive research can be highlighted as particularly influential, e.g. schema theory, information processing theories of problem solving and reasoning, levels of processing in memory, general competencies for thinking, mental models, and metacognitive processes. The underlying theme for learning is to model the processes of interpreting and constructing meaning, and a particular emphasis was placed on the instantiation of models of knowledge acquisition in the form of computer programmes (e.g. Anderson and Lebiere 1998). Knowledge acquisition was viewed as the outcome of an interaction between new experiences and the structures for understanding that have already been created. So building a framework for understanding becomes the learner's key cognitive challenge. This kind of thinking stood in sharp contrast to the model of learning as the strengthening of associations.

The cognitive account saw knowledge acquisition as proceeding from a declarative form to a procedural, compiled form. As performance becomes more expert-like and fluent so the component skills become automatized. Thus, conscious attention is no longer required to monitor the low-level aspects of performance, which become better described as associations, and cognitive resources are available for more strategic levels of processing. The computer tutors developed by Anderson and co-workers (Anderson *et al.* 1995) are all based on this 'expertise' view of learning.

Increasingly, mainstream cognitive approaches to learning and teaching have emphasized the assumptions of constructivism: that understanding is gained through an active process of creating hypotheses and building new forms of understanding through activity. In school-level educational research the influence of Piaget has been very significant, in particular his assumption that conceptual development occurs through intellectual activity rather than by the absorption of information. Piaget's constructivist theory of knowledge (1970) was based on the assumption that learners do not copy or absorb ideas from the external world, but must construct their concepts through active and personal experimentation and observation. Many studies have shown that students' abilities to understand something new depends on what they already know. Educators cannot build expertise by having learners memorize experts' knowledge. New knowledge must be built on the foundations of already existing frameworks, through problem-solving activity and feedback.

Piaget did not favour the direct teaching of disciplinary content, although he was arguing against the behaviourist bottom-up variety, rather than the kind of meaningful learning advocated by Bruner (1960). Indeed, the fundamental tension between what Newell (1980) called weak methods, a focus on generic skills, and strong methods, domain-specific, persists as an unresolved issue in higher and further education.

Collins *et al.* (1989) argued that we should consider concepts as tools, to be understood through use, rather than as self-contained entities to be delivered through instruction. This is the essence of the constructivist approach in which the learners' search for meaning through activity is central. Nevertheless, it is rather too simplistic to argue that constructivism has emerged directly from a cognitive perspective. As we have seen, in its emphasis on learning-by-doing, and the importance of feedback, it leans partly towards the associationist tradition. In its emphasis on authentic tasks it takes much of the situative position (see below). The emergence of situated cognition was itself partly dependent on the influence on mainstream cognitive theory of Lave's socio-anthropological work (Lave 1988). Vygotsky's (1978) emphasis on the importance of social interaction

velopment of higher cognitive functions continues to influence construc-
dagogy. Some theorists (e.g. Duffy and Cunningham 1996) distinguish
n cognitive constructivism (deriving from the Piagetian tradition), and
socio-cultural constructivism (deriving from the Vygotskian approach).

Activities of constructing understanding have two main aspects:

- interactions with material systems and concepts in the domain;
- interactions in which learners discuss and reflect on their developing understanding and competence.

The emphasis on task-based learning and reflection can be seen as a reaction
to the rapid development of multimedia and hypermedia in the 1980s and early
1990s, in which a tendency for technology-based practice to resurrect traditional
instructionist approaches was evident. Here the main focus was on the delivery
of materials through which information can be more effectively transmitted by
teachers and understood by learners. Indeed, for a while in the early 1990s, these
trends were working in opposite directions: the research community was uniting
around some key ideas of learning which emphasized the importance of the task-
based and social context, while the policy makers were seizing on the potential of technology-enhanced learning to generate efficiencies through powerful
methods of delivering information. There are recent signs that, while still not
perfectly congruent, these are no longer in opposition. Since the development
of the web, both have converged on communication as a key enabling construct.

The situative perspective

The social perspective on learning has received a major boost from the gradual
reconceptualization of all learning as 'situated'. A learner will always be
subjected to influences from the social and cultural setting in which the learning
occurs, which will also, at least partly, define the learning outcomes. This view of
learning focuses on the way knowledge is distributed socially. When knowledge
is seen as situated in the practices of communities then the outcomes of learning
involve the abilities of individuals to participate in those practices successfully.
The focus shifts right away from analyses of components of subtasks, and onto
the patterns of successful practice. This can be seen as a necessary correction
to theories of learning in which both the behavioural and cognitive levels of
analysis had become disconnected from the social. Underlying both the situated
learning and constructivist perspectives is the assumption that learning must be
personally meaningful, and that this has very little to do with the informational
characteristics of a learning environment. Activity, motivation and learning are
all related to a need for a positive sense of identity (or positive self-esteem),
shaped by social forces.

Barab and Duffy (2000) have distinguished two rather different accounts of
situated learning. The first can be regarded as a socio-psychological view of

situativity. This emphasizes the importance of context-dependent learning in informal settings and leads to the design of constructivist tasks in which every effort is made to make the learning activity authentic to the social context in which the skills or knowledge are normally embedded ('practice fields'). Examples of this approach are problem-based learning (Savery and Duffy 1996), and cognitive apprenticeship (Collins 2006). Here, the main design emphasis is on the relationship between the nature of the learning task in educational or training environments, and its characteristics when situated in real use.

The second version of situated learning is based on the idea that with the concept of a community of practice comes an emphasis on the individual's relationship with a group of people rather than the relationship of an activity itself to the wider practice, even though it is the practice itself that identifies the community. This provides a different perspective on what is 'situated'. Lave and Wenger (1991) characterized learning of practices as processes of participation in which beginners are initially relatively peripheral in the activities of a community and as they learn the practices their participation becomes more central. For Wenger (1998), it is not just the meaning to be attached to an activity that is derived from a community of practice: the individual's identity as a learner is shaped by the relationship to the community itself. The concept of vicarious learning (Mayes et al. 2001) is also based on the idea of learning through relating to others. Strictly, this occurs through observing others' learning, as for example in a master class. A great deal of conventional classroom-based learning is vicarious, and there are obvious ways in which this kind of learning is enhanced through computer-mediated communication.

There are perhaps three levels at which it is useful to think of learning being situated.

Situated learning at the community of practice level: At the top level is the social-anthropological or cultural perspective, which emphasizes the need to learn to achieve a desired form of participation in a wider community. The essence of a community of practice is that, through joint engagement in some activity, an aggregation of people comes to develop and share practices. This is usually interpreted as a stable and relatively enduring group, scientists for example, whose practices involve the development of a constellation of beliefs, attitudes, values and specific knowledge built up over many years. Yet a community of practice can be built around a common endeavour, which has a much shorter time span. Greeno et al. (1998) give examples of communities of practice that more closely resemble the groups studied in the social identity literature (e.g. Ellemers et al. 1999). Some examples are a garage band, an engineering team, a day care cooperative, a research group or a kindergarten class. It is worth noting that these are exactly the kind of groups described as activity systems in the approach that has come to be known as Activity Theory (Cole and Engeström 1993; Jonassen and Rohrer-Murphy 1999).

For long-term stable communities there are two different ways in which the community will influence learning. First, there is the sense most directly addressed by Wenger – someone aspires to become a legitimate participant of a community defined by expertise or competence in some field of application. The learning in this case is the learning of the practice that defines the community. This is the learning involved in becoming an accredited member of a community by reaching a demonstrated level of expertise, and then the learning involved in continuous professional development. This may be formal, as in medicine, or informal, by being accepted as a wine buff or a political activist. The second sense is that of a community of learners, for whom the practice is learning *per se*. That is, a very broad community identified by a shared high value placed on the process of continuous intellectual development.

Situated learning at the group level: At the next level of situatedness is the learning group. Almost all learning is itself embedded in a social context – the classroom, or the tutorial group, or the virtual computer-mediated communication (CMC) group or even the year group. The learner will usually have a strong sense of identifying with such groups, and a strong need to participate as a full member. Such groups can have the characteristics of a community of practice but here the practice is the learning itself, in a particular educational or training setting. Or rather it is educational practice, which may or may not be centred on learning. While there have been many studies of learning in informal settings (e.g. Resnick 1987), there are comparatively few ethnographic studies of real groups in educational settings to compare with the many studies of group dynamics in work organizations (see Greeno *et al.* 1998).

Situated learning at the level of individual relationships: Finally, learning is experienced through individual relationships. Most learning that is motivated by the other levels will actually be mediated through relationships with individual members of the communities or groups in question. The social categorization of these individuals will vary according to the context and nature of particular dialogues. Sometimes their membership of a group will be most salient, in other situations their personal characteristics will be perceived as more important. Such relationships will vary according to the characteristics of the groups involved, the context within which they operate, and the strength of the relationships (Fowler and Mayes 1999). With the explosion of web-based phenomena of social networking and game-based learning this analysis has taken on a new importance for pedagogy. It has brought into focus the potency of shared experience as a key component of social learning.

Technology-enhanced learning and the learning cycle

It is possible to view these differing perspectives as analysing learning at different levels of aggregation. An associationist analysis describes the overt activities, and the outcomes of these activities, for individual learners. A cognitive analysis attempts a level of analysis that describes the detailed structures and processes that underlie individual performance. The situative perspective aggregates at the level of groups of learners, describing activity systems in which individuals participate as members of communities. There will be few current examples of approaches that derive from taking just one level of analysis and neglecting the others. Most implementations of technology-enhanced learning will include blended elements that emphasize all three levels: learning as behaviour, learning as the construction of knowledge and meaning, and learning as social practice.

We conclude that each of the three perspectives described above is integral to learning. It seems appropriate to regard them as perspectives rather than theories, since each is incomplete as an account of learning. It is tempting to regard them not as competing accounts but as stages in a cycle (see Mayes and Fowler 1999). The three perspectives address different aspects of the progression towards mastery of knowledge or skill, with the situative perspective addressing the learner's motivation, the associative perspective focusing on the detailed nature of performance, and the cognitive on the role of understanding and reflecting on action. Each of these perspectives is associated with a particular kind of pedagogy, and each is capable of being enhanced through technology. A handout summarizing the three perspectives and their implications for teaching and assessment is provided in Appendix 1.

There is quite a long tradition of describing learning as a cycle through stages, with each cycle focusing in turn on different perspectives (Fitts and Posner 1967; Rumelhart and Norman 1978; Kolb 1984; Mayes and Fowler 1999). Such a representation of learning also carries the advantage of describing learning as iterative. Welford (1968), for example, reported work that demonstrated that practice will lead to performance improvements that proceed almost indefinitely even on simple perceptual-motor tasks. Learning should not be thought of as being completed when an assessment has been successfully passed. However, as it proceeds from novice to expert, the nature of learning changes profoundly and the pedagogy based on one stage will be inappropriate for another. Depicting our three perspectives as a cycle invites the learning designer to consider what kind of technology is most effective at what stage of learning. Fowler and Mayes (1999) attempted to map broad pedagogies onto types of technology,

---

Box 1.1 Learning for its own sake

It seems likely that many of the learners choosing to study on MOOCs (massive open online courses) are participating in the kind of lifelong learning tradition that has always provided learning for its own sake, rather than learning that leads to qualifications. The adult learning and lifelong learning literatures draw on what is essentially a fourth perspective on learning theory – that of humanistic psychology. This approach has stressed the importance of personal psychological growth and underpins the work of, for example, Mezirow (2009, transformational learning) and Kolb (1984, experiential learning). However, as with constructivist pedagogy in general, with its emphasis on reflection this strand of learning theory can also be traced back to John Dewey (1933).

distinguishing between the technology of presenting information (primary), the technology of supporting active learning tasks and feedback (secondary), and the technology of supporting dialogue about the application of the new learning (tertiary). Such a model is attractive as a design framework since it gives maximum scope for using technology strategically: addressing different pedagogical goals in different ways.

When we consider the current landscape of technology-enhanced learning another kind of model suggests itself, based perhaps on a simple dimension of locus of control. At one end of this dimension we have institutional virtual learning environments (VLEs), with their emphasis on standardization. These are at the institution-in-control end of this dimension. At the other end is an environment that empowers learners to take responsibility for their own learning to the point where they make their own design decisions. The currently popular notion of the personalization of learning environments moves us part of the way along this dimension, although it depends whether the personal choices offered allow the learner to shape the learning environment in a way that really influences pedagogic control. Some of the rapidly developing web tools for learning do provide the fully empowered e-learner with great flexibility in control of their own learning through processes allowing rich dialogue with others with whom the learner can identify. More than any previous educational technology, current tools allow the rapid identification of like-minded others, and allow learning relationships to drive both direct communication and the sharing of relevant information.

We might bring these ideas together in the following way. The stages represent a cycle that starts with the social. Motivation to start and continue learning will

---

Box 1.2 Self-regulated learning

Self-regulated learning is especially important for constructivist pedagogies. Successful self-regulation is necessary for learning independently: goal-directed, having a sense of self-efficacy, a willingness to commit, and metacognitive awareness. These attributes seem particularly important for what Weller (2011) has called 'the pedagogy of abundance', where a learner can independently access and explore enormous amounts of seemingly relevant content. Theoretically, the concept of self-regulated learning is quite hard to pin down since it lies in an area where cognitive, behavioural, affective and motivational processes all apply. Some aspects of self-regulated learning suggest a trait – a relatively enduring ability for learning effectively – but other aspects seem trainable, implying a situated learning dimension. A comprehensive socio-cognitive model of self-regulated learning is described by Pintrich (see Schunk 2005) involving phases of planning, monitoring, control and reflection. Nicol and Macfarlane-Dick (2006) have described how feedback from formative assessment can help to encourage self-regulated learning in higher education students.

be derived from communities and peers. This represents the situative perspective and it is served by the various technologies which allow the identification of, and communication with, others who will share in, or in some way contribute to, the learning experience. Gradually, personal ownership of the learning activities becomes necessary for the derivation of meaning and the construction of understanding. Learning tasks come into play. These will involve the production of outputs that can only be achieved through understanding. This brings the cognitive perspective into focus. The learner will interact with subject matter, but in a way that manipulates it actively. What are usually regarded as the pedagogical inputs, learning objects, should rather be outputs, created by the learner. To reach this point, however, it will at times be necessary to subject oneself as a learner to the discipline of bottom-up mastery of the components of a task, so an associationist perspective will underpin pedagogy at key moments. As learning progresses, so the learner will benefit from checking progress with peers, and engaging in dialogue about the refinements of the developing understanding, and the associated skills, so the cycle can continue for as long as necessary.

Other chapters in this book offer a range of different approaches to learning design underpinned by the general principles discussed here. In Chapter 2, Beetham develops our taxonomy further. In Chapter 6, Oliver et al. take the notion of constructive alignment and use it to explore learning designs with conceptual change as their goal. In Chapter 5, Conole uses the three perspectives described here in a taxonomy for describing learning activities, tools and resources.

Conclusions

We have offered a mapping of theoretical accounts of learning onto pedagogical principles for design. We have attempted to frame this account within a familiar curriculum design model, with its stages of describing intended learning outcomes, designing teaching methods and learning environments to achieve them, assessments to measure how well they have been achieved, and an evaluation of whether the stages are properly aligned. Most of this will now be familiar territory. For the training of skills we adopt an associative account, with its emphasis on task analysis and practice; for deep learning of concepts constructivist pedagogy is emphasized, with a learner actively involved in the design of his or her own learning activity. Giving meaning to the whole process is an engagement with the social setting and peer culture surrounding it.

As our understanding of technology-enhanced learning matures, so our appreciation of the importance of theory deepens. This view is one that rather challenges the conventional rationale of learning design. For most educational outcomes, theory points us clearly in a particular direction. Learners, in communities and other groups, but also individually, should be encouraged to take responsibility for the achievement of their own learning outcomes. As technology-enhanced learning tools become truly powerful in their capability, and global in their scope, so it becomes more feasible to remodel the educational enterprise as a process of empowering learners to take reflective control of their own learning. This view challenges current assumptions about how far institutions can put a boundary around a learning experience.

A virtual learning environment may be seen as representing a 20th century instantiation of the role of institutions in attempting to manage the process. In peer-to-peer social networks, and in MOOCs (see Box 1.2), we begin to see a 21st century view. Now that peer-to-peer learning is facilitated in a powerful way, and on a global scale, we see how learning can be socially situated in a way never previously possible. The Internet gives every course in every institution a potentially global span. Learning theory emphasizes the importance of this, but it does not provide us with a clear understanding of how to exploit it efficiently within the context of a mature educational infrastructure. Positioning empowered individual learners at the centre of the technology-enhanced learning design process will clearly impact on the role of the educator but it is not yet clear how that role will evolve. What is clear is that theory and practice must be aligned within a coherent and workable model of education.

References

Anderson, J.R. and Lebiere, C. (1998) *The Atomic Components of Thought*, Mahwah, New Jersey: Lawrence Erlbaum.

Anderson, J.R., Corbett, A.T., Koedinger, K.R. and Pelletier, R. (1995) 'Cognitive tutors: lessons learned', *Journal of the Learning Sciences*, 4 (2): 167–207.

Barab, S.A. and Duffy, T.M. (2000) 'From practice fields to communities of practice', in D.H. Jonassen and S.M. Land (eds) *Theoretical Foundations of Learning Environments*, New Jersey: Lawrence Erlbaum.

Biggs, J. (1999) *Teaching for Quality Learning at University*, Buckingham: Society for Research in Higher Education and Open University Press.

Bruner, J. (1960) *The Process of Education*, Cambridge, MA: Harvard University Press.

Cole, M. and Engeström, Y. (1993) 'A cultural-historical approach to distributed cognition', in G. Salomon (ed.) *Distributed Cognitions: Psychological and educational considerations*, New York: Cambridge University Press.

Collins, A. (2006) 'Cognitive apprenticeship', in R.K. Sawyer (ed.) *The Cambridge Handbook of the Learning Sciences*, Cambridge: Cambridge University Press.

Collins, A., Brown, J.S. and Newman, S.E. (1989) 'Cognitive apprenticeship: teaching the crafts of reading, writing and mathematics', in R.B. Resnick (ed.) *Knowing, Learning and Instruction: Essays in honour of Robert Glaser*, New Jersey: Lawrence Erlbaum.

de Freitas, S. and Jameson, J. (eds) (2012) *The Technology-enhanced Learning Reader*, London and New York: Continuum Press.

Dewey, J. (1933) *How We Think* (revised edn.), Boston: D.C. Heath.

Duffy, T.M. and Cunningham, D.J. (1996) 'Constructivism: implications for design and delivery of instruction', in D.H. Jonassen (ed.) *Educational Communications and Technology*, New York: Simon and Schuster Macmillan.

Ellemers, N., Spears, R. and Doosje, B. (eds) (1999) *Social Identity: Context, commitment, content*, Malden, MA: Blackwell.

Fitts, P. and Posner, M. I. (1967) *Human Performance*, Monterey, CA: Brooks/Cole.

Fowler, C.J.H. and Mayes, J.T. (1999) 'Learning relationships: from theory to design', *Association for Learning Technology Journal*, 7 (3): 6–16.

Gagné, R. (1985) *The Conditions of Learning*, New York: Holt, Rinehart and Winston.

Greeno, J.G., Collins, A.M. and Resnick, L. (1996) 'Cognition and learning', in D.C. Berliner and R.C. Calfee (eds) *Handbook of Educational Psychology*, New York: Simon & Schuster Macmillan.

Greeno, J.G., Eckert, P., Stucky, S.U., Sachs, P. and Wenger, E. (1998) 'Learning in and for participation in work and society', paper presented at US Dept. of Education and OECD Conference on How Adults Learn, Washington DC, April 1998.

Jonassen, D.H. and Land, S.M. (2000) *Theoretical Foundations of Learning Environments*, Hillsdale, NJ: Lawrence Erlbaum.

Jonassen, D.H. and Rohrer-Murphy, L. (1999) 'Activity theory as a framework for designing constructivist learning environments', *Educational Technology Research and Development*, 47 (1): 61–80.

Kolb, D.A. (1984) *Experiential Learning: Experience as the source of learning and development*, Englewood Cliffs, NJ: Prentice-Hall.

Lave, J. (1988) *Cognition in Practice: Mind, mathematics and culture in everyday life*, Cambridge: University of Cambridge.

Lave, J. and Wenger, E. (1991) *Situated Learning: Legitimate peripheral participation*, Cambridge: Cambridge University Press.

Mayes, J.T. and Fowler, C.J.H. (1999) 'Learning technology and usability: a framework for understanding courseware', *Interacting with Computers*, 11: 485–97.

Mayes, J.T, Dineen, F., McKendree, J. and Lee, J. (2001) 'Learning from watching others learn', in C. Steeples and C. Jones (eds) *Networked Learning: Perspectives and issues*, London: Springer.

Mezirow, J. (2009), An overview on transformative learning, In K. Illeris (ed.) *Contemporary Theories of Learning*, London: Routledge.

Newell, A. (1980) 'One final word', in D.T. Tuma and F. Reif (eds) *Problem Solving and Education: Issues in teaching and research*, New Jersey: Lawrence Erlbaum.

Nicol, D.J. and Macfarlane-Dick, D., (2006) 'Formative assessment and self-regulated learning: a model and seven principles of good feedback practice', *Studies in Higher Education*, 31 (2): 199–221.

Piaget, J. (1970) *Science of Education and the Psychology of the Child*, New York: Orion Press.

Resnick, L.B. (1987) 'Learning in school and out', *Educational Researcher*, 16: 13–20.

Resnick, L.B. and Resnick, D.P. (1991) 'Assessing the thinking curriculum: New tools for education reform', in B.R. Gifford and M.C. O'Connor (eds) *Changing Assessment: Alternative views of aptitude, achievement and instruction*, Boston: Kluwer.

Rumelhart, D.E. and Norman, D.A. (1978) 'Accretion, tuning and structuring: three modes of learning', in J.W. Cotton and R.L. Klatzky (eds) *Semantic Factors in Cognition*, Hillsdale, NJ: Erlbaum.

Savery, J.R. and Duffy, T.M. (1996) 'Problem-based learning: an instructional model and its constructivist framework', in B.G. Wilson (ed.) *Constructivist Learning Environments: Case studies in instructional design*, NJ: Educational Technology Publications.

Schunk, D.H. (2005) 'Self-regulated learning: The educational legacy of Paul R. Pintrich', *Educational Psychologist*, 40, 85–94.

Shanks, D.R. (2010) 'Learning: from association to cognition', *Annual Review of Psychology*, 61: 273–301.

Thomas, M.S.C. and McClelland, J.L. (2008) 'Connectionist models of cognition', in R.K. Sawyer (ed.) *The Cambridge Handbook of the Learning Sciences*, Cambridge: Cambridge University Press.

Vygotsky, L.S. (1978) *Mind in Society*, Cambridge, MA: Harvard University Press.

Welford, A.T. (1968) *Fundamentals of Skill*, Methuen: London.

Weller, M. (2011) *The Digital Scholar: How technology is changing scholarly practice*, London: Bloomsbury Academic.

Wenger, E. (1998) *Communities of Practice: Learning, meaning, and identity*, Cambridge: Cambridge University Press.

Wilson, B.G. and Myers, K.M. (2000) 'Situated cognition in theoretical and practical context', in D.H. Jonassen and S.M. Land (eds) *Theoretical Foundations of Learning Environments*, New Jersey: Lawrence Erlbaum.

Chapter 2

Designing for Active Learning in Technology-Rich Contexts

Helen Beetham

Editors' introduction

In the Introduction we stated that good design applies theoretical principles to specific cases of use. This chapter considers how design principles have been developed from theories of how people learn (see Mayes and de Freitas, Chapter 1) and how these can be applied to learning with digital technologies. The learning *activity* is presented as a helpful focus for design, and Activity Theory is used to develop a model of design practice that focuses on different aspects of activity.

Introduction

What design principles can be derived from the theoretical discussions of the previous chapter? All three approaches – which I term associative, constructive and situative – emphasize the central importance of activity on the part of the learner. Several decades of research support the view that it is the activity that the learner engages in, and the outcomes of that activity, that are significant for learning (e.g. Tergan 1997; Gholson and Craig 2006). There is no reason why the introduction of new digital tools and materials should challenge this emphasis, and the emergence of Learning Design as a paradigm in the early years of the century (see McAndrew and Goodyear, Chapter 8) was a sign that the learning technology community had refocused its interest on the activities undertaken by learners, after a period when the design of tools and resources had been the main concern.

It is useful to distinguish activities from tasks (see also Goodyear and Carvalho, Chapter 3). In a formal educational setting, tasks are usually defined *for* learners within the framework of the curriculum. Activities are engaged in *by* learners in response to the demands of a task. Although good teachers and learning designers will provide guidance as to how tasks might be carried out, for example by offering access to specific resources and environments, different learners will still have their own ways of proceeding. This is particularly true during the period of consolidation or practice that is another common principle of all three theoretical approaches.

Theorists also stress the need for integration across activities, whether associatively (building component skills into extended performance), constructively (integrating skills and knowledge, planning and reflecting), or situatively (developing identities and roles). The two principles of consolidation and integration help to explain why learning activities are never fully and sufficiently defined by the terms of the task. Once real learners are presented with a task, their own interpretation of what is required set against their personal aspirations for learning, along with factors in their social, physical and technical environment, will all influence what emerges.

One difference between the three theoretical schools described in the previous chapter is the degree to which learners' own meaning-making and aspiration are significant in task design. In an associative model, 'good' task design does not depend on learners sharing or even understanding the principles that govern the designer's thinking: if they follow the requirements of the task and do not fail in any of its components, they should learn in the ways predicted. For constructive theorists, the outcome of an activity is much more dependent on whether learners understand and integrate the task requirements into their own structures of awareness. Social constructive and situative theories place much more emphasis on the meaning of the activity to the learner, embedded in a social system that gives the activity value and influences how its roles, rules and aims are understood.

From each of these theoretical schools, however, learners and their activities are at the centre of interest. Partly because of their contingent and emergent nature, learning activities are perhaps the most pedagogically meaningful focus of design for learning.

Different theories: different emphases

If there are many agreed design principles (consolidation, integration, feedback etc), as I have just indicated there are also substantially different emphases that arise from the different theories about how people learn (see Chapter 1). These can be briefly summarized as follows.

*   *Authenticity of the activity*: Apprenticeship and work-based learning depend on activities arising 'naturally' from a highly authentic context (situative learning). Lab and field activities are designed to develop complex skills from real-world encounters, but the context is artificially manipulated to be supportive of learning, e.g. made safer, less complex, or more clearly signposted. Associative learning depends not on authenticity but on rehearsing skills and concepts in a highly structured way, hence the artificiality of the setting may be necessary.
*   *Formality and structure*: Learning activities may be highly structured and carefully sequenced, perhaps because this format has been shown to help fast and accurate learning, or they may be poorly defined, allowing learners

to develop their own approaches. Highly structured activities can often be expressed as a linear sequence while open-ended activities will more likely be represented as a problem space, a scenario, or a set of options.

- *Retention/reproduction versus reflection/internalization*: When the focus is on accuracy of reproduction, learners will be given opportunities to practise the required concept or skill until they can reproduce it exactly as taught. When the focus is on internalization, learners will be given opportunities to integrate a concept or skill with their existing beliefs and capabilities, to reflect on what it means to them, and to make sense of it in a variety of contexts.

- *The roles and significance of other people*: Much learning involves learners in relationship with a more expert other person, but the role of this person – instructor, mentor, facilitator, absent author – differs. Peer learners also have different roles to play, with some design approaches emphasizing the necessity of collaboration and social meaning-making, and others emphasizing the development of self-reliance.

- *Locus of control*: Related to roles is the question of how decisions about the learning activity are made. Who determines when a learning activity is completed? Who controls the timing of and criteria for assessment? Some approaches favour strong tutor or designer control, giving learners the security to focus on the skill or concept at hand, while others insist on giving learners more autonomy in order to make sense of the task and its requirements for themselves.

A checklist of approaches to learning and their implications for design is provided in Appendix 1. In the rest of this chapter I explore the decisions that have to be made in designing for learning activities in settings where digital technologies are available. Designers may approach these decisions already committed to a specific theoretical approach, or already decided on how the issues of authenticity, formality, and locus of control, etc. will play out in a specific context. On the other hand, practitioners' theoretical inclinations may only emerge as they reflect on the decisions they have taken (see Masterman, Chapter 4).

Defining a learning activity

We are interested here to define a learning activity in a way that supports the design process, including the design decisions to be made, the information required to support these decisions, and how theories or principles can be applied. From this perspective, a learning activity can helpfully be defined as *a specific interaction of learner(s) with other(s) using specific tools and resources, orientated towards specific outcomes*. Examples of learning activities might include solving problems, comparing and evaluating arguments, researching a topic, presenting ideas, or negotiating goals.

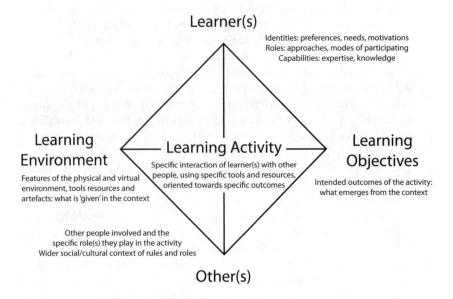

Figure 2.1 An outline for a learning activity

Figure 2.1 shows an outline for a learning activity with its component elements. When practitioners were consulted about their own design practice at a series of workshops, these were the elements they considered it necessary to describe and share (Masterman *et al.* 2005; Masterman, Chapter 4). The specific arrangement of elements in this diagram is derived from Activity Theory (see e.g. Engeström 1999), an approach which has proved productive for learning technology researchers in recent years (e.g. Issroff and Scanlon 2002; Margaryan and Littlejohn 2008; Cecile 2012).

Because a learning activity – or interaction – emerges as the learner engages in a task, the elements identified here are in practice highly interdependent on one another, and their final shape may only be clear when the activity is completed. As Goodyear and Carvalho note (Chapter 3), these elements need to be understood as a system of activity and not as a checklist. Nevertheless, in formal learning, elements of the activity are often prepared for separately, and different elements may be focused on. In highly learner-centred contexts such as research projects or key skills acquisition, the needs and goals of the learner will be of first concern. Pragmatically, access to specific resources or opportunities to relate to others are usually constrained, so access to these supporting features may be decisive. In formal, curriculum-based education, the desired learning outcome(s) will typically the starting point for design.

Designing for learning outcomes

A learning outcome is some identifiable change that is anticipated in the learner. In associative accounts of learning the anticipated change will be observable from learners' behaviour, such as the capacity to perform actions skilfully or to express concepts accurately. Constructive accounts of learning might be more interested in cognitive changes, but assessment would reveal that learners have a different conceptual framework for understanding a situation or the capacity to solve new kinds of problem. Situative accounts of learning will lead to outcomes that are observable in context, such as learners participating in new situations, occupying more expert roles, or acting in accordance with situational rules and expectations. Generally speaking it is the designer of the learning opportunity who defines its overall purpose – indeed the term 'design' is often synonymous with 'purpose' or 'intention'. However, learners must be motivated to achieve the outcome, either because it reflects their personal development goals, or because they can see its place in a wider curriculum or learning context to which they have committed themselves.

In line with the focus on activity, contemporary curriculum practice in the English speaking world is for learning outcomes to be expressed in the form *learners will be able to [verb] [qualification]* where the verb describes the kind of activity that learners will undertake (e.g. solve, describe) and the qualification describes the context, scope or method to be used (e.g. solve quadratic equations; describe the impact of recent legislation on childcare services). Outcomes can even be written in a way that defines different levels of attainment and how these will be graded (see e.g. Dick and Carey 1990) but in most educational systems this kind of detail is covered in the assessment regime. Taxonomies for defining learning outcomes, such as Bloom's (1956) or Biggs' (see Biggs and Tang 2007), are routinely taught in introductory courses for teachers in post-compulsory education, so they exert a strong cultural influence. Learning outcomes have now been endorsed by the Bologna Process as the 'basic building blocks' of higher education across the European community (Adam 2008).

One criticism of learning outcomes and associated taxonomies (e.g. Brady 1996) is the tendency for designers to consider separately those outcomes that concern knowledge, skills and values. While these distinctions can provide a useful check that different aspects of the learning experience are being designed and assessed for, in conceptual terms the separation can be unhelpful. It seems unlikely for example that conceptual skills are acquired independently of specific concepts to practise them on, and this is borne out by the strong association between students' motivation to acquire skills and the perceived relevance of the skills-based activities to their future goals (Lizzio and Wilson 2004). In fact, the close relationship between varieties of knowledge and varieties of conceptual activity is the main reason why designing for learning requires subject-specific expertise.

An important implication of the interconnectedness of skills, concepts and values is that digital capabilities need to be carefully framed in learning outcomes. On the one hand, if such capabilities do not appear in the intended – and assessed – outcomes, learners may not see digital technology as an integral part of their experience. On the other hand, designers must decide whether such capabilities warrant their own specific outcomes – conferring a special status – or whether outcomes should be written to encompass the possibility that digital technologies might be used in a wide range of activities, and to support a wide range of learning goals.

Outcomes-based design does require learners to adhere very closely to a curriculum and its assessment goals. In doing so, it may foster a strategic approach, with learners valuing only those tasks that lead transparently to assessment outcomes (Hussey and Smith 2003). Written outcomes may focus on aspects of learning that are easy to assess, neglecting, for example, learners' developing values, their capacities to learn, and subtle or unanticipated outcomes. However, outcomes can be written to focus on broad capabilities, giving learners room to demonstrate these in a variety of ways and even to discover new approaches not considered by the designer. Assessing the activity process as well as the end product is another way of helping learners to value unanticipated outcomes and to develop a repertoire of approaches to the task at hand. Appendix 2 provides a taxonomy of digital and information literacy and a version of Bloom's taxonomy, both developed at UK universities to support the writing of meaningful outcomes that encompass digital approaches and capabilities.

The current generation of digital technologies is, in fact, well suited to supporting open-ended outcomes. Simulations and virtual research tasks can be used to foster exploration; blogs and e-portfolios allow learners to collate evidence towards broadly defined learning goals; social and collaborative technologies can be used to capture learning in process as well its outcomes. The fact that learners have access to a wide range of tools and services in support of their learning militates against too stringent a definition of how a task should be accomplished. However, more broadly defined outcomes will always mean that a wider range of approaches need support and feedback. The resulting designs may be more learner-centred, but only if there are sufficient teaching resources to support the range of learner responses effectively.

Designing for learners

An outcomes-based or curriculum-led design approach assumes that learners respond to instruction in similar ways, and differences that are not related to performance on task are generally ignored. In contrast, a 'learner-centred' approach to curriculum design (Lea *et al.* 2003; Kember 2009) begins with the different aspirations, preferences and resources that learners bring to a task. Agendas such as accessibility, inclusion and widening participation favour a design ethos that takes learner differences as a starting point rather than an inconvenience (Dagger *et al.* 2005).

There are two challenges involved in taking a learner-centred approach, and both have new aspects in a technology-rich environment. The first is to know, among the many ways learners can vary from one another, which are significant to the learning at hand (see Appendix 3 for some more prompt questions about learners). Depending on the task and context, it may be necessary to consider learners'

1   subject-specific experience, knowledge and competence;
2   access needs, including any physical and sensory disabilities;
3   motives for learning, and expectations of the learning situation;
4   prior experience of learning, especially learning in the relevant mode (e.g. online);
5   preferred approaches to learning (see Box 2.1);
6   social and interpersonal skills;
7   digital and information literacy.

These differences interact in complex ways. ICT competence, for example, is not a stand-alone issue but can impact on a wide range of other factors, including learners' confidence, choice of location and support requirements (Lockitt 2004). A review of individual differences in e-learning (Sharpe et al. 2009) concluded that learners' feelings about the technologies they were offered could be key to their learning, especially feelings of frustration and alienation. More recent work has found that cultural attitudes (Yoo and Huang 2011) and teacher confidence or anxiety (Greener 2009) can profoundly influence learners' experiences with technology. Digital capability is not independent of other differences among learners such as their gender, culture, first language, and home background. Learners cannot therefore be treated as a bundle of disparate needs: they make sense of the tasks they are set in terms of their own identity and goals, and they may experience tasks quite differently when different technologies – with all the social and cultural meanings that they carry – are involved. When any novel technology is introduced, teachers need to build in formative checks or opportunities for self-reporting by learners to establish how their experience is being influenced.

The second challenge in learner-centred design is dealing effectively with learner variance. In the past, instructional design aimed to provide adaptive learning, matching materials and system responses to learners' performance on tasks or to some diagnostic measure of their aptitude or 'style' of learning. Apart from the technical challenges of adaptive systems, the theoretical validity and benefits of such an approach are controversial (e.g. Pashler et al. 2009). It is not obvious, for example, that learners should be accommodated in their preferences. Deeper learning may come about when learners take responsibility for their own learning and are challenged to develop alternative strategies. Also, while individualized instruction banishes the frustrations of cohort learning, it also does away with its many advantages.

Box 2.1 'Learning styles' and multimodality

There is no doubt that learners can gain insights into their own processes of learning, and that teaching improves when differences in learners' approaches are recognized. Of particular interest in learning design have been theories that learners prefer different representational formats – holistic versus serial, for example (Pask 1988), or linguistic versus spatial (Gardner 1994). There is little evidence, however, for learners having intrinsic 'styles' of learning which are stable over time and independent of setting (Coffield *et al.* 2004; Pashler *et al.* 2009). Rather there is good evidence that learning is better retained if learners have access to a variety of representational media (Tindall-Ford *et al.* 1997).

The learning styles debate has been played out on the terrain of cognitive science. From an entirely different theoretical perspective, Kress and van Leeuwen (2002) and Kress *et al.* (2006) have championed the idea that contemporary knowledge production is inherently multimodal. This leads him to the surprisingly similar conclusion that learners must practise communicating ideas in a wide range of different media.

In recent years, interest in e-learning has moved decisively away from adaptive systems towards blended learning, in which a more learner-centred experience is offered through a combination of learning modes – one-to-many, private, and collaborative learning – enhanced through the use of available technologies. Classroom-based technologies such as voting systems, and live interactive technologies such as video conferencing and online classrooms, all offer a greater repertoire of educational interactions. Asynchronous technologies allow learners more control over the time, place and pace of their learning, while the resources of the World Wide Web and – for more confident learners – the opportunity to connect with learning communities worldwide mean that the curriculum no longer defines the learning experience but rather provides a starting point for exploration. Social and public technologies open up new ways for learners to record evidence of their learning and showcase their outcomes.

For learners to feel empowered rather than overwhelmed by these opportunities, they must be supported in the different choices they make. Increasingly this means that learners must become digitally literate, judging for themselves which digital communications are of value, and which tools and services support their learning goals. This is why, despite their access to a world of learning opportunity, digital learners remain dependent on skilled practitioners to provide guidance, feedback and developmental support (Sharpe and Pawlyn 2008). This is also why learner-centred design should include opportunities to assess and progress learners' capacities to learn for themselves, including their capacity to use digital tools and resources for educational ends.

When this chapter was originally written in 2006, it seemed radical to suggest that learners might take more responsibility for their own learning in this way.

In the intervening years the compass has moved further towards involving learners as co-producers in the process of design (see Winn and Lockwood, Chapter 14). What matters for the purposes of this chapter is that learners should be considered as the primary actors in their own learning. Tasks can be designed to structure learners' experience in particular ways, resources and technologies can have designs on learners of different kinds as we shall consider next, and learners can have more or less involvement in those design choices. But in the end it is only the conscious activity of the learner that can lead to the kind of changes we recognize as learning, and the more consciously they are engaged in the process of design for their own learning, the more lasting the learning gains are likely to be.

Designing with digital resources and technologies

The Introduction to this book argued that the use of digital technologies changes the meaning of a learning activity, subtly or profoundly. The technologies available in the learning environment, and how learners are encouraged to use them for specific activities, are therefore essential aspects of design.

It is worth remembering that we are concerned here with *designed artefacts*, which include physical devices such as digital cameras and microscopes, data recorders of various kinds, mobile devices and tablets, laptop computers, and sensors contained in these devices (e.g. for location, orientation, light levels, etc.). Representational artefacts – web pages, data sets, software and systems – are also designed in a variety of media. User interfaces mediate between information/data and learners, and these too are designed at a minute level of detail to structure users' experiences and actions.

Here, the activity system of Engeström allows a new layer of complexity to be introduced. The artefacts which mediate the learning activity are themselves outcomes of earlier activities of design, and they carry traces of that activity system with its own framing of the learner as user, and its own intended outcomes. The properties of a designed artefact are sometimes referred to as their 'affordances' for a particular use: in this case their affordances for learning (after Gibson 1979). Here, however, we will talk about tools and resources in terms of how they *mediate* learning. This emphasizes that artefacts can have different meanings in different activity systems, and that the purposes for which artefacts are designed and the ends for which they are actually used need not be the same (see e.g. Oliver 2006). One point at which Activity Theory differs from Actor Network Theory (see Goodyear and Carvalho, Chapter 3) is that artefacts are understood as transitional objects between activity systems. As outcomes of their own design process they reify certain purposes, roles, rules and divisions of labour; and as components of the learning activity process they mediate new, emergent outcomes and relationships. Artefacts are never, in Activity Theory, conceived as actors themselves but as mediators of human actors' intentions, through complex and interrelated activity systems.

When computers were first used in educational contexts, it was very clear which digital artefacts were designed *for learning*. Certain computers – the BBC micro for example – were specifically marketed for the classroom. 'Educational software' was designed to be run on these computers, though aspirational parents might have bought such software and installed it on a 'home computer'. In the UK, considerable public funding was invested in educational software for university students (Tiley 1996), though it is interesting to recall that unless the software designer's educational aspirations were a near-perfect match with those of the lecturer, there was little chance of the software being adopted. Use of the software violated teachers' perceptions of their role as the main designers of learning opportunity for 'their' students. In other words, there were conflicts around the rules, roles, and divisions of labour in the larger system.

Today, educational artefacts are more likely to support a repertoire of activities than a specific learning experience. Electronic whiteboards and lecture-hall technologies are designed to enhance particular modes of teaching/learning interaction. Dedicated software continues to be developed to support specific academic or professional practices, but again these support a wide repertoire of activities. Examples would be reference management software, qualitative and quantitative data analysis tools, computer assisted design systems, and of course managed learning environments.

However, many digital artefacts encountered by learners will not have been designed for learning at all. Whether they are using apps on a mobile platform or web services via a browser, most students access academic content and communicate academic ideas through the same channels they use for entertainment or arranging a date. This has the benefit of making access to learning opportunities non-threatening, at least to digitally connected learners. But it also throws up the potential for confusion and blurring of boundaries. It poses new problems for designers, as a critical component of the activity system is – at least potentially – beyond their control.

The situation with digital resources is rather similar. In response to the overwhelming volume of material available online, public funding has shifted from developing educational content to providing guided access to content of educational value. The Open Educational Resources movement (see Pegler, Chapter 9), though it has other transformational features, is at one level simply the latest manifestation of the desire to differentiate content *designed for learning* from all the other content available online. While the skills of information design remain important to professional designers, today's educators are far more likely to be referring students to open repositories, or releasing their own lectures as open content, than to be designing resources from scratch. Another novel factor in the landscape of learning resources is the increasing availability of primary data, whether this is public social data, digitized original texts, or the openly available outputs of publicly funded research. Why invest time in producing secondary resources with pedagogic features 'built in' when learners can be directed towards primary resources and supported in this encounter with a flexible pedagogy that is 'built out'?

Rather than mandating the use of specific educational technologies or resources, then, a sound design for learning will take into account what available artefacts can mediate the task effectively and what kinds of choice learners should have in this regard. Except in cases when a discipline-specific system needs to be mastered, as previously discussed, it is more important for a designer to consider whether and how digital technologies can be advantageous than to 'design in' a particular solution.

Diana Laurillard's Conversational Theory of Learning (Laurillard 2002; see also Sharpe and Oliver, Chapter 10) has been particularly influential on thinking about the choice and use of digital technologies for learning. Laurillard distinguishes five different media types – narrative, communicative, interactive, productive and adaptive – which makes it easier to think about digital tools in terms of how they mediate learning activities. However, with the convergence of information and communication media that we have seen in the past decade, and the availability of multiple apps or web services on a common platform, it can be difficult to maintain Laurillard's distinctions. Looking at the intersection of web 2.0 knowledge practices with established modes of learning and teaching, Scott Wilson (2006) identifies five ways in which the new web-service-based environment offered potential for learning. In my adaptation of his original model, they are: discovering; developing and sharing ideas; collecting, gathering, recording and remixing/editing; solving problems and developing techniques; and working with others. For each of these activity types I will outline in general terms what the considerations for learning may be, though developments at the interface of digital and academic knowledge practice are currently so rapid that even to do this is to offer a hostage to fortune (see Figure 2.2).

Most subjects require learners to engage in *discovery* tasks such as searching databases, finding and judging online resources, undertaking tests and experiments, or exploring real-world or simulated situations. These are activities

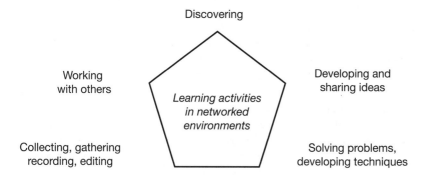

Figure 2.2 Five types of learning activity

that may be mediated by digital tools and instruments, or may take place in an entirely virtual space such as the Visible Human Project (National Library of Medicine 2006–2012). As we live and work in an increasingly designed, artefactual environment, the latter kind of learning becomes arguably more relevant and 'real'. In situational discovery tasks, digital simulations can offer risk reduction, reproducibility, accuracy, and cost savings, but in doing so they may attenuate features of the situation – such as human contact with a client, or bodily sensations – that are in fact critical to learning. A virtual experience can, however, be useful in advance for familiarization or mastering the component skills of field or lab work so that learners are prepared to gain from the real-world encounter. Digital instruments including personal devices – image, video and audio recorders in smartphones – are widely used for capturing data in discovery settings. In informational discovery tasks, students must learn not only to find and evaluate resources but also to manage the outcomes of their researches, whether in local databases or through tagging, storing, distributing etc. in the cloud.

Tools for developing and sharing representations in different media are often used more confidently by learners than by teaching staff themselves. Presentation software, data visualization apps, animation tools, video editing suites, wikis and blogs, even lightweight app development tools are accessible to a large and growing number of learners. But while learners may have some of the relevant skills, they do not often understand the rules of academic communication. This is where an open-ended design, which prescribes criteria of academic judgement but not the forms in which it is expressed, can allow teachers to draw on learners' digital know-how in exciting ways. As always, though, teachers need both time and confidence if they are to assess different representations fairly and provide useful feedback. The portability of digital representations is of huge advantage in feedback and peer review. Having their productions made public is a charged situation for learners, and while it can be highly motivating it does need to be approached gradually and with full consent.

Collecting, gathering, recording and remixing of content is regarded by some commentators as the bane of digital culture, or at least the aspect most antithetical to 'good' educational practice. Plagiarism detection software is now used almost universally in higher education in the US, UK and Australia and regular opinion pieces in the academic press decry students' 'cut-and-paste mentality' (Moiseff 2005) and their inability to respect, let alone achieve, originality of thought. There is evidence that students' approaches to writing have indeed changed (Kress and van Leeuwen 2002; Lenhart *et al.* 2008), but the same is true of academics. In fact, students' practices in this area can be seen in a positive light as a form of active note-taking and (re)constructing academic discourse. Setting explicit tasks of aggregation, repurposing and revision helps these practices to become more reflective. Students can be encouraged to capture moments in their learning using personal digital devices, to use cloud-based services such as Dropbox or Evernote to aggregate resources in different media, and then to make sense of these collections using mind mapping, tagging, social libraries such as delicious or pearltrees, or even emerging semantic tools. Digital storytelling is a technique that encourages learners to reflect on digital artefacts relevant to their development, while patchwork texts are being used for assessment in some courses (e.g. Brand *et al.* 2008; Arnold *et al.* 2009).

Solving problems and *developing techniques* are among the most discipline-specific of tasks, but some common observations can be made. Most subject disciplines and their research and professional specialisms are developing new methods rapidly as digital technologies emerge and as new uses for them are tried by those at the cutting edge of their field. Some of these new methods are enhancing practice, while others – such as text encoding in literary subjects, or geotagging in subjects where data has a locational component – are changing the game entirely. There is much exciting interdisciplinary work taking place, with digital networks helping to break down traditional boundaries between subject areas and their methods. So critical considerations for designers are:

- how early to introduce students to digital methods – some teachers feel the 'traditional' way of solving problems or analysing data can help learners appreciate the underlying purpose better;
- how to address the changes taking place in the subject area – some teachers feel this gets in the way of grasping central tenets and methods, while others feel it is motivating for students to know that their discipline is evolving fast.

Solving authentic problems and developing their own novel approaches are inherently motivating for students, but can be high risk. Particularly when introducing new methods, it is a good idea to allow space for exploration and play. Group work can be a particularly useful approach, allowing students to draw on different resources and share the risk. Knowing that different approaches are possible can help students become more conscious of method and more critical of the technologies involved, but only if this kind of reflection is explicitly encouraged.

Almost any of the foregoing tasks could be carried out *collaboratively*, but some digital tools exist specifically to mediate learning interactions between people, and these are dealt with more thoroughly in the following section.

No technologies should be introduced to the learning situation without consideration of learners' confidence and competence in their use. Ideally the learning should also extend that competence, for example by having learners explore different functions, make choices about use of a tool, and integrate it with more familiar tools in their repertoire. The use of personal and social technologies is an essential aspect of the construction of personal identity (Turkle 1995) and can help learners bridge the gap between their existing skills and values and the kinds of literacy required in formal education (Kukulska-Hulme and Traxler, Chapter 16). Yet unless they are encouraged to make these connections, learners may feel very uncertain about bringing their digital practices into formal study contexts.

Designing for interaction with others

Most learning involves interaction with a more expert other person. Associative theories of learning demand a teacher who is skilled not only in the subject matter but in guiding learners through structured activities. Situative accounts call for an expert mentor, while teachers committed to a constructive approach require a wide range of skills – negotiating outcomes, supporting learner discussion, giving relevant feedback and responding to learners' different needs.

Dialogue with peer learners is also highly valued by many theorists. Vygotsky (1986) argued that learning is a socially mediated activity in the first instance, with concepts and skills being internalized only after they have been mastered in a collaborative context. Constructivists following Piaget (2001), and in computer-mediated learning, Papert (1993), give dialogue a secondary role but agree that it supports the individual processes of reflection and abstraction. There is in fact evidence that some learners prefer to learn alone, but this is typically at advanced levels when they have already mastered the relevant skills in more supportive contexts. Opportunities for dialogue are considered crucial in most approaches to learning design.

Some or all of these interactions can now be mediated via digital means. In fact the best candidates for 'new' theories of learning in the digital age have emerged from the capacity of learners to be extensively and continuously interconnected with others, as well as with informational artefacts. Theories such as networked learning (Goodyear *et al.* 2004) and connectivism (Siemens 2005) propose that both the enhanced capacity to form connections and the potential of those massively interconnected networks to 'act' and learn in their own right are critical to learning in the digital age.

If they are to participate effectively in a digital society, learners need multiple opportunities to communicate and collaborate, to negotiate roles and identities, and to build their reputation in digital networks. But designers need to be aware that the use of digital media for learning interactions can profoundly change roles and relationships (McConnell 2005). For example, in asynchronous environments expertise can be contributed more equitably, turn-taking becomes less significant, and many face-to-face markers of difference are removed. The explicit nature of asynchronous dialogue makes it good for negotiating ground rules and building shared understanding. However, there are studies which report students being uncomfortable with these demands, for example struggling with the learner locus of control (Crook 2002), with the fact that personal work is visible to peers (Ramsey 2003) or with being dependent on other learners' contributions for critical aspects of the experience (Capdefero and Romero 2012).

In most collaborative environments it is possible for learners to control privacy settings – that is to decide which communications are public, which are for specific others, and which are for private reflection. But these are not skills that students should be assumed to have simply because they are avid users of social media. The capacity of digital services to collect their private information, and the uses to which their digital traces may be put by others, are critical issues for learners to appreciate. At the same time, well-designed learning tasks can help learners collect and showcase achievements that they are happy to be made public, and allow them to build a positive identity online.

Designing for effective collaboration is discussed in more detail in Jones (Chapter 13). Here it is important to note that designing for digital collaboration requires attention to participants' roles, and to making explicit the ground rules and expectations. These must include addressing how learners' work will be kept private, even if public services are being used to share material, and how their work may be made public, if this is explicitly a goal of the learning activity. Although many teachers report success through strongly directing and structuring learners' encounters online, the digital environment can provide an opportunity to break with established modes of teaching/learning discourse.

Conclusions

This chapter has outlined considerations for design that arise from theories about how people learn (see Mayes and de Freitas, Chapter 1) and the experience of applying these theories to learning with digital technologies. But 'good' design does not always move in a linear fashion from theory to principle to practice. It can evolve from a range of practical examples without ever being formally articulated (see Sharpe and Oliver, Chapter 10), remaining a kind of shared expertise, or 'theory-in-use' (Argyris 1997). The application of 'sound' principles is therefore only one facet of the design process: it is also important to understand how practitioners actually *do* design for learning (see Masterman, Chapter 4), to evaluate what is being done and to describe and share effective designs with others (see Ellaway, Chapter 12, and Dalziel, Chapter 15). This is particularly true in a rapidly changing context, where new opportunities and threats – including new kinds of learner and learning organization – are continually challenging established practices of design.

References

Adam, S. (2008) Learning Outcomes: Current Developments in Europe, report for the Scottish Government. Online. Available at http://www.ond.vlaanderen.be/ hogeronderwijs/bologna/BolognaSeminars/Edinburgh2008.htm (accessed 31 July 2012).

Argyris, C. (1997) 'Learning and teaching: a theory of action perspective', *Journal of Management Education*, 21 (1): 9–27.

Arnold, L., Williams, T. and Thompson, K. (2009) 'Advancing the patchwork text: the development of patchwork media approaches', *International Journal of Learning*, 16 (5): 151–66.

Biggs, J. and Tang, C. (2007) *Teaching for Quality Learning at University* (3rd edn), Buckingham: SRHE and Open University Press.

Bloom, B.S. (ed.) (1956) *Taxonomy of Educational Objectives: The classification of educational goals*, New York: MacKay.

Brady, L. (1996) 'Outcome based education: a critique', *Curriculum Journal*, 7 (1): 5–16.

Brand, D., Durose, M., Walker, S., Fryatt, S. and Baron, S. (2008) 'Patchwork texts', *Mathematics Teaching*, 211: 22–5.

Capdeferro, N. and Romero, M. (2012) 'Are online learners frustrated with collaborative learning experiences?', *International Review of Research in Open & Distance Learning*, 13 (2): 26–44.

Cecile, S. (2012) 'Activity Theory and qualitative research in digital domains', *Theory Into Practice*, 51 (2): 83–90.

Coffield, F., Moseley, D., Hall, E. and Ecclestone, K. (2004) Learning styles and pedagogy in post-16 learning: A systematic and critical review. London: Learning and Skills Research Centre. Online. Available at http://www.lsda.org.uk/files/PDF/1543. pdf (accessed 31 July 2012).

Crook, C. (2002) The campus experience of networked learning', in C. Steeples and C. Jones (eds) *Networked Learning: Perspectives and issues*, London: Springer-Verlag.

Dagger, D., Wade, V. and Conlan, O. (2005) 'Personalization for all: making adaptive course composition easy', *Educational Technology and Society: Special Issue on Authoring of Adaptive Hypermedia*, 8 (3): 9–25.

Dick, W. and Carey, L. (1990) *The Systematic Design of Instruction* (3rd edn), New York: Harper Collins.

Engeström, Y. (1999) 'Activity Theory and individual and social transformation', in Y. Engeström, R. Miettinen and R.-L. Punamaki (eds) *Perspectives on Activity Theory*, Cambridge: Cambridge University Press.

Gardner, H. (1994) 'Multiple intelligences theory', in R.J. Sternberg (ed.) *Encyclopedia of Human Intelligence* Vol. 2, New York: Macmillan.

Gholson, B. and Craig, S.D. (2006) 'Promoting constructive activities that support vicarious learning during computer-based instruction', *Educational Psychology Review*, 18: 119–39.

Gibson, J. (1979) *The Ecological Approach to Visual Perception*, Boston: Houghton Mifflin.

Goodyear, P., Banks, S., Hodgson, V. and McConnell, D. (2004) 'Research on networked learning: An overview', in P. Goodyear, S. Banks, V. Hodgson and D. McConnell (eds) *Advances in Research on Networked Learning*, London: Kluwer Academic Publishers.

Greener, S. (2009) 'e-Modeling – helping learners to develop sound e-learning behaviours', *Electronic Journal of e-Learning*, 7 (3): 265–71.

Hussey, T. and Smith, P. (2003) 'The uses of learning outcomes', *Teaching in Higher Education*, 8 (3): 357–68.

Issroff, K. and Scanlon, E. (2002) 'Activity theory and enhancing learning: using technology in higher education', *Journal of Computers and Learning*, 18 (1): 77–83.

Jonassen, D. (2000) 'Toward a design theory of problem solving', *Educational Technology Research and Development*, 48 (4): 63–85.

Kember, D. (2009) 'Promoting student-centred forms of learning across an entire university', *Higher Education*, 58 (1): 1–13.

Kress, G. and van Leeuwen, T. (2002) *Multimodal Discourse: The modes and media of contemporary communication*, London: Edward Arnold.

Kress, G., Jewitt, C., Ogborn, J. and Charalampos, T. (2006) *Multimodal Teaching and Learning: The rhetorics of the science classroom*, London: Continuum.

Laurillard, D. (2002) *Rethinking University Teaching: A framework for the effective use of learning technologies* (2nd edn), London: Routledge.

Lea, S.J., Stephenson, D. and Troy, J. (2003). 'Higher education students' attitudes to student centred learning', *Studies in Higher Education*, 28 (3): 321–34.

Lenhart, A. *et al.* (2008) Writing, technology, and teens. A report from the Pew Internet & American Life project. Pew Foundation. Online. Available at http://www.pewinternet.org/Reports/2008/Writing-Technology-and-Teens.aspx (accessed 31 July 2012).

Lizzio, A. and Wilson, K. (2004) 'First year students' perceptions of capability', *Studies in Higher Education*, 29 (1): 109–28.

Lockitt, B. (2004) *Adult, Community and Work Based Learning: E-learning*, Cheadle, Cheshire: 3T Productions.

McConnell, D. (2005) 'Examining the Dynamics of Networked E-learning Groups and Communities', *Studies in Higher Education*, 30 (1), 23–40.

Margaryan, A. and Littlejohn, A. (2008) 'Repositories and communities at cross-purposes: issues in sharing and reuse of digital learning resources', *Journal of Computer Assisted Learning*, 24 (4): 333–47.

Masterman, L., Lee, S., Beetham, H., Knight, S. and Francis, R. (2005) 'Supporting effective practice in learning design: an evaluation of the Learning Activity Management System (LAMS)', paper presented at Computer Assisted Learning: Virtual Learning conference, Bristol, April 2005.

Moiseff, A. (2005) 'Report on deterring plagiarism seeks to foster academic integrity', interview given to Elizabeth Omara-Otunnu for Advance, University of Connecticut. Online. Available at <http://advance.uconn.edu/2005/050919/05091902.htm> (accessed 31 July 2012).

National Library of Medicine (2006–2012) The Visible Human Project. Online. Available at <http://www.nlm.nih.gov/research/visible/visible_human.html> (accessed 31 July 2012).

Oliver, M. (2006) 'The problems with affordance', *E-Learning*, 2 (4): 402–13.

Papert, S. (1993) *Mindstorms: Children, computers and powerful ideas*, New York: Perseus.

Pashler, H., McDaniel, M., Rohrer, D. and Bjork, R. (2009) 'Learning styles: Concepts and evidence', *Psychological Science in the Public Interest*, 9: 105–19.

Pask, G. (1988) 'Learning strategies, teaching strategies, and conceptual or learning style', in R. Schmeck (ed.), *Learning Strategies and Learning Styles*, New York: Plenum Press.

Piaget, J. (2001) *The Language and Thought of the Child*, London: Routledge Modern Classics.

Ramsey, C. (2003) 'Using virtual learning environments to facilitate new relationships', *International Journal of Management Education*, 3 (2): 31–41.

Sharpe, R. and Pawlyn, J. (2008) 'The role of the tutor in blended e-learning: experiences from interprofessional education', in R. Donnelly and F. McSweeney (eds) *Applied eLearning and eTeaching in Higher Education*, New York: IGI Global.

Sharpe, R., Beetham, H., Benfield, G., Lessner, E. and de Cicco, E. (2009) Learners' Experiences of E-learning Synthesis Report: Explaining Learner Differences. Joint Information Systems Committee. Online. Available at www.jisc.ac.uk/media/documents/programmes/elearningpedagogy/lxp2finalsynthesis.pdf (accessed 31 July 2012).

Siemens, G. (2005) 'Connectivism: A learning theory for the digital age', *International Journal of Instructional Technology and Distance Learning*, 2 (1): 3–10.

Tergan, S. (1997) 'Misleading theoretical assumptions in hypertext/hypermedia research', *Journal of Educational Multimedia and Hypermedia*, 6 (3–4): 257–83.

Tiley, J. (1996) 'TLTP: Teaching and Learning Technology Programme', *Ariadne*, Issue 4 (July 1996). Online. Available at http://www.ariadne.ac.uk/issue4/tltp (accessed 31 July 2012).

Tindall-Ford, S., Chandler, P. and Sweller, J. (1997) 'When two sensory modes are better than one', *Journal of Experimental Psychology: Applied*, 3 (4): 257–87.

Turkle, S. (1995) *Life on the Screen: Identity in the age of the Internet*, New York: Simon and Schuster.

Vygotsky, L. (1986) *Thought and Language*, Cambridge, MA: MIT Press.

Wilson, S. (2006) 'Web services/web 2.0 and e-learning'. Blog post. Online. Available at http://zope.cetis.ac.uk/members/scott/blogview?entry=20060621135746 (accessed 15 August 2012).

Yoo, S.J. and Huang, D.W. (2011) 'Comparison of Web 2.0 technology acceptance level based on cultural differences', *Journal of Educational Technology & Society*, 14 (4): 241–52.

Chapter 3

The Analysis of Complex Learning Environments

Peter Goodyear and Lucila Carvalho

EDITORS' INTRODUCTION

In this chapter, Goodyear and Carvalho argue that an understanding of how people learn in complex, technology-rich environments requires more than an inventory of elements. It calls for analysis at the level of the whole system of human and non-human actors, in which learning emerges dynamically: an analysis they term ecological or architectural. They go on to describe the physical and social architectures that frame learning and a variety of possible connections between the material/digital elements of the system and human/learner activity. Through two case studies they draw out relationships between micro and macro levels of the learning system, and balance explanations based on the material affordances of digital artefacts with those based on human sense-making.

Introduction: analysis for design

Pedagogy, as the art and science of helping other people learn, can be practised in a variety of ways, including through direct face-to-face teaching. Our work seeks to understand and inform pedagogy that is enacted more indirectly as *design for learning* – that is, where people committed to facilitating other people's learning carry out their work primarily through the design of worthwhile learning tasks and/or the design of appropriately supportive learning resources. Given the focus of this book, our attention is on designs in which digital resources play a significant part, though we will argue that design often works best when it takes a more holistic approach – working with networks of interacting digital and non-digital entities. In this chapter, our focus is on analysis for design. Analysis connects with design in a number of ways, e.g. through needs analysis – a classic starting point for a structured design process (Crandall *et al.* 2006). It also plays a major role in evaluation – informing judgements at the end of a design cycle, about whether something is working well, and about what might need to be improved (Reigeluth and Carr-Chellman 2009).

Our approach to analysis is rather different. Its distinctiveness arises from these four observations:

1   Design rarely takes place on a 'green field' site. Analysis needs to be able to capture what exists already, not just what success would look like. Design activity can then make proposals that will work within, and improve upon, an existing set of constraints and possibilities.
2   Many things affect any single learning process. So analysis must be able to represent a complex array of influences, some of which are human, some physical – including digital.
3   Competence, which is one way of describing the end goal for a learning process, rarely resides in the head of a learner. Rather, a person's competence is usually entangled in, and dependent on, a set of social and physical relationships – such that a more expansive view of competence includes that person's ability to assemble and hold together the entities needed for the task at hand. When analysis is used to create a description of competence, or of a desired state of affairs – a smoothly working system – it needs to be able to deal with such complexity.
4   Since a number of influential models of learning involve some kinds of apprenticeship, authentic engagement in practice, legitimate peripheral participation, experiential learning, etc., then the kind of description created by analysis in (3) is needed if designers are to see what else they may need to help set in place to support such processes of learning through engagement in practice.

We employ the term 'learning environment' with some trepidation, since it is widely used but rarely explained in writing about learning technologies. It is a term that appears to work neatly when the focus is on an individualized learner and their physical environment, side-stepping questions about whether it is reasonable to describe other people as part of one's environment, or whether 'learning environment' can be used to describe the (shared) habitat of a collection of learners (Goodyear 2000a). As will become clear, our use of the term is *relational* – person and environment are mutually entailed; there is no person without an environment and no environment without a person (or organism) dwelling in it (Ingold 2000).

Shifting the focus of analysis from discrete devices to ecologies and networks

Later in this chapter we sketch two contrasting learning situations to illustrate our argument for a more systemic approach to analysis. Both situations involve a number of digital technologies, as well as other elements that combine to have educationally consequential effects. Some of these elements were designed for the situation, some were selected by teachers or designers, some had other ways of 'coming to hand' when students were engaged in their work. A thorough analysis needs ways of identifying *and connecting* diverse kinds of elements, including the physical, digital and human; texts, tools and artefacts; tasks, rules and divisions of labour. Producing an inventory of components is not enough, because functioning depends on structure – on relationships between parts. Nor does it make much sense to try to identify the contribution to learning made by a single component. Outcomes depend on interactions between multiple entities. Rather, we need forms of analysis that match the complexity of contemporary learning challenges – holistic, ecological or architectural rather than fragmenting, reductionist modes of thought.

We argue that richer, *socio-material* analyses of learning environments provide knowledge that fits well with the needs of design and designers. We suggest that providing better ways of thinking about analysis, evaluation and design can help dislodge unhelpful habits of thought – especially those that try to isolate intrinsic merits of particular tools, media or pedagogies. We also argue that such analysis sharpens perception of the boundary between what can be designed, and what must emerge at learntime.

Our approach to analysis shifts the focus from individual elements of an educational innovation to the system level (e.g. Luckin 2010; Ellis and Goodyear 2010; Boys 2011; Westberry and Franken, 2013). It starts by recognizing that learning activity takes place in complex, messy, dynamic situations, in which interactions between elements produce conditions that are more or less supportive of learning.

> ... knowledge generation ... [is] ... a joint exercise of relational strategies within networks that are spread across space and time, and performed through inanimate (e.g. books, mobile phones, measuring instruments, projection screens, boxes, locks) as well as animate beings in precarious arrangements ... Learning and knowing are performed in the processes of assembling and maintaining these networks, as well as in the negotiations that occur at various nodes comprising a network ... Things – not just humans, but the parts that make up humans and non-humans – persuade, coerce, seduce, resist and compromise each other as they come together.
>
> Fenwick *et al.* 2011: 10

Actor Network Theory (ANT), as used by Fenwick and colleagues, is one of a number of perspectives that can be used to try to capture some of this complexity. We remain agnostic about some of the key ideas associated with ANT – such as whether it is reasonable to attribute agency to artefacts. But, like other schools of thought implicated in the materialist turn, ANT sensitizes us to the ways in which material objects influence human activity (see also Boivin 2008; Sorensen 2009; Bennett 2010; Fenwick and Edwards 2010; Miller 2010; Johri 2011). It reminds us that matter matters. Ecological psychology similarly challenges presumptions about the superiority of mind over matter (Gibson

1977, 1986). From Gibson's work, educational technology has appropriated one of its core and most contested concepts – the idea that objects have *affordances* which shape the behaviour of people who encounter them (Laurillard 1987; Norman 1999; Conole and Dyke 2004; Oliver 2005, 2011; Turner 2005; John and Sutherland 2005; Dohn 2009). 'Affordance' does a great deal of work in educational technology – partly because it sidesteps issues about technological determinism without suggesting that technology choices can be arbitrary. But as Harry Collins has observed:

> The terms 'afford' and 'affordance' are lazy terms … these terms merely paper over deep cracks in our understanding … of why, given the extraordinary interpretive capabilities of humans, anything affords any one interpretation better than any other … something hidden and mysterious is going on whenever the terms 'afford' and 'affordance' make their appearance.
>
> Collins 2010: 36

We will come back to this issue shortly. For now, the key points are as follows: (1) analysing or evaluating learning activity in context cannot sensibly be reduced to enumerating the pedagogical affordances of individual tools, devices or artefacts; (2) instead, a more systemic approach is needed, in which learning and the things that influence it are seen as connected in webs or 'assemblages'; (3) how we conceptualize the functioning of the web has serious consequences for how we analyse and explain what happens – 'affordance' turns out to be just one of several useful terms.

Design and its products

Much of the learning that students do is accomplished without direct supervision. In such circumstances, with only very limited opportunities for teachers to carry out real-time repairs, good design is crucial. Since analysis and design need a shared conceptual framework, if they are to be mutually informing, then we offer the following sketch of design and its legitimate products. It consists of three broad principles, each of which is unpacked in a subsequent section (see Goodyear 2000b; Goodyear and Retalis 2010, for further information).

1   Design for learning is chiefly concerned with the design of good learning tasks – well-crafted suggestions of good things for people to do, if they are to achieve some desired learning outcome.
2   Design for learning must also attend to the social and physical setting – ensuring (as far as is possible) that all the resources needed for learning come to hand.
3   Design for learning needs to work fluently across scale levels: linking macro, meso and micro.

Design for learning is chiefly concerned with the design of good learning tasks

Task design typically results in the production of *texts* – often in the form of a specification of what should be done. Students interpret these texts and their subsequent learning activity can be understood as an improvisation that is informed – but rarely determined – by the text. It is often through their interpretation of key texts (such as course outlines and assignment specifications) that students unravel what is required from them in a given situation. This is rarely a straightforward process. On the one hand students will bring their own beliefs and experiences about how such activity is to be completed (Biggs and Tang 2007; Prosser and Trigwell 1999; Ellis and Goodyear 2010) and their ability to keep task specifications in mind, as activity unfolds, will be constrained by working memory. On the other hand it is necessary that students are able to recognize and realize the relevant meanings associated with the pedagogic/ learning context they are in (Bernstein 2000). Students' interpretation of what should be done – including the designers' intentions – requires that they are able to identify implicit social values associated with knowledge and practices within a particular context. That means that students will need to 'translate' a number of cues that are communicated to them along with the text. (Such cues can appear in a variety of modes including verbal, written, images or through implicit and subtle signs in the learning environment.) Once students understand the 'rules of the game', they then may be able to act and produce (texts and other artefacts) according to what is expected of them. Some of these implicit social values reflect underlying organizing principles structuring knowledge in particular fields of practice (Maton 2000; Carvalho, Dong and Maton 2009). They underlie the way in which pedagogical communication takes place, regulating teachers'/designers' practices and shaping, for example, the ways a task is proposed. Consequently, task design also involves incorporating ways of expressing the broader social context of the proposed learning activities so that students know the 'rules' for the context they are in. In short, tasks – as designed objects – need to be understood as (a) nested in an *architecture of tasks* (tasks make sense in relation to sub-tasks and supra-tasks), and (b) located within what might be called an *epistemic architecture* – a structure of knowledge and ways of knowing peculiar to a discipline, profession or practice.

Design for learning must also attend to the social and physical setting

Design that is attending to the physical and social setting(s) within which learning activity is expected to unfold typically results in the identification, selection, recommendation and/or creation of texts, tools and artefacts that the designer believes will be useful. It also results in suggestions to students about how they might work with others – proposing divisions of labour, grouping, and/or the allocation of roles. As with task specifications, these socio-material design components should normally be understood as resources on which students *may* choose to draw – even when their use is mandated, students find themselves some wriggle room (Goodyear and Ellis 2010). Moreover, working with and in a complicated network of people, tools, artefacts and places is neither an automatic nor a dependable process: what works needs to be seen as an accomplishment (Law and Mol 2002; Rabardel and Beguin 2005).

Design for learning needs to work fluently across scale levels

Design for learning gravitates towards the meso-level (Jones *et al.* 2006; Jones, Chapter 13). By this we mean that, in practice, educational design attention tends to be drawn to the design of learning tasks that run over hours or days, rather than years or seconds. It is better aligned to the layout of rooms or the recommendation of specific texts than to macro considerations (replanning the campus; restocking the library) or to the minutiae of students' choices of pen, paper, or workmate. That said, the devil can often be in the detail and also macro-level phenomena can place powerful constraints on what happens at the meso-level. So while design tends to focus on the meso, it cannot safely ignore chains of influence that run from macro to micro and back again. The interrelations between tools, artefacts and other material/digital resources for learning can be thought of as constituting a *physical architecture*. Similarly, interpersonal working relationships, divisions of labour, roles etc. make sense within what might be called a *social architecture*.

In sum, whether we are trying to analyse an existing learning situation, or design a new one, we need ways of conceiving of the networks of interacting people, objects, activities, texts etc. that shape learning activities and outcomes. We need to be able to detect global forces at work in local artefacts, and to account for the mutual shaping done by language, minds and things (Gibson and Ingold 1995; Miller 2010).

Connecting assemblages of tools and artefacts to human activity

An analysis of the relations between such things as digital tools and resources, on the one hand, and learning outcomes, on the other, needs to be informed by some defensible ideas about how the former can be said to influence the latter. Causality is multiple and complex. Evaluative or analytic approaches that assume simple linear causal paths are unlikely to be helpful. How then to frame analysis of learning environments so that we stand some chance of connecting (a) that which is designed to (b) valued educational outcomes? If one finds it sufficient to equate learning with authentic engagement in a social practice, then this is a one-step argument. If one also values some associated change in the understanding or skills of a learner, then two steps are needed to complete the connections (see Mayes and de Freitas, Chapter 1).

We take an *activity-centred* position on this: what matters is what the learner *does* – physically, mentally and emotionally (Shuell 1992; Biggs and Tang 2007). Different kinds of knowledge are acquired in different ways – through the activation of different kinds of mental processes, for example (Ohlsson 1995, 2011). So the nature of the learner's activity is part of the link between the material world and their learning outcomes. The other missing link is between the material world and activity. This is where the over-used idea of affordance is normally asked to weave its magic. It is usually a mistake to try to isolate some intrinsic properties of tools, resources, places, etc. and connect them to learning. Rather, as Nicole Boivin argues: 'material properties are always properties relative to people, as James Gibson's concept of affordances reminds us … what is important is not just materiality, but *the coming together of materiality and embodied humans engaged in particular activities*' (Boivin 2008: 167, emphasis added).

The quotation we took from Harry Collins (above), about 'affordance' being a 'lazy' term, was arguing that the extraordinary interpretive capabilities of people undermine the explanatory power of 'affordance'. It is true that people are extremely versatile sense-makers, but that does not mean that they linger in interpretive mode prior to every action. What needs to be acknowledged here is that human action can involve deliberation and interpretation but it can also be rapid, fluid and seemingly automatic. Rather than insist on the primacy of either 'affordance' or 'interpretation' in explaining relations between material objects and human activity, we would argue that both play a role, much of the time. One way to think about this is to consider Daniel Kahneman's argument that humans rely on two systems of mental operation – tuned to 'thinking fast and slow'. Kahneman (2011) describes two 'systems in the mind':

> System 1 operates automatically and quickly, with little or no effort and no sense of voluntary control … System 2 allocates attention to the effortful mental activities that demand it … The operations of System 2 are often associated with the subjective experience of agency, choice and concentration.
>
> Kahneman 2011

We suggest that affordances are involved when System 1 is running the show; interpretation invokes System 2. This immediately provides a more flexible and robust way of accounting for links between the material/digital world, learner activities and learning outcomes. For example, providing learners with scaffolding for their activities, by offering them guidance in the form of digital texts, necessarily invokes System 2, increases cognitive load, but also opens opportunities for interpretation and reflection on the designer's intentions. Design can substitute other forms of computer-based guidance for texts – e.g. through the use of interface icons, or other forms of procedural support, that afford one action rather than another. This allows System 1 to do what is needed, reducing cognitive load but sacrificing opportunities for reflection in order to expedite action. (Neither of these approaches is intrinsically better. Design involves trade-offs.)

This leads to a view of analysis that can hypothesize a variety of connections between the material/digital world, learner activity and outcomes – involving various mixtures of affordance and interpretation; fast thinking and slow; visceral, behavioural and reflective responses, or hot and cool cognition (Norman 2005; Thagard 2008). It also helps resolve thorny problems about technological determinism and human agency (Oliver 2011) since few, if any, encounters with technology are single-stranded.

Much of the literature that aims at explaining relations between technology and human action takes a social, cultural or semiotic view, within which characteristics of tools and artefacts are of little interest.

> In subsuming material studies into general semiotic and social paradigms, we highlight certain aspects of material meaning, but at the same time *we occlude recognition of what makes material things different from words and signs* – indeed what makes material things really interesting in their own right.
>
> Boivin 2008: 155, emphasis added

> Such examples allow us more clearly to see how the *actual physical properties of things* – rather than just the ideas we hold about them – instigate change, by placing constraints on some activities and behaviours, and making possible, encouraging, or demanding, other types of behaviour.
>
> ibid.: 166, emphasis added

Like Boivin, we think that analysis needs to account for ways in which technology – and the material world more generally – influences human perception and action, without recourse to deterministic arguments. Objects in the material world carry physical properties such as their size, weight, shape, colour and temperature, which may or may not have been intended as part of their design. Digital tools and artefacts affect a narrower range of senses, but have qualities that can change in an instant. We also need to acknowledge that embedded into the particular way any material object is designed is an intention of how form and function were to meet. The object itself thereby carries values from, and choices made in, the design process. Either way, through their physical properties and embodied intentions, designed objects will have an effect on human perception and action.

Illustrations: analysing the architecture of productive learning networks

Illustration 1: Field training of paramedics (iPads in the wild)

This case study came to our attention when one of our part-time master's students began discussing her ideas about a dissertation project. (We have changed a few details, to preserve anonymity.) Her original suggestion was that she might try to evaluate the effects on learning of the introduction of iPads – the context being one of the courses in her School of Health Sciences. She sketched how she might do this – with some students having school-provided iPads and others not. The first opportunity to do this would be on a field trip – an exercise in which students who are learning to be paramedics would take part in the search for, and treatment and evacuation of, some people injured while hiking in the mountains. (This exercise has been run annually for a number of years. The casualties are played by actors. Qualified mountain rescue personnel take a major role in running the exercise. The iPads were new.) We did not encourage our master's student to run the experiment that she had in mind. Rather, we suggested that, at least at first, she should take a more exploratory approach – roving around while the exercise unfolded, making field notes, and trying to identify and describe as carefully as possible the mix of things that seemed to influence the activities and their outcomes.

Her field notes mentioned that the iPads were used (but not often). She also noted the use of: compasses, maps, GPS devices, torches, whistles, ropes, binoculars and walkie-talkies. These were just the tools for navigation and communication. Then there were stretchers, bandages, scissors, watches (for measuring a pulse), stethoscopes, medications and syringes – objects involved in the initial 'treatment' of the actor/casualties once they had been located. A reasonably complete account would also take in these actor/casualties (semi-skilled), the mountain rescue volunteers (very skilled), the tutors (semi-skilled) and the students (often lost, cold and confused). Obvious though it might seem, the design and evolution of this exercise also necessitated being in the mountains. The difficulties of traversing rough terrain, locating a casualty when hidden in a valley or by vegetation, coping with poor visibility and communicating without mobile phones all played a substantial role in the exercise. Proper clothing is also important. A conventionally minded instructional designer might be forgiven for thinking that good boots and a warm, waterproof coat are things for the students to provide. But those who forgot these important items were unable to complete the exercise. And which instructional design guideline tells you that fingerless gloves are useful when trying to use an iPad on a cold mountain?

Among many other things, this example illustrates how important it is that students are able to recognize the relevant meanings of the pedagogical context in which they find themselves: relating ways of knowing with material circumstances. Pedagogical interactions on the mountain involved very different 'rules of the game' compared to those in a 'normal' classroom. Students had to be able to identify a different 'language' and those who could not recognize the essential rules within this context were then unable to participate fully in the experience.

From the perspective of the organizers as the 'designers' of the exercise, emphasis was placed on the technical knowledge associated with understanding drugs, first aid etc; on the use of technical devices (e.g. iPads), and on life-saving procedures. These were seen as the essential knowledge for completing the exercise, and some issues related to the effects of the environment were overlooked, or their influence underestimated. The organizers assumed that key aspects of the knowledge needed to work effectively in the mountain environment would come from the students' prior personal experience – and therefore, they 'should already know' that boots and coats were essential elements, given the material circumstances. As a result, in spite of whatever knowledge they had about life-saving procedures, using technology remotely and so on, those who did not know about the need for coats, gloves and boots in rough terrain failed to learn much from the experience.

We cannot easily portray the whole network of tools, artefacts, activities, people and attributes of the physical terrain in a single image. But Figure 3.1 begins to capture some of the relationships involved in (more or less) successful execution of this field exercise.

Our analysis suggests that successful participation in the exercise involves:

- learning to use each tool, at least with sufficient fluency to be able to act according to the established protocols, but ideally with a level of automaticity that binds tool and action in a smooth flow;
- integrating the use of the tools into a web of activity, involving smooth effective action, coordination with others, focus on the priority goals, etc.;
- turning the individual and aggregate experiences of the exercise into learning that lasts.

The point of the exercise, for each student, is not just to master the individual tools but to participate in the construction of a coordinated web of activity that

Figure 3.1 A (partial) network of objects and activities

can result in a successful rescue, minimizing danger to participants, and leaving traces (in some kinds of memory) that mean doing something like this again will not feel entirely new.

Illustration 2: Online learning for educational leadership

Our second case involves an online professional development programme for schoolteachers taking on curriculum leadership positions. (Again, unimportant details have been altered to protect anonymity.)

A number of elements of the programme are quite conventional. There is an online induction module, introducing the participants to the technology being used, to a number of key ideas about educational leadership, and to the overall scope and goals of the programme. Through direct experience of the resources, teaching methods, user interface, tasks and collaborative learning activities that will be used in the main part of the programme, participants have an opportunity to work out whether the programme will suit them, and whether they will be able to cope with its demands. Thirty per cent of participants quit during or immediately after the induction module.

The remaining participants then tackle 12 'structured learning modules' (SLMs), each of which introduces them to a set of ideas that the course team believes to be relevant to understanding curriculum leadership. Once the participants have completed four of these modules, they are allowed to join an online community of practice, within which they are encouraged to discuss issues with peers. Once all the SLMs are completed, participants work in small groups to design curriculum implementation projects that they will carry out in their own schools. The designs are peer-reviewed. The rubric for the peer review includes criteria that reflect and encourage the use of concepts, techniques, etc. that were presented in the SLMs. Thus far, some 200 projects have been designed and published for peer review by the programme participants.

An analysis of what is working well and what might be improved would conventionally focus on the quality of the resources being made available in the SLMs, the timeliness and helpfulness of online tutors' support, the ease of use of the online tools, participants' experiences and their assessment of the extent and usefulness of their own learning. All of these are important, but they tell less than the whole story, and an analysis of the case that was restricted to these elements would not – we contend – provide an adequate basis for others to design similar educational programmes.

Not least, the fact that this programme draws on problems that emerge in participants' own educational practice – and is intended to help solve those problems – means that the participants' schools (in all their complexity) have to be counted in as learning resources. People without access to such resources could not participate successfully in the programme. Moreover, these school-based 'resources' are outside the sphere of things that the programme providers can design. (The programme providers/designers can specify requirements – e.g.

that participants must have a leadership role with respect to curriculum change in some part of their school's work. But they cannot design these important parts of the network of activities, texts and resources on which participants will draw.)

Participants bring their school-based 'resources' to the mix and associated with each of these resources is a specific set of underlying principles structuring knowledge practices. That is, knowledge practices within each school reflect implicit values within that specific context, which shape participants' practices and the way they see leadership and curriculum. As various participants come into the pedagogical context of the online environment to exchange ideas about leadership and curriculum, they bring also their own beliefs and values, which will need to be negotiated with the beliefs and values of other participants, whose practices are shaped by their own experiences of their school-based resource. A participant with a background in science may see knowledge practices in a different way than a participant with a background in arts. Or a participant's views about leadership may reflect their experiences at different levels of hierarchy, such as being a Coordinator or a Principal. The context of the experience may also be influenced by the complexities that shape working in a city school versus in a remote area, an established versus a new school, and so on. As these participants come 'together' to exchange notions about leadership and discuss curriculum issues within the online environment, they do so from their own perspective, from where they are positioned within the field. The design of the pedagogical context where they interact needs to address these differences, acknowledging that diverse underlying values are likely to be present.

This use of the local working context as a resource for online learning is not uncommon in design for professional development, but we have found very little in the instructional design literature that helps capture or think about key issues here, other than in general terms.

Conclusions

In this chapter, we have suggested that approaches to analysing complex learning environments will be more productive, and will align better with the knowledge needs of designers, if they help map the webs of heterogeneous elements that shape learning activity. In particular, we have argued that neither affordance nor interpretation provides a sufficient explanation for the connections between that which is designed and the learner's activity. Our illustrations show how tasks (and activities) sit within nested architectures, such that what a person is doing at any one point only makes sense in relation to a web of other tasks (and activities), the accomplishment of which may well be distributed quite widely in time and space, and across the material, human and digital. We have also tried to show something of the complexity of the networks of tools, artefacts, places, practices, ways of knowing and interpersonal relationships that are implicated in designed learning situations. Successful designs for learning find ways of embracing this complexity. Sharp analytic skills help us understand such designs, and learn from them.

Acknowledgements

We gratefully acknowledge the financial support of the Australian Research Council through grant FL100100203: *Learning, technology and design: architectures for productive networked learning.* We also thank Helen Beetham for insightful comments on an earlier draft of this chapter.

References

Bennett, J. (2010) *Vibrant Matter: A political ecology of things*, Durham: Duke University Press.

Bernstein, B. (2000) *Pedagogy, Symbolic Control, and Identity: Theory, research, critique* (Revised edn), Oxford: Rowman & Littlefield.

Biggs, J. and Tang, C. (2007) *Teaching for Quality Learning at University: What the student does* (3rd edn) Buckingham: Open University Press.

Boivin, N. (2008) *Material Cultures, Material Minds: The impact of things on human thought, society and evolution*, Cambridge: Cambridge University Press.

Boys, J. (2011) *Towards Creative Learning Spaces: Re-thinking the architecture of post-compulsory education*, New York: Routledge.

Carvalho, L., Dong, A. and Maton, K. (2009) 'Legitimating design: a sociology of knowledge account of the field', *Design Studies*, 30 (5): 483–502.

Collins, H. (2010) *Tacit and Explicit Knowledge*, Chicago: University of Chicago Press.

Conole, G. and Dyke, M. (2004) 'What are the affordances of information and communication technologies?', *ALT-J: Research in Learning Technology*, 12 (2): 113–24.

Crandall, B., Klein, G. and Hoffman, R. (2006) *Working Minds: A practitioner's guide to cognitive task analysis*, Cambridge, MA: MIT Press.

Dohn, N. (2009) 'Affordances revisited: articulating a Merleau-Pontian view', *International Journal of Computer-Supported Collaborative Learning*, 4 (2): 151–70.

Ellis, R. and Goodyear, P. (2010) *Students' Experiences of E-Learning in Higher Education: The ecology of sustainable innovation*, New York: Routledge Falmer.

Fenwick, T. and Edwards, R. (2010) *Actor Network Theory in Education*, London: Routledge.

Fenwick, T., Edwards, R. and Sawchuk, P. (2011) *Emerging Approaches to Educational Research: Tracing the sociomaterial*, Abingdon: Routledge.

Gibson, J. (1977) 'The theory of affordances', in R. Shaw and J. Bransford (eds), *Perceiving, Acting, and Knowing: Toward an ecological psychology*, Hillsdale, NJ: Lawrence Erlbaum Associates.

Gibson, J. (1986) *The Ecological Approach to Visual Perception*, Hillsdale, NJ: Lawrence Erlbaum Associates.

Gibson, K. and Ingold, T. (eds) (1995) *Tools, Language and Cognition in Human Evolution*, Cambridge: Cambridge University Press.

Goodyear, P. (2000a) 'Environments for lifelong learning: ergonomics, architecture and educational design', in J. M. Spector and T. Anderson (eds) *Integrated and Holistic Perspectives on Learning, Instruction and Technology: Understanding complexity*, Dordrecht: Kluwer Academic Publishers.

Goodyear, P. (2000b) 'Seeing learning as work: implications for understanding and improving analysis and design', *Journal of Courseware Engineering*, 2: 3–11.

Goodyear, P. and Ellis, R. (2010) 'Expanding conceptions of study, context and educational design', in R. Sharpe, H. Beetham and S. de Freitas (eds) *Rethinking Learning for a Digital Age: How learners are shaping their own experiences*, New York: Routledge.

Goodyear, P. and Retalis, S. (2010) 'Learning, technology and design', in P. Goodyear and S. Retalis (eds) *Technology-enhanced Learning: Design patterns and pattern languages*, Rotterdam: Sense Publishers.

Ingold, T. (2000) *The Perception of the Environment: Essays in livelihood, dwelling and skill*, Abingdon: Routledge.

John, P. and Sutherland, R. (2005) 'Affordance, opportunity and the pedagogical implications of ICT', *Educational Review*, 57 (4): 405–13.

Johri, A. (2011) 'The socio-materiality of learning practices and implications for the field of learning technology', *Research in Learning Technology*, 19 (3): 207–17.

Jones, C., Dirckinck-Holmfeld, L. and Lindstrom, B. (2006) 'A relational, indirect, meso-level approach to CSCL design in the next decade', *International Journal of Computer-Supported Collaborative Learning*, 2 (2–3): 35–56.

Kahneman, D. (2011) *Thinking, Fast and Slow*, New York: Farrar, Straus and Giroux.

Laurillard, D. (1987) 'The different forms of learning in psychology and education', in J. Richardson, M. Eysenck and D. Warren Piper (eds) *Student Learning: Research in education and cognitive psychology*, Buckingham: Open University Press.

Law, J. and Mol, A. (eds) (2002) *Complexities: Social studies of knowledge practices*, Durham: Duke University Press.

Luckin, R. (2010) *Re-Designing Learning Contexts: Technology-rich, learner-centred ecologies*, New York: Routledge.

Maton, K. (2000) 'Languages of legitimation: The structuring significance for intellectual fields of strategic knowledge claims', *British Journal of Sociology of Education*, 21 (2): 147–67.

Miller, D. (2010). *Stuff*, Cambridge: Polity Press.

Norman, D. (1999) 'Affordance, conventions and design', *Interactions*, 6 (3), 38–43.

Norman, D. (2005) *Emotional Design: Why we love (or hate) everyday things*, New York: Basic Books.

Ohlsson, S. (1995) 'Learning to do and learning to understand: a lesson and a challenge for cognitive modelling', in P. Reimann and H. Spada (eds) *Learning in Humans and Machines: Towards an interdisciplinary learning science*, London: Pergamon.

Ohlsson, S. (2011) *Deep Learning: How the mind overrides experience*, Cambridge: Cambridge University Press.

Oliver, M. (2005) 'The problem with affordance', *E-Learning and Digital Media*, 2 (4), 402–13.

Oliver, M. (2011) 'Technological determinism in educational technology research: some alternative ways of thinking about the relationship between learning and technology', *Journal of Computer Assisted Learning*, 27: 373–84.

Prosser, M. and Trigwell, K. (1999) *Understanding Learning and Teaching: The experience in higher education*, Buckingham: SRHE/Open University Press.

Rabardel, P. and Beguin, P. (2005) 'Instrument mediated activity: from subject development to anthropocentric design', *Theoretical Issues in Ergonomic Science*, 6 (5): 429–61.

Reigeluth, C. and Carr-Chellman, A. (eds) (2009) *Instructional Design Theories and Models*, Volume 3, New York: Routledge.

Shuell, T. (1992) 'Designing instructional computing systems for meaningful learning', in M. Jones and P. Winne (eds) *Adaptive Learning Environments*, New York: Springer Verlag.

Sorensen, E. (2009) *The Materiality of Learning: Technology and knowledge in educational practice*, Cambridge: Cambridge University Press.

Thagard, P. (2008) *Hot Thought: Mechanisms and applications of emotional cognition*, Cambridge MA: MIT Press.

Turner, P. (2005) 'Affordance as context', *Interacting with Computers*, 17: 787–800.

Westberry, N. and Franken, M. (2013) 'Co-construction of knowledge in tertiary online settings: An ecology of resources perspective', *Instructional Science*, 41 (1): 147–64.

Chapter 4

The Challenge of Teachers' Design Practice

Liz Masterman

EDITORS' INTRODUCTION

Masterman's chapter reminds us that there is much to be learned from practitioners themselves as they engage with the day-to-day realities of learners and learning. She describes four research studies into how practitioners design for learning in complex settings and what considerations they take into account when framing tasks, resources and courses of study. Design for learning emerges as a social practice, governed by precedent and habit, constrained by pragmatic issues such as class size and timetabling, and informed by 'a range of intellectual and socio-cultural influences' of which designers may not always be fully conscious. Masterman's work has aimed not only to describe design practice more thoroughly but to support the development of tools that could enhance that practice. Although she is hopeful that 'a supportive digital tool which is rooted in a principled theory of educational processes' can be accepted by practitioners, she notes the difficulties – computational, theoretical, and organizational/political – that such a project must still overcome.

Introduction

A major strand in research into design for learning over recent years has been the development of supportive digital tools that guide teachers' thinking through the process of planning and constructing new learning experiences, and revising existing ones. Specifically, these tools have the twin aims of simultaneously supporting teachers' current design practice and stimulating them to innovate, both in their overall approach to design and in their use of digital technologies. The tools themselves are described by Conole (Chapter 5), who designates them 'pedagogy planners'. However, their design and deployment hinges on an understanding of teachers' design practice and the setting in which they carry it out. This chapter maps, and critically analyses, that problem space through a review of empirical work conducted, in part, by the author and colleagues. Specifically, it addresses:

- teachers' conceptualization of, and their approach to, the activity of design;
- four factors that bear on their design practice: students' needs and preferences, theory, the findings of educational research and the nature of the discipline;
- the socio-cultural context in which design practice takes place.

The chapter concludes by exploring the implications of the evidence uncovered for developing supportive digital tools, expressed as a number of tensions between actual practice and the compromises entailed in computational support for that practice.

Researching design in the real world

Studying teachers' design practice yields two benefits. First, it allows the principles of educational design to be held up against real-world processes and heuristics, and second, it can inform the development of computational tools and computer-assisted processes to support those practices. In focusing on the latter benefit, this chapter draws on knowledge accumulated from four projects, with reference also to the broader body of research.

The initial projects were exploratory studies. The *Learning Design Tools Project* gathered data on teachers' use of generic tools such as word processing, presentation tools and mind-mapping software in designing for learning, while *Design for Learning in Virtual Learning Environments: Insider Perspectives* explored the practice of designing and representing learning activities in virtual learning environments (VLEs) (Masterman and Vogel 2007). The later projects, *Phoebe* (Masterman and Manton 2011) and the *Learning Designer* (Laurillard *et al.* 2012), built successively on the findings of the first two in developing and evaluating two contrasting tools to support the practice of design for learning. Data from practitioners were collected during the requirements gathering phase of each project.

Conducting research into a process which is often tacit, incremental and distributed poses methodological challenges, particularly a reliance on lecturers' self-reports. Each project outlined in the previous paragraph adopted one or more of the following techniques: online questionnaires, interviews, workshops in which specific instances of practice were recorded (albeit in an artificial context), and inspection of design artefacts such as lesson plans and VLE course areas. However, it is the interviews conducted by the *Learning Designer* project that furnish many of the examples cited in the remainder of this chapter, conducted with ten *informant practitioners* (IPs): experienced lecturers, staff developers and learning technologists working in universities in the UK. Congruence of the findings, both among the four projects, and between them and other work, suggests the existence of a set of common, or core, features in teachers' design practice that permits cautious generalizations to be made.

Teachers' conceptualization of design

Broadly speaking, the literature distinguishes two dimensions to design for learning, theorized as Learning Design: (1) the creation of structured sequences of learning activities; and (2) a way to represent and share practice (Dalziel 2009). IPs' conceptualizations, elicited by the interview question 'What does the term "learning design" mean to you?', were concentrated on the first of these dimensions. In this respect, structure was considered as a property that emerged from fluidity and negotiation: as one lecturer expressed it, 'the interplay of aspects of learning and how together they would come up to […] an optimal situation which would enable learning'.

Some lecturers distinguished between 'design' and 'planning'. Planning involves laying out the constraints in terms of, for example, time, location, number of students, learning outcomes and content (i.e. a mixture of logistical and pedagogic factors), while design pays attention to what can be achieved within those constraints that will engage and activate the students, and have an impact on both the pedagogic and affective planes.

For a number of lecturers, contextual constraints functioned as a spur to creativity. For example, although a session might be officially billed in the timetable as a 'lecture', one lecturer designed whatever activities she felt were most conducive to students' learning. Being creative might also entail being subversive; for example, another person insinuated online assessment into her programme even though it was not permitted by university regulations, by simply designating the online tasks as part of students' coursework.

The perception of a creative aspect to design recalls the duality inherent in the notion of design. Design can be, simultaneously, the application of 'systematic principles and methods' and 'a creative activity that cannot be fully reduced to standard steps' (Winograd 1996: xx, xxii). However, for some teachers the two concepts are not symbiotic but mutually exclusive. Even though design for learning (conceptualized as 'Learning Design') is explicitly rooted in social constructivism (Oliver et al. 2002), one IP found the term at odds with his own conceptualization of education:

> It has echoes for me of going back to, kind of, Instructional Design. […] some things in education […], they're explorations to see where you're going and to see where you get to. They're not plans to get to a particular place.

Teachers' approach to the practice of design

The overarching practice of design for learning has been operationalized in a hierarchical model through the concept of layers by Boyle (2010), and in a cyclical (process) model by Beetham (Chapter 2). The testimonies reported here are largely derived from design practice at Boyle's 'session' layer: that is, individual lectures, seminars, practicals and other classes that are typically one to three hours in duration and either stand alone or belong to a superordinate layer such as a module or course. In terms of the four interrelated activities in Beetham's design cycle – creating, instantiating, realizing and reviewing – the testimonies focus on 'creating'; namely 'the specification of higher-level properties associated with the learning design – such as aims, learning outcomes, student characteristics, teaching approach and method of assessment – as well as the activities that the learners will carry out' (Masterman and Manton 2011: 230).

Some teachers start with pre-defined learning outcomes, while others structure their plan around a set of activities negotiated with their learners. Teachers may also take different routes through the task, some mapping out learning materials while creating the plan and others creating all such learning materials afterwards (i.e. during the 'instantiating' activity). One IP captured the messiness of the design process across multiple layers as one juggles interrelationships, dependencies and multiple actors:

> I mean, that's a module, um, and that links in … so you've got six of those across or whatever and it links down from … but the problem then is your programme design has to go from [year one to] year three. Now that's where I start to get so confused because you know, your [student] has to be able to do this at year three.

Another lecturer visualized the early stages of the design process as a circle, with the topic in the middle and the other factors to be considered around the edge. Only when she had obtained her 'big picture' did she switch to the linear (time-based) approach imposed by the VLE. A third person employed a picturesque horticultural metaphor: 'the "compost heap" approach where you throw stuff in and you've got a very big pile and then you can start throwing, taking things out of it […] But then you've got to structure what remains.'

The overall strategy adopted by any one teacher can be a function of personal proclivity and institutional practice: the careful structuring of learning designs by one IP resulted both from a highly formal background in teacher training and from the course format: he had to create a 'logical fit' among a seminar that he would be teaching, a lecture that would have already been given by someone else, and a reading list that had likewise been compiled by a third party.

Finally, returning to Beetham's cycle, we should note that the 'creating' activity can never be wholly dissociated from the others, since a design may need to be adapted in response to contingencies that arise during the learning session itself (the 'realizing' activity), or a 'reviewing' activity may lead to components of the design being added, modified or dropped.

Factors bearing on teachers' approach to design

Entwistle *et al.* (2000) and Bennett *et al.* (2011) have noted a propensity among lecturers to reproduce the teaching that they themselves experienced, and this was echoed by at least one lecture in the *Learning Designer* interviews: 'you either think they're great and emulate them, or you think they're terrible and try and do something else. Or, you have no idea what to do other than to imitate.' Other influences on teachers' approach uncovered by the four projects reflect previous research: for example, university policies, lecturers' freedom to vary the curriculum and the frequency of opportunities to design new courses or revise existing ones (Bennett *et al.* 2011).

In the next four sections we address additional factors that, to varying extents, can influence teachers' approach to creating learning designs: students, theory, educational research and the discipline in which they teach.

Student-related factors

The centrality of the undergraduate experience, which is now enshrined in UK government thinking (BIS 2011), was strongly apparent among IPs. Indeed, for one lecturer the very will to teach begins with the desire to share one's knowledge with students. Another had been prompted to explore the role of digital technologies through passion for the kind of learning experience that she could offer students. However, students may also exert direct pressure on teaching staff to make more use of technology: 'The students also make demands: "Can you provide this work online for us so that we can actually ... ?", and therefore people slowly start coming out of their own cocoons' (lecturer).

In the main, student-related factors act as constraints rather than enabling factors. Large class sizes can make it difficult even for enthusiasts to innovate. Culture, gender and ethnicity pose additional challenges: for example, in one IP's university 51 per cent of students were from black or minority ethnic communities, and he felt that the 'white middle-class culture' and 'western view of knowledge' promulgated in British universities was 'very alien' to them.

The emphasis on developing graduate attributes to ensure that students are fit for the labour market has also come to the fore in recent years. It is manifested, in part, in a drive towards digital literacy and towards the greater use of technology-enhanced learning. As one lecturer commented:

> If we don't do any sort of blogs, podcasts, internet searches, if we don't get the students using their mobile phones, if we don't introduce them to any of these technologies as part of the curriculum, what kind of graduates are we sending out?

Two other lecturers exploited the possibilities of technologies to scaffold students' self-management skills in an unexpected manner. They turned the 'anytime, anywhere' maxim of technology-enhanced learning on its head, by using the timed release functionality in their VLEs to make sure that students did their work within an allotted time.

Theory

Researchers generally consider that theories of learning and theory-informed frameworks play a key role, not merely in ensuring 'good pedagogical design' (Mayes and de Freitas 2004; Ravenscroft 2001), but also in countering tendencies towards 'technological determinism' (Conole 2008). The interviews with IPs in particular suggested that the value of theory lies above all in providing insights into the underlying mechanisms of teaching and learning. Indeed, one person drew an illuminating distinction between *theories of learning* – explanatory theories of how people come to learn, but which he felt contained insufficient constraints to be of use in guiding design practice – and *theories of teaching* – practical frameworks to support specific teaching and learning approaches, which may nevertheless be based on learning theories. In this way, theory can both inform the activity of creating a learning design and fulfil an explanatory function in the activity of reviewing (reflection):

> What the reflection can lead you to is the point where you go, 'Well, this is not working but I don't know how to fix it', which then needs to be – you need to be able to head into the theory behind it to work out why it's not working and then you could fix it yourself.

Of course, theory is not applied uncritically. Although a number of lecturers spoke of being influenced by a variety of theories, these had become interwoven into their general worldview and they rarely set out to implement a specific one; for example:

> ... there's kind of a lot of complexity around there, and it's not as simple as saying, 'Oh yes, I'm a, you know, I'm a constructivist or a social constructivist, or a this, or a that, or [...] I look at Piaget' ... I think they all do influence, but I don't think there's one correct one.

Finally, a few lecturers took a deliberately atheoretical stance; for example: 'in the end what's going to inform my decisions are time, number of students, [...], the things that they have to get done'. Moreover, even lecturers who cited theories extensively admitted that pragmatic issues were their primary consideration.

Research-informed teaching

Evidence from the *Learning Designer* project suggested that lecturers can be content with anecdotal accounts of practice from others within their discipline community, perhaps because of the element of trust that comes from belonging to a community of like-minded (and like-practising) individuals. A number of IPs even indicated the existence of negative attitudes towards education as a field of research in its own right, reflecting findings by, inter alia, Nuthall (2004).

However, lecturers are increasingly aware of the value of evidence-based practice to curriculum design and to the choice of assessment methods. Although time and other commitments are predictable logistical barriers, this self-report from a learning-technologist-cum-staff-developer suggests that social technologies are providing more adventurous practitioners with access to inspirational pedagogic developments:

> a combination of Google Reader and Twitter, I think and just, you know, explore the blogosphere [...] you just find some nice blogs that you like and just RSS-feed them and you tend to get all the information you need. Also through Delicious, actually, colleagues that are on Delicious they find stuff and they will send me the link.

Nature of the discipline

The extent to which discipline differences determine lecturers' academic practice is unclear (see Young 2010), but the interviews with IPs did indicate some durable influences. One staff developer suggested that social scientists may have less time for concepts such as learning styles because of a perceived lack of empirical evidence. Moreover, modelling professional practice within their teaching may, for example, lead law lecturers to adopt an element of formality, and sociology lecturers to adopt a more observational position.

The dominant research methodology within a particular discipline was perceived to influence lecturers' attitudes towards reusing materials created by other teachers, as shown in these quotations from a lecturer and a staff developer respectively:

> One of the functions that other people's stuff has is teaching me how to do it by looking at examples. And classicists are more prone to doing that, I think, than some other disciplines, just on the grounds that we're very used to looking at examples and recovering patterns in the way that we work for research.

> ... if people are stuck on 'Will this [be] better?', the definition of 'better' depends on what your research background is and 'Does there have to be an experiment in which a control group did this and X was applied in this situation and equalled Y?' If that's the only way you can be convinced, which may be to do with your discipline background, that's quite different from what you might read in a case study from somebody from the social sciences who is talking about a number of factors working together to bring about this change and no requirement for experimental model.

Content acts as another barrier to the cross-disciplinary fertilization of learning designs and design ideas. To surmount it, one must discern something of relevance to one's own teaching in terms of structure or approach. Sometimes it is possible to see this for oneself, but sometimes other people must act as a catalyst. A humanities lecturer vividly described a moment of enlightenment in this respect: perceiving the relevance to her own field of the pedagogy underlying a reusable learning object developed for physics:

> I […] got this lovely example of fulcrum, load and effort and a car crashing into a wall. […] I thought, 'Well that's not what I do because I don't teach a concept that can be grasped like that.' And there was this moment, and I can't remember what anybody said, but […] I had an epiphany because I suddenly went, 'Oh, so when I'm teaching that means I could do this!'

The socio-cultural context

Exploring the socio-cultural context in which design is practised yields two key themes: (1) the role of communities and (2) sharing and reuse.

Design is an inherently social act, even when carried out in isolation. Every teacher is part of at least one community, whether this is formally constituted (e.g. an institution or special interest group) or an informal grouping of people who share a common interest. Communities can overlap (in that someone may belong to both a university department and a scholarly society), or be nested within each other (e.g. a department within an institution). They may be long-lived (as in colleges and universities) or convene for a short time only (e.g. a workshop to share effective practice).

Together, communities constitute the socio-cultural context for teachers' design practice: for example, how that practice is prescribed (curriculum planning bodies), carried out (practitioners), enabled (support staff) or promoted ('communities of practice'). A panoply of policies, strategies, conventions, procedures, guidelines and norms can be formulated by different groups within the community (or supra-community organizations such as governments) for different purposes. Within an institution, they may include curriculum planning and operational concerns such as timetabling, booking procedures for information technology facilities, software purchasing policies and student attendance. On the broader plane, they may extend to national information and communications technology strategies, which will themselves impact on institutional practices.

Staff developers can play a key role in brokering innovation within and across the different communities in an institution, both through cascading new ideas for practice ('promoting things to staff development staff who are running [courses in university teaching] is a really quick way in': staff developer) and through modelling good teaching practice to the lecturers who are studying on these courses.

Informal communities close to the chalk-face were particularly valued by IPs in the *Learning Designer* project, largely for the element of trust that comes from close acquaintance. As one lecturer noted in answer to a question about reusing other lecturers' materials, 'having somebody that you trust who teaches and works in the department tell you that it's there makes it way more likely to get used than if university planning committee tells you that it's there.' Direct contact with another human being is also invaluable in helping lecturers to frame the pedagogic problems for which they seek help: 'you need somebody to look at it and then in a tactful constructive way point out that actually, you know, something else is going on here' (staff developer).

Both the *Phoebe* and *Learning Designer* projects uncovered potential tensions between innovative practice by individuals and institutional strategies for implementing technology-enhanced learning. Top-down initiatives may centre on 'endorsed' (Kennedy *et al.* 2011) tools (primarily the VLE) or on course design and validation processes. However, the VLE may not be universally used; moreover, individual members of staff may experiment additionally with other, unendorsed, tools. For a learning technologist interviewed by the *Learning Designer* project, a bottom-up approach is the optimal way to effect changes in practice:

> Do you wait for the change to come from the top – well, maybe it will – or, you know, can you take a sort of a guerrilla approach and maybe change one or two here, there and everywhere, and then that will feed through to committees or it will feed through to colleagues, or you get a dialogue going within these communities of practice, you know, it has to happen somewhere.

Turning to the second theme of the socio-cultural context, we noted earlier that sharing one's learning designs and associated materials with other teachers and, conversely, using or drawing inspiration from their materials, form a cornerstone in theoretical approaches to design for learning. They are also predicated on the truism that teachers' practice takes place within a broader socio-cultural context. Although sharing and reuse featured in the interview data collected by the *Learning Designer* project, they did not explicitly fall into IPs' conceptualization of design for learning. Instead, the mediational role of communities was prominent. For example, lecturers can be more receptive to materials even from external sources if the latter are recommended by a trusted body, such as the staff development team or a professional organization: 'so they're getting my kite-mark on it, my stamp of approval. But they don't mind that it's somewhere else, particularly if it's good' (staff developer).

Implications and conclusions

The findings from the four projects, supported and supplemented by existing research, have painted a complex, composite picture of the design process that has to do with the dispositions of individual practitioners and a range of intellectual and socio-cultural influences on them, as well as the nature of the process itself. The data support the literature suggesting that this process is 'a social practice that involves orientation to historical precedents, accessible resources [and] local values' (Oliver 2002: 13–14) rather than 'an elegant pathway from goals, to objectives, delivery, reception and so on' (Knight 2001: 374).

None of the projects was expected to lead to a definitive understanding of practice; in particular, the interviews conducted by the *Learning Designer* project were part of an iterative design-based study and were therefore intended mainly to yield a multifaceted working truth from which user requirements (and, hence, design features) could be elicited for a supportive digital tool.

The possibility that digital tools and other strategies can support current practice and advance lecturers' thinking has been established by Bennett *et al.* (2011), and this chapter has explored that problem space further. As a result, a number of aspects in which digital support could potentially be provided can be readily derived from the preceding sections. Examples include assistance in writing learning outcomes consonant with Bloom's taxonomy; the inclusion of 'bite-size' distillations of educational research findings in 'help' topics that address specific pedagogic challenges; and a repository in which learning designs can be shared for the purposes of collaboration, or for inspiration or adaptation. It is also possible to identify outcomes of other strands of research that might be co-opted as features of such a tool: for example, providing different graphical representations (visualizations) to show different facets of a learning design (Oliver *et al.*, Chapter 6) or introducing patterns in order to overcome discipline differences as a barrier to reuse (McAndrew and Goodyear, Chapter 8).

Even so, there remain some problematic implications for the deployment of digital tools to support and extend teachers' thinking: namely, providing computational support for cognitive actions in an 'ill-defined' domain, positioning these tools vis-à-vis theory, and the politics of deployment. These three areas provide a focus for our concluding reflections.

A number of authors have equated the process of planning and designing learning experiences – whether labelled 'learning design' (Donald *et al.* 2009) or 'instructional design' (Jonassen 2008) – to the solving of problems in ill-defined domains (Lynch *et al.* 2006). Such problems lack a single definitive solution; there is no set of steps for the user to follow that will guarantee success; and the solution chosen depends largely on how the solver conceptualizes the problem. In terms of computational support, this means providing guidance that makes the design 'problem' more tractable for the teacher without overly constraining their choices. As data from the *Phoebe* project show, a paradox can exist in which some users perceive a tool as being too flexible, and others as too structured (hence, militating against creativity) (Masterman and Manton: 2011). In addition, the problem of achieving a shared understanding between tool and user can risk either simplistic 'recipe'-style guidance, or guidance that is so vague as to leave novice teachers unsure whether a design decision is a 'good' or 'bad' one (unpublished data from the *Learning Designer* project).

Moreover, during the initial phase of planning the teacher shuffles content, pedagogic approach and so forth in a process of rapid iteration. This is often done using paper and pencil tools or mind-mapping software, for example, because designers need space to lay out their embryonic design or the opportunity to move elements around freely. The computer is used to record the design once these essentials have been decided. The digital tools designed to support pedagogic planning may therefore not be giving support at the time when it is most needed. This particularly elusive stage of the design process needs further empirical study for us to understand it more fully and determine how intelligent digital support might be offered.

In the same way that no technology to support students' learning can be pedagogically neutral (Kanuka and Rourke 2008), so no technology to support the planning of that learning can be agnostic *vis-à-vis* theory. This applies not only to the theories and frameworks that may inform different parts of the tool (for example, Bloom's taxonomy or Biggs' model of constructive alignment for ensuring that learning activities are matched to outcomes), but also to the theoretical assumptions about teaching and learning that imbue the tool itself. For example, the label 'learning activities' as a generic term for what goes on in class implies a different slant on the teacher–student relationship from the label 'teaching activities'.

Given the multiplicity of theoretical influences on teachers and their stitching together into individual and idiosyncratic worldviews, a supportive digital tool which is rooted in a principled theory of educational processes may be more acceptable to practitioners than one which is built on a prescriptive framework for practice or on a theory of learning that gives no clues for its realization in an actual learning experience. The case for Learning Design is particularly strong in view of the spontaneous espousal of its key principles by the lecturers interviewed.

When exploring the socio-cultural context of design earlier in this chapter we uncovered tensions between top-down and bottom-up approaches to innovation, particularly in relation to technology-enhanced learning. Unless carefully managed, the deployment of supportive digital tools for teachers' design practice may have substantial implications for relations between the institution and the individual teacher. Commenting on qualitative data from the *Phoebe* evaluation, Masterman and Manton note the risk of

> a perceived tension between a top-down management-directed deployment – with its implications of conformity and enforced adherence to standards – and the bottom-up voluntary espousal of a tool that individual teachers perceive as genuinely relevant to their personal practice and supportive of their creativity.
>
> Masterman and Manton 2011: 242–3

Although the institution must play a central role in exploiting the full benefit of these tools, this must be done in such a way that lecturers feel that they 'own' the tool as well.

To conclude, in reviewing lecturers' self-reported design practice we can discern a number of tensions, or balances to be achieved by the developers of digital tools to support teachers in the creation of learning designs. These include an inherent tension in the very concept of 'design' (method versus creativity); theory-informed versus pragmatic approaches to the design task; the ill-defined nature of learning design versus its systematization into an ontology to underpin computational support; and conformity versus creativity (the disjuncture between completing formal documentation and designing for students' learning).

These tensions are not readily resolvable, and each development team must take its own stand in relation to them, dependent on the user group for which it is designing the tool. Moreover, some of these tensions lie beyond their control, as they emerge from the manner in which the finished product is deployed in their institutional context. Hence, we can argue, the social and institutional influences brought to bear on the deployment of the tool within a particular community are at least as important as the functionality, look and feel of the tool itself. The question is, to what extent can – and should – developers take these broader influences into consideration in software design?

Acknowledgements

Portions of the text have been taken from the chapter by Masterman and Vogel in the first edition of this volume. The author acknowledges with appreciation the work of Mira Vogel in the original publication.

The *Learning Designer* project was funded from 2008–2011 by the ESRC-EPSRC TLRP TEL programme, grant ref. RES–139–25–0406. The partnering institutions were: Institute of Education (lead), Birkbeck University of London, University of Oxford, London School of Economics and Political Science, Royal Veterinary College and London Metropolitan University.

References

Bennett, S., Thomas, L., Agostinho, S., Lockyer, L., Jones, J. and Harper, B. (2011) 'Understanding the design context for Australian university teachers: implications for the future of learning design', *Learning, Media and Technology*, 36 (2): 151–67.

BIS (2011) *Higher Education: Students at the Heart of the System*. White Paper. London: Department for Business, Innovation and Skills.

Boyle, T. (2010) 'Layered learning design: Towards an integration of learning design and learning object perspectives', *Computers & Education*, 54: 661–8.

Conole, G. (2008) 'New schemas for mapping pedagogies and technologies', *Ariadne*, 56: 1–14.

Dalziel, J. (2009) 'Prospects for learning design research and LAMS', *Teaching English with Technology*, 9 (2): i–iv.

Donald, C., Blake, A., Girault, I., Datt, A. and Ramsay, E. (2009) 'Approaches to learning design: past the head and the hands to the HEART of the matter', *Distance Education*, 30 (2): 179–99.

Entwistle, N., Skinner, D., Entwistle, D. and Orr, S. (2000) 'Conceptions and beliefs about "good teaching": an integration of contrasting research areas', *Higher Education Research and Development*, 19 (1): 5–26.

Jonassen, D.H. (2008) 'Instructional design as design problem solving: an iterative process', *Educational Technology*, 48 (3): 21–6.

Kanuka, H. and Rourke, L. (2008) 'Exploring amplifications and reductions associated with e-learning: conversations with leaders of e-learning programs', *Technology, Pedagogy and Education*, 17 (1): 5–15.

Kennedy, G., Jones, D., Chambers, D. and Peacock, J. (2011) 'Understanding the reasons academics use – and don't use – endorsed and unendorsed learning technologies', in G. Williams, P. Statham, N. Brown and B. Cleland (eds) *Changing Demands, Changing Directions*. Proceedings ASCILITE Hobart 2011.

Knight, P.T. (2001) 'Complexity and curriculum: a process approach to curriculum-making', *Teaching in Higher Education*, 6 (3): 369–81.

Laurillard, D., Charlton, P., Craft, B., Dimakopoulos, D., Ljubojevic, D., Magoulas, G., Masterman, E., Pujadas, R., Whitley, E.A. and Whittlestone, K. (2012) 'A constructionist learning environment for teachers to model learning designs', *Journal of Computer-Assisted Learning*. DOI: 10.1111/j.1365–2729.2011.00458.x

Lynch, C., Ashley, K., Aleven, V. and Pinkwart, N. (2006) 'Defining ill-defined domains; a literature survey', in V. Aleven, K. Ashley, C. Lynch, and N. Pinkwart (eds) *Proceedings of the Workshop on Intelligent Tutoring Systems for Ill-Defined Domains at the 8th International Conference on Intelligent Tutoring Systems*, Jhongli (Taiwan): National Central University.

Masterman, E. and Manton, M. (2011) 'Teachers' perspectives on digital tools for pedagogic planning and design', *Technology, Pedagogy and Education*, 20 (2): 227–46.

Masterman, L. and Vogel, M. (2007) 'Practices and processes of design for learning', in H. Beetham and R. Sharpe (eds) *Rethinking Pedagogy for the Digital Age* (1st edn), London and New York: Routledge.

Mayes, T. and de Freitas, S. (2004) JISC e-Learning Models Desk Study Stage 2: Review of e-learning theories, frameworks and models. Bristol: JISC. Online. Available at http://www.jisc.ac.uk/uploaded_documents/Stage 2 Learning Models (Version 1).pdf (accessed 8 April 2012).

Nuthall, G. (2004) 'Analysis of why research has failed to bridge the theory-practice gap', *Harvard Educational Review*, 74 (3): 273–307.

Oliver, M. (2002) Creativity and the Curriculum Design Process: A Case Study, York: Higher Education Academy. Online. Available at http://www.heacademy.ac.uk/resources/detail/resource_database/id153_Creativity_and_the_curriculum_design_process_a_case_study (accessed 8 April 2012).

Oliver, R., Harper, B., Hedberg, J.G., Wills, S., and Agostinho, S. (2002) 'Formalising the description of learning designs', in A. Goody, J. Herrington and M. Northcote (eds) *Quality Conversations: Research and development in higher education*, Volume 25, Jamison, ACT, Australia: HERDSA, pp. 496–504.

Ravenscroft, A. (2001) 'Designing e-learning interactions in the 21st century: Revisiting and rethinking the role of theory', *European Journal of Education*, 36 (2): 133–56.

Winograd, T. (ed.) (1996) *Bringing Design to Software*, New York: ACM Press.

Young, P. (2010) 'Generic or discipline-specific? An exploration of the significance of discipline-specific issues in researching and developing teaching and learning in higher education', *Innovations in Education and Teaching International*, 47 (1): 115–24.

Chapter 5

Tools and Resources to Guide Practice

Gráinne Conole

EDITORS' INTRODUCTION

Conole's chapter builds on Masterman's – and references some of the same initiatives – by turning our attention to the computation tools that have been developed to support the process of design for learning. Her chapter provides a review of these tools and considers the key features and functions of each, along with how they may support practitioners in guiding their design practice. The tools and resources covered include visualization tools, pedagogical planners and specialized learning design resources. She concludes with an ecological model in which design tools and associated resources support practices of design in an integrated and sustainable way.

Introduction

In recent years there has been considerable development in terms of learning design tools and resources (e.g. Lockyer *et al.* 2008). This chapter begins by describing a set of conceptual learning design views. These demonstrate the ways in which different elements of a learning design can be represented. They range from high-level conceptual overviews of the design through to detailed views, which map how the learning design tasks are related to associated resources and tools. The visualization tools reviewed include: the Learning Activity Management System (LAMS), WebCollage, Courseware Development Methodology for Open instructional Systems (CADMOS) and CompendiumLD. The pedagogical planners reviewed include: DialogPlus, *Phoebe* and the *Learning Designer*. The specialized learning design resources reviewed include the ways in which Pedagogical Patterns and Open Educational Resources can be used to guide practice. Finally, the ways in which generic tools such as spreadsheets and mind maps can be used to represent learning designs is described.

Discussion of these state-of-the-art tools is intended to give an overview of the typical features of different types of tools. The focus is not on the tools *per se*, but is more of a discussion of how different functionality can enable practitioners to rethink their teaching practice. In particular the affordances (Gibson

1979; Conole and Dyke 2004) of the tools will be discussed and how these influence the way in which practitioners design. The relationship between visualization – and the tension between accurate, authentic representation and more fluid, creative representation – and guidance/support in the design process is discussed towards the end of the chapter. The chapter concludes with a set of principles for learning design. Likely avenues of future research are also discussed, including the notion of working towards a dynamic learning design ecology.

Conceptual learning design tools

The Joint Information Systems Committee (JISC)-funded Open University Learning Design Initiative (http://www.open.ac.uk/blogs/OULDI/) created a series of conceptual learning design views that can guide a designer through the process of creating a learning intervention. These include: a course map view, a course dimensions view, a pedagogy profile, a learning outcomes map and a task swimlane (Conole 2013). This section will show how these can be used to represent a specific learning intervention, which aims to help financial investors develop emotional regulation skills. This work was carried out as part of the EU-funded X-Delia project (eXcellence in Decision-making through Enhanced Learning in Immersive Applications) (http://www.xdelia.org).

The course map view enables the designer to think about four aspects of the learning intervention: (1) what guidance and support will be provided? (2) what types of content and activities are the learners engaged with? (3) what forms of communication and collaboration are involved? and (4) what types of reflection and demonstration are there? Figure 5.1 shows the course map for the X-Delia learning intervention. It shows that the guidance and support are in the form of a user-guided pathway. In terms of content and activities, the learner completes an online survey and then works through a series of games and videos. There is no collaboration involved, but learners are able to discuss their learning in an online forum. Finally, in terms of reflection and demonstration, they receive diagnostic feedback after completing the online survey in the form of tailored video feedback. They also complete a reflective diary.

Figure 5.2 shows the pedagogy profile for the learning intervention. It shows the amount of time the learner engages in the following activities: assimilative activities (reading, listening, viewing), information handling (such as manipulating data in a spreadsheet), communication, productive (creating an artefact for example), experiential (practising or mimicking), adaptive (modelling or simulation). It also shows the amount of time the learner will spend on assessment activities. In this intervention the learners are expected to spend a considerable amount of time communicating in the online forum.

The next view is the course dimensions view (Figure 5.3). This provides more detail on the four categories associated with the course view map described above. In this example, there is a high degree of course-created resources and activities and there is a strong guided learning pathway.

Figure 5.1 The course map view

Guidance and support
Linear guided pathway

Content and activities
Online survey, 2-index game, survey, AUC and SI game with sensors as input, mindfulness (exercise, smartphone app and game)

Communication and collaboration
Online forum

Reflection and overview
Diagnostic feedback via video, reflective diary

Summary
regulating the disposition effect and awareness of emotional regulation

Keywords
Smartphone app, survey, serious games and finance, emotion, sensors

Figure 5.1 The course map view

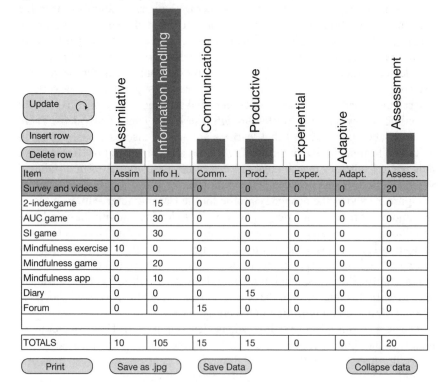

Item	Assim	Info H.	Comm.	Prod.	Exper.	Adapt.	Assess.
Survey and videos	0	0	0	0	0	0	20
2-indexgame	0	15	0	0	0	0	0
AUC game	0	30	0	0	0	0	0
SI game	0	30	0	0	0	0	0
Mindfulness exercise	10	0	0	0	0	0	0
Mindfulness game	0	20	0	0	0	0	0
Mindfulness app	0	10	0	0	0	0	0
Diary	0	0	0	15	0	0	0
Forum	0	0	15	0	0	0	0
TOTALS	10	105	15	15	0	0	20

Update
Insert row
Delete row

Print   Save as .jpg   Save Data   Collapse data

Figure 5.2 The pedagogy profile

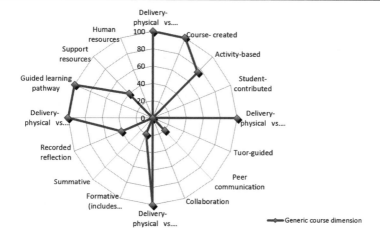

Figure 5.3 The course dimensions view

The task swimlane view (Figure 5.4) shows the learning pathway, i.e. the sequence of tasks that the learner is expected to take and any associated tools and resources.

The final view (Figure 5.5) is the learning outcomes map, which enables the designer to ensure that the learning outcomes are constructively aligned to the activities and assessment (Biggs 1999).

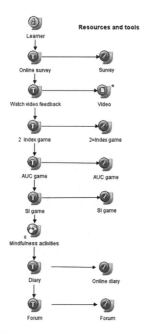

Figure 5.4 The task swimlane view

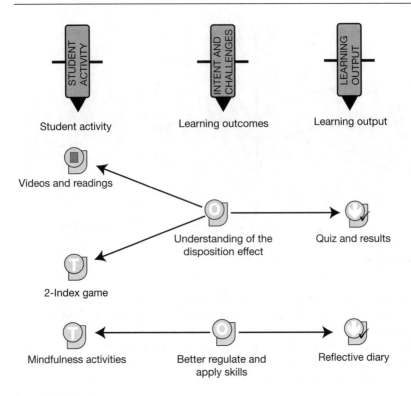

Figure 5.5 The learning outcomes map

The course map and course dimensions views were produced in an Excel spreadsheet. The pedagogy profile was produced using an online tool. The task swimlane and learning outcomes map were produced in CompendiumLD. Each view was saved as a jpeg and collated in PowerPoint.

Visualization tools

In the next chapter, Oliver *et al.* describe the work of the Australian University Teaching Committee (AUTC)-funded learning design project (http://www. learningdesigns.uow.edu.au/), which developed a learning design representation centred on three core aspects of the design process: the tasks undertaken, the associated resources involved and the support provided for the learning activity (Oliver and Herrington 2001). These are represented as three columns and are shown as a temporal design sequence. Many of the tools discussed in this section replicate to some extent this generic design representation.

Learning design visualization tools provide an environment in which a designer can create and represent a learning design. Four tools are discussed: LAMS, WebCollage, CompendiumLD and CADMOS.

LAMS

The Learning Activity Management System (LAMS) (http://www.lamsinternational.com/) was one of the first visualization tools to be developed back in 2002. It has a simple graphical interface. Users can drag and drop from a predefined set of activities, such as quizzes, voting, discussion, etc. These activities can be linked into a learning activity sequence. Dalziel (2011) describes LAMS as 'a web-based environment for the creation, sharing, running and monitoring of learning designs'.

A number of assumptions underpinned the development of the system. First, it was designed to implement the concept of learning design and, in particular, the representation of different instructional strategies (such as problem-based learning, role-play, etc.). Second, the design environment enabled the user to see the learning design in action. Third, the aim was to create a common language for communicating designs.

In the first version of LAMS, it was only possible to create linear designs. LAMS v2 enabled branching – where the teacher could assign students to particular pathways – and optional sequences – where the student could choose which pathway to complete.

Dalziel describes how a learning activity 'What is greatness?' can be represented in LAMS (Dalziel 2003) and then be repurposed for a different context. Figure 5.6 shows a screenshot of the 'What is greatness?' activity.

LAMS provides teachers with an easy-to-use authoring environment to create structured content and collaborative tasks (called sequences). Dalziel (2011)

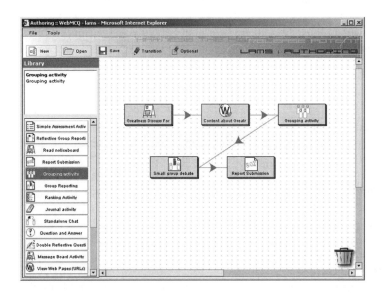

Figure 5.6 The 'What is greatness?' learning design represented in LAMS

notes that LAMS is used by thousands of teachers in more than 80 countries. However, he concedes that its use is mainly by early adopters, and earlier evaluation of the tool showed that it was not being implemented across institutions to a significant extent (Masterman and Lee 2005). Dalziel hypothesizes that practitioners may lack the necessary visualization skills to use LAMS effectively and therefore they might need embedded guidance and support.

LAMS also includes an Activity Planner which provides a set of templates based on good e-teaching practices. Templates include advice on using and repurposing these templates for different learning contexts. The planner is described by its developers as having the following uses:

- To share methods used by others.
- To inspire teachers to adopt a new teaching strategy and support them in doing so.
- To help teachers make theoretically informed decisions about the development of learning activities and choice of appropriate tools and resources to undertake them.
- To provide design ideas in a structured way, so that relations between design components are easy to understand.
- To combine a clear description of the learning design, and offer a rationale that bridges pedagogical philosophy, research-based evidence and experiential knowledge.
- As a database of existing learning activities and examples of good practice which can then be adapted and reused for different purposes.
- To encode the designs in such a way that it supports an iterative, fluid, process of design.
- As a mechanism for abstracting good practice and metamodels for learning (Ghiglione 2009).

WebCollage

WebCollage or WebInstanceCollage (http://pandora.tel.uva.es/wic/) is a web-based graphical authoring tool, which enables users to create collaborative or assessment sequences. Underpinning the tool are collaborative and assessment pedagogical patterns. The designs created can be exported as IMS Learning Design (IMS LD) (http://www.imsglobal.org/learningdesign/) packages. The tool builds on earlier work and in particular the Collage and InstanceCollage tools.

Hernández-Leo et al. (2006) describe the initial development of the tool as drawing on the application of the notion of collaborative pedagogical patterns. Pedagogical patterns (Goodyear 2005; Goodyear and Retalis 2010) are essentially structured examples of best practice and are derived from the work of Alexander (1977) in architecture. Hernández et al. describe a number of Collaborative Learning Flow Patterns (CLFPs), including the Jigsaw and Pyramid patterns. They then go on to show how the Collage tool provides a mechanism for users to choose and implement such CLFPs. They conclude with a summary of the initial evaluation of the tool with practitioners who did not have learning design expertise. Overall the evaluation was positive as the following quote illustrates: 'It helps to think in terms of collaborative learning and its previous arrangement'.

One of the nice features of WebCollage is that it represents pedagogical patterns as visual metaphors. For example, for the Jigsaw Pattern, working in groups of four, in the first stage, each student investigates a part of the problem. In the second stage, they get together with members of other groups who have investigated the same part of the problem and they share their findings to develop a better understanding. In the final stage, they return to their group and collectively share each part of the problem.

CompendiumLD

CompendiumLD was adapted from an existing mind mapping tool, Compendium, produced by the Open University. It enables the user to represent designs visually and show the connections between the tasks the learners are intended to do and any associated tools and resources. The activities of the teacher can also be represented. The adaption included a set of learning design icons, which represent the different components of a learning design, such as: roles (student, teacher, etc.), resources, tools, outputs, learning outcomes, and tasks. Conole *et al.* (2008) provide more background on the technical development of CompendiumLD. Figure 5.7 shows an example of a design created in CompendiumLD. The representation is similar to a LAMS sequence, but unlike LAMS, it is not runnable, although designs can be exported in a range of formats from a jpeg to an interactive website. The representation is also similar to the tasks, support and resources representation produced by the AUTC learning design project, described in the next chapter.

In addition to the standard icon set available in Compendium (which includes icons to promote brainstorming such as question, answer, note, URL, etc.), CompendiumLD includes a set of stencils specifically for learning design. These are:

- *LD-OU*: This consists of the core design icons, which include: tasks, resources, tools, roles, outputs, assignments and an overarching map icon.
- *Sequence mapping*: A stencil to help with laying out the learning activity.
- *Approaches to learning design*: These consist of a set of predefined design sequences, for example, a template for the task swimlane representation described earlier in the chapter.
- *LD-Conditional stencil*: These enable the user to include conditions in the design pathway.

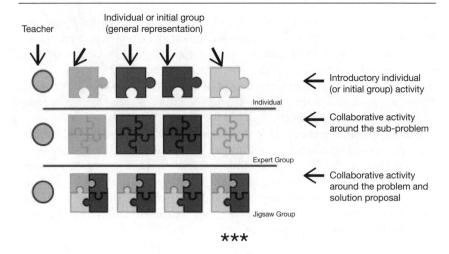

Figure 5.7 The jigsaw pedagogical pattern

Figure 5.8 shows an example of a design created with CompendiumLD. This is a group activity where each student researches a particular country and then shares their findings on a group wiki. They then post comments on a forum and get feedback from the tutor. The lines show which tools and resources are connected with each task. CompendiumLD has been extensively trialled through numerous workshops. Overall evaluation of the tool is positive, users can see the benefits of representing designs visually and said that the process helped them articulate their design process and also enabled them to identify any gaps or flaws in the design. The representations also made the design more explicit and shareable.

Brasher (2010) carried out an evaluation of the use of the tool on the Open University's H800 course. The analysis focused on student and tutor postings in the course discussion forum. Ninety-two of the 136 students registered on the course participated in the course forum, of these 78 created a CompendiumLD map, seven created a map and a visual representation using another tool and four did not create anything.

Most students thought that the tool was user-friendly, although it required an investment in time to become familiar with the interface. They liked the way in which colour was used and the different icons for different elements of a design. They also liked the way in which the tool enabled them to produce a clear, struc-tured output. Students felt that the representation produced was useful in that it did summarize the essence of an activity. Encouragingly, they also felt that the visual representation could reveal aspects of a design that are not obvious from a textual representation. They stated that it was particularly useful for brain-storming a design.

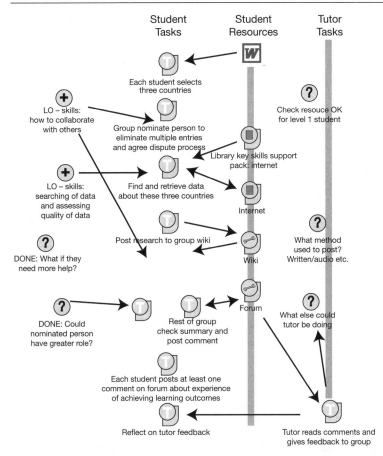

Figure 5.8 A learning design sequence produce with CompendiumLD

On the negative side, some students found the tool very frustrating and time-consuming to learn and use. Others felt that generic mapping tools, like MindManager, Cmap or Twine were more intuitive. Some of the students felt that the representation was essentially linear in nature and hence could not be used to produce more circular designs or ones with multiple pathways. Other negative comments included the fact that there is a potential to 'overdesign' and hence become too focused on the mechanism/process, and some were very sceptical of the return on investment of mapping out learning activities, stating that a textual lesson plan is quicker to produce and arguably more useful.

Potential uses that they cited included the following. First, that the tool could be used as a means of sharing design ideas among a team of tutors. Second, that for a complex design, the CompendiumLD representation could provide a useful mechanism for articulating the key steps and interdependences. Third, it could be used with students as a means of representing the course instructions and making the design intention explicit. Fourth, it could help with planning the overall logistics of a course – particularly for complex courses.

CADMOS

CADMOS (Courseware Development Methodology for Open instructional Systems) (http://cosy.ds.unipi.gr/cadmos/) is a relatively new learning design tool. Designs created with CADMOS can be exported as IMD LD level A and B. There are two aspects to it. The conceptual model enables the designer to describe the learning tasks that a learner will complete, along with the support tasks that the teacher provides. Each activity is related to a resource (digital content) like text, music or video files. The conceptual model of a unit of learning looks like a concept map or a tree structure, whose root is the title of the unit of learning and whose children are the learning and support tasks. Each task is related to one learning resource (learning object or learning service) (Retalis 2011).

A learning or support task might be simple or composite. A composite task consists of many simple tasks that are all assigned to one actor e.g. a student, a teacher, a pair of students, etc. So a composite task and its simple tasks should be assigned to the same actor. The second part is the learning design flow model, which defines the sequence of the execution of the activities described in the conceptual model. It consists of swimlanes for each of the actors; each swimlane defines the order in which the correspondent actor performs the tasks. Figure 5.9 shows a screenshot of the conceptual flow model. In this example there are three swimlanes: student, teacher and peer group. Each swimlane shows the activities that each actor is expected to undertake.

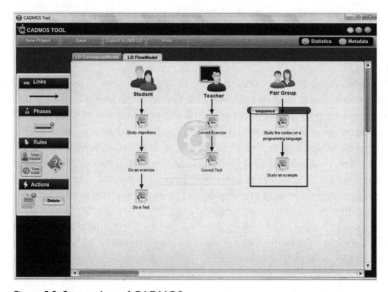

Figure 5.9 Screenshot of CADMOS

Katsamani and Retalis (2011) reported on an initial evaluation of the tool, which indicated that overall users liked CADMOS. The majority claimed that they were satisfied with both the approach and the tool. All of them said that the use of CADMOS was simple and that it was easy to create a learning design. Over half were satisfied with the guidance that was provided to them during the learning design process. The most important remark was that all of the student designers said that the design approach via the two visual learning design model views was helpful. The creation of the conceptual model and the modification of the flow model were considered to be simple and easy. The majority stated that the presence of ready-to-use design templates would have helped them and two-thirds said that they appreciated the fact that they could reuse existing learning designs.

Pedagogical planners

In addition to the visualization learning design tools described above, a number of pedagogical planners have also been developed. These provide more structured guidance on the design process. Three are described here: DialogPlus, *Phoebe* and the *Learning Designer.*

Cameron (2010) states that pedagogical planners describe the core elements that need to be considered if a learning design is to be successful. They help a designer create a clear and definable structure to their design process. Aspects include: the characteristics of the learner, the pedagogical approaches used, the types of technologies and activities involved, the learning environment, the roles and the learning outcomes. She lists a number of uses of these tools:

- as step-by-step guidance to help make theoretically informed decisions about the development of learning activities and the choice of appropriate tools and resources;
- to inspire users to adopt new teaching strategies;
- to provide design ideas in a structured way, so that the relationships between design components are easy to understand;
- to combine a clear description of the learning design and offer a rationale, which bridges pedagogical philosophy, research-based evidence and experiential knowledge;
- as a database of existing learning activities and examples of good practice that can then be adapted and reused for different purposes;
- as a mechanism for abstracting good practice and metamodels for learning;
- to produce 'runnable' learning designs intended for direct use by students;
- to encode the design in such a way that it supports an iterative, fluid process of design.

DialogPlus

DialogPlus was created through the JISC/NSF-funded DialogPlus project (http://www.dialogplus.soton.ac.uk/). It provides support and guidance on creating a learning design. The core objects on the site are 'nuggets' which are individual learning designs. The tool is based on an underlying taxonomy (Conole 2008) that describes the components involved in a learning design. Two other publications provide more detailed descriptions of the tool (Conole and Fill 2005; Bailey *et al*. 2006) and hence only key salient features are described here.

The toolkit centres on the notion of a learning activity, which is defined as consisting of three elements:

• The context within which the activity occurs, this includes the subject, level of difficulty, the intended learning outcomes and the environment within which the activity takes place.
• The learning and teaching approaches adopted, including the theories and models used.
• The tasks undertaken, which specifies the types of tasks, the techniques used, associated tools and resources, the interaction and roles of those involved and the assessments associated with the learning activity.

Sections of the toolkit guide the designer through each of these aspects and provide references and supportive text to enable the designer to make informed decisions. For example, different pedagogical approaches are described, along with suggestions about how they can be instantiated through the use of different technologies. So, for example, reflective practice can be supported through use of blogs, collaboration can be facilitated via the use of group wikis and role-play can be supported through online virtual worlds such as Second Life.

A learning activity has an associated set of intended learning outcomes. To achieve these the learner works through a sequence of tasks. Examples of tasks include: reading papers, discussing ideas, accessing databases, extracting or manipulating data, answering questions, and making decisions. Task techniques include: brainstorming, exercises, fieldwork, role-play, reflection or drill and practice exercises. Advice is offered on which tasks might be appropriate in different contexts. Interactions possible include: individual learning activities, one-to-many, student-to-student, student-to-tutor, group- or class-based interactions. When undertaking tasks, participants in the learning activity are assigned appropriate 'roles', such as individual learner, group participant, facilitator, tutor or presenter. Assessment can include diagnostic, formative or summative assessment or there may be no assessment at all associated with the activity.

Resources include: web pages, databases, video streams and interactive maps. Tools include: search engines, discussion boards, spreadsheets, media players, blogs, e-portfolios, wikis and social networking sites. The tasks and associated roles undertaken to achieve the prescribed learning outcomes occur within a particular context with characteristics, which include a description of the subject domain (for example physical geography or Spanish), the level (e.g. introductory), the perceived skills which will be used or acquired (e.g. numeracy, critical analysis, etc.), the time anticipated for completion of the activity (e.g. two hours), and any associated prerequisites (e.g. a requirement that the learners have successfully completed an earlier course, or the need for particular skills – for example IT skills or a certain level of language skills).

In addition to context and tasks, the toolkit includes taxonomies and models for learning and teaching approaches based on the work of Mayes and de Freitas (see Chapter 1).

Figure 5.10 shows a screenshot of part of the tool. It shows a learning design that is concerned with the use of Microsoft Excel. It is possible to work through the tool in sequence or flexibly. The toolkit was evaluated with geographers involved in the DialogPlus project and through a series of workshops with other practitioners at conferences. In general, evaluation of the toolkit was positive. Practitioners found the structure and guidance of the toolkit valuable and found it easy to use. A potential drawback of the toolkit is that despite the fact that designers can choose which component to complete when, it still feels like a relatively linear approach to design, which does not resonate with actual design practice. In addition, the format is primarily text-based, and hence does not harness the power of visualization tools discussed earlier.

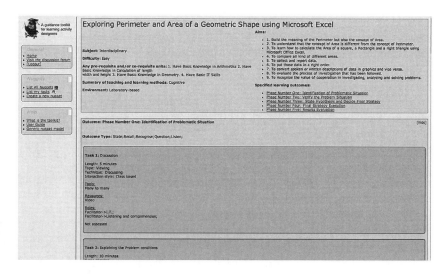

Figure 5.10 Screenshot of DialogPlus

Phoebe

Phoebe (http://www.phoebe.ox.ac.uk/) takes the form of an online wiki. It provides structured guidance and detailed information on the different components of a learning design outlined above. Figure 5.11 shows a screenshot of *Phoebe*. The screen is divided into two parts. One part provides a template for the designer to complete on each aspect of the design. The other part provides in situ guidance on each of the components.

In the example shown, the user completes the learning outcomes and potential teaching resources on the right-hand side. Details of the learning outcomes are described on the left hand-side to enable the designer to make informed design decisions. A particularly valuable aspect of *Phoebe* is the considerable amount of information that is available to guide the designer through completing the various stages of the design. The guidance includes information on: contextual information associated with the design, learning outcomes, assessment, the characteristics of the learners, possible learning activity sequences, contingencies to take account of and a space for reflection. There is also extensive information on teaching approaches and techniques. Of particular use are the sections on 'what technologies can I use for a particular activity?' and 'what can I do with a particular tool?'

Masterman and Manton (2009, 2011) argue that *Phoebe* was designed around teachers' actual practice rather than theory. They organized a number of evaluation events, where participants were able to try out the tool and were then asked to complete an online survey. A key strength was that *Phoebe* could be used as both a planning tool and a reference system. The latter was considered to be

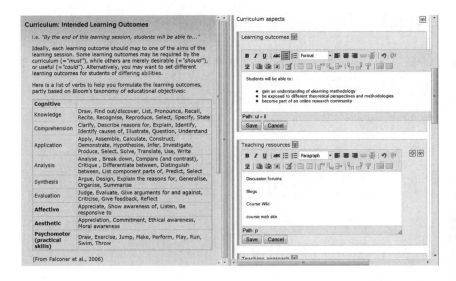

Figure 5.11 Screenshot of *Phoebe*

particularly useful for novice designers. It would be useful if it were embedded into institutional quality assurance processes. Opinions were divided as to whether *Phoebe* provided a structure linear guidance or a flexible tool. Users valued the fact that *Phoebe* provided access to designs created by other teachers. However, use of the tool *per se* did not necessarily result in transformation of practice, with many using the tool to mimic existing practice.

The Learning Designer

The *Learning Designer* tool (https://sites.google.com/a/lkl.ac.uk/ldse/) was derived from the London Pedagogical Planner tool and *Phoebe*. It is underpinned by the Conversational Framework developed by Laurillard (2002). The aims of the tool are: to give educational practitioners support for innovating with interactive, adaptive, reflective, discursive and collaborative learning designs, and to support lecturers and educational practitioners in building learning technologies into courses with tight budgets (Laurillard and San Diego 2007). It adopts a modelling perspective through mapping tasks to resources and attempts to align the design with specific pedagogical approaches. It adopts a user-orientated approach and plans to integrate the tool with the LAMS tool described earlier. The first screen invites the user to complete general information about the learning intervention. It is also possible to ensure that the topics covered, assessment and learning outcomes are mapped, i.e. constructively aligned (Biggs 1999). Designers indicate how much time learners are expected to spend on the following types of activity: attending, investigating, discussing, practising and articulating (Laurillard 2002). The planner takes the user through a series of design decisions, displaying their consequences in multiple dynamic numerical and graphical representations of their learning design. Figure 5.12 shows a screenshot of part of the tool. In addition, the tool includes links to a library of existing pedagogical patterns that users can download and adapt (http://thor.dcs.bbk.ac.uk/projects/LDSE/Dejan/ODC/ODC.html).

Generic tools

In addition to the specialized tools and pedagogy planners described so far, it is also possible to use generic tools such as mind mapping tools and spreadsheets. The X-Delia learning intervention described earlier used an Excel spreadsheet to create two of the views. Mind mapping tools are particularly useful, as they provide a means of mapping out and linking the various components of the design (such as the activities, tools and resources in the learning activity). An example is the Cmap tool (http://cmap.ihmc.us/), which has a node and link interface. In addition text can be added to the links between the nodes. Figure 5.13 shows an example Cmap being used to represent a learning outcomes map for a blended design workshop.

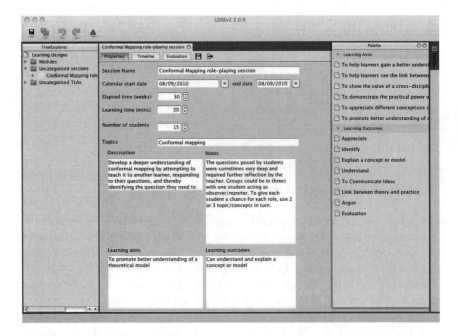

Figure 5.12 The *Learning Designer* tool

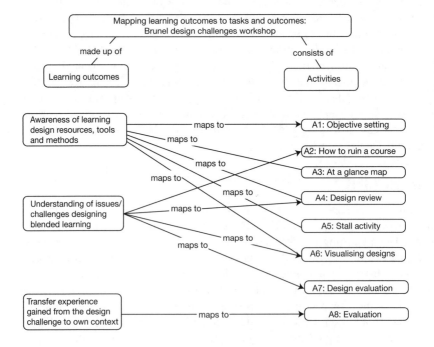

Figure 5.13 A learning design created using Cmap

Learning design resources

In addition to the learning designs discussed in the first half of this chapter, there are also a range of resources to either support design practice or provide examples of good practice. In particular we have seen the growth in the past ten years of the Open Educational Resource (OER) movement and there are now hundreds of high-quality OER repositories worldwide. These can be used as learning resources or as inspiration for teachers – to get ideas or to take and repurpose existing OERs. The OPAL initiative (http://www.oer-quality.org) analysed 60 case studies of OER repositories and abstracted a set of OER practices around the creation, use and repurposing of OERs. The practices were: strategies and policies, barriers and success factors, tools and tool practices, and skills development and support. These were translated into a series of guidelines for OER stakeholders (learners, teachers, institutional managers and policy makers), which can be used by organizations to first benchmark their existing OER practices and then articulate a vision and implementation plan. Many of the learning design tools described earlier in the chapter also have associated with them repositories of existing learning designs. Similarly the AUTC learning design site described in the next chapter provides a rich set of learning designs descriptions across the following types of pedagogical approaches: collaborative learning, conceptual/procedural development, problem-based learning, project/case study learning and role-play.

Goodyear argues that pedagogical patterns provide a useful means of addressing the growing demand for advice about effective, time-efficient ways of using ICT to support learning (Goodyear 2005; McAndrew and Goodyear, Chapter 8). The architect, Alexander, developed the notion of patterns. A pattern

> describes a problem, which occurs over and over again in our environment, and then describes the core of the solution to that problem, in such a way that you can use this solution a million times over, without ever doing it the same way twice.
>
> Alexander *et al.* 1977

Goodyear suggests that there are two ways of formulating a pedagogical pattern: from the bottom up – capturing recurrent problems and solutions – or from the top down – through structuring the problem space of design and sketching relationships between patterns.

Finally, social and participatory media offer a wealth of ways in which teachers can share and discuss learning and teaching ideas. There are now many special interest groups (SIGs) on social networking sites like Facebook, LinkedIn, Ning and elgg. In addition more specialized educational sites have emerged such as SOMETU (http://sometu.ning.com/), LeMills (http://lemill.net/), Connexions (http://cns.org/), and Cloudworks (http://cloudworks.ac.uk). Finally, many practitioners are now using microblogging sites like Twitter to share and discuss learning and teaching ideas. New tools continue to emerge at a phenomenal rate, and it will be interesting to see in the future which tools dominate.

Discussion

This discussion will focus on some of the underlying principles behind the types of tools described in this chapter. Arguably, many of these tools align to a socio-cultural theoretical perspective (Engeström *et al.* 1999; Daniels *et al.* 2007). This is because design is a messy, creative, interactive practice grounded in real-life contexts. The concept of mediating artefacts (Conole 2008) from Activity Theory is particularly useful, both in terms of the mediating artefacts that can guide the designs – such as the tools and associated resources described in this chapter – and also in terms of the final learning designs, which are themselves mediating artefacts that can be shared and discussed with other practitioners. This socio-cultural perspective makes learning design as a field distinct from Instructional Design, which tends to focus more at the level of multimedia and is grounded in positivism (Reigeluth and Carr-Chellman 2009).

Figure 5.14 provides an illustration of the application of the concept of mediating artefacts in the design process. The figure shows that as a teacher is creating a learning activity or resource, they use a range of mediating artefacts to guide their design practice. These might be design concepts, learning design tools, dialogues with other practitioners or exploration of relevant activities. The outcome is the learning activity or resource and an associated design that can be made explicit through a range of learning design representations (see Conole 2013). These can then be rendered through a variety of learning design tools of the kind discussed earlier. The created learning activity or resource and the associated learning design can then be used or repurposed by other teachers or learners.

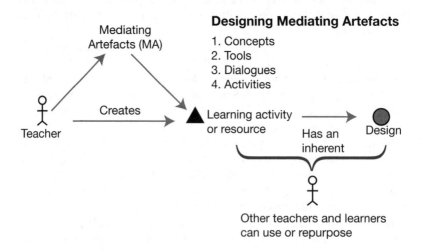

Figure 5.14 Learning design mediating artefact

In terms of principles, I want to draw out seven main ones. The first is that, as the previous chapter demonstrates, teachers are bewildered by the plethora of tools available and lack the skills necessary to make informed learning design decisions. Therefore a key facet of all the tools is that they attempt to provide practitioners with some form of guidance and support around their design practice. The aim is to help them shift from an implicit, belief-based approach to design to one that is more explicit and design-based (Conole 2009). Evidence of the evaluation of the use of these tools shows that they do help shift practitioners from a focus on content to activities and the learner experience. The second is that many of the tools use the power of visualization as a means of representing the designs. These can then be shared and discussed with others. The third is that there is a tension between design representations that are rigorous, precise and perhaps machine runnable and those that are more creative and closer to real practice. Derntl *et al.* (2010) argue that designing for learning needs both 'beauty' and 'precision'; and they show how different design languages can be used to present these. They state that:

> We are in no way suggesting that beauty and precision are in opposition to one another, nor even that they are mutually exclusive concerns. We make the distinction merely to further stress the competing demands on instructional designers for maintaining a grand view of the learning experience while also addressing the myriad details of an effective end product.

The fourth is that there is an issue about what level of in-context support and guidance is provided to the designer and how such support can be created on the fly from up-to-date and authoritative sources. The CompendiumLD tool includes a walled garden Google search, which searches across a number of predefined well-known and validated sources against a set of keywords (Brasher *et al.* 2008). However, in the future much more sophisticated personalized help needs to be developed. The fifth is the fact that learning designs are both a product and a process. In the first instance the designer engages with various learning design mediating artefacts to guide their design process, through a creative, iterative and messy process. Then their final design is a product, which represents a particular moment in time in the design process. The sixth is that, as Masterman outlined in the previous chapter, there are two dimensions of learning design: (1) the creation of structured sequences of learning activities, and (2) a way to represent and share practice. Finally, it is clear that the inherent affordances of different learning design tools will have an impact on how the practitioner goes about the design process. For example, because the LAMS tool focuses on tools as conceptual elements, the design process is likely to be tools-focused. In contrast, the social networking site Cloudworks focuses on sharing and discussion and so emphasizes the dialogic aspects of design.

I believe we are at an interesting watershed in terms of learning design research. We have made significant steps forward in the field over the past ten years or so and now have a much richer understanding of design practices and mechanisms for promoting them. The tools developed along the way have enabled us to explore these in real-world contexts; some focus on visualization, others on dialogue and sharing, and others on guidance/support. All three of these different types of scaffolds are important and support the practitioner in different ways. What is needed next is to try to combine these elements, not necessarily into one monolithic tool, but through the creation of some form of dynamic learning design ecosystem. As a first step towards this, the key researchers in the field have been meeting as part of an EU-funded group, the LDGrid (http://www.ld-grid.org/). A key output of the group is to produce a concise, comprehensive and accessible set of resources for practitioners and learners to help them adopt more learning-design-based thinking and practices. The group has held a number of workshops and has an evolving set of learning design resources.

Conclusions

This chapter has described a range of tools for visualizing learning designs. It has described the functionality of each, supported by illustrative examples. Where appropriate, data from evaluation of the use of the tools have been included. In addition, a set of conceptual learning design views was described. It is evident that visualizing designs is a powerful way of helping teachers to rethink their design practice and make more informed design decisions. Furthermore, the created designs help make the design more explicit and hence shareable. Evaluation of the use of these tools, along with the empirical evidence gleaned through a series of interviews with teachers about their design practices, has given us a richer understanding of the design process and the role of visualization.

Further research is needed to build on this substantial body of work. In particular, it would be good to develop a holistic or perhaps a distributed online learning design tool, which would enable the designer to oscillate between the different visualizations. Alongside this would be in situ help, of the kind provided in the DialogPlus toolkit and the *Phoebe* wiki. Finally, in order to share and discuss designs, social networking spaces such as the Cloudworks site are needed for learners and teachers to share and discuss learning and teaching ideas. The evolving resources collated by the LDGrid team are a useful starting point in terms of mapping the current status of the field.

The next stage will be to try to formulate what an evolving learning design ecology and community would look like and how it might be realized in practice. Figure 5.15 provides an illustration of what this learning design ecology might look like and, in particular, the relationship between the different tools and resources and how they might feed into the design process.

At the heart of the diagram the learning design process is represented in the CompendiumLD tool (see Figure 5.8). This representation shows the roles of those involved in the learning activity (for example, learner and tutor) and their

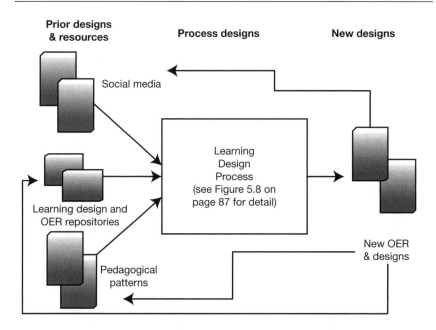

Figure 5.15 A learning design ecology of the future

associated tasks as a temporal sequence. In addition there are columns showing which resources and tools are associated with each task and how the tasks map to the intended learning outcomes. On the left-hand side of the diagram are the potential sources of input that the designer might draw on. This includes interaction with peers through social media (such as Twitter or the academic social networking site Cloudworks), examples of good practice from learning design and OER repositories, as well as more formally structured examples of good practice in the form of pedagogical patterns. The designer can use these as inspiration to guide their design or indeed incorporate elements into the learning pathway. The outputs of the design process are new OERs or learning designs, which can iteratively feed back into the wider community for further use or repurposing.

Only time will tell whether or not this vision will be realized. However, as is evident in the narrative in this chapter and others in this book, practitioners need guidance and support to help them make pedagogically informed design decisions that make innovative use of new technologies. The evaluations of the learning design tools and conceptual views described in this chapter are positive overall. They do appear to help designers rethink their design practice and shift from a focus on content to learning activities and the learner experience. Furthermore, it is evident that social and participatory media can provide a mechanism for practitioners to share and discuss their learning and teaching ideas.

References

Alexander, C. (1977) *Pattern Languages*, New York: Oxford University Press.
Alexander, C., Ishikawa, S., Silverstein, M., Jacobson, M., Fiksdahl-King, I. and Angel, S. (1977) *A Pattern Language: Towns, buildings, construction*, New York: Oxford University Press.
Bailey, C., Zalfan, M.T, Davis, H.C., Fill, K. and Conole, G. (2006) 'Panning for gold: designing pedagogically-inspired learning nuggets', *Educational Technology and Society*, 9 (1): 113–22.
Biggs, J. (1999) 'What the student does: teaching for enhanced learning', *Higher Education Research and Development*, 18 (1): 57–75.
Brasher, A. (2010) *Evaluation report on the use of CompendiumLD on the OU's H800 course*. Milton Keynes: The Open University.
Brasher, A., Conole, G., Cross, S., Weller, M., Clark, P. and White, J. (2008) 'CompendiumLD – a tool for effective, efficient and creative learning design', paper presented to 2008 European LAMS Conference: Practical Benefits of Learning Design, Cadiz, Spain, June 2008.
Cameron, L. (2010) 'Could pedagogical planners be a useful learning design tool for university lecturers?', *The University of the Fraser Valley Research Review*, 3 (2). Available at http://journals.ufv.ca/rr/RR32/article-PDFs/2-cameron.pdf (accessed 15 August 2012).
Conole, G. (2008) 'Capturing practice, the role of mediating artefacts in learning design', in L. Lockyer, S. Bennett, S. Agostinho and B. Harper (eds) *Handbook of Learning Designs and Learning Objects*, New York: IGI Global.
Conole, G. (2009) 'Capturing and representing practice', in A. Tait, M. Vidal, U. Bernath and A. Szucs (eds) *Distance and E-learning in Transition: Learning innovation, technology and social challenges*, London: John Wiley and Sons.
Conole, G. (2013) *Designing for Learning in an Open World*, New York: Springer.
Conole, G. and Dyke, M. (2004) 'What are the affordances of information and communication technologies?' *Association for Learning Technologies Journal*, 12 (2): 113–24.
Conole, G. and Fill, K. (2005) 'A learning design toolkit to create pedagogically effective learning activities', *Journal of Interactive Media in Education Special Issue: Advances in Learning Design*. Online. Available at http://www-jime.open.ac.uk/2005/08/ (accessed 15 August 2012).
Conole, G., Brasher, A., Cross, S., Weller, M., Clark, P. and White, J. (2008). 'Visualizing learning design to foster and support good practice and creativity', *Educational Media International*, 45 (3): 177–94.
Dalziel, J. (2003) 'Implementing learning design: the Learning Activity Management System (LAMS)', paper presented to ASCILITE, Adelaide, Australia, December 2003.
Dalziel, J. (2011) 'Visualizing learning design in LAMS: a historical view', in C. Alexander, J. Dalziel, J. Krajka and R. Kiely (eds) *LAMS and Learning Design*, Volume 2, Nicosia: University of Nicosia Press.
Daniels, H., Cole, M. and Wertsch, J.V. (2007) *The Cambridge Companion to Vygotsky*, Cambridge: Cambridge University Press.
Derntl, M., Parrish, P. and Botturi, L. (2010) 'Beauty and precision: weaving complex educational technology projects with visual instructional design languages', *International Journal on E-Learning*, 9 (2), 185–202.

Engeström, Y., Miettinen, R. and Punamäki, R.L. (1999) *Perspectives on Activity Theory*, Cambridge: Cambridge University Press.

Ghiglione, E. (2009) *LAMS Activity Planner*. Online. Available at http://wiki. lamsfoundation.org/x/1ACu (accessed 31 July 2012).

Gibson, J.J. (1979) *The Ecological Approach to Visual Perception*, Hillsdale, New Jersey: Lawrence Erlbaum Associated.

Goodyear, P. (2005) 'Educational design and networked learning: Patterns, pattern languages and design practice', *Australasian Journal of Educational Technology*, 21 (1): 82–101.

Goodyear, P. and Retalis S. (2010) *Technology-enhanced Learning: Design patterns and pattern languages*, Rotterdam: Sense Publishers.

Hernández-Leo, D., Villasclaras-Fernández, E.D., Asensio-Pérez, J.I., Dimitriadis, Y., Jorrín-Abellán, I.M. and Ruiz-Requies, I. (2006) 'COLLAGE: A collaborative learning design editor based on patterns', *Educational Technology and Society*, 9 (1): 58–71.

Katsamani, M. and Retalis, S. (2011) 'Making learning designs in layers: the CADMOS approach', paper presented to IADIS e-Learning 2011, Rome, Italy, July 2011.

Laurillard, D. (2002) *Rethinking University Teaching: A framework for the effective use of learning technologies* (2nd edn), London: Routledge.

Laurillard, D. and San Diego, J.P. (2007) 'Development and testing of a "Pedagogic Planner"', paper presented to Center for Distance Education (CDE) Fellows Conference, Institute of Education, University of London.

Lockyer, L., Bennett, S., Agostinho, S. and Harper, B. (2008) *Handbook of Research on Learning Design and Learning Objects: Issues, applications and technologies*, Hershey: IGI Global.

Masterman, L. and Lee, S. (2005) Evaluation of the practitioner trial of LAMS – final report, JISC. Online. Available at http://www.jisc.ac.uk/uploaded_documents/ LAMS%20Final%20Report.pdf (accessed 31 July 2012).

Masterman, L. and Manton M. (2009) 'Pedagogic theory and pedagogic planning in digital worlds', paper presented to Computer Assisted Learning (CAL) Conference, Brighton, England, March 2009.

Masterman, L. and Manton (2011) 'Teachers' perspectives on digital tools for pedagogic planning and design', *Technology, Pedagogy and Education*, 20 (2): 227–46.

Oliver, R. and Herrington, J. (2001) *Teaching and Learning Online: A beginner's guide to e-learning and e-teaching in higher education*, Perth: Edith Cowan.

Reigeluth, C.M. and Carr-Chellman A.A. (2009) *Instructional-Design Theories and Models*, Volume III, New York: Routledge.

Retalis, S. (2011) 'CADMOS tool', email 1/9/2011.

Chapter 6

Describing ICT-Based Learning Designs that Promote Quality Learning Outcomes

Ron Oliver, Barry Harper, Sandra Wills, Shirley Agostinho and John G. Hedberg

EDITORS' INTRODUCTION

This chapter describes a framework by which various types of learning design can be described according to whether their primary focus is rules, strategies, incidents or roles. Developed from the work of Jonassen (2000), the framework provided a theoretical basis for selecting exemplary learning designs for inclusion in the Australian University Teaching Committee (AUTC) project: *Information and Communication Technologies and Their Role in Flexible Learning*. The authors outline the selection and description of these exemplars, alongside the communication of principles of 'high quality learning', as a national project. Although the examples themselves are somewhat dated now, the classification system and the approach to visualizing designs remains relevant today, while the model has proven value in communicating learning design ideas accessibly to practitioners. Chapter 7 – new in this edition – builds on and updates the work described here.

Introduction

The widespread implementation and use of virtual learning environments (VLEs) and courseware management systems (CMS) in higher education today provide many teachers with the opportunity to create engaging and effective learning settings. The ongoing activities to develop online content in the form of learning objects, delivered seamlessly through standardized digital repositories, can provide many digital resources for teachers looking to make meaningful use of learning technologies (e.g. Oliver *et al.* 2005; Harper *et al.* 2005). The plethora of technology supports and digital tools and resources for learning has garnered strong interest among teachers in the use of technology as an integral and mainstream component of course delivery. However, while educational theory has for many years advanced the practice of more constructivist and authentic approaches to e-learning, many technology supports and templates can encourage the use of more conventional, structured and linear approaches. For example, much of the work in describing standards for learning objects as building blocks for online learning, presupposes very directed and structured presentation modes (Rehak and Mason 2003). In the meantime, teachers are still looking for theoretical and practical guidance in the design of effective e-learning strategies and activities (Littlejohn 2004).

This chapter describes outcomes from a project funded by the Australian Committee for University Teaching: *Information and Communication Technologies and Their Role in Flexible Learning* (AUTC 2003). The project involved the development of a framework for distinguishing between learning designs and a means for providing a formal description of each design. The project identified a number of ICT-based learning designs that promoted high quality learning outcomes and developed generic descriptions of each to facilitate their reuse in settings beyond their original context. The resulting set of learning designs has since been used in practice by a large number of higher education teachers to support quality learning outcomes.

Learning designs

In classrooms where teachers and students interact with each other, the learning setting tends to be governed and led by the teacher. In planning such lessons, a teacher plans learning activities for the students that can engage them and provide an experience from which learning would result. In technology-facilitated settings, the role of the teacher in learning activities is often less direct. Learners must make many decisions for themselves which otherwise might have been made by the teacher. Electronic learning settings typically provide students with notes, activities and directions to guide their learning. These notes, activities and directions are created by teachers but not necessarily the same teachers who are involved with the students.

As explained in the Introduction to this book, we use the term learning design to describe a representation of the learning experience to which students are exposed. For example, students might be required to read a chapter from a text and to glean certain information. They may be asked to use certain information to plan an approach to solving a given problem. They may be formed into groups and required to gather information and to produce a report. These tasks are part of a learning design, a deliberately planned set of experiences that are intended to help them to learn. A learning design typically involves descriptions of the learners and a space where they act with tools and devices to collect and interpret information through a process of interaction with others (e.g. Britain 2004). Learning designs involve descriptions of learning environments and spaces that are typically quite flexible and in many ways different from the sequences that have previously characterized instructional design strategies.

While the literature abounds with descriptions of the forms of learning settings that support quality learning outcomes, there is considerably less information available that provides discrete and detailed descriptions of teaching and learning processes in forms that teachers can understand and apply. Britain (2004) describes this process of designing for learning as creating a learner workflow. The value of designing for learning lies in the fact that teachers can use the resulting learning designs to plan the learning experiences that learners need to achieve the planned learning outcomes. Well-designed workflows can cater for the needs of individual learners. They can provide motivating and stimulating environments to maintain learner interest and they can provide the supports learners need to work beyond their comfort zones as they develop their skills, knowledge and understanding. Well-designed learner workflows also provide scope for students to choose the activities in which they will engage, recognizing the need for learners to assume some ownership of their learning experiences. At the same time, learner workflows, if well articulated and described, can be used over and over again by other teachers and students to achieve other learning outcomes.

With the high levels of interest and activity in the development and sharing of learning objects, there is growing interest in learning designs. The interest stems from the fact that learning objects by themselves can provide limited advantage to teachers. Learning objects, however, when utilized with sound learning designs to create meaningful learning experiences, can deliver far more beneficial outcomes.

Learning designs that support quality learning outcomes

There are a wide variety of forms which students' learning experiences can take in higher education settings. In Chapter 1, Mayes and de Freitas describe three perspectives that they argue embrace contemporary teaching and learning processes with respect to e-learning. The perspectives are described as associationist, cognitive and situative. When applied to the design of learning environments, each of the perspectives leads to learning experiences with particular forms of learning outcomes.

It was the intent in our project to explore ICT-based learning designs that could support quality learning outcomes. By this we mean learning outcomes which involved conceptual change and a deep understanding of the unit content. The project sought expert opinion to determine what constituted 'high quality learning' and, in conjunction with feedback from the project team, developed a set of principles that described high quality student learning in higher education (Boud and Prosser 2002). The principles used a learning perspective to characterize the essential elements of a learning design with the potential to foster high quality learning in higher education. These are described as:

- *Learner engagement*: A consideration of learners' prior knowledge and their desires and building on their expectations
- *Acknowledgement of the learning context*: A consideration of the implementation of the learning design and its position within the broader programme of study for the learner.

- *Learner challenge*: Seeking active participation of learners, encouraging learners to be self-critical and supportive of learners' ampliative skills.
- *Provision of practice*: Encouraging learners to articulate and demonstrate to themselves and their peers what they are learning (Boud and Prosser 2002).

These principles can also be traced in the examples of curriculum design practice outlined in Part II of this volume. In different learning contexts some of these principles may be more prominent than others; however, all four principles are important in any higher education context. The principles are holistic in that they incorporate both learning outcomes and learning processes and are based on the premise that learning arises from what students experience from an implementation of a learning design. Designers need to examine their learning designs from the perspective of their impact on learning, that is, placing themselves in the 'students' shoes' and thus examining their learning designs from the student perspective.

The conventional art of instructional design has previously been very well defined and many guidelines and models have been developed to guide instructional designers in the process of developing instructional sequences (e.g. Dick and Carey 1990; Gagné *et al.* 1992). Instructional design for learning settings that promote the quality learning outcomes described above involves a far more complex and nuanced process. Jonasssen (1994) argues that there cannot really be any firm models guiding the design of constructivist settings since knowledge construction is so context-specific. Lefoe (1998) argues that learning design theory provides principles and general concepts by which learning environments can be planned, rather than rigid guidelines. Despite these challenges, our project sought to produce what Masterman and Manton (2011) call 'manifest' designs as distinct from the more rough and ready sketches, the tacit rules of practice that teachers typically employ and which are not readily shared, which they call 'latent designs'.

Establishing a framework to describing learning designs

In our project, we needed to be able to articulate clearly the nature and scope of different forms of learning design in ways that would enable a design to be applied across a variety of settings and disciplines. We required some strategy by which the various learning designs could be described, and variations and instances accommodated. We were guided in our efforts by the work of Jonassen (2000), which provides a useful framework based on his notion of Activity Theory. Activity Theory provides a means to focus on the actions of a learner within an activity system, which involves a group pursuing a learning goal in a deliberate fashion.

The Jonassen (2000) framework describes learning designs as a range of activity or problem settings comprising 11 problem types in a continuum from activities that involve the application of rules, through those based on incidents and events, through to activities that involve strategic planning, and activities whose solutions are based on learners' performances.

When the problem types of Jonassen (2000) were further explored, there appeared three discrete forms of learning design within the 11. These discrete forms each encompassed a number of the problem types and appeared capable of being used to further categorize potential learning designs. The problems encompassed within Jonassens' descriptions are typically either of a rule-based, an incident-based, or a strategy-based form. Our inquiry suggested a fourth type of learning design: role-based. The four types of learning designs that emerged from this form of analysis and development are shown in Table 6.1. The learning designs are discrete and follow what might be seen as a continuum describing the scope of their complexity and openess. Table 6.1 shows these forms and provides descriptions of each type of learning activity and the forms of learning outcome that are associated with each.

The nature of the various learning designs described in Table 6.1 can be further demonstrated and exemplified by considering the forms of tasks, supports and learning resources that each would require in a learning setting (Oliver and Herrington 2001). Table 6.2 uses this strategy to further exemplify and distinguish the four types of learning design suggested by this process.

Table 6.1 A framework for a learning design typology

Learning design focus	Description	Learning outcomes
Rule-based	The learning task requires learners to apply standard procedures and rules in the solution. For example algorithmic approaches, the application of given procedures and rules.	A capacity to meaningfully and reflectively apply procedures and processes.
Incident-based	The learning activity is based on learners' exposure and participation to events or incidents of an authentic and real nature. The learning is based around activities that require learners to reflect and take decisions based on the actions and events.	Understanding procedures, roles and an ability to apply the knowledge.
Strategy-based	Learning is based on tasks which require strategic planning and activity.	A capacity to apply knowledge in meaningful ways in real-life settings.
Role-based	The learning is achieved through learners' participation as a player and participant in a setting which models a real-world application. Learners apply judgements and make decisions based on understanding of the setting in real-time scenarios.	An understanding of issues, processes and interactions of multi-variable situations.

Table 6.2 Characteristic elements of learning designs

Learning design focus	Learning tasks	Learning resource	Learning supports
Rule-based processes	Closed tasks, logical and bounded tasks in authentic settings, procedural sequence of manipulations, projects and inquiry-based forms.	Case-based materials, authentic resources, multiple sources, algorithmic descriptions and tutorials.	Collaborative learning, teacher as coach/ guide, opportunities to articulate and reflect.
Incident-based processes	Story-based tasks with disambiguate variables, case analysis tasks.	Incident/event descriptions and scenarios, case materials, theoretical underpinnings.	Collaborative learning, opportunities to articulate and reflect, teacher as coach/ guide.
Strategy-based processes	Complex and ill-defined tasks, decision-making tasks, trouble shooting tasks, diagnosis solutions, strategic performance tasks.	Authentic resources, multiple perspectives, expert judgements, theoretical underpinnings sample tasks and solutions.	Teacher as coach, collaborative learning, peer assessments, opportunities to articulate and reflect.
Role-based interactions	Assumption of roles within real-life settings, assuming the role, playing the role in scenarios.	Procedural descriptions, role definitions, resources to define and guide role, scenarios, theoretical underpinnings.	Learners assume individual roles, teacher as moderator, opportunities to articulate and reflect.

Describing learning designs in generic forms

In order to provide a consistent means to describe the underpinning elements in each learning design, the project developed a temporal sequencing strategy based on the three critical elements of learning environments proposed by Oliver and Herrington (2001). These elements are the learning task, learning resources and learning supports. To enable a visual representation of the learning design as in Figure 6.1, learning tasks are shown as a rectangle, learning resources as a triangle and supports as a circle. The following sections describe generic categorizations of the discrete types of learning designs using the temporal representation describing the interactions of the tasks, resources and supports. The sections also include examples of particular learning settings designed around such learning designs, which form part of the AUTC Learning Designs resource collection (AUTC 2003). Readers wishing to explore any of the designs further can access the examples described in the sections from the web addresses provided in the references.

Rule-based designs

Figure 6.1 shows a temporal sequence for the form of learning design we have designated rule-based design. Rule-based designs are those that are primarily comprised of closed tasks whose completion requires the application of some form of rules, procedures or algorithms. In rule-based learning designs, the resources which learners use include the procedural and system descriptions needed for the application 'and the environmental supports necessary for learners to achieve success in their efforts'. The learning is achieved through learners applying standard procedures and rules in developing a solution. For example, algorithmic approaches involve the application of given procedures and rules in defined ways to effect a solution. The tasks need to provide learners with opportunities to meaningfully and reflectively apply procedures and processes to specific closed, logical and bounded tasks. Figure 6.1 shows a possible form of this learning design using developed schema. It was intended in the project to determine if there was a generic form of representation that could be used to describe rule-based learning designs. As we explored a number of different rule-based learning designs in different settings and disciplines, it became evident that our system for describing the design yielded a variety of forms when applied to the different settings.

An example of a rule-based learning design is in the example *Communicating with the Tired Patient* (Liaw *et al.* 2002). This is a learning setting produced on a CD-ROM which aims to assist medical students with their clinical communication skills, and to help them develop an integrated biopsychosocial approach to identifying a patient's problems. Students are asked to play the role of the doctor in a simulated clinical interview. As the doctor, students listen to up to four audio options comprising questions they could potentially ask the patient. The student selects what he or she believes to be the most appropriate question given the current state of the interview and then views the patient's response via an audio/visual display. Students are able to see the ramifications and implications

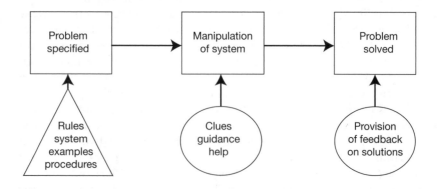

Figure 6.1 A temporal sequence describing a rule-based learning

of asking different questions by listening to and observing the patient's response. Students are challenged to reflect on specific sequences in their interview through expert 'Comments and Questions'. As students progress they are able to view a transcript of the interview at any time which allows them to review the questions they have asked, the patient's response, the expert comments made and their own notes. Students can complete an introductory tutorial before they begin an interview and they are supported by a glossary and a library of micro-skill resources as they conduct their interview. A full description of the learning setting and strategies for its reuse in other settings is provided. Figure 6.2 shows a detailed form of the underpinning learning design.

Incident-based learning designs

In an incident-based learning design, the learning activity is based on learners' exposure to, and participation in, events or incidents of an authentic and real nature. The learning is based on activities that require learners to reflect and take decisions about the actions and events. The temporal sequence shows learning based on a description of the incident, elaboration of that incident through reflection, a group or individual process to find a solution or to come to a decision, declaration of a solution or decision, and provision of feedback on the solution or decision. Incident-based learning designs can be supported through learner collaboration and through opportunities to articulate and reflect on the learning

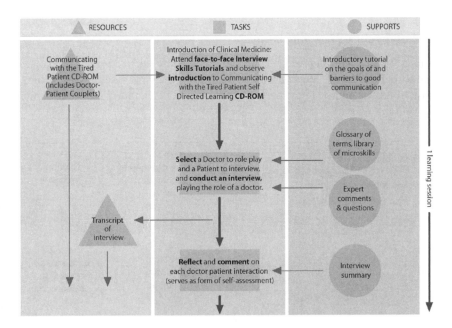

Figure 6.2 A description of the learning design in *Communicating with the Tired Patient*

provided by a teacher acting as a mentor. The learning is based on activities that require learners to reflect and take decisions based on the incidents and events that are represented. The setting requires a range of resources to provide rich descriptions and information about the incident and event upon which the learning is based (Figure 6.3).

An example of an incident-based learning design is *Real-Life Cases in Multimedia* (Bennett 2002). The learning environment is centred on a collaborative project task in which students who are enrolled in a graduate-level educational technology subject develop a multimedia package for a real client. The exploration of the problem is supported by an analysis of two real-life cases, through individual writing, and small group and whole class discussions. These real-life cases give students a 'behind-the-scenes' look at two large interactive multimedia CD-ROM projects, with access to interviews with the key designers and archival documents. Students work together in teams of three or four to develop their project designs and solutions. Each team member assumes a particular role and responsibilities typical of a real-world multimedia development team. The final phase of the learning design requires students to reflect on their experiences through individual and collaborative writing tasks. Appropriate social and technological supports are integrated into the learning environment, including access to class meetings and tutorials, computer laboratories and online discussion and file storage. A full description of the learning setting and strategies for its reuse in other settings is provided on the AUTC site. Figure 6.4 shows a detailed form of the underpinning learning design.

A strategy-based learning design

Strategy-based learning designs are characterized by such activities as complex and ill-defined tasks, decision-making tasks, some trouble shooting tasks, diagnosis solutions and strategic performance tasks. The temporal sequence shown

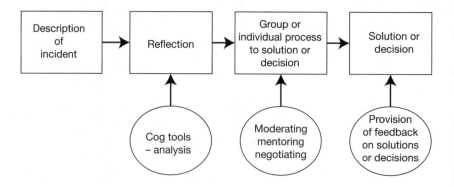

Figure 6.3 A temporal sequence describing an incident-based learning design

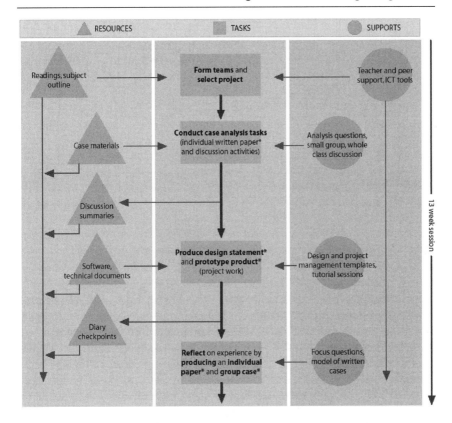

Figure 6.4 A description of the learning design in *Real-Life Cases in Multimedia*

in Figure 6.5 suggests a learning design where learners undertake a series of activities and at the same time interact with a variety of resources and learning supports. The process involves specification of the strategic problem, elaboration of that problem through reflection, a group or individual process to carry out the task, declaration of a solution or outcome from the tasks and reflection on the learning process.

In strategy-based learning designs, learning is based on tasks that require strategic planning and activity. The environment requires authentic resources that support multiple perspectives, provide such elaborations as expert judgements, and which also provide descriptions of theoretical underpinnings. Typically learners are also provided with sample tasks and solutions, cases, tactics, strategies and treatments. Support is provided through a teacher acting as a coach and facilitator, and often through collaborative learning tasks involving such strategies as peer assessments and the provision of meaningful opportunities and contexts for articulation and reflection.

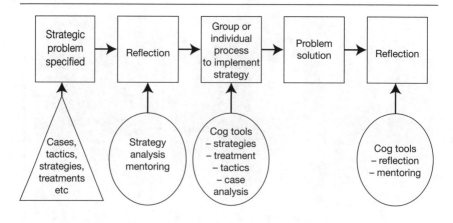

Figure 6.5 A temporal sequence describing a strategy-based learning design

An example of a strategy-based learning design is *Investigating Mathematical Assessment Strategies* (Herrington *et al.* 2002). The learning experience provided to students in this environment is one where students are given the opportunity to reflect on the appropriate use of assessment strategies in mathematics in much the same way that practising teachers might. Rather than learning a raft of different strategies one by one, and possibly not really knowing when to apply them, students are not given any direct instruction on the various strategies. Instead they are given a realistic problem (there are five) presented in the form of two documents (such as memos and letters) not unlike being given such a task in real life. The students then, in groups, use a range of resources and personal perspectives provided on a CD-ROM to investigate the task. They then present their findings also in a realistic, if simulated, context, as if they were presenting at a staff meeting or information night for parents. In this way, students can understand that a good knowledge of assessment strategies can be useful within a variety of contexts, and they have a broad range of strategies, beyond the standard pencil and paper test, that they can draw on as teachers of mathematics. Figure 6.6 shows a detailed form of the underpinning learning design.

Role-based learning design

In role-based learning, learners acquire skills, knowledge and understanding through the assumption of roles within real-life settings. The design typically involves some purposeful and directed preparation and role-playing in scenarios that have been developed to provide the forms of learning opportunities sought in the objectives. The temporal sequence shown in Figure 6.7 involves the declaration of learner role, online dialogue to clarify this role, presentation of a

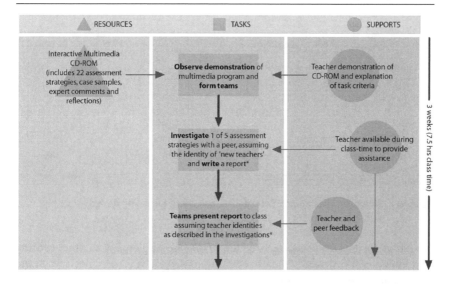

Figure 6.6 A description of the learning design in *Investigating Mathematical Assessment Strategies*

dilemma to resolve, online dialogue to resolve the dilemma within the perspective of a role, a possible negotiated resolution to the dilemma and reflection on the process.

In role-based settings, learning is achieved through learners' participation as a player and participant in a setting, which models a real-world application. Learners apply judgements and make decisions based on understanding of the setting in real-time scenarios. They require an array of resources to support the learners' role including procedural descriptions, role definitions, resources to define and guide roles, scenarios, topical content and cases. Typically the role of the teacher is that of a moderator and mentor, who creates opportunities for the learners to articulate and reflect on their learning experiences.

An example of a role-based learning design is *Political Science Simulation* (Yasmeen and Fardon 2002). This learning setting has political science students engaging in a role-play simulation which spans a period of five weeks and has students assuming the role of members of the United Nations Security Council. The Security Council has been convened to discuss the critical issue of the sanctions imposed on Iraq. The learning design has been divided into the three critical phases normally associated with role-play activities: planning and preparation, interaction, and reflection and evaluation. The first phase sees students preparing for the activity by researching their particular role. For this they are provided with specific references for their role and general references regarding international diplomacy, both electronic and paper-based. The next phase involves both face-to-face and electronic communication in the form of

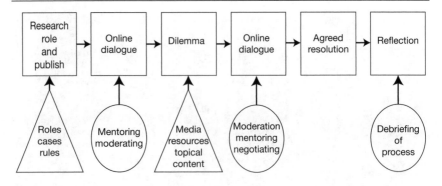

Figure 6.7 A temporal sequence describing a role-based learning design

'meetings' of the UN Security Council and secret diplomacy via the website. The final phase involves students reverting to themselves and reflecting on the process and experience, leading to a collaborative group report. Facilitation of the activity by tutors is critical, particularly during the interaction phase.

A comprehensive Designer Template, plus a number of checklists and associated documentation were provided to guide the design and implementation of such an online role-play model. These resources are included in the AUTC site. Figure 6.8 shows a detailed form of the underpinning learning design.

Conclusions

When we reflect on the processes and products from the project, a number of interesting issues appear to emerge. The first relates to the success of the temporal sequence framework we developed to adequately describe learning designs. This framework appears to provide a means to describe what we see as the critical elements in a learning design description. The framework provides an efficient means to represent teachers' plans for a learning experience by providing a representation for tasks, resources and supports together with the various connections between them and an indication of their various positions demonstrated in a temporal fashion. Among the team members it was found that when presented with a sequence, we could generally agree as to whether or not it provided an adequate description of a particular learning design. What was interesting was that given a particular learning approach, for example, an instance of a problem-based learning setting, the members of the team would usually provide quite different representations of this approach using the temporal sequence framework.

It was apparent that the difficulty lay in identifying the critical elements in the learning approach being investigated. In a problem-based case, for example, there is a degree of interpretation involved in identifying the particular tasks that learners might be required to undertake. One teacher might describe the first task

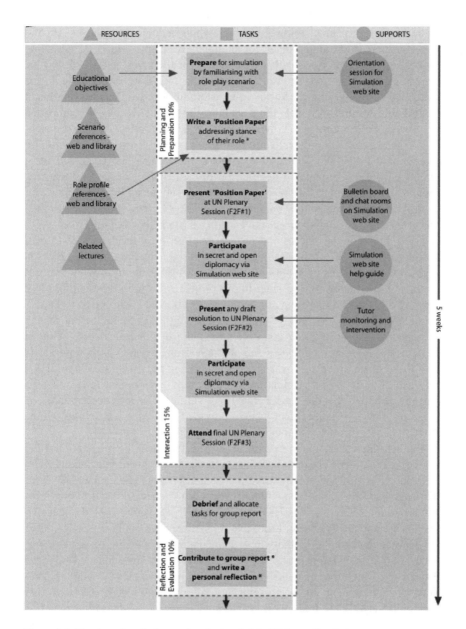

RESOURCES   TASKS   SUPPORTS

Educational objectives

Scenario references - web and library

Role profile references - web and library

Related lectures

Planning and Preparation 10%

Prepare for simulation by familiarising with role play scenario

Write a 'Position Paper' addressing stance of their role *

Orientation session for Simulation web site

Interaction 15%

Present 'Position Paper' at UN Plenary Session (F2F#1)

Participate in secret and open diplomacy via Simulation web site

Present any draft resolution to UN Plenary Session (F2F#2)

Participate in secret and open diplomacy via Simulation web site

Attend final UN Plenary Session (F2F#3)

Bulletin board and chat rooms on Simulation web site

Simulation web site help guide

Tutor monitoring and intervention

Reflection and Evaluation 10%

Debrief and allocate tasks for group report

Contribute to group report * and write a personal reflection *

5 weeks

Figure 6.8 The learning design underpinning *Political Science Simulation*

in the sequence as 'identifying a problem' whereas another might see the first task in a more microscopic form, for example, 'developing and understanding the context' followed by 'creating a boundary for the investigation'. It became clear to us that consistent and reliable use of this model would likely require a controlled vocabulary for the various elements and very detailed descriptions of the learning settings to enable the vocabulary to be applied. As we completed the project, we recognized that the temporal sequence framework would benefit from considerably more investigation and inquiry. The learning design toolkit (Conole and Fill 2005) appeared to support these thoughts. Designed for a similar purpose, it provided a detailed set of elements for describing learning designs and appeared to fill some of the gaps we recognized in our framework.

Another issue we found ourselves discussing often during the project concerned the size and scope of the learning designs that we were seeking to describe. In many classrooms and instructional settings, teachers tend to plan learning experiences for their students as single sessions. For example, a lesson might involve a series of experiences based on a plan, do and review process completed in an hour-long session. In our project, we were investigating some learning designs that represented a complete unit of study, with up to 100 hours of student activity. The relative sizes of these learning designs meant that in one instance the description could contain quite detailed elements, while in the semester-long course the elements in the learning design would necessarily have to be much broader. It was recognized among the group that it would be very useful to develop a schema that in some way constrained the size of the learning design so that the same elements could be used in each description. The Learning Activity Management System provided a very elegant solution to the problem of size through its modular approach (Dalziel, Chapter 15).

Another interesting outcome concerned the fact that the various learning approaches that were chosen for inclusion in the project were selected based on their perceived learning quality against such criteria as engagement, context, challenge and practice. In the temporal sequence framework used to provide a representation of the various learning designs, these elements of the learning designs are noticeably absent. More than this, there does not necessarily appear to be any logical way to include these elements in the learning design descriptions, despite their importance. It has been noted that the sequence provides a means by which the elements can be ordered but does not provide a framework for their content. Again, this appears to be an issue that could be further explored to enable the framework to more accurately provide a representation for different learning designs.

While the project has now been completed, it highlighted a number of pressing areas for further inquiry. It highlighted the challenges in categorizing and describing learning designs and the need for further work, some of which was taken up by other researchers (e.g. Littlejohn 2004; Conole and Fill 2005). There remains no agreed formal process for categorizing learning designs, and while strategies for describing designs are emerging – and are described elsewhere in this volume – an overarching typology is still to be described. Important in this process will be ways of expressing different contexts and ensuring that the language used can be understood by all teachers. The next chapter describes how some of these challenges have been taken up. We remain inspired by the enthusiasm that many researchers still retain for these areas of inquiry.

References

AUTC (2003) *Australian University Teaching Committee Project: Information and Communication Technologies and Their Role in Flexible Learning*. Online. Available at http://learningdesigns.uow.edu.au (accessed 31 July 2012).

Bennett, S. (2002) *Description of a technology-supported constructivist learning environment that uses real-life cases to support collaborative project work*. Online. Available at http://learningdesigns.uow.edu.au/exemplars/info/LD1/index.html (accessed 31 July 2012).

Boud, D. and Prosser, M. (2002) 'Key principles for high quality student learning in higher education: A framework for evaluation', *Educational Media International*, 39 (3): 237–45.

Britain, S. (2004) *A review of learning design: Concept, specification and tools*. Online. Available at http: <http://www.jisc.ac.uk/uploaded_documents/ACF1ABB.doc (accessed 31 July 2012).

Conole, G. and Fill, K. (2005) *A learning design toolkit to create pedagogically effective learning activities*. Online. Available at http://www-jime.open.ac.uk/2005/08/ (accessed 31 July 2012).

Dick, W. and Cary, L. (1990) *The Systematic Design of Instruction*, Glenview: Harper Collins.

Gagné, R.M., Briggs, L.J. and Wagner, W.W. (1992) *Principles of Instructional Design*, New York: Holt, Rinehart, and Winston Inc.

Harper, B., Agostinho, S., Bennett, S., Lukasiak, J. and Lockyer, L. (2005) 'Constructing high quality learning environments using learning designs and learning objects', paper presented at the 5th IEEE International Conference on Advanced Learning Technologies, Kaohsiung, Taiwan, July 2005.

Herrington, A., Herrington, J., Sparrow, L. and Oliver, R. (2002) *Description of investigating assessment strategies in mathematics classrooms*. Online. Available at http://learningdesigns.uow.edu.au/exemplars/info/LD2/index.html (accessed 31 July 2012).

Jonassen, D. (1994) 'Thinking technology: Toward a constructivist design model', *Educational Technology*, 34 (3): 34–7.

Jonassen, D. (2000) 'Toward a design theory of problem solving', *Educational Technology Research and Development*, 48 (4): 63–85.

Lefoe, G. (1998) 'Creating constructivist learning environments on the Web: The challenge in higher education', paper presented at the Australasian Society for Computers in Learning in Tertiary Education annual conference, University of Wollongong, December 1998.

Liaw, S., Kennedy, G., Marty, J., Judd, T., Keppell, M. and McNair, R. (2002) *Description of Communicating with the Tired Patient (Version 2.0)*. Online. Available at http://learningdesigns.uow.edu.au/exemplars/info/LD46/index.html (accessed 31 July 2012).

Littlejohn, A. (2004) *The Effectiveness of Resources, Tools and Support Services Used by Practitioners in Designing and Delivering e-Learning Activities.* Online. Available at http://www.jisc.ac.uk/uploaded_documents/Final%20report%20(final). doc (accessed 31 July 2012).

Masterman, L. and Manton (2011) 'Teachers' perspectives on digital tools for pedagogic planning and design', *Technology, Pedagogy and Education,* 20 (2): 227–46.

Oliver, R. and Herrington, J. (2001) *Teaching and Learning Online: A beginner's guide to e-learning and e-teaching in higher education,* Mt Lawley: Edith Cowan University.

Oliver, R., Wirski, R., Wait, L. and Blanksby, V. (2005) 'Learning designs and learning objects: where pedagogy meets technology', in C. Looi, D. Jonassen and M. Ikeda (eds) *Towards Sustainable and Scalable Educational Innovations Informed by the Learning Sciences,* Amsterdam: IOS Press.

Rehak, D. and Mason, R. (2003) 'Keeping the learning in learning objects', in A. Littlejohn (ed.) *Reusing Online Resources: A sustainable approach to e-learning,* London: Kogan Page.

Yasmeen, S. and Fardon, M. (2002) *Description of Political Science Simulation Exercise.* Online. Available at http://learningdesigns.uow.edu.au/exemplars/info/LD25/index. html (accessed 31 July 2012).

Chapter 7

Learning Designs as a Stimulus and Support for Teachers' Design Practices

Shirley Agostinho, Sue Bennett, Lori Lockyer, Jennifer Jones and Barry Harper

EDITORS' INTRODUCTION

This chapter builds on and brings up to date the work described in Chapter 6. The authors report on a decade of empirical work with teaching practitioners, which has led them to conclude that learning designs – by which they mean a specific form of graphical representation and explanatory text – are usable by university teachers. Designs are referred to for guidance and inspiration, in what the authors see as an example of case-based professional learning. Having a classification system seems to support this, even though it is not directly related to subject area. An important finding is that learning designs from the AUTC project can support the integration of pedagogy, technology and content knowledge in practitioners' design thinking.

Introduction

In the global higher education sector, university teachers are being challenged to improve student learning by effectively integrating new pedagogies and technologies. Quality teaching and educational experiences are considered critical to equip a diverse range of students with the lifelong learning skills essential for full participation in contemporary society.

Educational design has emerged as an important issue with research and development work focused on ways in which university teachers can be supported to design learning experiences for students. A key challenge in this area of inquiry has been the representation of effective designs in forms that can be easily understood by teaching practitioners and thus reusable. This has led to the term 'learning design' being applied to various means for documenting teaching and learning practice to facilitate sharing and reuse by teachers.

Some significant investments have been made to build repositories and/or tools that allow university teachers to document, model, implement, share and adapt educational design ideas, so as to build on good design practice. One of the first large-scale projects in Australian higher education was the *Information and Communication Technologies (ICT) and Their Role in Flexible Learning* project (http://www.learningdesigns.uow.edu.au), commissioned by the former Australian Universities Teaching Committee (AUTC) in 2000. This project involved the identification, evaluation, documentation and dissemination of high quality education examples that involved the use of ICT. The outcome of the project, hereafter referred to as the Learning Designs (LD) Project, was a repository of contextualized examples and generic guides called Learning Designs. These Learning Designs were units of study that were described through a graphical representation comprising the sequence of learning activities, supports and resources of the education experience (hereafter referred to as the Learning Design Visual Sequence (LDVS)) and descriptive text. The textual description provided a summary statement and design team details, detailed the tasks, resources and supports, explained the implementation context and provided a reflective comment by the original designers in terms of the pedagogy employed and any evaluative research conducted.

Chapter 6 explained the LD Project in terms of the project team's initial thinking about a taxonomy to classify the different learning foci of the collated Learning Designs. Harper and Oliver (2009) have detailed the project's final implemented taxonomy: see also Agostinho *et al.* (2008) for an explanation of how the LDVS was derived. This pioneering work led to a series of research studies and projects conducted by the authors spanning the past 10 years. This body of work provides important insights about strategies that allow teachers to publish, search for and comment on learning and teaching ideas (irrespective of ICT integration), as well as developing tools to support aspects of the educational design process.

This chapter synthesizes our research work and explains it within the context of international research on learning designs. The chapter is structured in accordance with the following key research questions that have guided our research, particularly within the Australian higher education context:

- How can learning designs from the LD Project be reused by teachers?
- Can a learning design be consistently and clearly represented?
- How can learning designs support university teachers in designing quality learning experiences?
- How can learning designs be used as a stimulus for teacher design thinking?

The chapter concludes by summarizing our work and suggesting future research directions.

Reusing and adapting learning designs

Building directly on the LD Project through qualitative studies of how teachers engage with learning designs, we are developing a deeper understanding of the role learning designs can play in supporting teachers' design processes. This line of research began in 2004 with a study investigating four members of a teaching team who redesigned a large first-year pre-service teacher subject (Bennett *et al.* 2004; Bennett *et al.* 2005).

The teaching team's aim was to adopt a problem-based approach customized to meet the needs of students from the different course specializations (Primary, Early Childhood, and Physical and Health Education). All were experienced teachers from the Faculty of Education, but none had previously used learning designs. Participants were observed and interviewed during a design workshop in which they selected and adapted a problem-based learning design (selected from the LD Project) to suit their context. A key finding from this study was that participants preferred the contextualized examples, which described the design as implemented in its original context, in preference to a more generic 'guide' (Bennett *et al.* 2004). Similar findings have been reported in later studies (e.g. Falconer *et al.* 2007). Furthermore, participants used the graphical representation, the LDVS, and textual description to become familiar with the design, but thereafter relied on the LDVS to develop their ideas further.

A larger study commencing in 2007 used a multiple case study approach to investigate the design processes of eight university teachers over 6 to 12 months as they selected and adapted a learning design from the LD Project, and then implemented and reflected on this learning design (see Jones *et al.* 2009, 2011). The university teachers were recruited via Australian professional associations focused on teaching and learning, were drawn from four universities and represented a range of disciplines and teaching experience. Data was collected during the pre-design, design, implementation and reflection phases of the design, and comprised interviews, unit of work documents and websites, researcher observations and field notes.

The research was guided by two questions:

1   How do university teachers design a unit of work using a learning design?
2   How does the use of a learning design impact on university teachers' development of technological, pedagogical and content knowledge?

Three main findings from the study are explained below.

Learning designs could be readily understood and reused

Participants of all experience levels were able to effectively select, apply and adapt previously documented learning designs according to their own needs. Specifically, the participants selected learning designs that aligned with their pedagogical goals, and in seven out of eight cases participants worked from contextualized examples rather than the generic guides. Interestingly, they did not limit themselves to designs from their own discipline. The finding that participants were able to understand and apply contextualized designs originating from disciplines other than their own suggests that the practice of 'translating' learning designs into more generic forms, which was one objective of the LD Project, may be unnecessary. This finding plus the similar finding in the Bennett *et al.* (2004) study suggests that the contextual detail included in a learning design adds to its reusability.

Learning designs were used for design ideas and benchmarking

The learning designs were mainly used for design ideas. Participants initially selected learning designs that had aligned with their pedagogical goals and then creatively adapted the details to suit their needs. Thus, for most participants the learning design was a source of ideas, rather than a model to replicate. In fact, early in the study a number of participants expressed an aversion to being 'restricted' by a prescribed design template. Participants also used the learning design LDVS and text in a variety of ways, specifically:

- as an outline of the pedagogical process (text and LDVS);
- to focus their design steps and activities (text and LDVS);
- for clarification of detail (text);
- as a checklist for resources, tasks, supports and their connections (LDVS);
- in one case, to document and map design thinking (LDVS).

In addition to design ideas and guidance, most participants (7 or 8) used the learning designs as benchmarks or models of good practice with which to compare their previous design thinking and work. Comparing the design ideas of their work against their chosen learning design provided participants with an indication of 'quality' of their designs and some participants reported this comparison gave them more confidence in their abilities and knowledge as a designer.

Learning designs supported integration of technology, pedagogy and content

One of the significant outcomes of using learning designs was the observed and reported impact on participants' integration of technology, pedagogy and content. The study drew on the notion of pedagogical content knowledge (PCK) (Shulman 1986), which attempts to describe the thinking a teacher undertakes when deciding how to teach a particular concept effectively, that is how they combine their knowledge of content with their knowledge of pedagogy. This idea has been extended to incorporate technology, hence the concept of Technological Pedagogical Content Knowledge (TPCK) (Mishra and Koehler 2006). TPCK refers to the thinking required of a teacher to determine how technology should be integrated with effective pedagogy to teach a particular concept. The study found:

- Designing with a learning design was reported to impact on PCK and/or TPCK in six of the eight cases.

- Participants designing new units of work or completely redesigning a unit of work tended to report an impact on PCK rather than TPCK.
- Participants working on smaller changes to more established learning designs reported an impact on their TPCK.

The difference in impact for participants working on new designs compared with participants refining more established designs suggests that, for university teachers designing units of work that will not be fully online, the design goals and thinking occur in two stages: first, there is a focus on PCK, which is followed by integration of technology. This is not to say that these participants did not use technology or did not have future plans for greater technology use. However, the goals expressed by the participants suggested, even among experienced technology users, that they saw the development and integration of technology as a longer-term goal to develop over multiple iterations. This is supported by the finding that participants revising more established learning designs reported focusing more on the reorganization and refinement of existing content in relation to the pedagogical sequence and then on how this refinement of existing content could be integrated within the online environment. This is an area of interest for future research.

The results of these two studies, which address research question one (*How can learning designs from the LD Project be reused by teachers?*), provide important insights into the utility of learning designs, in terms of how they are represented, how they are used for different purposes and in different design contexts, and the outcomes that might be achieved. Overall these two studies have shown that the learning designs from the LD Project can be reused by teachers as the participants from these two studies were able to select, understand and then adapt learning designs to implement in their contexts. Furthermore, the contextualized description was deemed a useful support in the design process and perhaps preferable to the more generic learning design 'guide'. Learning designs can be seen as a way to generate and inspire ideas rather than serve as a 'prescriptive pedagogy' and provide models of good practice against which university teachers can compare their own design thinking and work.

It is pertinent to note that research studies such as the two explained here follow design activities conducted over a sustained period. Data collection is thus intensive and time-consuming, thereby limiting the number of participants that can be included in a study. Further research to investigate emerging questions about the role of discipline, teaching expertise and context is a necessary extension of this work.

Representing and describing learning designs

As stated in the previous chapter, the learning design representation derived from the LD Project – i.e. the LDVS and accompanying text – provided the opportunity for further investigation about how learning designs could be described and represented. Below is a summary of two studies that address research question two: *Can a learning design be consistently and clearly represented*? The first study focused on the perceived usefulness of the learning design representation format of the LD Project. The second study examined whether the actual learning design descriptions provided in the LD Project repository described a learning design sufficiently so that it can be easily understood. The findings are explained below.

Study 1: Perceived usefulness of the LDVS to support university teachers' practice

This study, reported in Agostinho (2011), explored how university educational designers and teachers used the LDVS in their own teaching practice and how it supported their design processes. Eleven participants were interviewed. Most of them had used the LDVS to produce their own visual representation of their own teaching (8 of 11) or had adopted the '*tasks, resources, supports*' framework in a tabular written form to document their teaching ideas (2 of 11). Some of the eight participants made their own particular modifications to the visual sequence to suit their needs, such as substituting symbols in the visual representation, i.e., using a 'cloud' image instead of a triangle to represent resources; adding an extra support column to represent how teachers could be supported when implementing the learning design, and representing the visual sequence in a horizontal rather than a vertical orientation.

Of the 10 participants that had either created their own LDVS or applied the 'tasks, resources, supports' framework, the purpose for doing so was: to document their own teaching ideas, or use it as a design tool to discuss teaching ideas with colleagues, or to use their LDVS as an analysis tool to reflect on their learning design to check their understanding and see if anything (such as tasks, resources or support) was missing.

Overall, all participants thought that the LDVS was useful in their teaching as the visual aspect provided an overall summary of the learning design, the structure of tasks, resources and supports, helped participants better understand their learning designs, was simple to use and they could adapt the visual format to suit their needs. This study provides some evidence for the LDVS being a useful tool to support a university teachers' design process. The study's limitations were that use of LDVS was based on participants self-reporting retrospectively, and that it did not investigate how the LDVS formalism could be used as a way to encourage reuse of other people's designs. A richer insight would be to observe teachers while engaging in design to gain a deeper understanding of how tools such as LDVS could be used to support the design process. The study by Jones, explained above, addressed these limitations by monitoring the design processes of university teachers' use of learning designs from the LD Project.

There is evidence of further uptake of the LDVS as a mechanism to document learning designs – interestingly from practitioners with no direct involvement in the original LD Project (for example, see Cooner 2010; and Elliott *et al.* 2010).

Study 2: Determining what constitutes an 'effective' learning design description

Since completion of the LD Project, an international agenda has contributed to further understanding about how learning designs can be represented to facilitate sharing and reuse, the definition of a 'learning design' has evolved, several learning design presentations have emerged and significant technical developments have been made in terms of interoperability (see Falconer *et al.* 2007; Lockyer *et al.* 2009; Masterman 2006; and Tattersall and Koper 2005). Thus this second study arose from the need to revisit the literature and examine more recent thinking about what constituted an 'effective' learning design description and compare that with the learning design representation and descriptions in the LD Project.

This literature review (reported in Agostinho *et al.* 2009), which included international research from 2004–2008 about practitioners' perceptions of different learning design representations, found that an 'effective' learning design description should provide the following:

- clear and explicit description of the pedagogy of the learning design;
- some form of 'quality' rating about the learning design, e.g., evaluative findings; and
- explicit guidance/advice about how the learning design could be reused.

An instrument was developed based on these characteristics to analyse the 32 contextual examples in the LD Project. Six learning design descriptions were considered effective descriptions (refer to Agostinho *et al.* 2009) and formed the basis for the research team to further develop and refine to serve as input into a larger study, explained below.

Learning designs as supports for university teachers

A larger-scale study, funded by the Australian Research Council, began in 2007 to examine a missing piece evident in the learning designs literature, that is: how teachers actually design; the extent to which they have freedom to innovate with their designs; and the lack of practical, relevant and flexible supports and tools to help university teachers as they design. This investigation provides some answers to the third research question: *How can learning designs support university teachers in designing quality learning experiences?*

The research study consisted of three phases (illustrated in Figure 7.1).

The first phase of the research focused on investigating how teachers design learning experiences as a basis for considering what role design support tools might play. Despite the significant body of research into university teachers' conceptions of teaching and substantial funding invested in learning design approaches and tools, surprisingly little is known about how teachers actually

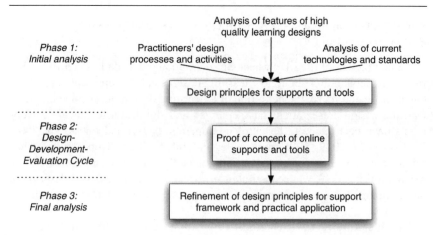

Figure 7.1 Phases from the Australian Research Council project Improving University Teaching: Creating strategies and tools to support the design process

design. Thirty Australian university teachers were recruited from three broad disciplinary groupings: the Sciences, the Arts, and the Professions (see Bennett *et al.* 2011 for the discipline grouping rationale). Participants were interviewed about their design practices. The semi-structured protocol posed questions about the contexts in which teachers worked, their conceptions of teaching and learning, their disciplinary background, their usual practices when designing a unit for the first time and when revising a unit they had previously taught, the key influences on their design decisions and the supports they used. Key findings from this phase of the study are presented below (see Bennett *et al.* 2011 for a detailed account).

Australian university teachers can exercise a high degree of autonomy in terms of design, and this suggests there may be opportunities for teachers to consider using reusable learning designs. Specifically, 40 per cent of participants taught in a context in which there was no set curriculum, thus allowing them the freedom to design units according to their own preferences and the needs of their students. More than half of the participants (60 per cent) taught within a set curriculum for which there were pre-set guidelines to follow, such as predetermined learning outcomes and required content to cover. Yet, the majority of these teachers explained that there was still flexibility within this structure for them to decide how the units should be designed. All but two participants cited institutional structures as having some impact on their design decisions. Specifically, planning processes determined how often major changes could be made to units, assessment policies provided broad guidelines on the types of strategies that could be used and in what combination, and class schedules determined what teaching and learning contexts were available. Two participants stated the institutional policies did not restrict their design decisions in any way.

Participants were regularly involved in both the design and redesign of new units. Most had been involved in designing a unit from scratch (83 per cent) and a majority described revising a unit each time they taught it to continually improve it (73 per cent). This suggests that participants experienced both continuity and variation in their teaching commitments. Eighteen (60 per cent) explained that they tended to teach the same units each year, and this was particularly so for those involved in large, core units. However, there were also opportunities to teach new units, often on more specialized topics with smaller cohorts. Only seven (23 per cent) worked alone when designing a unit, while the reminder engaged in both team and individual design. Group design usually occurred when undertaking overall planning of a degree programme or specialization, and in the case of large subjects involving a team of teaching staff. Smaller units, such as advanced level electives, were usually designed by one teacher, though often in consultation with colleagues.

Overall, these findings suggest that the Australian university context has some of the necessary preconditions for adoption of learning design and design support tools, as teachers have scope to make key decisions about how and what they teach. While helpful in providing insights into teachers' design practices, data from 30 Australian participants limits the ability to derive general conclusions. The research team is now undertaking further interviews with a view to developing an online survey to collect data across an international context.

Phases 2 and 3 of this study investigated how learning designs could serve as online support for teachers within an online learning management system (LMS). The rationale for this investigation was that the lack of embedded design support limits existing approaches because a teacher must either start with an empty shell or use a pre-existing contextualized unit of work. Neither of these options offer guidance in situ about opportunities for different teaching and learning strategies, or when and why certain tools might facilitate those strategies when adapted to different contexts. The idea of embedding design support within the online environment of a learning management system is an entirely new strategy to supporting online design. None of the major LMSs currently embed specific supports for designing for effective learning. All provide functions to help teachers create and arrange content, and add communications tools. All provide technical support manuals. Recent developments have focused on expanding the range of teaching and learning tools available within an LMS or developing visual interfaces to help teachers create 'digital lesson plans' external to the LMS that can be stored and used by others (Conole and Fill 2005; Dalziel 2007; Masterman and Manton 2011), but none offer guidance within the LMS about how the tools might be used to promote high quality learning.

The first step (Phase 2) was to assess the learning designs developed for the LD Project according to a more rigorous set of criteria to determine their quality, relevance and adaptability. An evaluation framework developed and applied to the LD Project repository resulted in six of the original set of 32 exemplars being appropriate for further development (this study is explained above and reported in Agostinho *et al.* 2009). The research team then refined these six learning designs to simplify the pedagogical expression and developed a proof of concept in the form of supports through embedded learning designs and design tools in the LMS, Janison Toolbox (www.janison.com.au).

Phase 3 of the research investigated the use of international standards for sharing educational designs and integrating digital resources. These had been the focus of intense technical research, but with little practical application in education. One priority was the IMS Learning Design (IMS-LD) specification, which provides a standardized computer language developed specifically for describing educational processes (Koper and Tattersall 2005). The underpinning concept was that a single lesson or whole course could be saved as an IMS-LD document and then read into any LMS compliant with the standard (illustrated in Figure 7.2).

After creating a lesson or course in an LMS and saving it as an IMS-LD document, a teacher could share it within a teaching team, institution or digital library, allow it to be edited in any other LMS that complies with the standard, and the new version could be saved as a new IMS-LD document. This approach would not only make particular lessons or courses sharable so that they can be reused and adapted by others, but the learning designs on which they are based could also be shared and reused. Work conducted on this aspect of the project to date demonstrated that while technically feasible, production of a fully operating system involved complexity beyond the scope of the grant. Work did not continue beyond this point because, despite being the only specification available for interoperability of online learning, IMS-LD has not been incorporated into learning management systems and support tools. As to the reason for this, perceptions of complexity have been considered a main barrier to adoption yet there is continuing debate about the lack of adoption of IMS-LD (Derntl *et al.* 2012).

Overall, the main insights from this research study are:

- Within the Australian context, the use of learning designs as supports for university teachers is feasible and beneficial.

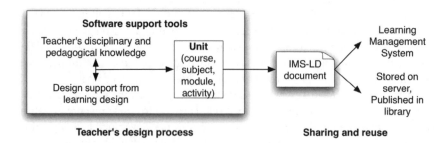

Figure 7.2 Applying international standards for sharing and reuse

- Learning design descriptions that provide contextual detail, offer advice on how to reuse, and provide evaluative data can be deemed effective descriptions.
- Incorporating learning designs within an LMS in the form of design guidance is worthy of further exploration.
- Technical interoperability, while technically feasible, is not a fruitful research direction unless there is widespread adoption of IMS-LD by LMS designers and the sector generally.

Can learning designs be a stimulus for teacher design thinking?

A key goal for the LD Project was one of reusability, that is, providing examples of good education and technology integration practice for teachers to apply to their own context. This focus was consistent with other projects concurrently undertaken worldwide which were interested in practical and technical aspects of creating design collections (e.g. Conole and Fill 2005). Since then, some related work has considered socio-cultural aspects of sharing such types of designs among teachers (e.g. Dalziel 2007; Margaryan and Littlejohn 2008).

The research reported in this chapter has gone beyond the original LD Project to better understand the context in which Australian university teachers design and have a sense of how learning designs might support them in their design activities. However, the limitations of this work and related research internationally make room for a more focused theoretical exploration of how learning designs can be of influence on an individual cognitive level.

In essence, learning designs are cases of teaching practice. They describe an instructional solution to educational problems – what to teach, how to teach, for which learners. As such, the use of learning designs can be theoretically linked to case-based reasoning. Capturing such problems and solutions as a case in the form of a learning design removes some, but not all, context-specific information, allows for understanding and sharing, and the process of adapting the design to an individual's teaching text allows for the development of a new understanding of the case and/or new cases. These are key characteristics of materials that support case-based reasoning (Kolodner *et al.* 2004).

The future agenda for this research team is to investigate the theoretical basis for learning designs in terms of their effectiveness in stimulating design thinking. Specifically, the research direction is to ask our fourth research question posed in this chapter: *How can learning designs be used as a stimulus for teacher design thinking?*

The aim is to test how case-based reasoning might occur as an individual teacher engages with the process of selecting, interpreting, adapting and implementing a learning design. From an individual cognitive perspective, the methodological challenge is to investigate this largely unobservable process. Preliminary work has been undertaken with schoolteachers to investigate the efficacy of the Learning Design graphical representation in the K–12 education context in terms of supporting the design thinking process. Initial findings suggest learning designs may be a useful way to communicate the thinking that can guide the design of a multi-lesson, cross-disciplinary unit of work.

Conclusions

This chapter has presented a decade of research inspired from the LD Project. Our research work has provided insight into usability of learning designs and their efficacy in generating teaching ideas. Overall we have shown that learning designs – i.e. the graphical representation and the accompanying text – are usable by university teachers irrespective of both the discipline of the original design and the discipline of the teacher using the design and thus can promote reuse. University teachers report that learning designs are useful in providing a point of inspiration or reference for their own design ideas in their own teaching context.

Our research has also provided a richer understanding of the Australian higher education teaching context and thus the parameters in which university teachers design. This understanding, in future, can be compared to other contexts in other countries. It also provides a basis for further research in the area of teacher design thinking. The practical outcomes for the work reported here and future research can lead to further development of tools and supports to aid teachers in their process of design.

References

Agostinho, S. (2011) 'The use of a visual learning design representation to support the design process of teaching in higher education', *Australasian Journal of Educational Technology*, 27 (6): 961–78.

Agostinho, S., Harper, B.M., Oliver, R., Wills, S. and Hedberg, J. (2008) 'A visual learning design representation to facilitate dissemination and reuse of innovative pedagogical strategies in university teaching', in L. Botturi and S. Stubbs (eds) *Handbook of Visual Languages for Instructional Design: Theories and practices*, Hershey, PA: Information Science Reference.

Agostinho, S., Bennett, S., Lockyer, L., Kosta, L., Jones, J. and Harper, B. (2009) 'An examination of learning design descriptions in an existing learning design repository', in R.J. Atkinson and C. McBeath (eds) *Same Places, Different Spaces*, Proceedings ASCILITE Auckland 2009, Auckland: The University of Auckland. Online. Available at http://www.ascilite.org.au/conferences/auckland09/procs/ (accessed 15 August 2012).

Bennett, S., Lockyer, L. and Agostinho, S. (2004) 'Investigating how learning designs can be used as a framework to incorporate learning objects', in R. Atkinson, C. McBeath, D. Jonas-Dwyer and R. Phillips (eds) *Beyond the Comfort Zone: Proceedings of the 21st ASCILITE Conference*, Perth: ASCILITE. Online. Available http://www.ascilite.org.au/conferences/perth04/procs/bennett.html (accessed 31 July 2010).

Bennett, S., Agostinho, S. and Lockyer, L. (2005) 'Reusable learning designs in university education', in T.C. Montgomerie and J.R. Parker (eds) *Proceedings of the IASTED International Conference on Education and Technology*, Anaheim, CA: ACTA Press.

Bennett, S., Thomas, L., Agostinho, S., Lockyer, L., Jones, J. and Harper, B. (2011) 'Understanding the design context for Australian university teachers: implications for the future of learning design', *Learning, Media and Technology*, 36 (2): 151–67.

Conole, G. and Fill, K. (2005) 'A learning design toolkit to create pedagogically effective learning activities', *Journal of Interactive Media in Education*, 8: 1–16.

Cooner, T.S. (2010) 'Creating opportunities for students in large cohorts to reflect in and on practice: Lessons learnt from a formative evaluation of students' experiences of a technology-enhanced blended learning design', *British Journal of Educational Technology*, 41 (2): 271–86.

Dalziel, J. (2007) 'Building communities of designers', in H. Beetham and R. Sharpe (eds), *Rethinking Pedagogy for a Digital Age: Designing and delivering e-learning*, London and New York: Routledge.

Derntl, M., Neumann, S., Griffiths, D. and Oberhuemer, P. (2012) 'The conceptual structure of IMS Learning Design does not impede its use for authoring', *IEEE Transactions on Learning Technologies*, 5 (1): 74–86.

Elliott, K., Boin, A., Irving, H., Johnson, E. and Galea, V. (2010) *Teaching scientific inquiry skills: A handbook for bioscience educators in Australian universities.* Online. Available at http://www.altc.edu.au/resource-teaching-scientific-inquiry-skills-melbourne–2010 (accessed 31 July 2010).

Falconer, I., Beetham, H., Oliver, R., Lockyer, L. and Littlejohn, A. (2007) *Mod4L Final Report: Representing Learning Designs*. Online. Available at http://www.academy. gcal.ac.uk/mod4l/ (accessed 31 July 2010).

Harper, B. and Oliver, R. (2009) 'Developing a taxonomy for learning designs', in L. Lockyer, S. Bennett, S. Agostinho and B. Harper (eds) *Handbook of Research on Learning Design and Learning Objects: Issues, applications and technologies*, Hershey, New York: IGI Global.

Jones, J., Bennett, S. and Lockyer, L. (2009) 'Investigating lecturers' use of learning designs to support technology enhanced course design', in T. Bastiaens *et al.* (eds), *Proceedings of World Conference on E-Learning in Corporate, Government, Healthcare, and Higher Education*, Chesapeake, VA: AACE.

Jones, J., Bennett, S. and Lockyer, L. (2011) 'Applying a learning design to the design of a university unit: A single case study', in T. Bastiaens and M. Ebner (eds) *Proceedings of World Conference on Educational Multimedia, Hypermedia and Telecommunications*, Chesapeake, VA: AACE.

Kolodner, J.L., Owensby, J.N. and Guzdial, M. (2004) 'Case-based learning aids', in D.H. Jonassen (ed.), *Handbook of Research on Educational Communications and Technology*, Mahwah, NJ: L. Erlbaum Associates.

Koper, R. and Tattersall, C. (2005) (eds) *Learning Design: A handbook on modelling and delivering networked education and training*, Berlin: Springer.

Lockyer, L., Bennett, S., Agostinho, S. and Harper, B. M. (eds) (2009) *Handbook of Research of Learning Design and Learning Objects: Issues, applications, and technologies*, Hershey, New York: IGI Global.

Margaryan, A. and Littlejohn, A. (2008) 'Repositories and communities at cross-purposes: Issues in sharing and reuse of digital learning resources', *Journal of Computer Assisted Learning*, 24 (4): 333–47.

Masterman, L. (2006) *The Learning Design Tools Project: An evaluation of generic tools used in design for learning.* JISC. Online. Available at http://www.jisc.ac.uk/uploaded_documents/LD Tools Report v1.1.pdf (accessed 31 July 2010).

Masterman, E. and Manton, M. (2011) 'Teachers' perspectives on digital tools for pedagogic planning and design', *Technology, Pedagogy and Education*, 20 (2): 227–46.

Mishra, P. and Koehler, M. (2006) 'Technological pedagogical content knowledge: A framework for teacher knowledge', *Teachers College Record*, 108 (6): 1017–54.

Shulman, L. (1986) 'Those who understand: Knowledge growth in teaching', *Educational Researcher*, 15 (2): 4–14.

Tattersall, C. and Koper, R. (2005) 'Editorial: Advances in Learning Design', *Journal of Interactive Media in Education*, 1.

Chapter 8

Representing Practitioner Experiences through Learning Design and Patterns

Patrick McAndrew and Peter Goodyear

EDITORS' INTRODUCTION

This chapter considers alternative ways in which learning activities can be represented in order to be shared. In particular, it looks at a 'learning design' approach, where the aim is to build a formal description that can be handled by a computer and played to an end user. The strengths of this approach are considered in relation to the tools that are being developed to support the IMS Learning Design specification, and the portability of the resulting designs. The chapter goes on to consider an alternative approach that may have lower barriers to take-up by practitioners. 'Patterns' provide flexible descriptions that engage and challenge their users, and can be mapped to different contexts of use. A pilot patterns-based approach is described, whereby existing materials are reworked as online open content with patterns extracted and stored to assist the process of design in the future. This chapter has been only lightly updated since it first appeared in 2006, but as an expression of the ambitions of the learning design community – some of which have entered the mainstream of educational thinking – it remains relevant today.

Authors' introduction to second edition

At the time of the first edition, the topic of Learning Design was one of great interest within a specialized audience but had little impact on day-to-day approaches to teaching and learning. As time has moved on the balance has changed with the specialized focus on Learning Design and the way it can be represented much less of a topic for direct research. On the other hand learning design – no longer with capitals – is now a common part of the way teachers will discuss their approach to designing learning experiences. The consistent format that was a promise of some of the specifications remains a challenge, particularly in reuse, however relaxing the requirement to be able to produce courses that can be interpreted and run has made the barrier to engaging with the approach much lower. The simpler concept of patterns as ways to show how content can be used has, perhaps, been more resilient (see e.g. Derntl and Motschnig-Pitrik 2010), but has not moved into the mainstream as a shared concept for describing ways to teach and learn. The need for both concepts is illustrated by application to Open Educational Resources, where understanding of learning design can help build new models for teaching in the open, while the use of patterns helps those who need to find a suitable way to change and adjust content to new situations and contexts. The combination of free, properly licensed resources and the designs to make use of them gives a new direction and importance to this work. There must be some disappointment recorded that the proposed format that enabled reuse was not widely adopted; even so the structure and best practice set out remain a good basis as work continues on the best way to share content, share plans and encourage reuse alongside invention.

Learning Design

Learning Design (LD) is a specification that allows the representation of units of learning and, as such, is a candidate for the representation of practitioner experiences. While it may not have achieved the impact described by Bill Olivier, one of the architects of the specification, who stated that: 'the ability to share and modify LDs will enable us to build up better practice for eLearning – and that is the main aim of LD', nevertheless the overall approach has gradually changed the way people are working to develop online content. The barriers to more widespread impact have not been the complexity of working with design (Derntl *et al.* 2011) so much as the disruptive nature of the changes that it has required in educational practice (Johnson *et al.* 2011). In reviewing the state of Learning Design, Britain (2004: 2) drew the distinction between '"learning design" (small "l", small "d") as a general concept and "Learning Design" (Capital "L" and "D") as the concept specifically implemented in the IMS specification.' This is an important distinction, as discussion about learning design has encouraged a greater focus on activities and collaboration, which were the features that originally inspired the developers of Educational Modelling Language (EML) and the IMS Learning Design specification. However use of the specification itself has been inhibited by the lack of tools and limitations in the existing specification. For example, Dalziel (2003) commented on the absence of tools to support collaborative tasks and to allow for group creation and monitoring (see also Dalziel, Chapter 15).

Britain highlights in his first recommendation 'that the concept of learning design can be usefully distinguished from the implementational level' and that 'work needs to be conducted to examine the range of approaches to "designing for learning" in use by teachers and lecturers, and the software tools that are or could be used to support these activities' (Britain 2004: 25). Masterman (Chapter 4) discusses some of the research that has since been done to explore current practice in 'designing for learning'.

Given that Learning Design is a specification with few proven tools, it remains difficult to commit to the use of the complete specification. Tools available from development projects have been focused on proving that the specification is viable. Second-generation tools may offer greater usability and robustness, but they have been relatively slow to arrive. However, those who do invest in describing their own learning activities in the framework of Learning Design can expect to have improving support for the process of transferring these designs to learners in runnable form. Learning Design remains a good candidate for formally capturing activity descriptions and making them available for use in other circumstances. Even so, attempts to engage practitioners in the learning design approach have met with only partial success. This may reflect the poorly established nature of learning design within mainstream educational thinking, but could also indicate more fundamental difficulties with the transfer of standardized vocabularies and methods from an expert group to wider use.

Specific barriers to the adoption of Learning Design include the following.

*   *The lack of a way to describe learning tools.* There are very few generic descriptions of the services needed to run learning designs. For designs to be transferable a wide range of generic services need to be described, and then matched to appropriate local services at the point of delivery, but only a very limited number of services are included in the specification of Learning Design. This is proving problematic for projects seeking to transfer learning designs, such as the Sakai project (http://sakaiproject.org/), where work on describing such services has concentrated on developer support (e.g. Open Service Interface Definitions – OSIDs) and has yet to address how the different services should be represented at the design level. Working from the requirements end, the Learning Activity Management System (LAMS) (Dalziel 2003) has demonstrated that providing a set of configurable tools to support a range of pedagogically sound activities is very engaging to the teacher community, and, with the release of the LAMS Tools contract, offers a way to change the toolset inside the system. However, the representation and ways of working with tools have proved hard to represent in a way that is compatible with the LD specification.
*   *Difficulty in creating the designs.* The process of writing down a design – as described in the IMS Learning Design best practice guide – is time-consuming and technically involved. The process includes building use cases, representing activities through Unified Modelling Language (UML) diagrams and then codifying the design in Extensible Markup Language (XML). Only the last stage of this process is supported by the current range of software tools, and the result can be a rigid design that is transferable for reuse but does not engage the teacher or require any understanding of how the activity works before it can be taken and reused. This could mean that it is not reused in the most appropriate way.
*   *The tension of working with a complex specification.* The IMS Learning Design specification is powerful in that it includes support for programmed logic and flexibility in describing the sequence. But it can be initially

frustrating in the limited number of services that are explicitly supported, the verbose structures that need to be described in XML, and the lack of explicit support for either hierarchical or generic levels of design.

These issues may be addressed by using a less rigid approach instead of the Learning Design formulation. Possible structures include templates, lesson plans or simplified learning designs. One candidate is to take a patterns-based approach, drawing on experience from other fields that have aimed to share designs.

Patterns

Learning patterns (Goodyear *et al.* 2004) is an approach that looks to architectural design patterns (Alexander 1979) as a way to capture knowledge from designers and share it with practitioners. In particular it aims to consider patterns as a source for advice to reproduce the general forms of architecture without the expectation that any cases are exactly the same. Thus a pattern

> describes a problem which occurs over and over again in our environment, and then describes the core of the solution to that problem, in such a way that you can use this solution a million times over, without ever doing it the same way twice.
>
> Alexander *et al.* 1977: x

Applied to learning, the design patterns approach seeks to identify what needs to be provided as useful background, guidance and illustration in describing ways to assist learning. A pattern is seen as something that will not be reused directly but can help informed teachers build up their own range of tasks, tools or materials by drawing on a collective body of experience. This is quite different from the Learning Design paradigm, in which the design must be specified tightly enough to be implemented within a player: the pattern is *not* intended to supply a complete solution but rather to give enough guidance to support human intervention and variation in each reuse. This approach may be integrated with more specific solutions such as coded Learning Designs or LAMS sequences; however the focus is on producing abstracted descriptions that engage the designer rather than packaged answers.

The format for a pattern, adapted from Goodyear *et al.* (2004), is:

1   A *picture* (showing an archetypal *example* of the pattern).
2   An *introductory paragraph* setting the *context* for the pattern (explaining how it helps to complete some larger patterns).
3   Problem *headline*, to give the essence of the problem in one or two sentences.
4   The *body* of the problem (its empirical background, evidence for its validity, examples of different ways the pattern can be manifested).

5   The *solution*. Stated as an instruction, so that you know what to do to build the pattern.
6   A *diagrammatic representation* of the solution.
7   A *paragraph* linking the pattern to the smaller patterns which are needed to complete and embellish it.

Such patterns are then integrated into a pattern language by providing related components – the example given by Goodyear *et al.* is a *discussion group* pattern that draws on patterns for *discussion role, facilitator* and *discursive task*. This format seeks to encompass a range of useful aspects that need to be recorded to enable the reader to understand the reason for the pattern and the solution that is being addressed. The way in which a pattern is stored is not itself rigid, and other projects have used variations on the format, with alternative labels. However, the key is the ability to identify the three aspects of context, problem and solutions. It is interesting to compare this format with work done on how different representations of practice are used by practitioners (Sharpe and Oliver, Chapter 10).

The strength of the patterns approach is shown in communities that adopt them, such as the original architecture community and more recently also communities of software developers. In these communities, design patterns are usually drafted, shared, critiqued and refined through an extended process of collaboration. Thus patterns have the potential to contribute to the sharing of techniques between developers of learning activities.

In contrast to Learning Design, patterns offer informality and are open to different interpretations and implementations at the detail level. This can raise difficulties over shared vocabulary and a relative lack of descriptive power, as has occurred with learning-related metadata (see following discussion); on the other hand it can also be seen as allowing contributions with a lower overhead and encouraging users to engage with and challenge the contents of patterns rather than adopt them unchanged. A further stage is to develop a collection of learning patterns as part of a pattern language. There are emerging collaborative efforts to achieve this: for example the E- project, discussed in Goodyear *et al.* (2004), has produced sample templates and encouraged contributions, and the pedagogical patterns project (Sharp *et al.* 2003) has built on work on design patterns in computer science to consider the learning process.

Metadata and vocabularies

A barrier to the development of shared descriptions, whether in Learning Design or patterns, has been how to provide a way to summarize and search each design. Metadata is one approach to solving this. Metadata is informally defined as the 'information about information', but this is a flawed definition: the key to understanding some of the problems with metadata is to see it as a home for information that is about an object but which is not essential to the direct use of the object. For example, to read this chapter, you do not need to know the software that created it, the date it was written, or even the keywords used to catalogue it, yet these can all be considered as potentially useful items to capture. The problem is illustrated by the use of the word 'potentially'; the temptation then arises to record everything that might possibly be useful, resulting in much information that actually will never be used. To those involved in the development process there is little motivation to provide this information in a way that is accurate and reliable.

The development of metadata for learning objects, in particular IMS Metadata and its development into the Institute of Electrical and Electronics Engineers' (IEEE) Learning Object Metadata (LOM) in 2002 (see http://ltsc.ieee.org/wg12/) revealed that agreement about the different aspects of learning to record in the metadata was not enough; the vocabulary to be used for actually describing those elements was also vital. In early development of IMS Metadata specification, it was decided that appropriate vocabularies should be suggested while leaving the final choice to users. However, the suggested vocabularies have proved not to be sufficient (for example, some were based very specifically on the US model of education, others had been excessively simplified), and use of locally relevant vocabularies, such as course code systems internal to a university, have meant that the resulting metadata records are not transferable. The view represented in work on vocabulary description exchange (see http://www.imsglobal.org/vdex/) is that it is important to allow local vocabulary development, but to a transferable format and available from a public site for others to use. Within a sufficiently cohesive community collaborative work can lead to agreement on the use of a common vocabulary (e.g. Campbell *et al.* 2001).

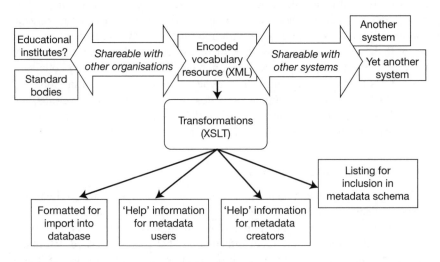

Figure 8.1 Mechanisms for exploiting vocabularies encoded using XML thesauri

Source: adapted from Brasher and McAndrew 2003

A proposed methodology for exploiting vocabularies for metadata is outlined in Figure 8.1, based on work led by Andrew Brasher (Brasher and McAndrew 2003). In this diagram the suggested approach is to represent the vocabularies using shareable thesauri containing not just the terms but additional explanation, hierarchies and relationships. This approach would be applied within a community by identifying the particular terminology that is in use and any specialist meanings that are attached to it. In this way, we can attempt to be clear about the meaning for its original audience and also prepare for a more transferable version for other audiences. This provides some of the same flexibility as the patterns approach, within a structured format.

Implementing a patterns approach for open content

The role of patterns is illustrated in Figure 8.2. This shows a hierarchy of representations, ranging from models of learning that can be drawn from theory, literature or existing examples (see for example Mayes and de Freitas, Chapter 1) through to patterns that can abstract a number of generic designs. At a more local level are instantiations based on how these designs are interpreted and matched to relevant learning materials and tools, and finally runnable versions in a suitable environment, e.g. LAMS, the Moodle virtual learning environment (VLE), or in a player for IMS Learning Design.

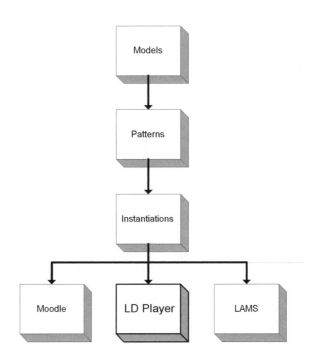

Figure 8.2
Patterns as part of the
development process

Patterns are intended to inspire new instantiations; however the model assumes that good patterns can be identified as part of the development process. The concept of what is 'good' can itself cause problems. If there is an available collection of designs or patterns then we would like to know that they are worth the effort to reuse. We would like to use the good patterns and avoid the bad ones (there is a view that it is valuable to record the bad as 'antipatterns' to serve as warnings to others (Brown *et al.* 1998). However, measuring the effectiveness of an educational technology and approach is notoriously difficult (Joy and Garcia 2000). Alexander, in his work on patterns (Alexander 1979: 19) gives an alternative by devising a 'quality without a name' (qwan): he states that 'This quality is objective and precise, but it cannot be named.' Alexander uses this concept to justify his listing of architectural patterns that will bring benefits, are somehow appealing and seem right, even if they have not been measured as better than others. This clearly raises a further question as to whether patterns are too subjective, but frees us from using only patterns that have passed through some kind of formal check.

In this view, patterns are proposals that are made with individual judgement that they possess sufficient quality but are then open to refinement and validation by the community to be proved in use. This approach fits well with the focus on community suggested by Sharpe and Oliver (Chapter 10). The source for patterns is, in general, the experience of those working on solutions to problems and in particular working with existing implementations. Any existing implementation will be set in a specific context and the format of a pattern encourages that to be described, but the overall premise is that the pattern can help inform reuse in a new context.

There has been some discussion of ways to automate extraction of patterns (Brouns *et al.* 2005), but these assume consistent structure for the material, such as already being encoded as IMS Learning Designs. In the Open University's OpenLearn project (http://www.open.ac.uk/openlearn) patterns are being piloted as a way to capture designs as part of a human process of academic transformation. OpenLearn provides free access to a range of educational materials, both for learners using the content within a learning environment, and for educators reusing and remixing the content in new contexts. Content is currently provided as XML structured files and as courses in the Moodle VLE (http://moodle.org). Eventually IMS Learning Design may also be used. The content set is derived from proven Open University materials designed to work within its taught courses, i.e. quality assured content intended to enable cohorts of students supported by tutors to meet particular learning objectives. The new context for this material is as online open content, where there is less control over timing and support, and activities must be viable in isolation from the associated course structures.

'Academic transformation' is the term used for the adjustments that need to be made to the content to make it available in this new context. A three-level view of the transformation sees the content as (a) maintaining its original integrity with unchanged intent, but being adjusted for the new platform; (b) keeping its essence but significantly changing some aspects; or (c) using the original as inspiration to be remixed into a new work. The initial focus is on material that will maintain its integrity. However, care is needed to identify what should be retained to keep academic integrity, what must be changed as it is too tied to the original context, and what might be open to change to take advantage of new tools and ways of learning in the new context.

Patterns have been introduced into this process as a tool to help academic transformers represent their interpretation of the original intent, and show how they intend to change the materials into the new context. A Pattern Analysis Template (PAT) based on the pattern structure has been used to capture the view of those involved in the process (see Figure 8.3). Once complete, the template provides a candidate pattern and will be available as an additional resource to educators seeking to reuse the material. The hope is that the patterns will build towards a pattern language, potentially giving educators an alternative way of understanding the intention behind peda-gogical source materials, alongside the instantiation intended for the learner. Patterns will help record how resources can be used and how the designer expects them to work. In the case of the material being used for OpenLearn, the original content does not have a corresponding pattern set and so the templates are gathering and sharing views on how both the original and trans-formed content operate.

While the evidence is that designers find it helpful to review the pattern analysis before directly working on the content, feedback indicates that this can also be an uncomfortable experience, leading to alternative, and some-times conflicting, views on the same material. These views may each be valid, and illustrate the different levels of perspective that are expected in a pattern language – in contrast to the approach that looks for a single 'runnable' instan-tiation. A tension has also been observed between extracting patterns that focus on the learning experience, and extracting those that focus on the provider's viewpoint and the requirements of the transformation. Both of these viewpoints are valuable and indicate there may be a case for making alternative perspectives explicit in the way that patterns are recorded.

The pattern format encourages a large amount of information to be entered into a relatively small space and, as with the metadata problem described previously, it is difficult to encourage a consistent approach that provides the relevant information. The academic transformers had example patterns to help them in completing new templates. Analysis of the linguistic structure of the examples and the new templates has indicated that the structure and language used in the example may have a significant influence on how the new templates are completed. Revised versions of these examples use clearer language to act as models and style guides for designers on how to word their own contributions.

Pattern Analysis Template

Completed by:
Date:
Comments:

Name: (short name to convey ideas to others)
Context: (what is needed to make this work, and any assumptions)
Problem: (background or statement of problem solved)
Solution: (key points any critical factors)
Diagram or illustration: (sketch out the solution or describe stages in words)
Related patterns: (similar sections, builds on another pattern)
Instantiation: (e.g. course name, section, chunk identifier, link)

Figure 8.3 The Pattern Analysis Template used by OpenLearn

Conclusions

Both patterns and learning design encourage the representation of activities alongside content, and this is important to encourage appropriate designs for learning with technologies. Perhaps the main distinction between the two approaches is that they aim in the one case to represent a design for a computer to understand and process, and in the other for a human being to understand and work with. Both of these aspects are important and deserve to be supported in a holistic approach to developing educational materials. In the Learning Design approach, if a unit of learning is described so that a computer can work out the roles that are involved, set up the unit's structure, and sequence the learners' access to the material, then we can be fairly sure that the description is complete and detailed enough. A pattern-based description will inevitably have lost some of the detail and may have failed to capture information necessary to reproduce the situation we want to describe. However, the key pedagogical points can now be made simply and argued for in a direct way, so that the human reader of the pattern can apply their own expertise. Rather than simply reproducing previous ideas, they can develop new ways of achieving the same goals that are suited to their own context. This matches well with Alexander's own vision for the use of patterns in architecture 'A pattern language gives each person who uses it, the power to create an infinite variety of new and unique buildings, just as his ordinary language gives him the power to create an infinite variety of sentences' (Alexander 1979: 167).

There are tensions between human-understandable and computer-understandable forms of representation, and a way forward is to combine these different representations to take advantage of their different strengths. A proposed model is to use patterns for human–human communication and either Learning Design or, more awkwardly, multiple VLE specific instantiations to provide the computer-interpretable form. Although there is limited practice in using patterns, the work within the OpenLearn project shows an approach that appears to focus attention on academic issues in working to reuse materials. Dimitriades *et al.* (2009) considered the ways that individual tasks could be made collaborative and examined attitudes to the use of designs and patterns. Sharing designs helped understanding of purpose, while the pattern approach helped inspire new ways to use open educational resources, pointing the way towards a mixed approach to meet the challenge of reusing the pool of such resources now available.

Acknowledgements

OpenLearn is supported by the William and Flora Hewlett Foundation in conjunction with the Open University. Patrick McAndrew is grateful for discussion with members of OpenLearn, in particular Giselle Ferreira, Andy Lane, Jerard Bretts, Stephen Bradley and Steve Godwin. The linguistic analysis of example patterns was carried out by John McAndrew of Macquarie University.

References

Alexander, C. (1979) *The Timeless Way of Building*, New York: Oxford University Press.

Alexander, C., Ishikawa, S., Silverstein, M., Jacobson, M., Fiksdahl-King, I. and Angel, S. (1977) *A Pattern Language: Towns, buildings, construction*, New York: Oxford University Press.

Brasher, A.J. and McAndrew, P. (2003) 'Metadata vocabularies for describing learning objects: implementation and exploitation issues', *Learning Technology Newsletter of IEEE LTTF: Special Issue*. Online. Available at http://www.ieeetclt.org/issues/january2003/index.html#9 (accessed 9 July 2012).

Britain, S. (2004) *A Review of Learning Design: Concept, specifications and tools*, JISC Project Report. Online. Available at www.jisc.ac.uk/uploaded_documents/ACF83C.doc (accessed 9 July 2012).

Brouns, F., Koper, R., Manderveld, J., van Bruggen, J., Sloep, P., van Rosmalen, P., Tattersall, C. and Vogten, H. (2005) 'A first exploration of an inductive analysis approach for detecting learning design patterns', *Journal of Interactive Media in Education*. Online. Available at http://jime.open.ac.uk/jime/article/view/2005-3 (accessed 9 July 2012).

Brown, W.J., Malveau, R.C. and Mowbray, T.J. (1998) *AntiPatterns: Refactoring software, architectures, and projects in crisis*, New York: John Wiley and Sons.

Campbell, L., Littlejohn, A. and Duncan, C. (2001). 'Share and share alike: encouraging the reuse of academic resources through the Scottish electronic Staff Development Library', *Association for Learning Technology Journal*, 9 (2): 28–38.

Dalziel, J. (2003) 'Implementing learning design: the learning activity management system (LAMS)', paper presented at ASCILITE 2003, Adelaide, December 2003. Online. Available at www.melcoe.mq.edu.au/documents/ASCILITE2003%20Dalziel%20Final.pdf (accessed 9 July 2012).

Derntl, M. and Motschnig-Pitrik, R. (2010) 'The practitioner's perspective on design patterns for technology enhanced learning' in P. Goodyear and S. Retalis (eds) *Technology-Enhanced Learning: Design patterns and pattern languages*, Rotterdam: SensePublishers.

Derntl, M., Neumann, S., Griffiths, D. and Oberhuemer, P. (2011) 'The conceptual structure of IMS Learning Design does not impede its use for authoring', *IEEE Transactions on Learning Technologies*, 5 (1): 74–86.

Dimitriadis, Y., McAndrew, P., Conole, G. and Makriyannis, E. (2009) 'New design approaches to repurposing open educational resources for collaborative learning using mediating artefacts', paper presented at ASCILITE 2009, Auckland City, New Zealand, December 2009. Online. Available at http://oro.open.ac.uk/19378/ (accessed 9 July 2012).

Goodyear, P., Avgeriou, P., Baggetun, R., Bartoluzzi, S., Retalis, S., Ronteltap, F. and Rusman, E. (2004) 'Towards a pattern language for networked learning', in S. Banks, P. Goodyear, V. Hodgson, C. Jones, V. Lally, D. McConnell and C. Steeples (eds) *Networked Learning 2004*, Lancaster: Lancaster University.

Johnson, M., Griffiths, D. and Wang, M. (2011) 'Positioning theory, roles and the design and implementation of learning technology', *Journal of Universal Computer Science*, 17 (9): 1329–46.

Joy, E.H. and Garcia, F.E. (2000) 'Measuring learning effectiveness: A new look at no-significant-difference findings', *Journal of Asynchronous Learning Networks*, 4 (1): 33–9.

Sharp, H., Manns, M.L. and Eckstein, J. (2003) 'Evolving pedagogical patterns: the work of the pedagogical patterns project', *Computer Science Education*, 13 (4): 315–30.

Chapter 9

The Influence of Open Resources on Design Practice

Chris Pegler

EDITORS' INTRODUCTION

Since the first edition of this book appeared in 2006, open education and openly licensed educational resources (OER) have become world-changing movements. This chapter explores some of the implications for designers of learning, when, for example, they may be designing for learners enrolled on remote campuses, at rival institutions, in workplaces and on home study courses, and learners who are not formally enrolled in education at all. Tracing the history of the movement in Reusable Learning Objects (RLOs), Pegler argues that while they offer similar potential for widening access to learning, OERs provide for other kinds of openness, including participation in open knowledge communities through the 'read-write practices' of the open web.

Introduction

Since Vest (2001) announced the Massachusetts Institute of Technology (MIT) would open its courses to learners beyond the institution there has been an impressive increase in access to open educational resources (OER) for reuse by learners and educators. After ten years MIT estimated that it had shared resources from 2000+ courses and reached 100 million people worldwide, and laid down an even bolder ambition to 'reach a billion minds' by 2021 (MIT 2011). However, while large-scale initiatives attract institutional and sectoral interest for their ability to showcase and advance new models of educational access, they also raise questions with design implications about the support, retention and recognition of learners who are not necessarily registered students. There has been disappointment in the evidence of uptake of OER by practitioners (i.e. their reuse) so far, consistent with the lack of reuse evidenced from earlier initiatives such as the push to adopt reusable learning objects in the 1990s. This reflects problems in tracking informal behaviour to accurately establish the extent of resource reuse (Masterman and Wild 2011). It also highlights the relevance of context and growing awareness of the importance of supporting, recording, sharing, developing and understanding wider open educational *practices* (OEP) to fully realize the potential of OER activity. The Open Education Quality Initiative (OPAL) project has defined OEP as: 'practices which support the (re)use and production of high-quality open educational resources (OER) through institutional policies, promote innovative pedagogical models, and respect and empower learners as co-producers on their lifelong learning path' (OPAL 2012), suggesting that understanding OEP is necessary to extend focus 'beyond "access"' and towards 'innovative open educational practices' (OPAL 2011). Open resources need to be understood in the wider context of open practices and the evolution in these, and reflected in new and existing approaches to learning design, if their potential is to be realized.

The notion of opening up education to reach a wider body of learners on the basis of innovative design of learning resources is not a new one. Open learning until 2000 was associated with removing or reducing the entry barriers to becoming a university student. This movement was linked to the establishment of alternative styles of institution such as the Open University in the UK (from 1969), Athabasca University in Canada (from 1970) and other, large-scale open universities including the largest university in the world Indira Gandhi National Open University (IGNOU) (from 1985). While these and other open initiatives widened participation in higher education by opening access, in the 21st century openness in education has taken on additional meanings that extend beyond enrolment of individual students on conventional award-bearing programmes.

Online connectivity has made it possible to open up and change the way that education is offered and experienced, moving academic practice towards open publication, open research, open science, open data, open innovation, open source and OER activities. Opening access to education has broadened to become an international cradle-to-grave objective. For example, Education for All, supported by UNESCO and the World Bank, has set a target that by 2015 all children, wherever they live 'will have access to and complete, free, and compulsory primary education of good quality' (UNESCO 2012). Such large-scale ambitions to open up educational access can only be addressed through development and sharing of open resources. In making those available and in opening up educational systems and activities to accommodate them, other changes also become possible or desirable.

Each newly open activity within the open education movement offers an alternative to an established 'closed' arrangement with potential to influence that arrangement. For example, as an open source virtual learning environment (VLE) Moodle, has established itself within mainstream online education, Blackboard, an established proprietary VLE provider, has announced plans to be more open itself by introducing a 'share' button to allow access to content on its platform for users other than registered students (Young 2011) and has also set up an open source services group. Such activity underlines the reality that in most institutions and on most courses, open activity coexists alongside more conventional approaches, part of a blend of open and restricted formats, methods, or tools. Some wholly open alternatives are being piloted, blending open resources with optional accreditation pathways, for example the OERu consortium pilot courses (Witthaus 2012), however these options are still experimental and untested. Currently the significance of OER for most students and teachers is as alternatives or additions to conventional teaching resources, rather than as complete replacements.

However, unlike the earlier open education initiatives, the emphasis in new forms of educational openness is not restricted to meeting the needs of registered students. A significant attribute of the new emphasis is the lack of boundaries. Open education does not exist solely *within* educational institutions and open learners are not limited to *registered students*. While the new open learning movement – often described as 'open education' – fosters broad objectives and long-term goals around wider engagement, individual educators and learners play a more direct and immediate role as a result of a more open learning landscape. This is particularly the case with OER activity, the focus for this chapter.

What are open educational resources?

An alternative, earlier (1998) term for OER is 'open content' (Wiley 2006). This phrase recognizes that resources used for learning need not be educational in origin or intent, for example a holiday picture posted on photo-sharing site Flickr (http://www.flickr.com/) can be used for educational purposes. However, the word 'content' suggests a relatively narrow and static range of items and led to preference for the term 'resource', with OER distinguished not by form, label, or origin but by openness to use. An open licence usually indicates the availability of the resource for new uses and users, identifying permissions additional to normal intellectual property rights (IPR), e.g. copyright. David Wiley in Hilton *et al.* (2010) described these as 4R activities:

- *Reuse*: the right to reuse the content in its unaltered/verbatim form (e.g., make a backup copy of the content).
- *Revise*: the right to adapt, adjust, modify, or alter the content itself (e.g., translate the content into another language).
- *Remix*: the right to combine the original or revised content with other content to create something new (e.g., incorporate the content into a mash-up).
- *Redistribute*: the right to share copies of the original content, the revisions, or the remixes with others (e.g., give a copy of the content to a friend).

Both learners and educators may be unaware that there is no automatic right to engage in 4R activity without additional permissions. Such activity already occurs in education *without* an open licence or equivalent arrangement, part of the unseen iceberg of using resources educationally and openly without permission (White and Manson 2011). Resources based on third-party content and copied, shared or adapted (i.e. used in 4R fashion) legally within the restrictions of a site licence or fair dealing cannot usually be *legally* opened to others to use. Open licensed resources allow transition of resources to new learning and teaching contexts and, where permitted, new formats and forms.

Resources which have been tested in educational contexts may inspire more confidence in terms of accuracy, effectiveness and persistence; however the purpose for which an open resource was created is immaterial if the resource allows revisions or remixes. Reusable learning objects (RLOs), other educational resources made available for use beyond their original context, were at their broadest defined as: 'Any entity, digital or non-digital, which can be used, reused or referenced during technology supported learning' (IEEE 2002). Many prominent OER researchers and practitioners previously researched or advocated RLO use (e.g. Wiley, Downes, McGreal, Anderson, Lamb, Mason and Weller) leading to description of OER as 'reusable learning objects with an open license' (Wiley and Downes 2009). A pragmatic definition of OER which acknowledges open arrangements other than licensing is: 'materials used to support education that may be freely accessed, reused, modified and shared by anyone' (Downes 2011). The licence may permit less openness than Downes suggests yet still be described as an OER. If any of Wiley's 4R activities is allowed this is not a conventional 'closed' resource.

The Creative Commons (CC) licence is the most widely applied open licence for sharing OER within education. In order to design for or with OER it is useful to understand its basic forms. The 'Attribution (CC-BY)' licence is the most open, setting no conditions other than that the creator be identified. This is not only a 'moral right' under international copyright law, but also the tenet of good academic practice. It forms the basis of all CC licences with other options applying additional restrictions on use, i.e.: 'non-commercial' (NC); 'no derivs' i.e. no revisions or remixing (ND); 'share alike' i.e. limiting versions or works based on it to the same level of open licensing (SA). Although permitting different levels of activity, the six CC combinations shown in Figure 9.1 are all *open* licences.

It is hard to overstate the importance of establishing the rights status of an open resource. Open licensing has paved the path for open education through schemes which are relatively easy for students and teachers to understand and use, and which facilitate online resource discovery focused on openness.

Approaches to OER design

As with other resources used in education, OER can be repurposed from existing educational activity or made anew. It can be adopted within traditional teaching practice (e.g. as printed handouts downloaded from an online repository), or as open educational practices online (OPAL 2011). Each approach can result in different levels of OER granularity (size). Taking one well-known example, MIT, OER replicates teaching activity on the MIT campus, e.g. recording lectures in progress and making these available as webcasts. The granularity is relatively large, based on the duration of the original lecture, with changes to the

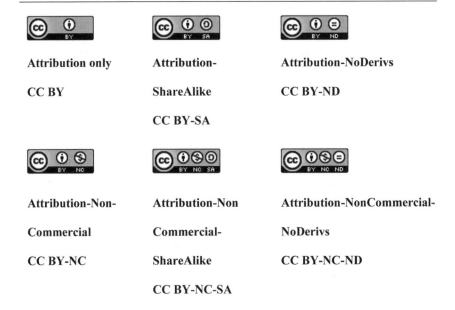

Attribution only	Attribution-	Attribution-NoDerivs
CC BY	ShareAlike	CC BY-ND
	CC BY-SA	

Attribution-Non-	Attribution-Non	Attribution-NonCommercial-
Commercial	Commercial-	NoDerivs
CC BY-NC	ShareAlike	CC BY-NC-ND
	CC BY-NC-SA	

Figure 9.1 The six Creative Commons open licences for OER

format rather than to the structure. In a similar way, OER within the UK Open University's OpenLearn platform is based on lightly repurposed versions of the distance learning units created for registered students. Both examples retain strong resemblance to their donor courses and are examples of 'open courseware', which directly addresses learners, with quality of the resource finish at least as high as that used for classroom instruction.

Alternative OER based on existing resources in use on education are more granular material elements e.g. PowerPoint slides, handouts, images, videos, games, quizzes or simulations. This may not be ready-to-use by learners, but can have appeal to educators who wish to blend these resources within a new learning design, or adapt them for a new context. Both types of resource – courseware and assets – are by-products of conventional education, which improves the potential for sustainability. There is a relatively small level of additional effort or skill required to make these resources open, so a smaller draw on institutional resources. In contrast, resources created purely as OER, with no connection to the normal business of the institution, require an exceptional flow of funding or effort, whether generating assets or courseware. Such activity may fill gaps in provision, or allow experimentation, but without significant institutional support are more likely to create discrete episodes in OER supply which ceases when external funding does, rather than a steady flow. This is not to suggest that made-as OER are less desirable. They may be the easiest route to transforming educational practice. If there is third-party material within an existing resource, or if it was written in a heavily contextualized manner, it may be impossible to easily convert it into an OER. This is one reason why creating new open resources rather than adapting existing ones may be preferred (McGill *et al.* 2010). Chapter 7 has suggested learning design pattern approaches that may be adopted when creating OER.

The openness of the licence does not *require* an open emphasis in use, so OER can be used in similar ways to closed equivalents. However, unlike conventional educational resources, OER offers opportunities for what Lessig (2008) described as read-write (RW) activity where users reinvent and create. This is in contrast to closed resources that restrict those options, leading to what Lessig described as read-only (RO) passive consumption. It is the openness of the OER within an increasingly open educational landscape that allows the creation of opportunities for more active engagement. The three examples below illustrate how openness in conjunction with OER can lead to RW practices through: transnational two-way sharing; the educator acting as DJ in remixing resources and; use and generation of OER in open online courses (OOCs) or massive open online courses (MOOCs).

Example 1: Gains in translation

To translate educational resources into other languages is not novel activity but is usually 'demand-led activity' directed at specified opportunities because of the high cost. Publication as OER allows users rather than suppliers to lead decisions to translate and can generate significant spread of resources. For example, over 1000 of the MIT open courseware courses have been translated into languages including Spanish, Portuguese, Chinese, French, German, Vietnamese and Ukrainian.

Translation of OER opens up access, but can also lead into two-way exchanges as the experience of UnisulVirtual in Brazil shows. In 2007 this Brazilian university, with support from the OLNet OER research project based at the Open University, identified resources offered within OpenLearn that would be useful to their students. The resources were translated into Portuguese and adapted and linked from the UnisulVirtual online learning environment as additional resources for their students.

Following this initial 'read-only' exchange of resources, UnisulVirtual made the Portuguese translations available through the OpenLearn LabSpace platform, and then identified some of its own resources which it wished to share back as OER (dos Santos 2012). They used LabSpace and adopted an open courseware format similar to the OU content, with translations into English as alternatives to the original Portuguese.

Labspace is an open access system which hosts remixes of OU OpenLearn content (available as XML format files) and other OER. While the level of support from OLNet, OpenLearn and LabSpace provided an unusually supportive environment for this activity, this example shows the reciprocity that is possible through OER activity.

Example 2: Mash-up resources: rip, mix, burn

Scott Leslie has expanded on the metaphor of 'Teacher as DJ' (Wiley 2005) to explain the potential of openness in drawing together resources from different sources. His emphasis is not only on using and creating OER, but on identifying open online tools and creating courses as experimental mash-ups of existing open content. Leslie identifies four main steps in the activity of open educator as DJ (Leslie 2010):

- Step 1: *Search* (Going through the bins);
- Step 2a: *Sample* (Getting the parts of the resources you need);
- Step 2b: *Capture your own track* (When you just can't find the right beat);
- Step 3: *Sequence* (Putting the pieces in order);
- Step 4: *Record* (Perform the set, teaching 'live' with OER).

This sequence captures a view of teaching with OER that commences with searching to establish what exists and builds from this. Although the creation of new resources only occurs if suitable alternatives do not exist, or cannot be repurposed to suit the new course, Leslie's examples emphasize the creative process possible using 'found' materials from a range of contexts. If resources sampled are open and allow derivatives they can be disaggregated and remixed within new learning designs. This approach expects creativity and originality in course design to feed from existing materials and ideas, rather than needing to start from scratch. The searching may inform and promote further unplanned activity and not simply meet the educator's immediate needs.

In the simplified four-step version above, Leslie's Teacher DJ combines and remixes to reflect educator preferences. Open online tools are key to allowing organization and syndication of the clippings within educational remixes. Although the tools and techniques suggested by Leslie may be unfamiliar or even feel inappropriate to some educators, his basic model is widely relevant. In this model, open course design starts with and responds to existing resources, uses open rather than proprietary tools and systems, and records (publishes) the resulting remix openly. By employing OER and tools which are interchangeable and freely available, the remixes and remix approach can be used with registered students, but are not limited to these. The approach suggests not only a *personalized* learning environment (PLE), but one which is also far more open than a conventional VLE.

Example 3: Open online courses (OOCs and MOOCs)

Examples 1 and 2 showed how closed practice can be extended through engagement with OER. The third example extends these, presenting educational activity that is more extensive and orchestrated yet retains the serendipitous emergent design potential of the first two examples.

An MOOC (massive open online course) is a relatively new teaching approach, originating in 2007 and not only providing access to assets, objects or courseware, but doing this as part of structured or negotiated open learning and teaching activity. Some formats of MOOC can seem very similar to conventional closed participation online courses, with published study schedules, periodic quizzes and lectures (online webinars) and online forums. However, because MOOCs address an unrestricted range of learners, the resources used need to be open and the course design flexible. Not only use of OER, but creation or remix of these by learners as well as educators is expected to occur, bringing significant amounts of user-generated resources into the 'course' activity. These remain available for participants and others to draw on afterwards. As Siemens has observed (Rheingold 2011) the institution does not own the space so cannot cut the connections when the course ends.

There has so far been no fee for engagement in MOOCs and relatively relaxed limits on who can participate. Registered students based at institutions offering the MOOC are likely to be significantly outnumbered by open learners who have no affiliation with it. For example in late 2011, an MOOC on artificial intelligence (AI) taught by Stanford professor Sebastian Thrun was capped at 160,000 enrolments from 190 countries, while only 200 Stanford students enrolled on campus (Lewin 2012). The exceptional 'class' size represents not only massive scale but massive diversity of background and motivation, adding to a distinctive feel of MOOCs as separate from mainstream education. If open education aims to remove barriers to accessing learning activity, MOOCs could be viewed as a high-profile manifestation of this potential.

George Siemens who has pioneered the MOOC approach to teaching provides this reflection on their special nature, suggesting that the openness is not an institutional gift:

> an open course starts as a shell with the instructor providing links, articles, and activities. From there, learners take course content and massage it, enhance it, extend it, clarify it, question it, and improve it. Passionate learners – the ones to take the time to improve a course – need a level of trust and transparency between course organizers. In an open course, the educator isn't the one showering participants with gifts of knowledge. The process of learning is iterative and the relationship is mutually beneficial. Participants do the course organizers as much of a favour in joining as the course organizers do in opening the course.
>
> Siemens 2011

Siemens notes the need for trust and transparency in MOOC design and teaching, referring in this blog post to the debate that raged when Stephen Downes, another MOOC pioneer, experimented by automatically subscribing learners to email alerts for forum discussions (Downes 2008). Within a conventional course such a decision might not be unexpected by students. There the teacher is 'in charge' of the design, leading and controlling communication within what is sometimes referred to as the 'walled garden' of the course or institution. However, discussion between Downes and his MOOC participants showed that some learners, particularly those who were not taking the course 'for credit' or saw their engagement as occurring within their 'free time' found this experiment in control over their study habits to be unacceptable. Emphasis on openness and co-creation can generate expectation that learners will have greater freedom to direct their own activity, including the power to change the direction of this. For example, there is greater freedom for MOOC participants to avoid engagement, dropping into and out of activity as they choose, initiating alternative activities or introducing new resources. These freedoms are not wholly positive aspects of OOC/MOOC approaches. While the numbers of learners registered can appear huge in comparison with conventionally taught courses, the course population can be subject to unpredictable fluctuation in both volume and constitution during and across presentations. Fini (2009), researching one of the earliest MOOCs, found that while 85 per cent of formal learners completed the whole course with assignments, only 6 per cent of informal learners did so. This was despite the fact that the majority of learners who responded to his research (84 per cent) said they were informally registered. While there may be low barriers to engaging in open online courses, there are also low barriers to exiting it.

The level of proactivity and achievement for successful open learners can be impressive with impact across the whole course community, encouraging conventionally designed courses to become open and reinvent themselves innovatively. The Digital Storytelling (DS106) course at the University of Mary Washington became open in Spring 2011 and illustrates the impact of openness on a formerly campus-based module which led to establishment of 'a radio station, a TV station, an assignment bank with over 280 contributions, and an explosion of creativity and fostered community like never before' (Groom 2012). The radio and TV stations allow course participants to broadcast for themselves, again recalling Lessig's read-write approach (Lessig 2008). By 2012 seven universities were basing formal teaching on participation in DS106 and the 1200-plus open online participants had generated more than 18,000 posts. The idea of the course as a community is central to this design of MOOC. To fund the expansion of the DS106 server and other improvements required to remain massively open, an appeal was made to the DS106 community and the modest funds required were pledged within 24 hours (Groom 2012), and nearly quadrupled within seven days, attracting more than 140 backers.

Not all open courses are informal in design, e.g. the AI Stanford course, however informal community activity can still occur around, within and outside formal MOOCs. Learners registered on the AI MOOC, and many who failed to or did not wish to register, set up Facebook groups (including in Thai and Spanish languages), Google groups and hangouts, a YouTube channel and Twitter feeds to support discussion and learning based on the MOOC content which was visible (The Rohan Aurora 2011). MOOCs and OOCs open the gate to the walled garden of education, but this form of open education does not require learners to enter that garden to access learning.

The openness continuum

As this chapter has emphasized, OER can be derived from a variety of sources and span types from component to course, encompassing both 'little' and 'big' OER (Weller 2010). Open resources can be blended with conventional 'closed' resources and used in closed designs for all types of learning activity, from individual, informal learning through to structured, massive teaching. Weller has talked about the value of 'little OER' made and shared as a result of individual initiative rather than in response to institutional push. This is an important distinction as participants in open learning typically have more choice and control to take initiative, including over the extent to which they engage with openness. The non-rivalrous nature of sharing of digital online resources allows many to access the same resource with fewer scale or supply constraints. The addition of open licences makes clear to potential users the limits, or lack of limits, to reuse. In combination these offer advantages not only in scaling up the use of educational resources, but also in facilitating changes in practice. The three examples explored in this chapter show how OER used openly can transform access, practice and course design.

Broadening the view from OER to the question: 'What are the implications to learning design of adopting open practices?', Conole and Pegler (Conole 2012) identified evidence of a continuum of open practice in use of OER addressing five facets of learning design – resources, activities, learning pathways, support and accreditation. Table 9.1 builds on this initial analysis.

Table 9.1 Examples and issues in design with OER

Learning design facets	Examples and issues
Resources	*Examples*: From big to little OER (Weller 2010) including multimedia resources directed at informal or non-formal learners (e.g. Khan Academy, iTunesU) and alternatives to conventional publishing outputs (e.g. open access journals and open textbooks). *Issues*: Sharing as OER has the potential to make previously private teaching practice public. Open resources provide opportunities to invite comment on work-in-progress (e.g. as in LORO and HUMBOX repositories) (OPAL 2010) and to showcase course content as marketing to attract students (Lane 2009). These two types of OER engagement present markedly different quality concerns, reinforcing the diversity of motives for sharing as well as using OER (Pegler 2012). Other concerns include responsibility for updating and for establishing confidence in sources (particularly when individual rather than institutional providers) (Pegler 2011).

Learning design facets	Examples and issues
Activities	*Examples:* These can range from conventional activity to innovative new approaches, or blends of these. *Issues:* There is greater opportunity for informed and motivated open learners to engage with what Cormier (2011) describes as rhizomatic learning (organic, without clear start or end and responding to context). Open education activity can be heavily structured, or emergent, with the choice of the technology used also open. However there are concerns about levels of interaction, retention and participation by many open learners, which can be far lower than those of registered students (Fini 2009; Lewin 2012). This may challenge the viability of some conventional approaches to learning activity.
Learning pathways	*Examples:* The OU's SocialLearn (sociallearn.open.ac.uk) allows learners and staff to share learning pathways informally while sites such as the Bussu language learning site (bussu.com) offer learning pathways based on an assessment of needs. *Issues:* Open education contributes to a 'pedagogy of abundance' (Weller 2011) so recommender systems and greater use of learning analytics are expected to grow in importance. Learners can otherwise 'drown' in the choice and waste time. The scaffolding that open learners need (given their diversity in motivation) may range from conventional (award-focused) to flexible and informal.
Support	*Examples:* Examples range from the serendipitous to the structured. Learner-led use of Facebook, Twitter and other social networks increasingly supports both conventional and open education. This can provide valuable culturally specific support in massive open courses (e.g. The Rohan Aurora 2011). However, formal open resources are valuable in supporting less confident students. Bridge to Success (b2s.aacc.edu) offers support based on OU access to study courses, to prepare to students to enter US community colleges (i.e. open education here aims at opening access to conventional education). *Issues:* The costs of providing formal support can be considerable. Providing this as an additional (paid for) aspect of open education on an opt-in basis is being explored. There is suggestion that without support open education principally benefits the already well resourced (Reich 2012).
Accreditation	*Examples:* OERu (OER University) is developing a scheme for formal low-cost accreditation for learners on open courses. Some open learning practitioners are also developing badges to note progress in a less formal, incremental fashion, to reward progress other than course completion. For example, the P2P University model offers skill and community engagement achievement badges (p2pu.org/badges/). *Issues:* Are standard forms of accreditation relevant? How important is assessment to open learners? If demonstration becomes an increasingly important assessment emphasis in the shift from knowledge acquisition to skills and competencies, how can this be effectively assessed in an open landscape? What assessment approaches are suitable for informal, non-formal and formal learners using the same content or studying the same course?

As this illustrates, for all five design facets there is a continuum of activity options possible. For example, in terms of open assessment both formal (institutionally accredited) and innovative non-formal (badging) schemes are evolving, with some overlap between the two. The new approaches to design that are emerging from open education illustrate that it is not only course economics that may be overturned by shifts to openness. There is a higher degree of choice and chance in open education for learners and educators. This presents an uncertain future and intriguing potential for learning designers.

References

Conole, G. (2012) 'Openness', *e4Innovation* blog, 27 March. Online. Available at http://e4innovation.com/?p=541 (accessed 31 July 2012).

Cormier, D. (2011) 'Rhizomatic Learning – Why we teach?', Dave's educational blog, 5 November. Online. Available at http://davecormier.com/edblog/2011/11/05/rhizomatic-learning-why-learn/.

dos Santos, A.I. (2012) *Open Educational Resources in Brazil: State-of-the-Art, Challenges and Prospects for Development and Innovation.* UNESCO. Online. Available at http://iite.unesco.org/publications/3214695/ (accessed 31 July 2012).

Downes, S. (2011) 'Open educational resources: a definition', Half an hour blog. Online. Available at http://halfanhour.blogspot.co.uk/2011/07/open-educational-resources-definition.html (accessed 15 August 2012).

Downes, S. (2008) 'Power and auto-subscribe forum discussion', *Connectivism and Connective Knowledge (CCK08)* MOOC forum. Online. Available at http://ltc.umanitoba.ca/moodle/mod/forum/discuss.php?d=1047 (accessed 31 July 2012).

Fini, A. (2009) 'The technological dimension of a massive open online course: the case of the CCK08 course tools', *The International Review of Research in Open and Distance Learning*, 10 (5). Online. Available http://www.irrodl.org/index.php/irrodl/article/view/643/1402 (accessed 31 July 2012).

Groom, J. (2012) 'Become a part of the first crowd-funded community-driven open online course on digital storytelling', Kickstarter fundraising website appeal 29 March http://www.kickstarter.com/projects/jimgroom/ds106-the-open-online-community-of-digital-storyte

Hilton, J., Wiley, D., Stein, J. and Johnson, A. (2010) 'The four R's of openness and ALMS analysis: frameworks for open educational resources', *Open Learning: The Journal of Open and Distance Learning*, 25 (1): 37–44.

IEEE (2002) *IEEE 1484.12.1–2002, Draft Standard for Learning Object Metadata,* 15 July, New York. Online. Available at http://ltsc.ieee.org/wg12/files/LOM_1484_12_1_v1_Final_Draft.pdf (accessed 31 July 2012).

Lane, A. (2009) *The institutional impact of OER*, paper presented at CETIS/OU OER Workshop, Milton Keynes. February 2009. Online. Available at http://www.slideshare.net/olnetchannel/the-institutional-impact-of-openlearn (accessed 31 July 2012).

Leslie, S. (2010) *The Open Educator as DJ – Towards a Practice of Educational Remix*, OLNET fellowship presentation podcast, 14 July, Milton Keynes. Online. Available at http://cloudworks.ac.uk/cloudscape/view/2140 (accessed 31 July 2012).

Lessig, L. (2008) *Remix: Making art and commerce thrive in the hybrid economy*, London: Bloomsbury Academic. Online. Available at http://www.bloomsburyacademic.com/view/Remix_9781849662505/book-ba–9781849662505.xml (accessed 31 July 2012).

Lewin, T. (2012) 'Instruction for masses knocks down campus walls', *New York Times*, 5 March. Online. Available at http://www.nytimes.com/2012/03/05/education/moocs-large-courses-open-to-all-topple-campus-walls.html?_r=2 (accessed 31 July 2012).

McGill, L., Beetham, H., Falconer, I. and Littlejohn, A. (2010) 'Business cases and benefits realisation', *OER Pilot Programme Synthesis and Evaluation Report*, August. Online. Available at http://www.caledonianacademy.net/spaces/oer/index.php?n=Main.BusinessCasesAndBenefitsRealisation (accessed 31 July 2012).

Masterman, L., and Wild, J. (2011) OER Impact Study: Research Report. Bristol, UK: JISC. Online. Available at: http://www.jisc.ac.uk/media/documents/programmes/elearning/oer/JISCOERImpactStudyResearchReportv1-0.pdf (accessed 31 July 2012).

MIT (2011) 'The next decade of open sharing: reaching one billion minds', MIT website. Online. Available at http://ocw.mit.edu/about/next-decade/initiatives/ (accessed 31 July 2012).

OPAL (2012) 'Open Educational Quality Initiative (OPAL) Progress Report: Public Part.' *Report from Open Educational Quality Initiative (OPAL)*, European Commission Education, Audiovisual & Culture Executive Agency, 12 Jan.

OPAL (2011) 'Beyond OER: Shifting focus to Open Educational Practices'. *Report from Open Educational Quality Initiative (OPAL)*. Online. Available at http://duepublico.uni-duisburg-essen.de/servlets/DerivateServlet/Derivate–25907/OPALReport2011-Beyond-OER.pdf (accessed 31 July 2012).

OPAL (2010) 'Deliverable 3.1: Scope of desk research and case study identification'. *Report from Open Educational Quality Initiative (OPAL)*, 16 April. Online. Available at http://www.slideshare.net/OPAL2010/opal-d3-v6-07052010 (accessed 31 July 2012).

Pegler, C. (2012) 'Herzberg, hygiene and the motivation to reuse: Towards a three-factor theory to explain motivation to share and use OER', *Journal of Interactive Multimedia in Education*, March. Online. Available at http://www-jime.open.ac.uk/jime/article/view/2012-04.

Pegler, C. (2011) 'Reuse and repurposing of digital online learning resources in UK higher education, 2003–2010', unpublished thesis, The Open University.

Reich, J. (2011) 'Open educational resources expand educational inequalities', *Educational Technology Debates*, December. Harvard University. Online. Available at https://edutechdebate.org/oer-and-digital-divide/open-educational-resources-expand-educational-inequalities/ (accessed 31 July 2012).

Rheingold, H. (2011) *George Siemens on Massive Open Online Courses (MOOCs)*, video interview, 5 May. Online. Available at http://www.youtube.com/watch?v=VMfipxhT_Co&feature=related (accessed 31 July 2012).

Siemens, G. (2011) 'Stanford AI MOOC: let's try transparency', *eLearnspace* blog, 9 Sept. Online. Available at http://www.elearnspace.org/blog/2011/09/09/stanford-ai-mooc-lets-try-transparency/ (accessed 31 July 2012).

The Rohan Aurora (2011) 'Top 10 study groups and resources for Stanford's open class on AI', *The Rohan Aurora* blog. Online. Available at http://therohanaurora.com/stanford-ai-open-class-resources/ (accessed 31 July 2012).

UNESCO (2012) *Education for All*, UNESCO. Online. Available at <http://www.unesco.org/new/en/education/themes/leading-the-international-agenda/education-for-all/> (accessed 31 July 2012).

Vest, C.M. (2001) 'MIT to make nearly all course materials available free on the World Wide Web', *MIT News*, 4 April. Online. Available at http://web.mit.edu/newsoffice/2001/ocw.html (accessed 31 July 2012).

Weller, M. (2010). Big and little OER. In: OpenED2010: Seventh Annual Open Education Conference, 2–4 November 2010, Barcelona, Spain.

Weller, M.J. (2011) *The Digital Scholar: How technology is transforming scholarly practice*, London: Bloomsbury Academic.

White, D. and Manson, M. (2011) *The Value of Reuse in Higher Education*, JISC. Online. Available at http://www.jisc.ac.uk/media/documents/programmes/elearning/oer/ OERTheValueOfReuseInHigherEducation.pdf (accessed 31 July 2012).

Wiley, D.A. (2005), Teacher as DL, blog post in Iterating towards openness, 28 December http://opencontent.org/blog/archives/227.

Wiley, D. (2006) 'Open source, openness, and higher education', *Innovate Journal of Online Education*, 3 (1). Online. Available at http://contentdm.lib.byu.edu/cdm/ singleitem/collection/IR/id/164 (accessed 31 July 2012).

Wiley, D.A. and Downes, S. (2009) *Wiley Downes Dialogue*. Discussion prior to Open Ed 2009 Conference, Vancouver. Online. Available at http://sites.wiki.ubc.ca/opened09/ index.php/Wiley_Downes_Dialogue (accessed 31 July 2012).

Witthaus, G. (2012) 'The OER university: from vision to reality', paper presented to OCWC/OER12 Cambridge 2012: Innovation and Impact – Openly Collaborating to Enhance Education, Cambridge, April 2012.

Young, J.R. (2011) 'In victory for open-education movement, Blackboard embraces sharing', *Chronicle for Higher Education*, 18 October. Online. Available at http:// chronicle.com/blogs/wiredcampus/in-victory-for-open-education-movement-blackboard-embraces-sharing/33776 (accessed 15 August 2012).

Part II

Designing for Learning in Context

Part I explored the many templates and processes that help us to understand the concept and principles of designing for learning. In contrast to the rationalistic undertones that pervaded the first edition of *Rethinking Pedagogy*, we saw in Part I that designs are now understood to be created and mediated. The renaming of Part I from 'Models for learning' to 'Principles and practices of designing' recognizes this shift in our thinking. Masterman (Chapter 4) and Agostinho *et al.* (Chapter 7) showed that the ways in which designers use the tools and resources provided for them are as important as the tools themselves. Designs are not created or used in isolation but are created and mediated by groups of people, working within the wider context of their course, department, institution and discipline. We now recognize the role of the context in which people make design choices and decisions, rather than emphasizing the choices *per se*.

If we accept that context is a determining factor in the application of technology in education, the challenge in Part II is to examine how designing for learning occurs in different contexts and what these fields contribute to our understanding of the design processes. In Part II we have allowed, even encouraged, the authors to use their experiences of working with practitioners to challenge our existing approaches to design for learning. These chapters ask: What influences the design process as it occurs? How might designs need to be contextualized for different disciplines? How are designs for learning activities incorporated into course designs?

Sharpe and Oliver (Chapter 10) begin our journey into the contexts in which design for learning takes place by examining the course or programme of study and specifically the role of the course team in the design process. They reveal the complexity and sensitivity of the course design process in practice, finding that designing for technology-rich courses is in practice rarely theoretically informed, more often pragmatic and iterative. They foreground the role of the team in this process and conclude that course teams are an important locus for professional development.

The next three chapters explore design processes within the broad discipline areas of: the arts (Harding and Ingraham, Chapter 11), the professions (Ellaway, Chapter 12) and the social sciences (Jones, Chapter 13). Each of these takes a slightly different approach. Harding and Ingraham remind us that design is a creative process and, as such, has much to learn from the creative subjects taught in our universities. Ellaway uses examples to illustrate the need for designs to be relevant and appropriate to the overall aims of the learning situation and, crucially, to our understanding of how students learn within that discipline. Jones takes this further, explaining that learning in the social sciences is understood as occurring through communication and dialogue, and looks at the infrastructures for technology-mediated learning which can support such ways of learning.

Winn and Lockwood (Chapter 14) expand our notion of context one step further, beyond course or discipline to institutional strategy, explaining how designing for learning can be shaped by the teaching and learning philosophy of the institution in which it takes place. In the case studies explored in this chapter, in an institution that is attempting to radically reconceive the role of the student, designers are encouraged to engage their students as important actors in the teaching and learning process. Such radical pedagogy is not commonly found, indeed it was this frustration with the lack of innovation potentially made possible by the availability of institutional virtual learning environments, which led James Dalziel (Chapter 15) to create a community for designers who were using the Learning Activity Management System (LAMS).

The LAMS community created six years ago is still active and is fundamentally different from other online repositories that might superficially look similar. This is an important point which brings together much of what we shall see in the chapters in Part II. Designing is an active process undertaken by real people in real contexts. Improvements to learning designs, which fundamentally influence the environments in which our students learn and experience learning, will not come from the existence of an innovative design *per se*. They will come from the sharing and adapting of designs by practitioners working within course teams, who share a language with which they can discuss the suitability of different designs for their local and wider context. Communities such as the LAMS community will have an important role to play in the future as places where designers can come together to share their ideas and respond quickly to rapidly changing technological environments.

The final two chapters show why communities such as LAMS will become increasingly important. In Chapter 16, Kukulska-Hulme and Traxler take a step back from the furious pace at which their work in supporting mobile learning has progressed, to reflect on what designers working in this field need now. In mobile learning, the pace of change has been determined by technological developments – not pedagogical or, even worse, institutional change timescales. This provides a fascinating case of the distinctiveness of designing for learning in technology-rich environments. Perhaps it is also harbinger of which we should take note. Kukulska-Hulme and Traxler propose that what educators need most now are design principles that they can turn to as they are faced with designing for learners living, working and studying in a technologically rich world. Indeed, if we look back, other chapters have also noted the benefits of having simple principles that can be applied by practitioners (Sharpe and Oliver, Chapter 10; Ellaway, Chapter 12).

What the discussion of mobile learning shows is that it is not going to be possible to predict how technologies are going to develop in the future. Rather than guess what the future might hold, the final chapter takes a futures approach, exploring a variety of possible futures that have been generated by many of this book's contributors. If we cannot design for an unknown future, how else can we prepare ourselves for the challenges to come? Part II shows that we will need design principles (Chapters 12 and 16), teams in which to discuss them (Chapter 10), whose members have an understanding of how students learn within their class (Chapters 11, 12, 13, 14), and communities in which to share and adapt the designs which result (Chapter 15).

Designing for Learning in Course Teams

Rhona Sharpe and Martin Oliver

EDITORS' INTRODUCTION

This chapter begins our exploration of design as a highly contextualized process by examining the role of the course and the course team in designing for learning. The authors argue that understanding how course design occurs is crucial to our being able to apply the principles and use the tools that were presented in Part I. They show that although educational rationales and design tools are available, the reality of making the designs real within a course is a complex process. As well as describing what is known about how course teams operate, they draw on evaluations of staff development interventions to offer advice for supporting staff through the process of designing for technology-enhanced courses.

Background

In 2006 we conducted a review of blended e-learning for the Higher Education Academy (Sharpe *et al.* 2006a). This review of over 300 studies of blended learning aimed to reveal evidence of the impact of blended learning on the student experience. We used a best evidence synthesis to identify key papers and conducted seven visits to institutions with reputations as long-standing implementers of blended learning. The visits enabled us to conduct interviews and provided us with access to unpublished literature and revealed practices that we could not know about as 'outsiders'. One of the main recommendations arising from this review was that an institutional focus on blended learning could be used as a driver for transformative course redesign. Transformative course redesign is important because when there is a concerted effort to redesign the curriculum, rather than bolt on a technology-mediated activity, such innovations are more likely to be pedagogically appropriate, innovative and sustained (Twigg 2005). Today, in these uncertain times, where funding models and technological developments are in flux, the ability to generate and embed radical pedagogies, with their innovative course designs, is going to be crucial for universities.

In this chapter, six years on from the blended learning review, we consider how attempts to transform the curriculum through the use of technology have progressed and what we have discovered about how to support practitioners through the process. We come from two starting points. First, as educational developers, we bring our knowledge of the literature and practice on curriculum design from beyond the field of e-learning. Our second starting point is that curriculum design is not unproblematic. Chiming with Beetham's commentary on the design of learning activities in Chapter 2, we have found that it is important to understand the practice of design – the design activity itself. Studies of routine curriculum design practice reveal the complexity and sensitivity of this process. Millen (1997), for example, demonstrated how the negotiation of content – such as which readings to put on the reading list – was an important way for academics to express their own professional identity in relation to the 'canon', contested or otherwise, that defined their field of study. Those engaged in course design have to deal not only with their own professional identity, but also with their role as sitting between institutional objectives (e.g. for blended or e-learning or for graduate attributes) and the student experience.

Approaches to course design

We start by examining three approaches to course design: rational – the approach most often recommended to new lecturers; theoretical – a common refrain of learning technologists to put the 'pedagogy before the technology', and indeed our starting point for *Rethinking Pedagogy*; and pragmatic – the approach which was seen most often in our 2006 review of blended e-learning. The following section explores how these approaches have been used, and assesses their suitability for course teams designing for e-learning.

Rational approaches

The most approaches to course design that are offered as guidance to practitioners frequently focus on rational planning. They outline a logical sequence starting with writing aims and learning outcomes and going on to identifying and sequencing topics, selecting teaching methods and resources, planning assessments and finally, evaluating the design (e.g. Turner 2002; Ramsden 2003; Stefani 2009). As discussed in Chapter 2, the learning outcomes are often given as the starting point, as they can be used to:

- define students' knowledge, understanding, intellectual and subject-specific skills at each level;
- clarify the purpose of the course;
- identify and prioritize which topics to teach, and in what depth;
- select appropriate teaching and learning strategies;
- and specify how students demonstrate their learning through purposeful assessment tasks.

Having specified these outcomes with sufficient clarity, the intention of these models is that practical decisions are then taken about how best to lead learners towards meeting these criteria. A rational model that has been hugely influential is the notion of the constructively aligned curriculum. John Biggs (1999) coined the term 'constructive alignment' to describe the way that effective teaching strategies deliberately align not just outcomes and assessment tasks but outcomes, *activities* and assessment tasks:

> The alignment in constructive alignment reflects the fact that the learning activity in the intended outcomes, expressed as a verb, needs to be activated in the teaching if the outcome is to be achieved and in the assessment task to verify that the outcome has indeed been achieved.
>
> Biggs and Tang 2007: 52

Biggs' exposition of curriculum alignment offers rational, technical tools for course designers, and its wide usage reflects the value of this approach for those who are new to formal curriculum design processes. One benefit has been that the principles of constructive alignment highlight the power of assessment to shape students' experiences – what Biggs (1999) describes as the 'backwash effect'. Although unanticipated outcomes frequently occur in learning – and ideally also receive feedback – it is considered essential that learners receive feedback on their performance in relation to the anticipated outcome. In compulsory education, ensuring assessment strategies are constructively aligned with the learning objectives has been described as 'feed forward', emphasizing the role of feedback through a process referred to as 'assessment for learning' (Black and William 1998).

However, the limitation of any such approach is the difficulty it has in representing the holistic experience of learners and the contexts and cultures in which they operate. For example, the discussion in Chapter 2 indicated that effective design should take into account the needs and preferences of individual learners, and of how they participate with others. Cousins (2012), in a thoughtful reflection on the influence of constructive alignment, commented on the need to recognize what goes on for learners beyond the planned curriculum:

> Not everything can be corralled into a web of consistency because so much happens at the subcultural level. Universities have formal and informal curriculum [sic] and we need to know more about how the two operate.
>
> Cousins 2012: 19

Oliver (2003) showed further that academics could simultaneously hold multiple notions of what the curriculum was. The simplest of these levels can be described as 'curriculum as syllabus'; this was nested within a more sophisticated notion of 'curriculum as map' (relating modules or other teaching events); and this in turn was located with a conception of the 'curriculum as plan for action', which was expressed in terms of ideas such as constructive alignment. Yet this was not the final layer. Even the planned curriculum was seen as contained within something else: a hidden curriculum, reflecting the values and politics surrounding teaching. This social context, which is so important in framing the curriculum, is rarely analysed in higher education, although it has been more extensively studied within schools. This context introduced issues such as approval by teaching committees (often seen as conservative), the difficulties of innovating on an inherited or co-taught course (especially for junior members of staff; this seemed particularly acutely felt by women), and the potential for 'treading on toes' when choosing what topics to include or exclude from a taught offering. Parallel to this 'nested' account was an alternative conception expressed by lecturers as 'curriculum as space' (or opportunity). Rather than something mechanical or plannable, this saw the curriculum as something performed; students were provided with opportunities ('spaces'), and the 'lived' curriculum emerged from the interactions of teachers and students as the course was enacted.

Oliver also found no academics used rational models of course planning during design, although some used them retrospectively to justify what they were doing, particularly if required to do so for a quality audit. The lack of rational planning and reconception of the curriculum uncovered by Oliver requires a different emphasis to be taken up when designing courses, highlighting the limits of design and the points at which professional artistry substitutes for mechanical analysis. It accords with the notion of providing people with what Feenberg (1999) calls 'room for maneuver'. Feenberg argues that all technologies and systems are 'underdetermined': in other words, they will be implemented and used in different ways, with the specificity of particular uses arising from the way in which groups with different interests have competed to influence processes of design and adoption. In the context of curricula, the creation of spaces provides opportunities for the formal specification of the curriculum as system to be renegotiated in the light of students' experiences.

Theoretically informed approaches

Another underpinning framework offered to designers is the recommendation to design a course around a theory of learning. If we are not clear how learning occurs, it will be very hard to design a course in a way that encourages students to learn. Theoretical models of learning, as discussed in Chapter 1, should provide useful frameworks for course designers.

Reviews from the UK and Australia confirm that the dominant model of learning influencing school and post-compulsory education is constructivism (Cullen et al. 2002; Eklund et al. 2003). A typical example is provided by Clark and James (2005) who present a rationale for their blended design based on principles of 'guided construction'. They describe the redesign of an introductory soil science module at the University of South Australia, where weekly online readings with question prompts were introduced instead of recommend readings from the course textbook. There were two lectures every week – the first was of a traditional type, at the end of which that week's course readings and questions were released. Students were expected to use the online discussion forum to work collaboratively on their answers before the second lecture, which was run in a question and answer format.

Situative learning is commonly used to underpin designs in professional and vocational education where courses aspire to develop the skills, attitudes and behaviours that will enable a learner to be judged as a competent practitioner by peers in the subject's profession (see Ellaway, Chapter 12). The professional skills might be quite specific to the discipline, for example, developing differential diagnosis in veterinarian science (Ellis *et al.* 2005), writing guidelines for users in computing (Oliver 2006), or negotiating and bargaining in world trade economics (Carr *et al.* 2004).

Designs can also be informed by models that have been developed specifically to understand how learning occurs in technological contexts. Laurillard (2002) identified 12 types of interactions that can be used to characterize learning. These take place within a Conversational Framework between teacher and student that involves description, adaptation, interaction and reflection. This would translate into the teacher attempting to describe some aspect of the subject and the student attempting to understand, the teacher setting a goal and both interacting and adjusting their actions and reflecting on them in the light of the feedback received.

Similarly, Siemens (2005) argued that learning theories need to reflect the technological developments of the time. In explaining his model of connectivism, Siemens proposed that learning derives from making connections, and that these connections are more important than the knowledge held by the individual. To Siemens, learning is 'a process of connecting specialized nodes or information sources' (p. 5). This has direct implications for the design of learning environments – although it also has radical consequences for ideas about what it means to be a learner. Since Siemens' account defines learning in terms of networks and connections, it makes little sense to try to assess learners in a generic way; learning becomes an effect of specific network configurations rather than a decontextualized property that a learner carries with them from setting to setting.

To what extent are learning theories used by course teams? Gordon *et al.* (2010), in a series of interviews planned to reveal lecturers' intentions for using technology, did find that staff were able to articulate the learning models that underpinned their e-learning design. However the 21 staff interviewed in this study had been on secondment to a Centre for Excellence in Teaching and Learning (CETL) and they noted how they had benefited from having time and technical support to develop their designs. This group may not be typical of most staff working on course redesigns. More realistically, our original blended e-learning review identified a number of studies where specific pedagogical principles had been identified as drivers for course design. These included being sensitive to the needs of learners as individuals (Graff 2003), active learning (Hinterberger *et al.* 2004), repetition and elaboration (Boyle *et al.* 2003), the requirement for prompt and frequent feedback (Morris and Walker 2006), or design principles relating to course outcomes (e.g. 'attention to detail') (Stubbs *et al.* 2006). Similarly, Masterman (Chapter 4) found that although lecturers refer to theory that influenced them, it does not lead a design, rather informs their own personal teaching principles. It seems that although courses may not be designed completely around a single learning theory, some aspects of theoretical models can be useful in informing design decisions.

Pragmatic approaches

Back in 2006 we found that the approach most commonly used to underpin the design of technology-enhanced courses was not rational or theoretical but pragmatic. We found that practitioners were often able to be explicit about the rationales for incorporating technology into their course redesigns where their rationales were prompted by practical challenges they faced in their teaching. At this time, the challenges involved teaching large groups and we highlighted a range of blended course designs that had been generated to tackle problems created by large group sizes. These included developing learning objects for difficult topics (Boyle *et al.* 2003), offering extension activities for some students (Oliver 2006), creating additional opportunities for feedback (Catley 2004), preparing students for practical work (Davies *et al.* 2005), promoting interactivity in class (Boyle and Nicol 2003), and creating opportunities for dialogue in smaller groups (Condron 2001).

The lecturers in both Masterman's (Chapter 4) and Gordon *et al.*'s (2010) interviews also talked about such practical 'logistical' concerns, although Gordon *et al.* thought that these masked more complex motivations. They found that rationales for e-lectures, initially expressed as coping with very large class sizes (around 700 students), actually were informed by notions of learner autonomy:

> This included the notion of the students being able to access this learning at times and places convenient to them. The designs described by them also included additional resources within the e-lecture for students to use according to their own perceived needs. The lecturers planned that the students would be able to repeat the lecture as often as required, to download the lecture as a handout if desired and to give the students some control over the time, place and pace of learning.
>
> Gordon *et al.* 2010: 540

Course redesign in practice may also be a pragmatic response to an institutional initiative. In two papers from Oxford Brookes University we have explained how teams have come together in a supported staff development setting to decide what changes to make to their courses in response to various institutional change agendas over a period of almost ten years, starting with blended learning and including assessment, internationalization and graduate attributes (Sharpe *et al.* 2006b; Dempster *et al.* 2012).

More broadly still, Comrie (2011) argues that drivers for programme redesign come 'from a changing economic and funding climate and a pedagogic driver to offer value to learner' (p. 251). Again, we see here the combination of the pedagogic and practical considerations uncovered by Gordon *et al.*

Supporting course design in practice

We have seen that rational approaches do not fully represent the reality of the course design process, which is likely to be a complex process, incorporating both the explicit and the hidden curriculum. Theoretical approaches are difficult to adopt in their entirety, although designers do find simple pedagogic principles useful, even when redesign might at first seem to be a pragmatic response to practical challenges. Transformative redesign of the curriculum may also be a valuable result of an institutional change agenda. With this better understanding of the actual approaches to course design in practice, the following section considers what support it is appropriate to offer those engaged with design projects.

Design principles

It may be that there is a middle way between the theoretical and practical approaches of providing design principles as scaffolds for course teams. A number of large-scale interventions are finding that broad design principles can be useful, provided that course teams are given the opportunity to develop, articulate and communicate them themselves. Such negotiation allows designers to take account of the context in which they operate. For example, the Oxford Brookes' Course Design Intensives (see Box 10.1) engage designers with Chickering and Gamson's seven principles of undergraduate education by thinking about the ways in which technology can be used to advance the seven principles (see Chickering and Ehrmann 1996). In an evaluation of the Course Design Intensives, which collated data from over five years of workshops with more than 200 participants, Dempster *et al.* (2012) found that participants valued the opportunity to re-examine their own pedagogy. This was facilitated by the facilitators' knowledge of models combined with opportunities to debate these principles. Some of the materials used in the Course Design Intensives are provided in Appendices 6, 7 and 8.

Other interventions are reporting similar findings. The Transforming and Enhancing the Student Experience through Pedagogy (TESEP) project led by Napier University promoted a social constructivist pedagogy based on the notion of 'learners in control'. The four TESEP teaching principles were shared widely and changes in teaching practices around them were negotiated by course teams

---

Box 10.1   The Course Redesign Intensive at Oxford Brookes University

Teams of staff undertaking projects identified as being strategically important are invited to come on the two-day Course Redesign Intensive experience. The two-day events allow the programme team to work on their redesign with additional support and resources on hand in the form of learning technologists, educational developers and other innovators. The aim is to bring additional development resources into the picture for a team in a concentrated way to get a quick result. By the end of the day teams will have designed the basic structure of a revised course, e.g. for delivery in the institutional virtual learning environment, and developed an action plan for development of the project.

The events recognize that e-learning courses do need high levels of planning. Course teams are taken through a guided planning process supported by such tools as fundamental decisions checklist (Appendix 6), prompts for blue skies thinking (Appendix 7), storyboarding, risk assessment, and culminating in a questioning consultation with critical friends (Appendix 8).

Dempster *et al.* 2012

---

and supported over an extended period (Smyth and Mainka 2009; Smyth 2007). At the University of Ulster, 'Viewpoints' workshops use a series of reflective tools to engage staff with general principles of assessment and feedback, information skills, learner engagement, and creativity and innovation (O'Donnell *et al.* 2012).

While such principles might be simplistic versions of learning theories, it is important that they are still based on what is known from the research literature about how students learn. Nicol (2007) reports that 'a key outcome of the REAP [Re-engineering Assessment Practices] project is the value of having robust formative assessment principles derived from the research when thinking about the design of assessment practices' (Nicol 2007: 677).

Iterative course design

The rational planning models of curriculum development tended to assume that a course is being designed from scratch. In reality it is exceptional for courses to be created without drawing on existing points of reference. Most course design work could be better described as redesign: updating, replacing, copying and adapting form the basis for most of the curriculum work academics describe themselves as doing (Oliver 2004). Courses are not usually planned and then implemented in discrete stages, but are designed iteratively over a number of years.

In 2006 we saw the importance of transformative course level designs as a way of characterizing blended e-learning. As many as three or four iterations of course design, development and implementation may be needed to complete the transition from traditional to blended e-learning course (Sharpe *et al.* 2006a).

Throughout the review, staff repeatedly identified engaging in course redesign as critical to their success. The valuable features of the course redesign were identified as:

- undertaking an analysis of the current course;
- collecting and making use of student feedback, undertaking the design as a team;
- designs which make explicit their underlying principles; and
- developing the course iteratively over a number of years.

The TESEP project similarly recognized that 'transformation often tended to be an "incremental" process rather than a "big bang approach"'. The 3E approach developed by TESEP engaged practitioners in a process of gradually changing their curricula to increase learner autonomy (Comrie 2011: 254).

Designing in teams

Design is increasingly being described as an activity that takes place with others. This may be seen as a way of providing opportunities for dialogue, which is a necessary element of professional learning (Falconer *et al.* 2007), or just for sharing ideas and building networks (Dempster *et al.* 2012). For others it is about bringing together different sources of expertise into an extended course team (Dempster *et al.* 2012; Armellini and Aiyegbayo 2010). Bringing together a team also encourages dedicated time to be set aside for the design work and for its validation as an acceptable academic activity (Aycock *et al.* 2002; Dempster *et al.* 2012). For Comrie (2011) collaborative course teams have extended between higher and further education institutions.

There have been recent calls for course teams to include students or, at the very least, to take into account the views and needs of students. There are a number of techniques to encourage course teams to view their designs from the student perspective, e.g. storyboarding. For example, the song 'Another tick in the box', produced by the Assessment Standards Knowledge Exchange from the words of students talking about their experiences of assessment, expresses the student experience in vivid, memorable ways (see http://www.brookes.ac.uk/aske/MultimediaResources/). However, Beetham's (2008) review of the Joint Information Systems Committee (JISC) Design for Learning Programme reports that, even where teams attempted to take learner needs and characteristics into account, they found it difficult in practice to design in a way that was genuinely learner-led (p. 23).

Although there has been much rhetoric about engaging students in curriculum design, a review of the literature conducted in 2008, shows how recent a development this is (Bovill *et al.* 2008). Bovill *et al.* found only three examples of students being proactively engaged in the course design process. This prompted them to go on and take a critical look at student involvement, looking at both the advantages and challenges. The outcomes of this review, which included focus groups with learners and teachers as well as desk research, were that although learners can gain clarity of expectations and awareness of learning process through observing course design, a move to co-creation of the curriculum is demanding of staff and students, and needs to be undertaken with care (Bovill *et al.* 2011). Some examples are starting to emerge of where such care is being taken to engage students as partners in the course design and delivery processes (Kay *et al.* 2010) and these are worth watching.

Design teams as a locus for professional development

It has become clear throughout this chapter that course design is not just about the specification of learning outcomes, activities and assessments, and the production of a final output such as a course description. Rather designing within the context of the course is a form of professional learning, as individuals engage with the issues, conventions, resources and practices of their institution and discipline. Through the activity of design, practitioners develop their knowledge through use, in much the same way as professional learning has been described in practice (Eraut 1994; Ellaway, Chapter 12). As professionals who are learning, practitioners draw on their prior experience and tacit knowledge in making design decisions. Seeing design as a professional learning activity helps to make recommendations about the kinds of support that would be usefully made available. Alongside the theories, models, tools and resources described in Part I of this volume, Falconer *et al.* (2007) recommend creating spaces for professional dialogue to take place. Interesting examples of this have been the creation of communities of inquiry to support practitioners through the design process (Garrison and Vaughan 2011; Vaughan 2010), for those using the Hybrid Learning Model (see http://cetl.ulster.ac.uk/elearning/hlm.php) and the Learning Activities Management System (Dalziel, Chapter 15).

As staff are increasingly busy, they are less likely to make time for formal development courses. However, this is a well-established pattern: studies of technology adoption in higher education inevitably identify 'time' as a barrier (Smith and Oliver 2000). Existing teaching and research commitments usually take priority over time for professional development, unless the course is perceived to be: relevant to well-recognized problems; practically oriented; valued by senior members of the organization; and preferably bearing some kind of recognition or certification. While staff can be directed to participate, coercion is likely to result merely in superficial engagement. A progressive response to this dilemma is provided by Armellini and Aiyegbayo (2010) who, in describing the Carpe Diem design programme, explain that it allows staff to 'seize two days' to engage in design activities. The two-day event is designed to address problems recognized by course teams, who work together with support from staff developers, learning technologists and others to develop and pilot possible solutions. The time released from other duties is taken as a mark of institutional commitment to the work.

Conclusions

Incorporating technology successfully requires the purpose of the course to be negotiated and made explicit, and involves consideration of the course contexts. This process of contextualization prompts reflection, negotiation and adaptation in what has traditionally been a private and tacit area of work. This important ongoing process of negotiation and renegotiation, as designs are shared and evolve, reveals why the 'one off' processes of rational course design have been so problematic, particularly if followed in a simple, formulaic manner.

As an alternative to traditional approaches to course design, we suggest that general design principles are a valuable scaffold, where they are derived from the research literature and combined with opportunities for staff to discuss them with colleagues. In such supported situations, teams that bring together colleagues with a mix of skills, in a protected time and space, will be able to make decisions about the role of technology in their courses, and embed them iteratively through changes over time. Supporting staff through the course redesign process will help them to respond to the changing challenges of their teaching situations and provide a local for their own professional development.

References

Armellini, A. and Aiyegbayo, O. (2010) 'Learning design and assessment with e-tivities', *British Journal of Educational Technology*, 41 (6): 922–35.

Aycock, A., Garnham, C. and Kaleta, R. (2002) 'Lessons learned from the hybrid course project', *Teaching with Technology Today*, 8. Online. Available at http://www.uwsa.edu/ttt/articles/garnham2.htm (accessed 25 August 2006).

Beetham, H. (2008) *Review of the Design for Learning programme phase 2* (June 2008). Bristol: JISC. Online. Available at http://www.jisc.ac.uk/whatwedo/programmes/elearningpedagogy/designlearn.aspx (accessed 8 July 2012).

Biggs, J. (1999) 'What the student does: teaching for enhanced learning', *Higher Education, Research and Development*, 18 (1): 57–75.

Biggs, J. and Tang, C. (2007) *Teaching for Quality Learning at University* (3rd edn), Buckingham: Society for Research into Higher Education and Open University Press.

Black, P. and William, D. (1998) *Inside the Black Box: Raising standards through classroom assessment*, London: King's College.

Bovill, C., Morss, K. and Bulley, C. (2008) *Curriculum design for the first year,* First Year Enhancement Theme Report, Glasgow: QAA (Scotland).

Bovill, C., Morss, K. and Bulley, C. (2011) 'Should students participate in curriculum design? Discussion arising from a first year curriculum design project and a literature review', *PRIME*, 3 (2): 17–25.

Boyle, J.T. and Nicol, D.J. (2003) 'Using classroom communication systems to support interaction and discussion in large class settings', *ALT-J, Research in Learning Technology*, 11 (3): 43–57.

Boyle, T., Bradley, C., Chalk, P., Jones, R. and Pickard, P. (2003) 'Using blended learning to improve student success rates in learning to program', *Journal of Educational Media*, 28 (2–3): 165–78.

Carr, T., Cox, G., Eden, A. and Hanslo, M. (2004) 'From peripheral to full participation in a blended trade bargaining situation', *British Journal of Educational Technology*, 35 (2): 197–211.

Catley, P. (2004) 'One lecturer's experience of blending e-learning with traditional teaching or how to improve retention and progression by engaging students', *Brookes eJournal of Learning and Teaching*, 1 (2). Online. Available at http://www.brookes. ac.uk/publications/bejlt/volume1issue2/academic/catley05_1.html! (accessed 25 August 2006).

Chickering, A. and Ehrmann, S.C. (1996) 'Implementing the Seven Principles: Technology as Lever', *AAHE Bulletin*, October: 3–6. Online. Available at <http:// www.tltgroup.org/programs/seven.html (accessed 8 July 2012).

Clark, I. and James, P. (2005) 'Blended learning: An approach to delivering science courses on-line', *UniServe Science Blended Learning Symposium Proceedings*. Online. Available at http://science.uniserve.edu.au/pubs/procs/wshop10/index.html (accessed 25 August 2006).

Comrie, A. (2011) 'Future models of higher education in Scotland: Can collaborative, technology-enhanced learning offer solutions?', *Campus-Wide Information Systems*, 28 (4): 250–7.

Condron, F. (2001) 'Using electronic resources to support dialogue in undergraduate small-group teaching: The Aster project', *ALT-J, Research in Learning Technology*, 9 (2): 39–46.

Cousins, G. (2012) 'Getting our students to engage: a review of two key contributions 10 years on', *Higher Education Research and Development*, 31 (1): 15–20.

Cullen, J., Hadjivassiliou, K., Hamilton, E., Kelleher, J., Sommerlad, E. and Stern, E. (2002) 'Review of current pedagogic research and practice in the fields of post-compulsory education and lifelong learning', Tavistock Institute, TLRP, ESRC. Online. Available at http://www.tlrp.org/pub/acadpub/Tavistockreport.pdf (accessed 30 March 2006).

Davies, A., Ramsay, J., Lindfield, H. and Couperthwaite, J. (2005) 'A blended approach to learning: added value and lessons learnt from students' use of computer-based materials for neurological analysis', *British Journal of Educational Technology*, 36 (5): 839–49.

Dempster, J., Benfield, G. and Francis, R. (2012) 'An academic development model for fostering innovation and sharing in curriculum design', *Innovations in Education and Teaching International*, 49 (2): 135–47.

Eklund, J., Kay, M. and Lynch, H. (2003) *E-learning: Emerging issues and key trends*, Australian National Training Authority.

Ellis, R.A., Marcus, G. and Taylor, R. (2005) 'Learning through inquiry: Student difficulties with online course-based material', *Journal of Computer Assisted Learning*, 21: 239–52.

Eraut, M. (1994) *Developing Professional Knowledge and Competence*, London: Falmer Press.

Falconer, I., Beetham, H., Oliver, R., Lockyer, L. and Littlejohn, A. (2007) *Mod4L Final Report: Representing learning designs*, Glasow: Glasgow Caledonian University.

Feenberg, A. (1999) *Questioning Technology*, London: Routledge.

Garrison, R. and Vaughan, N. (2011) *Blended Learning in Higher Education: Framework, Principles, and Guidelines* (2nd edn), Oxford: John Wiley and Sons.

Gordon, F., Booth, K. and Bywater, H. (2010) 'Developing an e-pedagogy for inter-professional learning: lecturers' thinking on curriculum design', *Journal of Interprofessional Care*, 24 (5): 536–48.

Graff, M. (2003) 'Individual differences in sense of classroom community in a blended learning environment', *Journal of Educational Media*, 28 (2–3): 203–10.

Hinterberger, H., Fässler, L. and Bauer-Messmer, B. (2004) 'From hybrid courses to blended learning: A case study', *ICNEE, 27–30 September 2004*, Neuchâtel, Switzerland.

Kay, J. Dunne, E. and Hutchinson, J. (2010) Rethinking the values of higher educa-tion – students as change agents? Quality Assurance Agency. Online. Available at http://www.qaa.ac.uk/Publications/InformationAndGuidance/Documents/Students ChangeAgents.pdf (accessed 8 July 2012).

Laurillard, D. (2002) *Rethinking University Teaching: A framework for the effective use of learning technologies* (2nd edn), London: Routledge.

Millen, J. (1997) 'Par for the course: designing course outlines and feminist freedoms', *Curriculum Studies*, 5 (1): 9–27.

Morris, L. and Walker, D. (2006) 'CAA sparks chemical reaction: Integrating CAA into a learning and teaching strategy', *Evaluation of the use of the virtual learning envi-ronment in higher education across Scotland*. QAA Scotland.

Nicol, D. (2007) 'Laying a foundation for lifelong learning: case studies of e-assessment in large 1st-year classes', *British Journal of Educational Technology*, 38 (4): 668–78.

O'Donnell, C., Galley, R. and Ross, V. (2012) 'The art of the designer: creating an effec-tive learning experience', paper presented at the Blended Learning Conference, University of Hertfordshire, June 2012.

Oliver, M. (2003) 'Curriculum design as acquired social practice: a case study', paper presented at the 84th Annual Meeting of the American Educational Research Association, Chicago, April 2003.

Oliver, M. (2004) 'Effective support for e-learning within institutions', unpublished project report, JISC practitioners research study project. Online. Available at http:// www.jisc.ac.uk/uploaded_documents/Effective%20support%20instit%20v2_ Martin_Oliver.doc (accessed 9 October 2006).

Oliver, R. (2006) 'Exploring a technology-facilitated solution to cater for advanced students in large undergraduate classes', *Journal of Computer Assisted Learning*, 22 (1): 1–12.

Ramsden, P. (2003) *Learning to Teach in Higher Education* (2nd edn), London: Routledge.

Sharpe, R., Benfield, G., Roberts, G. and Francis, R. (2006a) *The undergraduate experi-ence of blended e-learning: a review of UK literature and practice undertaken for the Higher Education Academy*. Online. Available at http://www.heacademy.ac.uk/4884. htm (accessed 9 October 2006).

Sharpe, R., Benfield, G. and Francis, R. (2006b) 'Implementing a university e-learning strategy: Levers for change within academic schools', *ALT-J, Research in Learning Technology*, 14 (2): 135–51.

Siemens, G. (2005) 'A learning theory for a digital age', *International Journal of Instructional Technology*, 2 (1). Online. Available at http://itdl.org/Journal/Jan_05/ article01.htm (accessed 15 July 2012).

Smith, J. and Oliver, M. (2000) 'Academic development: A framework for embedding learning technology', *International Journal of Academic Development*, 5 (2): 129–37.

Smyth, K. (2007) TESEP in Practice: The 3E Approach. Napier University. Online. Available at http://www2.napier.ac.uk/transform/TESEP_3E_Approach.pdf (accessed 8 July 2012).

Smyth, K. and Mainka, C. (2009) 'Embedding the TESEP 3E approach in the professional development of educators: a case study of the MSc blended and online education', in A. Comrie, J.T. Mayes, N. Mayes and K. Smyth (eds) *Learners in the Co-creation of Knowledge: Proceedings of the LICK 2008 Symposium*, Edinburgh: Napier University in association with TESEP.

Stefani, L. (2009) 'Planning teaching and learning: curriculum design and development', in H. Fry, S. Ketteridge and S. Marshall (eds) *A Handbook for Teaching and Learning in Higher Education* (3rd edn), London: Kogan Page.

Stubbs, M., Martin, I. and Endlar, L. (2006) 'The structuration of blended learning: Putting holistic design principles into practice', *British Journal of Educational Technology*, 37 (2): 163–75.

Turner, D. (2002) *Designing and Delivering Modules*, Oxford: Oxford Centre for Staff and Learning Development.

Twigg, C. (2005) 'Course redesign improves learning and reduces cost', *Policy Alert*, National Centre for Public Policy and Higher Education. Online. Available at http://www.highereducation.org/reports/pa_core/core.pdf (accessed 30 May 2005).

Vaughan, N. (2010) 'A blended community of inquiry approach: linking student engagement and course redesign', *The Internet and Higher Education*, 13: 60–5.

Chapter 11

The Art of Design

Derek Harding and Bruce Ingraham

EDITORS' INTRODUCTION

This chapter explores the impact of arts pedagogy on the process of designing for learning, not just for the arts but for all subject areas. Given that educational thinking is largely derived from social scientific perspectives, the authors ask whether approaches valued in the arts – especially criticism and aesthetics – can provide equally valid perspectives from which to examine the new media artefacts that are central to pedagogy in the digital age. They also open up the question of how design for learning, as a creative practice, can learn from other creative subjects that are taught in our universities and colleges.

Introduction

In this chapter we explore some of the ways in which the methodologies of the arts can be brought to bear on understanding the activity of designing learning opportunities in and for the contemporary electronically mediated world of education. In the course of this exploration we will highlight some examples of interesting practice drawn from the design of learning opportunities for the arts or of artistic practice in the design of learning opportunities for other disciplines. In speaking of the arts, we are referring to those disciplines covered in the UK by the following Higher Education Academy subject network centres: Art, Design and Media; English; History, Classics and Archaeology; Languages, Linguistics and Area Studies; PALATINE – Dance, Drama and Music; Philosophical and Religious Studies.

At the heart of our position lies the assumption that while education is often studied from the perspective of the social sciences, education is perhaps more art than science. From our perspective teachers may be said to reflect on their experience of their discipline and, like an artist, create (design) opportunities upon which students can (like a critic) reflect and by so doing further their understanding of the discipline. As such, the methods of both creating and interpreting aesthetic experiences are relevant to understanding how to design for learning not only for the arts, but for many disciplines.

In addressing the aesthetics of teaching and learning, we are not confining ourselves to a consideration of the practical tuition of the creative skills of such things as music, media, art composition or performance. Quite the contrary, while in some sense the act of artistic creation inspires our thinking, the focus here is more on the activity of interpreting and understanding the significance of aesthetic and other experiences. This activity is in arts pedagogy frequently embodied in a dialogic process that leads from one set of questions to another.

Still further we see these disciplines as lying along a spectrum from the more practical and skills-oriented (e.g. performing arts) to the, at times, explicitly scientific, like archaeology, which, as Foucault (1969) reminds us, provides perhaps the most paradigmatic model of the underlying process of semiosis that characterizes all knowing and consequently all learning. Ultimately this semiotic process, this activity of interpreting, provides the key to the discipline of the arts and it is this activity that we see as the key to the art of designing for learning.

Questions and artefacts

In the arts there are similarities in approach between disciplines but there are also important differences. A key similarity, which is pertinent here, is the artefactual critique which is a central activity in all arts disciplines. For this to occur two things are required – artefacts to interact with and strategies through which to critically engage with them. Contemporary technology provides previously unimaginable opportunities to deploy artefacts, which can then be used as the basis for activities for students to engage in.

These artefacts might be texts, images, voice recordings or moving images and might be available in a variety of formats. They might be part of the growing collections of digitized materials provided by the Joint Information Systems Committee (JISC), the Arts and Humanities Data Service or some other provider or, equally, they might be provided by the lecturer. The artefacts are intended to provide a stimulus for students to engage with in some way.

Although critical reflection on artefacts can take many forms, it is highly significant that the interaction between students, scholars and the artefacts of the discipline frequently takes the form of a dialogue, written or spoken, that leads from one set of questions to another. To some degree this reflects the difference between what Giddens (1984) described as mode 1 and mode 2 knowledge. Mode 1 emphasizes objectivity, rationality and universalism and the latter emphasizes contingency, application and contextualization. Interestingly, such a division was also reflected in the language chosen by discipline practitioners to describe key curriculum issues at a recent UK Higher Education Academy Symposium on e-Learning in Disciplines. In feedback from discussions arts practitioners used terms like 'critical thinking', 'reflection', 'evaluation', and 'contextualization' to describe key curriculum outcomes while representatives of maths and the natural sciences spoke of 'conceptualizing/modelling problems', 'developing/

extrapolating solutions', and 'testing and reflecting on solutions' (HEA 2006). In the context of the present discussion what we see is an emphasis on the process of thinking about a problem (of questioning) in the arts as compared with an emphasis on resolving problems, finding solutions (answers) in some other disciplines. It is this focus on the activity of questioning that is the key to the disciplines of the arts and, accordingly, to designing for learning in those disciplines.

In fine art the stimulus may be, for example, a painting, a photograph, a critique or a body of work, which students are required to respond to in some way. They may discuss the work's significance or explore a concept that it is intended to illustrate. This discussion might then inform further work. The stimulus will produce a response but not an 'answer'.

Classicists and philosophers might critically examine a set of texts (Kolb 1994) or be expressly concerned with conduct of philosophical discourse online as a subject for philosophical reflection (Carusi 2005) and, like languages, might have a concern with students being able to translate them. Languages was amongst the first of the disciplines of the arts to explore the potential of multimedia to enhance the process of acquiring essential language tools (see Box 11.1).

In the study of English or any other literature the focus lies on written texts and what they mean or say to different audiences. For example, in the field of English studies in the UK the work of the Duologue Project (Knights 2004) has attracted considerable attention in the area of supporting critically reflective dialogue online and Susana Sotillo (2006) reports on the use of instant messaging to provide another mechanism for freeing the dialogue from the geotemporal constraints of the classroom (see Box 11.2 for more examples from the Subject Centre for English).

The task of (re)presenting the complexity of such critically reflexive discourse has been of significant interest to the literary community; and from Landow's seminal work on hypertext (1992), and indeed earlier, many literary and other arts scholars have been interested in using hypertext as a mechanism for capturing the play of reflective discourse (e.g. Lee 1996 or Kolb 2000).

Recently, Taylor (2006) reports an experiment that links the process of discussion to the use of hypertext to help students construct and represent critical thinking in/on the history of art. In this case, the learners were in secondary rather than tertiary education, but the principle is readily transferable not only

Box 11.1 The CAMILLE Project

The CAMILLE Project was one of the first academically robust uses of fully featured multimedia to create a computer-mediated environment for learning (Levy 1997: 34–7). Initially a European project, CAMILLE continues at the Universitat Politècnica de Valencia.

CAMILLE (n.d.)

Box 11.2 The UK Subject Centre for English

The UK Subject Centre for English also provides a number of examples of projects and other resources using state of the art technology including a project led by Stuart Lee at Oxford using a tool called Media Stage (Lee, 2006; http://www.immersiveeducation.com/uk/MediaStage_Default.asp) to provide students with an opportunity to animate their interpretation of a theatrical text. Conversely, Salem (2005) reports on using the *commedia dell'arte* as a model for designing avatars to support collaborative learning. In both cases the students are being invited to reflect on a discipline through an aesthetic practice. In the first instance as directors, and in the second as performers.

---

from one level to another, but also across a range of disciplines. Using a tool called *Storyspace* students were provided with a mechanism for visualizing the complex of relationships that emerged in a critical reflection on a particular topic. Such representations can not only be used by students, but can also be appropriately and interesting used by scholars to represent reflective complexes (cf. Kolb 1994).

Taylor reminds us that the dialogic of learning is not limited to the student. She writes:

> According to Paulo Freire, 'Liberating education consists in acts of cognition, not transferrals of information. It is a learning situation in which the cognizable object (far from being the end of the cognitive act) intermediates the cognitive actors-teachers on the one hand and students on the other. Accordingly ... [t]he teacher is no longer merely the-one-who-teaches, but who is him or herself taught in dialogue with the students, who in turn while being taught also teach'.
>
> Freire 1994: 60–61 cited in Taylor 2006

Similarly in history the artefacts under study may take many forms in a variety of media from photographs to letters or public records. They might, for example, be a set of marriage records – they record the occupations of the bride and groom but also the witnesses – which the students might use to examine the occupational structure of a place. Just as with discussion this activity would be unlikely to produce answers but instead would produce a set of more detailed questions designed to guide further enquiry.

Clearly there are similarities between the pedagogies of arts disciplines that we can crudely model as follows:

- stimulus – the artefact or artefacts;
- activity – critical examination of the stimulus material usually with some question or questions in mind;
- outcome – greater understanding of the artefact/s.

The outcome however, would in practice contain a number of elements:

- evidence, i.e. observations; and
- conclusions – of two types:
  1 those which we can have some confidence about;
  2 the need for further examination.

What emerges from this process is in effect a new set of questions (see Box 11.3).

Although a similar model can be applied to each of the disciplines we are observing, the outcomes will reflect different concerns and the types of artefact will be different.

The active/act of interpretation

Understanding a work of art involves an active process during which the reader/viewer etc. interprets the semiotic structure of an object into a meaningful experience. In the arts, the term criticism is frequently used to describe the activity of reflecting on the process of interpreting the experience of reading a poem, seeing a play or whatever. At its best the role of the critic is to reflect on their experience of 'reading an object' and then to explain how and why they interpreted it as they did and, in so doing, perhaps provide some 'guidance' to help others understand their own experience of the artefact in question. This 'guidance' can and does reflect the theoretical infrastructure of the critic's discipline and can be highly contentious, or complicated, and forms the basis of much of the contemporary theoretical discourse in the arts and related disciplines. Consequently, thinking

---

Box 11.3 History example

Stimulus – marriage records for a particular place.

Activity – determining the occupations of those persons in the records. The question in mind here would be whether Eric Hobsbawm's (1991) assertion that half a million hand loom weavers were left to starve to death during the industrial revolution was accurate.

Outcome – the principal occupation turns out to be weaver and this is a period after Hobsbawm's.

Evidence – observations from the official records.

Conclusions:

Observation – There are more weavers than we should expect from Hobsbawm's claim since it seems to be the principal occupation.

Questions – Is this the case for other places? Is this the case for other periods? Can we say with confidence that Hobsbawm was inaccurate? What questions do we need to ask to have a greater degree of accuracy?

about the 'art of designing for learning' inevitably involves a consideration of such issues, but a thorough consideration of that range of issues lies well outside the scope of the present chapter.

However, we should note two things about our own perspective on this. First, the act of criticism does not apply only to works of art. It applies equally to the critically reflective evaluation of historical evidence, philosophical texts and, as we shall see, to the activity of understanding most things. Second, the critic's 'reading' of the art work/evidence is itself a document for interpretation. Indeed, at best, it is an independent work of art to be interpreted. Consequently any certainty about the meaning will tend to slip away in the 'semiotic drift' of interpretation and re-interpretation. However, this should not be understood as suggesting that meaning lies exclusively *in* the interpreter, or to deny the intrinsic substantiality of the objects *out there*. Rather this view represents an alternative to the traditional subjectivist/objectivist dichotomy that is usually understood as the key to Western European epistemology. There is, however, a third tradition that does not locate knowledge either in here or out there. In fact, it is not much interested in 'knowledge' at all. Rather it is interested in 'knowing'. That is, its locus of interest is in the interaction between in here and out there through which both become known and in the absence of which neither is known (has meaning). It is therefore the process/activity of knowing that is of interest rather than any putative learning or knowledge objects/commodities.

Although this emphasis on process rather than object has been a focus in much so-called post-modernist thinking, it should be seen not as something novel. It is part of a tradition that can be traced back in Western European thought to at least Plato. Plato's early dialogues (up to and including the *Phaedo*, *Symposium*, and *Phaedrus*) can easily be seen as dramatizations of the process of semiotic interpretation that lies at the core of post-modernism. Furthermore, the activity of dialogue and dialogics is, as we shall see in the next two sections, crucial to the pedagogical processes of the arts. Still further, while early post-modernism is an important element in this tradition, it is not the only recent element that is significant. Post-modernism has its roots in the arts, but there is also a cognate theoretical perspective that has its origins in the sciences. The American pragmatist John Dewey provides a particularly useful take on this. In three books, *Experience and Nature* (1926), *The Quest for Certainty* (1929), and *Art as Experience* (1934), Dewey articulates through the imagery of the scientific method the concept of epistemology as being concerned with knowing as a process. His position is significant because it lies at the root of the intellectual movement that eventually gives rise to the constructivist/constructionist perspectives that currently dominate much educational thinking.

Dewey argues that all knowing is allied to experimentation. We build up a theoretical model and test it against our experience and then refine the theory on the basis of the results, re-test the theory and so on, effectively ad infinitum, because we need to constantly test the accuracy of our models. Consequently, he argues that experimental science does not lead to knowledge of the objective world *out there*. Experimentalism is a process of knowing through which the knower forms a better understanding *in here* of what is *out there*. This applies across the whole spectrum of the activity of knowing for human beings. In day-to-day life we mostly do this without thinking about it. It is only when we are surprised by something that we bring this to consciousness. For example, if we encounter a *trompe l'oeil* or miss the last step, because the model of the world presented by our varifocals does not quite match the object out there, our knowledge of which is tested by a stumble. The stumble is a 'learning event'. It is the outcome of an experiment – putting our foot down expecting to find a step – from which we learn that our previous model was not entirely accurate.

What might this mean for the design of electronically mediated learning? From the perspective of the e-pedagogy researcher, it might mean that instead of collecting statistics, he or she might ask students to write reflective essays on their learning experiences and then reflect critically on those responses in order to inform design decisions. From the perspective of the e-pedagogy practitioner, it might mean designing resources, like some of those presented below, that are structured more like the subjects of the arts and that, accordingly, invite responses similar to such objects and are thus more susceptible to such analysis. This raises questions like: How do we design interactive events through which knowing will take place? How do we create environments that allow learners not to construct their own knowledge, but to engage in the activity of knowing (learning)?

As academics we do already have one good example of a technologically mediated environment for the creation of learning experiences and a reasonably robust methodology for their critical evaluation – books and book reviewing. Writing a book is a way of designing an interactive event through which learning takes place. The book is meaningless until someone reads it. Reading it is an interpretative activity during which learning takes place. In principle, as academics we know how to write books and we know people who can design them to facilitate their capacity to engender learning events. We also know how to critically evaluate them both through the peer evaluation that is part of the publication process and through the critical reviewing process that follows it.

This is less true for other contemporary media. In 'Scholarly Rhetoric in Digital Media' (2000) Ingraham addressed some of the issues about the kinds of expertise and literacies that may be needed by tutors and students if we are to use new technologies to create rich, technologically-mediated learning experiences. For example, we need better skills in the creation and interpretation of what in many respects are essentially televisual artefacts. There is an academic literature available from areas like media and cultural studies that can help us (see Levine and Scollon 2004). By acquiring these critical skills along with those that we already employ, we can perhaps begin to develop a methodology for what Papert (1987, 1990) called computer criticism. That is, we can move towards mechanisms for peer review and criticism akin to those through which academia monitors the quality of its printed publications. For example, *Vectors* is a relatively new academic journal publishing multimedia scholarship that can only be realized in an online format. Each of the articles in its first two issues represents a unique attempt to design the visual representation of scholarly discourse in ways that are self-evidently more aesthetic than scientific and to do so without undermining the scholarship or the learning opportunities created by engaging in such discourse.

One way of doing this may be to adopt critical strategies explicitly derived from the arts and apply them to new media learning artefacts. For example, in 'Ambulating with Megafauna' (2005) Ingraham undertook a narratological analysis of a televisually mediated learning opportunity, while Gouglas *et al.* (2006) report on using computer games to support the study of narratology. Similarly, we could apply such critical skills to the analysis of learning activities that we frequently seek to emulate in electronic environments. A lecture, for example, is self-evidently a theatrical performance. By better understanding what the performance elements contribute to the learning experience, we may be better able to create effective electronic analogues. Again, seminars involve a performance element and their effectiveness may owe more to the literary dialogics of Plato, Lucian or Bakhtin, than we normally take into account when considering the role of a moderator in an online discussion (Ingraham and Ingraham 2006).

In short, we need to critically review both what we are publishing and what we are proposing to publish in new media to our students if we are to build up a body of good practice. Such practice can itself be critically evaluated and so inform both our practice and that of our students in much the same way that our tacit knowledge of how to read and write academic books does. And, if we are not doing that, what are we doing? If we are not trying to use the technology to create something at least as good as books, why bother?

Interesting design

Throughout the chapter we have noted that a focus on creative activity is typical of the arts and that the methodologies (i.e. discussion) used to study the artefactual focus of these disciplines are to some degree themselves inspired by the methodologies employed in the creation of those artefacts. This remains true when we look at what constitutes, if not good design, at least interesting design in this field. Such design comes in a variety of guises which for convenience we can marshal into three types, the third of which may be seen as marking a transition between designing for the discipline and designing in the light of the discipline's artefactual foci. All three are valuable in their own way.

The first aspect of this is the overall design. What it looks like and how it works.

The second level of good design is adopting practices and ideas that have been tried and tested by others in the field and adapting them for local use. The work of the Teaching and Learning Technology Programme (TLTP) phase 3 funded Courseware for History Implementation Consortium (Chic) is a good example of adaptation for local use. A body of materials which had been created in the previous, TLTP phase 2, round of funding were used as core materials for use in other institutions and contexts. In each case they were adapted for local use and the results were evaluated with staff and students. Other initiatives have produced materials that can also be used or adapted in various ways such as the various rounds of the Fund for the Development of Teaching and Learning (FDTL), JISC and Academy initiatives from subject centres and the like. These provide a wealth of ideas that lecturers can draw upon to engage in good practice and there are people in the subject centres who are willing to help spread these ideas.

The third level of good design has, in a sense, already been mentioned in that there are those who add to the canon by exploring the cutting and some times precipitously bloody edge of the pedagogical envelope. Sometimes these risks do not produce the results we hoped for but we should still applaud them for trying. In some cases, quite spectacular results can arise which were not expected either. A case in point came about during the second stage of the Chic project (See Hall and Harding 2001) when Graham Rogers of Edge Hill College was asked 'If you could do anything you wanted online what would you do?' His response was something of a surprise and a challenge. He said, 'I would put my PhD online'. Once he had said it and those involved had thought it through, it made so much sense. Graham had access to all of the necessary materials, and the course could be designed around them in such a way that the students would follow the same steps that he did and consider the same evidence as he did, but without the struggle of finding the evidence. That would be readily available online.

Graham had little experience of the technology and did not have the skills to prepare the materials, but he did have the ideas and a sufficient understanding of his discipline to know which questions to ask. The project had access to skills and could fund materials production. This is how we add to the canon of e-learning. A good idea emerges at a time when the resources are available to make it happen. Graham's course was very successful and the students enjoyed doing it. It was also very cheap to produce, costing a few thousands of pounds for the data preparation and database design. Today it would be even easier and cheaper to do because the technology has moved on so far and has become more reliable.

Inconclusions

Clearly, it would be unreasonable to draw formal conclusions from the preceding discussion, but it is possible to make some observations and possibly point towards areas for further investigation. In this chapter we have observed that the disciplines of the arts tend to focus on the reflective analysis of artefacts/ evidence and that it now seems likely that most arts disciplines are going to become increasingly dependent on electronically mediated artefacts to stimulate the key reflective processes of learning. This means that tutors will need to reflect on how best to design the mechanisms through which the students are invited to engage with the evidentiary base of their discipline and record their reflections on it and we have suggested that aesthetic objects may provide valuable design models.

We have suggested that such design is occurring and is likely to occur on at least three levels – basic, adaptive, cutting edge. Of these, the first is currently the best understood, focusing as it does on issues of clarity and simplicity. The adaptive and the cutting edge involve more serious reflection on the capacity of the technology to support better (in the case of the adaptive) or novel and aesthetically provocative (in the case of the cutting edge) access to the evidence or mechanisms for reflecting upon that evidence or for (re)presenting those reflections.

To look at this from another perspective, the book and its derivatives have traditionally provided the primary technology for disseminating not only the evidence/artefacts upon which the discourse of the arts focuses, but also for capturing and (re)presenting that discourse. While this is likely to remain the case for the foreseeable future, it is also the case that as both the artefacts and discourse become increasingly electronically mediated in the ways we have been examining, the book is likely to become but one of many ways of mediating learning opportunities. In consequence, it is difficult to know at this stage what the primary mode of publication is likely to become and what the impact of that will be on how the discourse is conducted in the future.

Similarly, face-to-face dialogue has been and is likely to remain a key element in the conduct of the discourse of the arts. We have seen that new online models for the conduct of such interaction are emerging and these models blend into the new modes of publication. It is, again, difficult to predict what the hypermediated, asynchronous dialogics of the future may look like and how, if at all, they will relate to the traditional groves of Academe – except that, for the arts, the discourse, whatever its form, will always raise more questions than it answers.

References

CAMILLE (no date) *CAMILLE*, Online. Available at <http://www.upv.es/camille/> (accessed 24 August 2006).

Carusi, A. (2005) *Taking Philosophical Dialogue Online*. Online. Available at http://prs. heacademy.ac.uk/documents/articles/taking_philosophical_dialogue_online.html (accessed 7 June 2006).

Dewey, J. (1926) *Experience and Nature*, Chicago: Open Court Publishing Company.

Dewey, J. (1929) *The Quest for Certainty*, New York: Capricorn Books.

Dewey, J. (1934) *Art as Experience*, New York: Capricorn Books.

Freire, P. (1994 [1970]) *Pedagogy of the Oppressed*, New York: The Continuum Publishing Company.

Foucault, M. (1969) *The Archaeology of Knowledge*, London: Routledge.

Giddens, A. (1984) *The Constitution of Society*, Cambridge: Polity Press.

Gouglas, S., Sinclair, S., Ellefson, O. and Sharplin, S. (2006) 'Neverwinter Nights in Alberta: Conceptions of Narrativity through Fantasy Role-Playing Games in a Graduate Classroom', *Innovate*, 2(3). Online. Available at http://www.innovateonline. info/index.php?view=article&id=172 (accessed 7 June 2006).

Hall, R. and Harding, D. (eds) (2001) *Managing ICT in the Curriculum*, Middlesbrough: University of Teesside.

HEA (2006) *E-learning in the disciplines symposium*. Online. Available at http://www. heacademy.ac.uk/learningandteaching/ELDisciplinesCombinedReflections.doc (accessed 7 June 2006).

Hobsbawm, E.J. (1991) *The Age of Revolution 1789–1848*, London: Cardinal.

Ingraham, B. (2000) 'Scholarly rhetoric in digital media', *Journal of Interactive Media in Education*. Online. Available at http://www-jime.open.ac.uk/00/ingraham/ingraham-t.html (accessed 16 May 2003).

Ingraham, B. (2005) 'Ambulating with mega-fauna', in S. Bayne and R. Land (eds) *Education in Cyberspace*, London: Routledge.

Ingraham, B. and Ingraham, S. (2006) 'eQuality: a dialogue between quality and academia', *E-Learning*, 3 (1). Online. Available at http://www.wwwords.co.uk/ pdf/viewpdf.asp?j=elea&vol=3&issue=1&year=2006&article=11_Ingraham_ ELEA_3_1_web&id=62.254.64.17 (accessed 7 June 2006).

Kolb, D. (1994) *Socrates in the Labyrinth*, Eastgate Systems. Online. Available at http:// www.eastgate.com/catalog/Socrates.html (accessed 7 June 2006).

Kolb, D. (2000) 'Hypertext as Subversive', *Culture Machine*, 2, Online. Available at http://culturemachine.tees.ac.uk/frm_f1.htm (accessed 7 June 2006).

Knights, P. (2004) *The Duologue Project*. Online. Available at http://www.english. heacademy.ac.uk/duologue/ (accessed 7 June 2006).

Landow, G. (1992) *Hypertext: The convergence of contemporary critical theory and technology*, Baltimore: Johns Hopkins University Press.

Lee, S. (1996) *A Case Study: Teaching on the WWW Isaac Rosenberg's 'Break of Day in the Trenches'*, Online. Available at http://www.agocg.ac.uk/reports/mmedia/ rosenbrg/rose.pdf (accessed 7 June 2006).

Lee, S. (2006) *New Tools for Creative Interpretation: An investigative study using digital video and computer animation*. Online. Available at http://www.english.heacademy. ac.uk/explore/projects/archive/technology/tech16.php (accessed 7 June 2006).

Levine, P. and Scollon, R. (2004) *Discourse and Technology*, Washington, DC: Georgetown University Press.

Levy, M. (1997) *Computer-Assisted Language Learning*, Oxford: Clarendon Press.

Papert, S. (1987, 1990) 'Computer Criticism vs. Technocentric Thinking', published as 'M.I.T Media lab Epistemology and Learning Memo No. 1' (November 1990). Another version appeared in *Educational Researcher* (vol. 16, no. 1) January/February 1987.

Salem, B. (2005) 'Commedia virtuale: from theatre to avatars', *Digital Creativity*, 16 (3): 129–39.

Sotillo, S. (2006) 'Using Instant Messaging for Collaborative Learning: A Case Study', *Innovate*, 2 (3), Online. Available at http://www.innovateonline.info/index. php?view=article&id=170 (accessed 7 June 2006)

Taylor, P. (2006) 'Critical Thinking in and through Interactive Computer Hypertext and Art Education', *Innovate*, 2 (3), Online. Available at http://www.innovateonline.info/ index.php?view=article&id=41 (accessed 7 June 2006).

Chapter 12

Activity Designs for Professional Learning

Rachel Helen Ellaway

EDITORS' INTRODUCTION

In this chapter, design is examined within the context of designing for professional learning, where such learning is seen to be distinctive because it is concerned with practice, with application of knowledgem, and with skills development. Taking each of these in turn, Ellaway draws on existing conceptual frameworks and examples of technology-rich learning scenarios to show how design must be appropriate to the overall aims of the learning situation and to our understanding of how professionals learn and develop. For example, it is accepted that expert practice develops through a number of stages, hence design decisions must be appropriate to the stage of professional development at which the learning activity is targeted. Designs for learning in professional contexts must also prepare students for operating effectively within real-world situations, be concerned with the application of knowledge (rather than being limited to knowledge acquisition), and, at times, include opportunities for drill and practice that are necessary for skills development. In addition, professionals must learn to acquire the attitudes and understand the cultural norms of their professional community, and be able to work effectively within and across professional communities. This is a useful summary of the principles that underpin designing for learning in professional contexts. Ellaway observes that engaging in a design process can lead to real improvements such as the sequencing of learning activities to match learners' stage of development, or a closer alignment between simulation and real-world settings, which both contribute to development of practice. The challenge will be to formulate activity designs that truly represent, and can be used to analyse, the complexities of learning within the complex and dynamic situations developing professionals are presented with.

Professional education

The separation between professional education and the rest of the post-compulsory sector reflects both the social status of the professions (Eraut 1994) and their heterogeneity (Bines and Watson 1992). Professions are broadly defined by the responsibilities and privileges that set them apart from other occupations, usually in the form of power and privilege over others and the accountability for how that power is exercised. Professional education involves more than the simple acquisition of knowledge and skills; professionals are also socialized to become a member of a community of practice. Concepts of practice, expertise and competence are therefore central to the philosophy and conduct of professional education, as is developing the sense of accountability of the individual to their chosen profession and to society as a whole. Professional education is also defined by its relationship with a client base. For example, the primary beneficiaries of healthcare education are not students but patients. Other common characteristics include narrow post-qualification vectors, a predominant focus on workplace learning, external regulation and accreditation, and a fundamental dependence on practitioner educators.

While professional education often employs relatively generic designs for learning such as report writing or project work, these are reconstructed within the context of developing professional practice. For example, attendance and participation in even the most generic of designs – the lecture – is often framed in the context of professionalism; non-attendance or misbehaviour may be considered unprofessional and can have significant consequences. The development of practice informs all designs for learning in professional education.

Professional learners negotiate a professional development continuum that defines their progression from novice to expert (Dreyfus and Dreyfus 2005), each of which has different implications for design for learning:

1 *Novices* focus on acquiring the basic models and schemas that underpin professional practice with little exposure to the complexity of real-world practice. Designs for learning at this level are predominantly about presenting and learning the core schemas on which professional skills will be built. Learning here is largely based on knowledge acquisition using didactic or exploratory methods and simple but frequent testing of learners' developing knowledge.

2 *Advanced beginners* focus on applying and further developing the schemas they acquired as novices in structured contexts, often using various aspects of problem-based learning. Activities focus on predefined and simplified practice scenarios with low levels of risk and complexity and limited learner autonomy. Activities need to be rich in feedback on learner performance to ensure they build their schemas robustly and reliably.

3 *Competent practitioners* focus on acquiring and practising the application of their new skills, through being exposed to real-world practice situations – although still in carefully controlled settings – and being encouraged to identify connections between different aspects of their developing practice and the ways this may impact on their future clients, their colleagues and themselves.

4   *Proficient practitioners* focus on developing more advanced skills and a deeper conceptual understanding of their practice that allows for independent practice, self-correction and the ability to accommodate new knowledge and skills in their practice. Learning is increasingly reflective, focused on developing an increasingly mature practice model, and located within the context of practice.

5   *Experts* have moved significant components of their practice to preconscious processing allowing them to react intuitively, rapidly and consistently to complex problems. Despite these abilities, learning remains an essential part of maintaining expertise.

The value of design for professional learning is based, therefore, on its ability to support learners at different stages of their professional development. The need for adaptive designs for learning tied to a representation of the practice context is reflected in the widespread use of practicums (learning environments that approximate to aspects of real-world practice) and simulation (specific activities involving some kind of abstraction of real-world practice). The connection between these and other more specific designs for learning will be a recurring theme in this chapter, the overall aim of which is to provide an integrated approach to considering professional education as a coherent and discrete form of design for learning.

Activity Theory and design for learning

Design for learning is about defining and structuring learning activities (see Beetham, Chapter 2). Although there may seem little connection between designs such as lecturing and problem-based learning, the application of Activity Theory to the consideration of design for learning can provide a unifying set of concepts that identifies their connections, at least for professional education. The development of Activity Theory is fundamentally based on human activity systems as its primary unit of analysis. Engeström describes activities as consisting of subjects (learners) engaging in activities that have some object (or objective) that will achieve a desired outcome by using a range of tools (such as curricula) within a particular context (Engeström 1987) – see Figure 12.1.

Leont'ev (1977) considered three levels of granularity in activities: the activity as a whole (objectives); the specific ways in which the broad objectives are to be addressed (actions); and the stepwise processes that go to make up the actions (operations). Design for learning can be considered in a similar way; the design of what the learner does to negotiate the activity (operations such as click here, read this, discuss that); what the designed activity is supposed to do (actions such as learn this knowledge, develop that skill); and what the designed activity means (objectives such as satisfying accreditation or audit needs). The operations are essentially encoded into the tools and technologies used, actions are constructed around these operations and the goals consider the outcomes and what they mean in the broader educational programme context. These can be combined in a single model that can be applied to technology-mediated learning activities (Ellaway and Davies 2011) – see Figure 12.2.

Different participants in the design for learning process are typically involved with different activity levels. For instance, instructional designers are largely involved with encoding activities through the design and production of learning

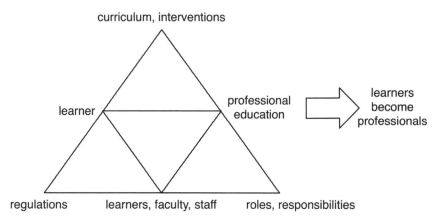

Figure 12.1 An activity model of professional education. A learner (subject) engages in a programme of study (object), in order to become a professional (outcome). In doing so they engage with tools and technologies such as curricula, lectures and libraries in the context of the regulations, other participants and the roles and responsibilities of all those involved in the programme

Source: after Engeström 1987

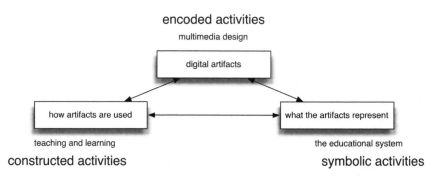

Figure 12.2 Three activity dimensions of design associated with an activity, in this case educational technologies

Source: after Ellaway and Davies 2011

artefacts, teachers are more concerned with the constructed interplay between learners and artefacts and the achievement of their immediate teaching objectives, and academic administrators are interested in meeting accreditation and other more symbolic requirements.

Activity systems: practicum and simulation

Activities exist as part of interwoven activity systems (Engeström 1993). A recurring challenge to professional educators is how to balance connections with real-world practice while minimizing the complexities and stressors of that practice to meet the needs of their learners. Each of the five stages of Dreyfus and Dreyfus' expertise model can be considered as an activity system in its own right as well as a part of a broader activity system. The unification of activities into activity systems allows us to better understand the educational or training environment and the activities within it. In the context of professional education, with its fundamental basis in real-world practice, activity systems are encapsulated in the twin concepts of practicum and simulation.

Although students may not fully engage as practitioners before qualification – typically for safety and liability reasons – they still need to experience and learn from situations that are appropriate to their level of training. Schön's conception of the practicum is 'a setting designed for the task of learning a practice. In a context that approximates a practice world, students learn ... by undertaking projects that simulate and simplify practice' (1987: 37). Although the practicum should 'usually fall short of real-world practice' and be 'relatively free of the pressures, distractions and risks of the real'. Professional education may start with somewhat abstract and simplified representations of practice, moving through increasingly complex models that are closer and closer approximations to the work of qualified professionals (Ellaway *et al.* 2009), again mirroring different stages in the development of expertise.

Simulation is also linked to real-world practice through aiming 'to replace or amplify real ... experiences with guided experiences, artificially contrived, that evoke or replicate substantial aspects of the real world in a fully interactive manner' (Gaba 2004). The use of simulation is well established for technical professions such as architecture, healthcare and the military, as well as less technical domains such as business and law. Forms of simulation range from practising simple manual tasks to dealing with complex multi-participant scenarios involving actors and a range of simulator technologies such as patient mannequins and flight simulators. Although simulation has been a part of professional education for centuries, developments in physical and computer engineering have expanded its use to become a part of the educational mainstream with immersive environments, robots, video games and virtual worlds increasingly employed for professional learning (Aldrich 2005; Quinn 2005).

Simulation and the practicum are essentially the same construct seen from different perspectives; simulation is concerned with activities, whereas the practicum represents and provides the environment for developing professional practice. It is perhaps important to note that simulation is not a single activity but a series of design patterns for designing specific activities. Simulation is therefore an activity method or an activity metadesign; a class of similar activity designs. Essential characteristics of the simulation metadesign include providing learner- rather than client-focused experiences, ensuring participant safety (particularly in otherwise dangerous situations such as mid-air emergencies or complex surgical procedures), providing meaningful and constructive feedback on learner performance, supporting repetitive practice, providing variation in the difficulty and focus of scenarios, enabling learners to try multiple strategies in controlled learning environments, and supporting defined outcomes and benchmarks (Issenberg *et al.* 2005).

Design for professional learning: knowledge

Developing knowledge is an essential part of professional education. However, professionals need to have more than the knowledge of their domain, they need to be able to apply their knowledge in practice. This is reflected in Miller's continuum from 'knowing what' to 'doing' (1990) and Eraut's assertion that the 'distinction between propositional knowledge which underpins or enables professional action and the practical know-how ... is inherent in the action itself and cannot be separated from it' (1994: 15).

While many designs for professional knowledge acquisition are shared with other domains in higher education (e.g. lectures, tutorials, independent study), problem-based learning (PBL) is perhaps most often applied to professional and vocational education (Savin-Baden and Wilkie 2007; van Berkel *et al.* 2010). PBL embeds the acquisition of knowledge in tasks that require learners to research, appraise and synthesize their developing knowledge in a simulated scenario. Although variations on the PBL design are used at different levels of professional development, the complexity and ambiguity of the problems encountered increase over time with the increasing expertise of those involved. For instance, typical problem-based learning activities used in the early years of training involve a group of eight or so learners working collaboratively with the problem introduced at the start of the week for group discussion. Learners then engage in research and asynchronous discussion during the week before coming together to present their solution to the problem at the end of the week. The pattern repeats the following week with a new problem and so on. PBL activities often require learners to take on different tasks, some doing research, some writing and others presenting the group's ideas. The division of labour (a key construct in Activity Theory) is clearly an essential part of design for learning. PBL designs shift to more individual and less structured challenges for more senior learners (such as for continuing professional development) or they merge into progressively more complex forms of simulation.

Knowledge is not just something to be acquired. The vast and ever-increasing amount of knowledge available to professionals means that knowing is no longer a matter of internalization, learners need to 'know how to know', particularly when knowledge is distributed across multiple sources. Designs for learning, such as PBL, also include significant aspects of finding, appraising and using knowledge resources such as research bibliographies and technical references.

Design for professional learning: skills

Professionals also need to develop the repertoire of skills and procedures that define their practice and, despite the unfashionable behaviorist aspects of 'drill and practice', much professional education still requires the acquisition of essential practical skills using repetitive practice. Basic skills are typically learned in relative isolation from each other (such as handling a scalpel or a dental drill) before being integrated in increasingly realistic simulation activities and eventually performed in real-world practice. Learners' competence in performing these skills must be tested at each stage and any problems identified and corrected before progressing to the next stage.

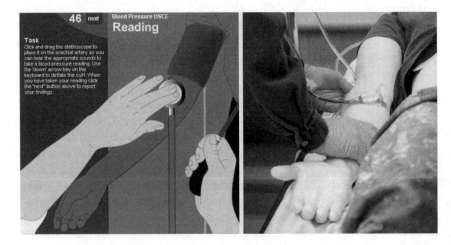

Figure 12.3 An onscreen simulation for learning the skills of measuring blood pressure (left) and a mannequin-based simulation where a learner is taking its pulse (right). The onscreen design is more abstract showing only the critical details required to undertake the task. The mannequin has more physical presence but is still abstract in the sense that it can only respond to learner interactions in certain predefined ways. While the activity in the onscreen simulation is entirely encoded into the simulator the activity around the mannequin is more emergent and dynamically constructed around the simulator

Fidelity and validity are common concepts used in considering different kinds of skills-based activities; fidelity in terms of the perceived relationship to practice, validity in terms of how consistently and efficiently the activity can support the development of the required skills. While validity is always required, fidelity is less important unless directly tied to validity. For instance, low fidelity simulators can, in the right circumstances, serve as well as more expensive and higher fidelity forms (Reznick 1993). Designs for learning skills need to follow the appropriate cognitive mapping between the simulated and real-world aspects of the skill to be valid and may combine psychomotor skills (see Figure 12.3) with reasoning and decision-making skills (see Box 12.1). Designs for learning for skill acquisition usually start with a brief overview of what the skill involves followed by the opportunity to practise the skill as often as is necessary to master it. All such designs are fundamentally dependent on good quality, regular and appropriate feedback to allow for correction and development through this repeated practice.

Design for professional learning: attitudes

Learners seeking to join a profession are required to do far more than learn about being a practitioner, they must adopt both their chosen profession's culture and ways of working (Lave and Wenger 1991). This socializing process involves the negotiation and acquisition of broader and often quite different forms of knowledge from those required in non-professional education contexts (Harter and Kirby 2004). For instance, Lincoln et al. (1997) identify interpersonal skills, standards of conduct and personal ethical competence as essential to learning a domain of practice in addition to technical competence. This is another area where design for learning takes on quite distinct professional characteristics.

Given the professional focus on the development of practice rather than knowledge alone, the portfolio-based designs for learning can act both as a developmental log and as a tracking mechanism to assure key outcomes and signifiers such as fitness to practise (Buckley et al. 2009). Indeed, while portfolios in science or humanities subjects are likely to be predominantly student owned and controlled, professional portfolios are more often directly integrated into teaching and assessment and involve higher levels of scrutiny and control. These activity structures can also be considered as designs for learning. Specific portfolio designs include logbooks and critical event analyses, personal and professional development planning, written case reports, progress tests, professional CVs, individual objectives and curriculum mapping, as well as more personal and formative diary entries. Portfolios can also be considered as learning meta-designs. While individual portfolio activities may involve making a reflective log or recording certain achievements or challenges, it is the longitudinal aggregate perspective of professional development and growth that is the portfolio's central design function.

Box 12.1 Virtual cases

Virtual Triage
Node: 14235

powered by
OpenLabyrinth

'*You are a medical student who has been involved in a traffic accident. Thankfully you are unhurt but there are three injured people around you. Examine each of them and then decide who you can help …*'

The previous statement is a typical starting point for a virtual case, an online simulation of a real-world situation. The learner is required to gather information, make decisions and take actions and then deal with the consequences of having done so. Virtual cases, although lacking the sensorial richness of embodied encounters, can support many different kinds of designs for learning such as critical decision making, exploring alternative strategies and metrics-based assessment, as well as providing triggers and resources for problem-based learning activities (Poulton *et al.* 2009). Virtual cases are also conceptually well aligned with Carroll's ideas of 'minimalist instruction' (1990) in that they allow for rapid engagement with meaningful tasks, while encouraging reasoning and improvisation, supporting error recognition and recovery and building upon prior learning using realistic situations.

Depending on the objectives of the activity, simple low-fidelity simulations (image- or text-based narrative hypermedia) can be as effective as high-fidelity 3D environments and very much easier to produce and sustain. The quality of the experience is less dependent on the fidelity of representation than it is on the emotional engagement arising from the challenges the activity presents.

Virtual cases are simulations with a strong design for learning component; the ways in which learners can work through the virtual case have to be designed, along with the encounters they face and the scenario as a whole, each component being structured to provide the appropriate learning experience to the task in hand. These three levels in a virtual case map to Leont'ev's activity levels; the scenario as a whole is the activity, the paths taken the actions and each challenge the operations. The virtual case is therefore an exemplar of Activity Theory entwined with design for learning.

Design for professional learning: teamwork and collaboration

Few if any professionals practice in isolation. The ability to work in teams is yet another essential aspect of professional education. Although designs for collaborative learning include some forms that have already been discussed (such as PBL), it is simulation that provides some of the most effective designs for learning in teams. For instance, the majority of health professional simulation is based on team-based scenarios where the task is to manage a critical incident as a team with the assumption that the participants have all of the component skills to meet the challenges but not necessarily the experience in applying their abilities in context and with others. These activities typically start with a short briefing that assigns roles and sets the scene for the task but otherwise gives few clues to what is about to happen. The scenario itself is then started, often involving an operator who can direct the progress of the scenario in reaction to what the participants do. Once the scenario has been completed both the team and the individuals within it are given debriefing (in role addressing practice issues) and feedback (out of role addressing learning issues).

Learners in these team-based activities may take on different roles, often outside their profession. Medical students in a resuscitation scenario may play the roles of triage nurse or respiratory therapist or these roles may be played by actors. Although there is a great interest in multiprofessional education (when students from different professions learn side by side) and interprofessional education (when students from different professions learn from and about each other) (CAIPE 1997), both introduce significant new challenges, not least of which are finding appropriate designs for learning for students from mixed curricula and divergent educational and professional cultures.

Discussion

These examples demonstrate how design for learning in professional education can be rich, nuanced and both convergent and divergent with design for learning in higher education as a whole. Despite the rich ecology of designs for learning, the use of design for learning as a conceptual tool and the more explicit use of learning designs in professional education remain somewhat limited, not least because of the technological associations of design for learning and the need to conduct much, if not most, of professional education in embodied rather than virtual spaces (Ellaway *et al.* 2008). Dalziel and Dalziel (2011) also identify the reluctance of educators in professional disciplines to accept generic learning design templates, preferring instead to use more abstract forms of design for learning that reflect their educational philosophies. However, there is increasing use of certain technology-mediated forms of design for learning in professional education, particularly around various kinds of scenario representation in simulation (see Figure 12.4).

Despite the relatively low profile of design for learning in professional education, there are many activity patterns in professional practice that can be used for structuring professional designs for learning. For instance, healthcare mnemonics can be used to structure learning designs: HEIDI (history, examination, investigations, diagnosis, and intervention in a patient consultation); ISBAR (introduction, situation, background, assessment and recommendation

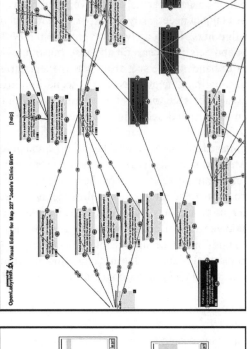

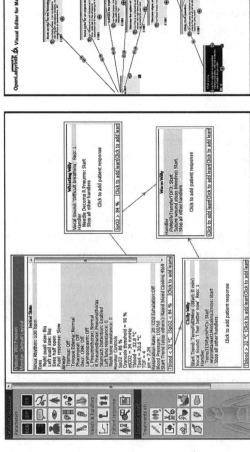

Figure 12.4 Sample scenario editor screens for the Laerdal SimMan mannequin (left) and the virtual case system OpenLabyrinth (right) illustrating some of the ways that design for learning is becoming more explicit in professional education. Both systems construct their scenarios from a series of branching interconnected nodes. The mannequin model models a great deal of complexity within the node (vital signs, trends and key interactions with the mannequin) with relatively simple branching to provide different outcomes. The virtual case model may place as much or greater emphasis on the topology of the decision paths taken by learners as on the content of any given node

in clinical communication); ABC (airway, breathing, and circulation in critical care); or OPQRST (onset, provocation, quality, region, severity, and time) for pain management. There are also professional designs for assessment, including key feature questions (KFQs – Farmer and Page 2005) and script concordance tests (SCTs – Fournier *et al.* 2008). The use of quality improvement tools, such as checklists and decision algorithms, can also be used as the basis for learning designs by creating activities that guide learners through narrative versions of the algorithms or test their ability to make the appropriate diagnoses and decisions.

The focus on embodied practice in professional education might be expected to lead to a lower uptake of technology-based designs for learning than in other educational domains. However, not only is there significant use of generic forms such as learning management systems and portfolios, there are also many domain- or discipline-specific forms being used, particularly various kinds of simulation. These designs for learning are increasingly blurring the transition into practice by bringing new technologies used in practice settings into the classroom. Indeed, it is arguable that the primacy of embodied practice tends to favour those technologies that align with real-world practice over those that diverge from it. This is reflected in the idea of 'economies of presence', essentially attaching more or less value to different kinds of presence, both physical and digital (Mitchell 2000). Designs for learning that provide the most appropriate forms and economies of presence also tend to be the ones that provide greater value in professional education.

Design for learning can also function as an integrating mechanism for different levels and forms of activities. The basic concept of IMS Learning Design is to sequence and connect different actions within an activity. Although tools such as the Learning Activity Management System (LAMS, see Dalziel, Chapter 15) provide the tools to realize these kinds of approaches, they generally treat each action (discuss, research, etc.) as a 'black box' that is independent of others in the activity. Simulation, on the other hand, needs to track the state of the emerging situation around which the activity revolves between and across multiple actions and in response to learner interactions. Examples of state-tracking may include a patient's vital signs or the balance sheet of a business or economic system. The ability to manage a global state model while connecting and integrating otherwise heterogeneous devices and activities is a significant challenge. Nevertheless, design for learning concepts can be used to integrate diverse learning technologies and techniques into single aggregate activities (Ellaway *et al.* 2010). By providing a form of semantic interoperability that simplifies the messaging between devices while tracking the progress of an activity with simple state-based rules, design for learning can be adapted to these complex and dynamic learning contexts.

As an example, a simulation activity may start with an online virtual patient action but at some key point – triggered by a learner, a teacher or a predefined rule – the focus can switch to a mannequin along with all of the simulated patient's vital signs. Subsequent actions may move the focus of the activity back and forth between different devices while referring to a common and dynamic state model. Although this work is largely experimental at the time of writing, it offers the possibility of creating seamlessly integrated and multimodal learning environments for professional education that depend on design for learning principles and therefore encourage educators to work more explicitly with design for learning tools and techniques.

Conclusions

The lens of design for learning offers much to professional education, both in terms of creating, evaluating and using specific activity designs and in considering the activity systems that constitute different activity domains. The key themes for design in professional learning are:

1   Although there is relatively little uptake and consideration of design for learning at a conceptual level, professional education is rich in domain-specific forms of design for learning.
2   Professional practice is intrinsically embodied and the progression towards such practice defines the values and culture of professional education as a whole.
3   Simulation and the practicum are two fundamental metadesigns in professional education. Simulation is about activities that approximate to practice whereas practicums are environments that approximate to practice.
4   Professional education involves more than academic learning or knowledge acquisition. Designs for professional learning also need to accommodate the socialization of the learner into a profession.

Design for learning can serve as a framework for research and development of new models for professional learning as well as for the critical appraisal and analysis of existing ones. By connecting design for learning concepts to Activity Theory we can generate a more comprehensive model of the activities used within professional education. It has been observed that research into professional e-learning regularly fails to adequately describe or even fully understand the intervention under consideration (Cook *et al.* 2008). Using the techniques and lenses of design for learning in professional education to model and report on activities in the context of research can significantly help to address these issues.

The general discourse in educational technology research has understandably tended to focus on generic approaches (Laurillard 2002; Jochems *et al.* 2004) while professional education has tended to develop its own discourses (Ellaway and Masters 2008). It remains a problem, resulting perhaps from professional education's inherent exclusivity, that what is normative within a professional education discipline is often unknown or misunderstood by those outside it. It is to be hoped therefore that the emerging design for learning discourse will facilitate better understanding of the nature and importance of profession-specific designs and facilitate a more aligned and proximal approach to e-learning across the professional education spectrum as a whole. By reifying these essential designs, design for learning would seem to offer substantial benefits to professional education, by making specific those designs and forms of learning that were otherwise tacit and unregarded by providing a common vocabulary and syntax to discuss and compare different forms of educational activity. There is great promise therefore – if at present largely unrealized – for learning design to increase the quality and quantity of scrutiny and review in professional educational practice. Furthermore, by binding design for learning with aspects of Activity Theory, the opportunities for innovative approaches to the research and development of professional education become all the more compelling.

References

Aldrich, C. (2005) *Learning by Doing*, San Francisco: Pfeiffer.

Bines, H. and Watson, D. (1992) *Developing Professional Education*, Milton Keynes: Open University Press.

Buckley, S., Coleman, J., Davison, I., Khan, K., Zamora, J., Malick, S., Morley, D., Pollard, D., Ashcroft, T., Popovic, C. and Sayers, J. (2009) 'The educational effects of portfolios on undergraduate student learning: a Best Evidence Medical Education (BEME) systematic review. BEME Guide No. 11', *Medical Teacher*, 31 (4): 282–98.

CAIPE (1997) 'Interprofessional education – a definition', *CAIPE Bulletin*, 13. Online. Available at http://www.caipe.org.uk/about–us/defining–ipe/ (accessed 13 March 2012).

Carroll, J. (1990) *The Nurnberg Funnel: Designing Minimalist Instruction for Practical Computer Skill*, Cambridge: MIT Press.

Cook, D., Levinson, A., Garside, S., Dupras, D., Erwin, P. and Montori, V. (2008) 'Internet–based learning in the health professions: a meta–analysis', *JAMA*, 300 (10): 1181–96.

Dalziel, J. and Dalziel, B. (2011) 'Adoption of Learning Designs in teacher training and medical education: Templates versus embedded content', *Proceedings of the 2011 International LAMS and Learning Design Conference*, Sydney, Australia. Available at http://lams2011sydney.lamsfoundation.org/docs/RP/Dalziel.pdf

Dreyfus, H. and Dreyfus, S. (2005) 'Peripheral vision: Expertise in real-world contexts', *Organization Studies*, 26 (5): 779–92.

Ellaway, R. and Davies, D. (2011) 'Design for learning: Deconstructing virtual patient activities', *Medical Teacher*, 33 (4): 303–10.

Ellaway, R. and Masters, K. (2008) 'AMEE Guide 32: e-learning in medical education Part 1: Learning, teaching and assessment', *Medical Teacher*, 30 (5): 455–73.

Ellaway, R., Dalziel, J. and Dalziel, B. (2008) 'Learning design in healthcare education', *Medical Teacher*, 30 (2): 180–4.

Ellaway, R., Kneebone, R., Lachapelle, K. and Topps, D. (2009) 'Connecting and combining simulation modalities for integrated teaching, learning and assessment', *Medical Teacher*, 31 (8): 725–31.

Ellaway, R., Cooperstock, J. and Spencer, B. (2010) 'Simulation integration for healthcare education, training and assessment', *Proceedings of Fifth International Conference on Digital Information Management (ICDIM)*, IEEE. Available at http://www.informatik.uni-trier.de/~ley/db/conf/icdim/icdim2010.html

Engeström, Y. (1987) *Learning by Expanding: An activity-theoretical approach to developmental research*, Helsinki: Orienta–Konsultit.

Engeström, Y. (1993) 'Developmental studies of work as a testbench of activity theory: Analysing the work of general practitioners', in S. Chaiklin and J. Lave (eds) *Understanding Practice: Perspectives on activity and context*, Cambridge: Cambridge University Press.

Eraut, M. (1994) *Developing Professional Knowledge and Competence*, London: Falmer Press.

Farmer, E. and Page, G. (2005) 'A practical guide to assessing clinical decision-making skills using the key features approach', *Medical Education*, 39 (12): 1188–94.

Fournier, J., Demeester, A. and Charlin, B. (2008) 'Script concordance tests: Guidelines for construction', *BMC Medical Informatics and Decision Making*, 8 (18). DOI:10.1186/1472–6947–8–18

Gaba, D. (2004) 'The future vision of simulation in health care', *Quality and Safety in Health Care*, 13: 2–10.

Harter, L. and Kirby, E. (2004) 'Socializing medical students in an era of managed care: the ideological significance of standardized and virtual patients', *Communication Studies*, 55 (1): 48–67.

Issenberg, S., McGaghie, W., Petrusa, E., Gordon, D. and Scalese, R. (2005) 'Features and uses of high-fidelity medical simulations that lead to effective learning: a BEME systematic review', *Medical Teacher*, 27 (2): 10–28.

Jochems, W., van Merriënboer, J. and Koper, R. (eds) (2004) *Integrated e-Learning: Implications for pedagogy, technology and organization*, London: Routledge Falmer.

Laurillard, D. (2002) *Rethinking University Teaching: A framework for the effective use of learning technologies* (2nd edn), London: Routledge.

Lave, J. and Wenger, E. (1991) *Situated Learning: Legitimate peripheral participation*, Cambridge: Cambridge University Press.

Leont'ev, A. (1977) 'Activity and Consciousness' *Philosophy in the USSR, Problems of Dialectical Materialism,* Progress Publishers. Online. Available at http://www.marxists.org/archive/leontev/works/1977/leon1977.htm (accessed 17 December 2011).

Lincoln, M., Carmody, D. and Maloney, D. (1997) 'Professional development of students and clinical educators', in L. McAllister, M. Lincoln, S. McLeod and D. Maloney (eds) *Facilitating Learning in Clinical Settings*, Cheltenham: Stanley Thornes.

Miller, G.E. (1990) 'The assessment of clinical skills/competence/performance', *Academic Medicine*, 65 (supplement): S63–7.

Mitchell, W.J. (2000) *e-topia: 'Urban Life, Jim – But Not As We Know It'*, Cambridge MA: MIT Press.

Poulton, T., Conradi, E., Kavia, S. and Round, J. (2009) 'The replacement of "paper" cases by interactive online virtual patients in problem–based learning (PBL)', *Medical Teacher*, 31 (8): 752–8.

Quinn, C. (2005) *Engaging Learning: Designing e–learning simulation games*, San Francisco: Pfeiffer.

Reznick, R. (1993) 'Teaching and testing technical skills', *American Journal of Surgery*, 165 (3): 358–61.

Savin-Baden, M. and Wilkie, K. (2007) *Problem–based Learning Online*, London: Routledge.

Schön, D. (1987) *Educating the Reflective Practitioner*, San Francisco: Jossey-Bass.

van Berkel, H., Scherpbier, A., Hillen, H. and van der Vleuten, C. (eds) (2010) *Lessons from Problem–based Learning*, Oxford: Oxford University Press.

Chapter 13

Designing for Practice
A View from Social Science

Christopher R. Jones

EDITORS' INTRODUCTION

This chapter is concerned with design for learning and approaches arising from the disciplinary context of the social sciences. It sets out from the identification of some core issues for design in the social sciences. It also examines the emergence of what has been called 'big data' and the use of networked devices and naturally occurring records in new kinds of research, including learner analytics. In accordance with the overall approach of the book, the chapter considers design at what the author describes as the meso level, clarifying that the focus is on activities within institutions and programmes and not on the macro level of global infrastructure, nor on the micro level of the detailed interactions of specific episodes of learning. The author takes an indirect view of design and examines key lessons from the social sciences that impact on the practice of design.

Design and the social sciences

The social sciences are a complex domain that includes a range of applied and pure sciences. The social sciences are diverse and the diversity between subjects is also found internally within subjects, especially with regard to the kinds of knowledge they are dealing with and traditions of teaching and learning. Because of the range of subjects included there is no single approach that could encompass design in this disciplinary area. However, it is possible to define the broad features of a design tradition derived from the social sciences. Key issues concerning design that arise out of the social sciences are communication and dialogue, the levels at which design for learning takes place and the indirect nature of the process of design.

Levels of design

Social science can contribute to an understanding of design in a learning context by identifying the ways design takes place. Design is undertaken at a variety of levels (see Beetham and Sharpe, Introduction). The design level this chapter focuses on is what I describe as the meso level (Jones *et al.* 2006a; Liljenström and Svedin 2005). That is, this chapter is not concerned with the global technological infrastructure or the design of national infrastructures including the design of broad learning environments. Nor is the chapter concerned with the immediate micro level day-to-day interactions in which and through which teaching and learning take place in locally situated conditions.

This chapter also proposes a more analytic use of the term 'meso level' to identify interactions in and with settings beyond the small group but which still retain a local focus that remains open to routine control and intervention. Meso also implies a time frame that is beyond the immediate interaction but which provides only a relative permanence and is not fixed for extended periods of time. Micro in this set of related concepts points to the contingent and highly local, whereas macro points to the level of interaction that has a general and relatively permanent character. Meso also points to *social practice* as the locus in which broader social processes are located and contingency is moderated by organization and planning (Schatzki 1996; Schatzki *et al.* 2001).

Infrastructures are located at both macro and meso levels in education. At a macro level 'universal service infrastructures' intended for all citizens (Hanseth and Lundberg 2001), such as search engines and social network sites, lie beyond the institution. Institutional infrastructures, such as learning lanagement systems (LMS), known in the UK as virtual learning environments (VLE), are examples of local meso level infrastructural elements. The LMS/VLE can be deployed according to local conditions and in some cases, for example the open source Moodle platform, designed for local conditions (Jones 2009). Infrastructures take the form of largely given elements for those involved in the day-to-day design process. The design of infrastructures for learning is not generally undertaken directly by the academic staff who are involved in the day-to-day running of courses and programmes. Infrastructure from this point of view is enacted in the micro interactions of day-to-day teaching practices and infrastructure can be conceived of as a process in which micro local and macro global factors combine. Infrastructures are factors that come into micro settings from outside and while they are enacted at a micro level, infrastructural elements cannot be designed or altered at this level alone. The use of an institutionally supported LMS is an example of this tension. The infrastructure implemented at one level comes into being when the LMS is locally deployed, but the design of the LMS and its selection are largely beyond the local and micro level context.

Guribye and Lindström provided the following definition of an infrastructure for learning:

An infrastructure for learning is a set of resources and arrangements – social, institutional, technical – that are designed to and/or assigned to support a learning practice.

Guribye and Lindström 2009: 105

Infrastructures for learning are commonly be designed by a variety of actors. Educational infrastructures are becoming intertwined with infrastructural elements that stand outside of educational institutions and which are neither designed for nor assigned to an educational purpose (Bolt *et al.* 2010). Increasingly design for learning needs to consider universal service infrastructures because they extend the range of contexts within which learning activity is intended to take place. Services such as Facebook, YouTube and iTunes are being integrated into educational institutions, and student learning practices, but they are significantly beyond institutional control. Universal services have institutional aspects such as the Open University (UK), which launched an iTunesU service in June 2008 (http://www.open.ac.uk/itunes/) and has made materials available via a YouTube channel (http://uk.youtube.com/theopenuniversity).

Indeterminacy: the indirect nature of design

The notion of design, as it is understood today, arose during the 14th and 15th centuries in Europe and implies the separation of thinking and doing:

> This is not to suggest for a moment that designing was a new activity. Rather it was separated out from a wider productive activity and recognized as an activity in its own right. Design can be said to constitute a separation of hand and brain, of manual and intellectual work, of the conceptual part of a work from the labour process.
>
> Cooley 1999: 59

Cooley goes on to suggest that the scientific method has influenced the characteristics that a process or design must display to be regarded as scientific: that design must be predictable, repeatable and quantifiable in mathematical terms. In contrast, ethnographic studies of the design process suggest a view that places design and designs as component parts of situated action (Suchman 2007). Design as situated action cannot have the characteristics that Cooley describes as the scientific method. From the perspective of situated action, design is an iterative process and the products of design are part of a deeply social and situated set of work practices (see also Sharpe and Oliver, Chapter 10). Design and the products of design – plans, representations, etc. – do not have a determining role, rather they form resources for action, available to inform the working practices of those involved in the design process.

The distinction between tasks and activities (see Beetham, Chapter 2) forms part of a broader design philosophy. Tasks are what designers set, they are prescriptions for the work the students are expected to do, while activity is what people actually do. Because students constitute their own learning context it should be expected that students' activity will often differ from the task that initiated it. The distinction between task and activity is mirrored by two further distinctions between space and place and between organization and community. Together these three distinctions are referred to as an indirect approach to learning and their relationships are shown in Figure 13.1.

As an example of this approach, Jones and Asensio (2001) examined a distance learning course and reported a post-assessment series of interviews within one tutorial group. The group had been divided up into sub-sets that had the task of preparing their final assessment in the form of a group project with an individually prepared component. Students interpreted their instructions in highly contingent ways that depended on the particular context in which each student found themselves. The responses to the set assessment task could be grouped into two broad understandings of the task, but they were affected by highly specific factors in each case (see Box 13.1). It is worth emphasizing that this course and assignment were well designed: the problems arose not from the design of the task itself but from factors affecting the students that were outside the course design process, and indeed in some cases outside of the learning environment. Similar cases have been reported more recently (see Box 13.2).

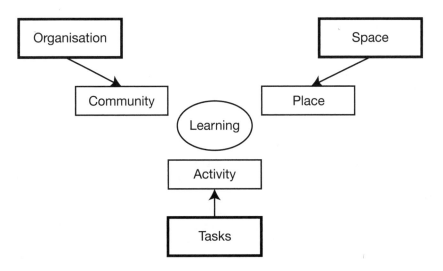

Figure 13.1 Design: an indirect approach

Source: Goodyear *et al.* 2001

Box 13.1   An example of two contrasting interpretations of instructions

(Interviewer in italics)
1   What did you conceive that task to be?
I would assume that it was more to continue the computer mediated conferencing as an exercise in itself for people to work together to sort of exchange ideas and irrespective of what the particular project was to work on. (Daniel)

2   What do you think the emphasis was?
Your personal individual, um your personal big 500 words or whatever
So the individual submission was ....
Was more important than the group work
And how about content and process if we split it that way?
Content
Rather than process ...
Rather than process and yet it's, I would argue the process probably took as much time as writing the content if not more (Lillian)

The two students were part of the same group working together to produce a joint report yet they had different understandings of the task they had been set. This was despite extensive documentary guidance provided in a 12-page assessment booklet. When prompted to re-read the booklet Daniel, who had identified the task as being to conduct group work, revised his view and conceded that content may indeed have been more important. There were two reasons offered by students in the group that shed light on why the group process dominated over the intention of the assessment criteria. First, the group process was novel and pervasive as they used the conferencing system throughout the course and were expected to work collaboratively using the system for two assessments. Second, the ability to communicate between students was a valued and novel element within the distance learning setting.

Source: Jones and Asensio 2001

The point being made here is that there is no simple way out of this design problem. There is no special kind of design that will make every student or even most students read instructions or any other kind of text in the same way. It points towards a social and iterative process of design in use that makes the artefacts and products of design only one part of the design process. In particular, it points to the need for good processes to take place during the enactment of a design to ensure its success. This is not simply an iterative approach to design because it suggests that a key point in the process takes place at the point of use, beyond the design process itself. In the case of assessment instructions, for example, checks can be made on students' understandings as the task is undertaken. It is suggested that the assumption should be made that design is not a once and for all activity of preparation but a process that is both iterative and includes the enactment of the design in use.

Box 13.2   Example of two students from the same course and university managing their environment in notably different ways

(Interviewer in italics)

B: I prefer to work in the lab because the software is there and everything's working. So it's easier for me that way.

Interviewer: And your choice was?

C: I kind of prefer to do it in my room because in the labs there's certain things you can't do and on your own computer you can. (Jones 2011: 110)

Both students were studying the same computing course and in the same interview the students contrasted their use of cut and paste for programming:

C: … I use quite a lot of online books because if I do code … if you have a book on paper you have to copy the code in, type it in yourself.

Interviewer: You have to retype it, yeah?

C: But then if you make like one mistake, if you like miss out a dot or something, it messes up and you can't understand why. But if they provide you with an example on the Internet and you copy and paste and then you know it works because it's exactly what they give you, if you know what I mean.

B: I prefer to do both. I like the books because it's something you can read. When I type it and if I get it wrong after a couple of attempts I'll just go to the website and copy the exact same code but I prefer to type it because it's like a learning process isn't it. (Jones 2011: 110)

Clearly these students, even when studying under the same general conditions, engaged in different practices which accorded with their particular approaches to learning. Source: Jones 2011

Design, communication and dialogue

A key area of design that has been influenced by social science approaches concerns issues of communication, collaboration and participation. The concern with communication and dialogue is perhaps the most characteristic concern of the social sciences as distinct from other subject areas.

Communication and dialogue have often been understood using the stronger terms cooperation and collaboration, which imply that activities are essentially social and depend fundamentally on the interactions between participants. The technological changes that enabled computer-mediated communication combined with social and situated views of learning to generate Computer Supported Collaborative Learning (CSCL) (Koschmann 1996; Stahl *et al.* 2006). The move to CSCL was related to, but not entirely the same as, a much longer tradition of cooperative or collaborative learning (Goodyear *et al.* 2012).

Social science research in pedagogy and new technology is closely related to the development of social and situated views of learning and the cultural turn in the social sciences (Engeström 1987; Hutchins 1995; Jameson 1998; Lave and Wenger 1991; Vygotsky 1986). The key feature of this re-orientation of the social sciences has been the central focus on social and cultural factors rather than the individual and psychology, or on the biological bases of learning. These factors had previously been heavily emphasized in behaviourist and cognitivist theories of learning. Compare Mayes and de Freitas (Chapter 1), or for a fuller discussion of this area see Jones *et al.* (2006b).

Many advocates of CSCL who hold a social or situated view of learning (for example, Stahl 2003) do not claim that it is a more efficient or a more effective learning process. Others, however, do see collaborative learning as superior to other forms of learning (see, for example, Johnson *et al.* 2000). For some writers, collaborative learning comes close to meaning 'learning' in general, as from a social or situated perspective *all* learning can be described as a social activity. Collaborative learning understood as social learning is not an approach that can be argued for; it is more like a descriptive enterprise setting out how people learn *in* and *through* social activity.

An alternative formulation to CSCL is networked learning, advocates of which argue that learning emerges from relational dialogue with online resources and others in learning networks or communities (McConnell *et al.* 2012, McConnell 2000). The networked learning conference series has been associated with the following definition of networked learning:

> learning in which information and communications technology (ICT) is used to promote connections: between one learner and other learners, between learners and tutors; between a learning community and its learning resources.
>
> Goodyear *et al.* 2004: 1

Networked learning has a close relationship to CSCL but it has some distinct features. It is less concerned with face-to-face collaboration around technology and is generally more concerned with remote interaction. It also tends to the large scale and is less concerned with small-scale collaboration such as in pairs and small groups. Networked learning also tends to focus on the use of generally available technologies rather than being concerned with the design and development of tools to support particular instances of cooperation and collaboration.

The key element of the definition of networked learning is the term *connections*. The notion of learning emphasized in this definition is a relational view in which learning takes place in relation to others and also in relation to an array of learning resources. Networked learning does not privilege any particular types of relationships between people or between people and resources and in this it differs from CSCL, which arose out of the reaction to cognitivist and individualist notions of learning (Koschmann 1996).

For CSCL the relationship between people is one of cooperation or collaboration, and though CSCL includes learning resources it does not draw particular attention to them. A danger that is present in CSCL is that the description of learning in terms of collaboration becomes a moral imperative, so that collaboration *ought* to be the way we learn. For these two reasons networked learning has been suggested as an alternative way of dealing with the concerns that gave rise to CSCL.

Networked learning sees cooperation and collaboration as special cases of the wider phenomenon of networks. The idea of networked learning has drawn on recent developments in network analysis and the tradition of social network analysis (De Laat and Lally 2004; De Laat *et al.* 2007; Haythornthwaite and De Laat 2010; Jones *et al.* 2006a; Jones 2004). From this perspective networks are composed of nodes and the ties or connections between them. Nodes can be individuals, or various kinds of social forms including organizations, communities and collectives (Dron and Anderson 2007). Nodes and the active agents in networks can be of different types, including non-human actors. Social network analysis has also been applied to CSCL and networked learning (Haythornthwaite and De Laat 2010; De Laat and Lally 2004; De Laat *et al.* 2007). From a social network perspective the research interest is in the nature of ties between participants and whether they are weak, strong or latent (Jones *et al.* 2009).

CSCL faces a potential challenge from web 2.0 because web 2.0 involves large-scale network effects and interaction in large groups (Dohn 2009; Kafai and Peppler 2011). Applications of web 2.0 in education include the collaborative use of blogs, wikis, virtual worlds and mobile social media (Dohn 2010). Although web 2.0 technologies blur the distinction between synchronous and asynchronous communications, web 2.0 remains primarily an asynchronous medium. This is because web 2.0 applications rely on scale for their efficacy. The architecture of participation at scale suggests that the value of a service increases with the number of users sharing the service. Design in web 2.0 may need to take place at the level of the social and technical infrastructures. Key issues for future work in relation to web 2.0 concern infrastructures and the levels between micro level interactions and macro level social and technical conditions (Jones *et al.* 2006a, Jones and Dirckinck-Holmfeld 2009).

Big data and learning analytics

Since the first edition of this book there have been significant developments in the social sciences and beyond captured by the term 'big data'. Big data, more properly known as data-intensive science, relies on the capture, curation and analysis of large collections of data. Data-intensive science opens up the possibility of detecting patterns in large data sets that would not be available without large-scale and widespread computing. In some opinions this leads to a 'fourth paradigm' (Hey *et al.* 2009) which questions the position of theory in scientific discovery (Anderson 2008). The fourth paradigm suggests a scientific development from empirical science, through a period of theoretical science to a recent rise in computational science. The fourth paradigm is claimed to be distinct because data is collected by instruments or generated from simulations, processed by software, stored in a computer and only at the latter stages of the process does it reach the scientist for analysis using data management and statistical techniques (Hey *et al.* 2009). This kind of data can be processed in such a way that it can be visualized, enabling the teacher or learner to make sense of them, rather than simply relying on software.

Currently, the anti-theoretical stance has taken on a new importance and Anderson has claimed that:

> This is a world where massive amounts of data and applied mathematics replace every other tool that might be brought to bear. Out with every theory of human behavior, from linguistics to sociology. Forget taxonomy, ontology, and psychology. Who knows why people do what they do? The point is they do it, and we can track and measure it with unprecedented fidelity. With enough data, the numbers speak for themselves.
>
> Anderson 2008

In a world of big data the idea that theory is at best irrelevant and at worst counterproductive is extremely dangerous. In educational technology the idea of learner analytics could be developed to suggest that simply by collecting enough raw data on students and educational interactions, persistent and perennial problems could be easily answered. The history of social science suggests that this is unlikely to be the case. There are known weaknesses in a reliance on numerical data and on 'big data' in particular (see, for example, boyd and Crawford 2011). In current conditions. in which there is arguably a flood of data, in which new data sources impact on all the disciplines that learning technology draws on, the limitations of an a-theoretical stance need to be highlighted.

Learner analytics are likely to feature in emerging debates as they relate closely to a trend towards business analytics and powerful policy and market interests (Brown 2011). In the educational arena learning analytics has been defined as:

> the measurement, collection, analysis and reporting of data about learners and their contexts, for purposes of understanding and optimising learning and the environments in which it occurs.
>
> LAK 2011, as reported in Ferguson 2012

It is rooted in earlier social science developments such as social network analysis, but it is driven by more immediate institutional and political concerns and the increasing availability of machine-readable data sets produced by digital technologies, including the learning management systems deployed in many universities (Ferguson 2012). Currently a number of universities are exploring how these large data sets can be managed and analysed to provide meaningful information to institutional managers, course teams, teachers and students. The data has had to be managed, curated and presented in relevant and usable forms in ways that will be familiar to many quantitative researchers in the social sciences. Learning analytics will require the application of a significant effort in the management and processing of the raw data collected by various systems. Indeed the social sciences have a considerable amount to offer this debate because as Bowker has noted, 'Raw data is both an oxymoron and a bad idea; to the contrary, data should be cooked with care' (2005: 184).

Conclusions

The social sciences have much to offer and to learn about the relationships between design for learning and the social practices of education. Social science has knowledge about the way technologies are related to social change. In particular, studies indicate that technology cannot simply determine social change. A key support for this was found in CSCL research which illustrates that technology is not an independent factor and cannot in any simple sense *cause* educational effects or any particular learner responses. Design in the social sciences and design for the social sciences is an exercise in choice, a way of setting the parameters within which technologies will be deployed. Design could be a response to perceived social pressures – the need for team working in the workplace for example – or it could be a choice to stand opposed to the general social trend that has been called networked individualism. Technologies do not decide such issues; rather these are the issues that can be central to design if it is thought of as more than simply a technical task.

Design choice can be exercised at many levels. I have introduced the analytic distinction between micro, macro and meso levels. At a macro level design is outside of the control of individuals and small groups and takes time to enact. The decisions and design choices made at the macro level are national, institutional and corporate. These are choices about national and global infrastructures, equivalent to roads and utilities. Which corporate platforms can provide universal services in education, what educational policies for e-learning will be developed and what will the organization of digital resources look like? These are choices typically made by collective bodies over time, and are not subject to local design until they are deployed in use. However, institutional choices are not beyond the influence of organized bodies and consistent pressure over time.

At the micro level precise designs can be developed for particular interactions. CSCL has generated a great deal of empirical work in this area, either examining individual systems in highly specific settings or studying close micro interactions. At this level design can be very detailed but it is subject to a high degree of contingency. The danger is that research can find it hard to move beyond the particular to the general. However, this is a fundamental problem that affects all levels of design, as noted below in relation to indirect design.

The level that I argue educational practitioners need to focus upon is the meso level of design. The meso level is focused on the medium term and decisions that small groups and individuals can easily make or influence. In universities, this might mean the department or course team, the design of a course rather than an individual interaction, and design that involves the use of systems and tools selected elsewhere. This level may soon become an interesting point of tension as institutions internalize some of the external services previously integrated at the meso level, and as learner analytics are integrated at a macro level, but require implementation at the level of the department, programme or course.

A fundamental point that a social scientific understanding can contribute to this field is the indirect nature of design. This is not a problem that can be dealt with by developing 'situated' designs or by setting up processes of design that can eliminate uncertainty. The cultural turn and the many varieties of social theories that flow from it, from post-modern and ethnomethodological to feminist, post-colonial and critical theory, point to a simple but hard to digest foundational issue. Every time a technology is deployed, every time a design is enacted, every time a plan is put into use, its meaning has to be disinterred from the technology, design or plan by those putting it into use for their own purposes. Design of the tasks we provide for students, the spaces we place students in and the organizations we set up for them can only indirectly affect the activities they generate from tasks, the places they make from spaces and the communities they build within organizations. Worse than that for those who believe in a formal design process: the active process of enactment means that not only can design never be *of* learning only *for* learning, but learning itself is only loosely related to the activities, places and communities our students create.

REFERENCES

Anderson, C. (2008) 'The end of theory, will the data deluge make the scientific method obsolete?', *Edge*. Online. Available at http://www.edge.org/3rd_culture/anderson08/anderson08_index.html (accessed 20 February 2012).

Bolt, B., Fitzgerald, M. and Jessen, S. (2010) 'Implementing Google Apps for faculty and staff', *Research Bulletin* 21, Boulder, CO: Educause Centre for Applied Research. Online. Available at http://www.educause.edu/ecar (accessed 20 February 2012).

Bowker, G.C. (2005) *Memory Practices in the Sciences*, Cambridge, MA: MIT Press.

boyd, d. and Crawford, K. (2011) 'Six provocations for big data', paper presented at the Oxford Internet Institute Decade in Internet Time Symposium, Oxford. September 2011.

Brown, M. (2011) 'Learner analytics: The coming third wave', Educause Learning Initiative brief April 2011. Online. http://www.educause.edu/Resources/LearningAnalyticsTheComingThir/227287 (accessed 20 February 2012).

Cooley, M. (1999) 'Human-centred design', in R. Jacobson (ed.) *Information Design*, Cambridge MA: MIT Press.

De Laat, M.F. and Lally, V. (2004) 'It's not so easy: Researching the complexity of emergent participant roles and awareness in asynchronous networked learning discussion', *Journal of Computer AssistedLearning*, 20 (3): 165–71.

De Laat, M.F., Lally, V., Lipponen, L. and Simons, P.R.J. (2007) 'Patterns of interaction in a networked learning community: Squaring the circle', *International Journal of Computer-Supported Collaborative Learning*, 2 (1): 87–104.

Dohn, N. (2010) 'Teaching with wikis and blogs: Potentials and pitfalls', in L. Dirckinck-Holmfeld, V. Hodgson, C. Jones, D. McConnell and T. Ryberg (eds) *Proceedings of the 7th International Conference on Networked Learning*, Lancaster: Lancaster University.

Dohn, N. (2009) 'web 2.0: Inherent tensions and evident challenges for education', *International Journal of Computer-Supported Collaborative Learning*, 4 (3): 343–63.

Dron, J. and Anderson, T. (2007) 'Collectives, networks and groups in social software for e-learning', in T. Bastiaens and S. Carliner (eds) *Proceedings of World Conference on E-Learning in Corporate, Government, Healthcare, and Higher Education 2007*, Chesapeake, VA: AACE. Online. Available at http://www.editlib.org/p/26726 (accessed 20 February 2012).

Engeström, Y. (1987) *Learning by Expanding: An Activity Theoretical approach to developmental Research*. Helsinki: Orienta-Konsultit Oy. Online. Available at http: http://lchc.ucsd.edu/mca/Paper/Engestrom/expanding/toc.htm (accessed 20th February 2012).

Ferguson, R. (2012). 'The state of learning analytics in 2012: A review and future challenges', *Technical Report KMI–12–01*, Knowledge Media Institute, The Open University, UK. Online. Available at http://kmi.open.ac.uk/publications/techreport/kmi–12–01 (accessed 21 June 2012).

Goodyear, P., Banks, S., Hodgson, V. and McConnell, D. (eds) (2004) *Advances in Research on Networked Learning*, Dordrecht: Kluwer Academic Publishers.

Goodyear, P., Jones, C. and Thompson, K. (2012) 'Computer-supported collaborative learning: instructional approaches, group processes and educational designs,' in J.M Spector, M.D. Merrill, J. Elen and M.J. Bishop (eds) *Handbook of Research on Educational Communications and Technology* (4th edn), New York: Springer.

Goodyear, P., Jones, C., Asensio, M., Hodgson, V. and Steeples, C. (2001) *Effective Networked Learning in Higher Education: Notes and guidelines*. Lancaster: Lancaster University. Available at: http://csalt.lansc.ac.uk/jisc/ (accessed 23 January 2013).

Guribye, F. and Lindström, B. (2009) 'Infrastructures for learning and networked tools – The introduction of a new tool in an inter-organisational network', in L. Dirckinck-Holmfeld, C. Jones and B. Lindström (eds) *Analysing Networked Learning Practices in Higher Education and Continuing Professional Development*, Rotterdam: Sense Publishers.

Hanseth, O. and Lundberg, N. (2001) 'Designing work oriented infrastructures', *Computer Supported Cooperative Work*, 10: 347–72.

Haythornthwaite, C. and De Laat, M. (2010) 'Social networks and learning networks: Using social network perspectives to understand social learning', in L. Dirckinck-Holmfeld, V. Hodgson, C. Jones, D. McConnell and T. Ryberg (eds) *Proceedings of the 7th International Conference on Networked Learning*, Lancaster: Lancaster University.

Hey, T., Tansley, S. and Tolle, K. (eds) (2009) *The Fourth Paradigm Data-Intensive Scientific Discovery*, Redmond, WA: Microsoft Research. Online. http://research.microsoft.com/en-us/collaboration/fourthparadigm/ (accessed 20 February 2012).

Hutchins, E. (1995) *Cognition in the Wild*, Cambridge, MA: MIT Press.

Jameson, F. (1998) *The Cultural Turn: Selected writings on the postmodern 1983–1998*, London: Verso.

Johnson, D. W., Johnson, R.T. and Stanne, M. B. (2000) *Cooperative Learning Methods: A meta-analysis*. Online. Available at http://www.tablelearning.com/uploads/File/EXHIBIT-B.pdf (accessed 20 February 2012).

Jones, C. (2011) 'Networked learning environments', in M. Keppell, K. Souter and M. Riddle (eds) *Physical and Virtual Learning Spaces in Higher Education: Concepts for the modern learning environment*, Hershey, PA: IGI Global.

Jones, C. (2009) 'A context for collaboration: The institutional selection of an infrastructure for learning', in C. O'Malley, D. Suthers, P. Reimann and A. Dimitracopoulou (eds) *Proceedings of the 9th International Conference on Computer Supported Collaborative Learning: CSCL2009: CSCL Practices*, Lancaster: University of Lancaster.

Jones, C. (2004) 'Networks and learning: communities, practices and the metaphor of networks', *ALT-J, Research in Learning Technology*, 12 (1): 82–93.

Jones, C. and Asensio, M. (2001) 'Experiences of assessment: using phenomenography for evaluation', *Journal of Computer Assisted Learning*, 17 (3): 314–21.

Jones, C. and Dirckinck-Holmfeld, L. (2009) 'Analysing networked learning practices: An introduction', in L. Dirckinck-Holmfeld, C. Jones and B. Lindström (eds) *Analysing Networked Learning Practices in Higher Education and Continuing Professional Development*. Rotterdam: Sense Publishers.

Jones, C., Dirckinck-Holmfeld L. and Lindström, B. (2006a) 'A relational, indirect, meso-level approach to CSCL design in the next decade', *International Journal of Computer-Supported Collaborative Learning*, 1 (1): 35–56.

Jones, C., Cook, J., Jones, A. and De Laat, M. (2006b) 'Collaboration', in G. Conole and M. Oliver (eds) *Contemporary Perspectives in E-learning Research*, London: RoutledgeFalmer.

Kafai, Y.B. and Peppler, K.A. (2011) 'Beyond small groups: New opportunities for research in Computer-Supported Collective Learning', in Spada, H., Stahl, G., Miyake, N. and Law, N. (eds) *Connecting Computer-Supported Collaborative Learning to Policy and Practice: CSCL2011 Conference Proceedings*. Volume I – Long Papers, University of Hong Kong: Hong Kong, China.

Koschmann, T. (ed.) (1996) *CSCL: Theory and Practice of an Emerging Paradigm*, Mahwah, NJ: Lawrence Erlbaum Associates.

Lave, J. and Wenger, E. (1991) *Situated Learning: Legitimate peripheral participation*, Cambridge: Cambridge University Press.

Liljenström, H. and Svedin, U. (eds) (2005) *Micro Meso Macro: Addressing complex systems coupling*, New Jersey: World Scientific Publishers.

McConnell, D. (2000) *Implementing Computer Supported Cooperative Learning* (2nd edn), London: Kogan Page.

McConnell, D., Hodgson, V. and Dirckinck-Holmfeld, L. (2012) 'Networked learning: a brief history and new trends', in L. Dirckinck-Holmfeld, V. Hodgson, and D. McConnell (eds) *Exploring the Theory, Pedagogy and Practice of Networked Learning*, New York: Springer.

Schatzki, T.R. (1996) *Social Practices: A Wittgensteinian approach to human activity and the social*, Cambridge: Cambridge University Press.

Schatzki, T.R., Cetina, K. and von Savigny, E. (eds) (2001) *The Practice Turn in Contemporary Theory*, London: Routledge.

Stahl, G. (2003) 'Meaning and interpretation in collaboration', in B. Wasson, S. Ludvigsen and U. Hoppe (eds) (2003) *Designing for Change in Networked Learning Environments: Proceedings of the International Conference on Computer Supported Collaborative Learning 2003*, Dordrecht: Kluwer Academic Publishers.

Stahl, G., Koschmann, T. and Suthers, D. (2006) 'Computer-supported collaborative learning: An historical perspective', in R. K. Sawyer (ed.) *Cambridge Handbook of the Learning Sciences*, Cambridge, UK: Cambridge University Press, pp.409–26.

Suchman, L. (2007) *Human–Machine Reconfigurations: Plans and Situated Actions* (2nd edn), New York and Cambridge UK: Cambridge University Press.

Vygotsky, L.S. (1986) *Thought and Language*, A. Kozulin (trans.), Cambridge, MA: MIT Press.

Chapter 14

Student as Producer is Hacking the University

Joss Winn and Dean Lockwood

EDITORS' INTRODUCTION

The previous chapters in Part II were concerned with the interaction between designers and design principles within disciplinary contexts. This chapter takes our understanding of context further, to encompass the teaching and learning philosophy and institutional strategy within which design takes place. Drawing on the example of the 'Student as Producer' project at the University of Lincoln, UK, the authors explain how curriculum design is expected to be informed by a view of the student as an active contributor to and collaborator in the knowledge creation process. When students are engaged to such an extent, they bring with them use of technology as a norm. Designs for radical pedagogy, facilitated by technology, need to consider their impact on the roles of the different actors involved. So, at Lincoln, staff and students have been encouraged to explore and experiment with technology together, with a particular focus on how openness is expressed and enacted within today's technologically rich environment. Here design is seen as a truly collaborative venture that brings staff and students together.

A dysfunctional relationship

The Centre for Educational Research and Development (CERD) was created in 2007 to lead the University of Lincoln's teaching and learning strategy, run post-graduate courses for the study of education and practice of teaching, and support the academic use of technology across the university. Since its inception, the theme at the heart of the Centre's work has been to reconnect research and teaching, the core activities of universities. Central to this objective is an attempt to reconfigure the dysfunctional relationship between teaching and research in higher education and a conviction that this can be best achieved by rethinking the relationship between student and academic. We call this project 'Student as Producer' and, since late 2010, Student as Producer (http://studentasproducer. lincoln.ac.uk) has been adopted as the de facto teaching and learning strategy for the University of Lincoln.

As such, Student as Producer is a university-wide initiative, which aims to construct a productive and progressive pedagogical framework through a re-engineering of the relationship between research and teaching and a reappraisal of the relationship between academics and students. Research-engaged teaching and learning is now 'an institutional priority at the University of Lincoln, making it the dominant paradigm for all aspects of curriculum design and delivery, and the central pedagogical principle that informs other aspects of the University's strategic planning.' (Student as Producer 2012)

Under the direction of Professor Mike Neary, Dean of Teaching and Learning, much of the work of CERD has been informed by the conviction that students should become producers rather than consumers of knowledge and of their own social world. By engaging students and academics as collaborators, we can refashion and reassert the very idea of the university.

The argument for Student as Producer has been developed through a number of publications that assert that students can and should be producers of their social world by being collaborators in the processes of research, teaching and learning (Neary 2008; Neary and Winn 2009; Neary 2010; Neary and Hagyard 2010). Student as Producer has a radically democratic agenda, valuing critique, speculative thinking, openness and a form of learning that aims to transform the social context so that students become the subjects rather than objects of history – individuals who make history and personify knowledge. Student as Producer is not simply a project to transform and improve the 'student experience' but aspires to a paradigm shift in how knowledge is produced, where the traditional student and teacher roles are 'interrupted' through close collaboration, recognizing that both teachers and students have much to learn from each other. Student as Producer aims to ensure that theory and practice are understood as praxis, i.e. a process of 'reflection and action upon the world in order to transform it' (Freire 2000: 51).

A critical, social and historical understanding of the university and the roles of researcher, teacher and student inform these aspirations and objectives. They draw on radical moments in the history of the university as well as looking forward to possibilities of what the university can become. Student as Producer is not dependent on technology but rather on the quality of the relationship between teacher and student. However, the extent to which technology can support, improve and even positively disrupt this relationship is key.

An important aspect of the project is redesigning the university's administrative and bureaucratic processes so that they align with and support the principles of Student as Producer. This is an organic process intended to engage administrative staff, academics and students in the development of curricula and course validation. As part of their curriculum design, academics are asked to:

- show ways in which the courses will include research-engaged teaching;
- consider issues of space and spatiality in their teaching practice;
- describe how they will write up their teaching as a scholarly research project;

- illustrate the ways in which they will use appropriate web technologies;
- demonstrate the extent to which students are involved in the design and delivery of programmes and courses, and
- show how the course enables students to see themselves having a role in creating their own future, in terms of employment, and to make a progressive contribution to society (University of Lincoln 2010).

Student as Producer regards students as expert users of the university's facilities and, following examples in other sectors, recognizes that student/user engagement is essential in the design and delivery of their own programmes and modules, i.e. the design of the idea of the university.

Student as Producer is not dependent on technology but recognizes that it is deeply embedded in modern university life, supporting, for example, the increasingly collaborative nature of research through discipline-specific Virtual Research Environments and the creation of Personal Learning Environments where teachers and students use technologies pragmatically, appropriate to their needs and capacities. Likewise, technology can be used to understand, map and visualize the uses of physical and virtual space and underwrites critical institutional functions penetrating deep into the overall 'learning landscape' of the university (Neary and Saunders 2011). Arguably, networked technology is now ingrained in the very 'idea of the university' and the social production of knowledge. It is not a matter of asking, 'What is the role of the Web in higher education?' but rather, 'What is the role of the university in the world of Web?' (Powell 2009).

Student as Producer recognizes what *The Edgeless University* called a 'time of maximum uncertainty and time for creative possibility between the ending of the way things have been and the beginning of the way they will be' (Bradwell 2009: 63). At a time when the higher education sector is being privatized and students are expected to assume the role of consumer, Student as Producer aims to provide students with a more critical, more historically and socially informed, experience of university life which extends beyond their formal studies to engage with the role of the university, and therefore their own role, in society. Pedagogically, this is through the idea of 'excess' where students are anticipated to become *more* than just student-consumers during their course of research and study (Neary and Hagyard 2010).

Through this 'pedagogy of excess', the organizing principle of university life is being redressed, creating a teaching, learning and research environment which promotes the values of experimentation, openness and creativity, engenders equity among academics and students and thereby offers an opportunity to reconstruct the student as producer and academic as collaborator. In an anticipated environment where knowledge is free, the roles of the educator and the institution necessarily change. The educator is no longer a delivery vehicle and the institution becomes a landscape for the production and construction of a mass intellect in commons, a porous, networked space of abundance, offering an experience that is in excess of what students might find elsewhere.

The remaining part of this chapter provides two case studies of how Student as Producer is infiltrating quite different areas of university life at Lincoln. The first discusses Student as Producer in the context of Deleuze and rhizomatic curriculum design, while the second looks at how the project is being applied to the development of an open institutional infrastructure, in which computer science students are redesigning and developing the tools used for research, teaching and learning.

Rhizomatic pedagogy

Gilles Deleuze, in the nineties, suggested that pedagogy would soon be caught up in an incessant 'decoding' and 'recoding' as capitalism mutated to seize upon the potential that digital flows of communication offered for unleashing energies hitherto accumulated in closed institutional sites. Notwithstanding digitality's crucial role in this mutation, Deleuze maintained that 'machines don't explain anything, you have to analyze the collective arrangements of which the machines are just one component' (1995: 175). A key question such an analysis would address is whether the exigencies of communication in this emergent situation will lead also to new 'lines of flight', new forms of resistance. If so, resistance would be more likely to turn around 'creation' rather than 'communication': 'Creating has always been something different from communicating. The key thing may be to create vacuoles of non-communication, circuit breakers, so we can elude control' (ibid.).

In a 2011 Student as Producer project, drawing on a CERD fund dedicated to enabling innovations in curriculum design, Lincoln School of Media lecturers Rob Coley, Dean Lockwood and Adam O'Meara embarked upon an experiment inspired by this thought of the interruptive vacuole with a level 2 Photography Projects module (taken, on this occasion, by 42 students). In hacking parlance, we might call this an 'exploit', a move designed to turn a system to one's own advantage and open up the possibility of something new happening. Consonant with the basic principles of Student as Producer outlined above, the design of the course was conceived as directly research-engaged. In this instance, tutors brought students' attention to bear on the concept of the rhizome – key to much of the tutors' own independent research – taken from Deleuze's work with Félix Guattari (Deleuze and Guattari 2004), suggesting that the semester's work could constitute a serious collaborative attempt to generate, in the encounter between this conceptual adventure and their practical work, new and original lines of enquiry for photographic image production.

There is insufficient space here to fully unfold the implications of the rhizome concept but, briefly, it indicates an attempt to break away from Western hierarchical – or 'arborescent' – models which encourage us to think in terms of the logic of representation and reproduction of already given structures. For Deleuze and Guattari, the rhizome – a flat, horizontal root-system – suggests the immanent, transformative connectedness of the world and constitutes a corrective to an arborescent logic of stand-alone 'trees'. The rhizome privileges the connecting line rather than the isolated point. It is an endlessly proliferating assemblage of lines which connect from the middle. Connectivity, without centre, boundaries, beginning or end, is the first principle of the rhizome. Related principles are heterogeneity and multiplicity. The rhizome ceaselessly self-differs. Further, it expresses a cartographic logic of production rather than a 'tracing' logic of reproduction. Constructed on the basis of fostering new connections, 'what distinguishes the map from the tracing is that it is entirely oriented toward an experimentation in contact with the real' (Deleuze and Guattari 2004: 13). In the rhizomatic, cartographic encounter, when tutor and student, and tutor/student and the real, come into contact, the world emerges anew in a process of mutual 'becoming'. Nothing is represented. Nothing is communicated, only created.

The module tutors envisaged that the rhizome concept would enable themselves and students, with photographic image production as the pretext, to connect up to each other and to the real in exciting ways which obviously could not be fully stipulated at the commencement of the project. It was hoped that the use of available digital technology would facilitate this – students were required to contribute ideas to a blog set up for the purpose of the project and encouraged to share and upload their work to Flickr, Vimeo and other online resources. It should be noted that tutors did not promote an uncritical embrace of the digital. The emancipatory potential of digital technologies is precisely something to be struggled for, part of what is at stake.

It is fair to say that students experienced some difficulty in grasping what was an unfamiliar way of framing our thinking and doing. In particular, there was much discussion of their anxieties with regard to how, given the foregrounding of rhizomatic connection and becoming, individual achievements would be recognized and assessed. Assurances were given that reasonable efforts to participate in the project would in themselves merit a pass mark as a baseline, regardless of 'quality' of final product, thus providing a safety net. However, tutors did not set out to suppress dissonant views, seeing these as a necessary part of the project. Connectivity should not imply consensus. The tutors agree with those running similar projects (which have taken the rhizome as the organizing principle for pedagogical experiments) that the key to such experiments lies in the insight that 'the community *is* the curriculum' (Cormier 2008). Where they differ, however, is in their greater insistence on the *political* valency of rhizomatic pedagogies. It is in this respect that elements of conflict should be welcomed. The community-curriculum learns in a moment of crisis, surrendering the consolation of reproduced knowledge. If nothing is at stake, is anything truly learnt? Rhizomatic pedagogy embraces collective movement of thought, generating new styles of thinking. Mobile thought is creation from the middle, in and through others as mediators. This perspective shatters the complacency of received truths, common knowledge. It demands a community of mediators who connect in order to make things happen, to invent in the space between individuals, rather than merely to agree. The tutors hoped that what would transpire would be a collective, intervallic spirit of invention fostering an immanent transcendence of traditional tutor and student roles and relationships.

The project evolved to encompass group outings to make images and stitch them together as a 'pack', an exploit from which a new assemblage promised to emerge within the old. The pack generated its ideas and images, culminating in a provocative exhibition in a public space in Lincoln city centre on a busy afternoon. In the time since the project came to an end, sufficient positive feedback has been gathered from both tutors and students to merit further investigation of this approach to teaching and learning. The experiment has been a frequent talking point for the students who were involved and its resonances continue to be felt – something new most certainly occurred.

In this instance, rhizomatic pedagogy aimed to foster a rhizomatic photographic practice, a way of producing images collectively that disrupts the traditional representational paradigm of photography. This has to be as much about exploring the techniques, methods, research ethos and social context of image production as about the eventual images produced. Throughout, process was foregrounded over product, which meant frustrating the expectations of some students. In relation to technology, tutors proposed that a tutor–student rhizome might hack photography as a kind of serious play rather than maintain a strictly instrumental orientation to the camera and associated conventions. To be more specific, it was deemed imperative for the project to critically interrogate the default assumptions tutors and students have with regard to how to teach and learn photography. Expectations of both parties have typically revolved around the notion that an individual will be instrumentally orientated towards the camera as a means of representing some aspect of the external world as skilfully as possible in order to be rewarded with a good grade. The rhizome project, tutors suggested, would work with different assumptions. These are that the group finds itself in the middle of an emergent situation, to which it critically attends by perceiving, thinking and making images with machines, i.e. cameras. It also reflexively attends to its own assumptions and expectations and the logic inherent in the camera, because these also are connected and germane to the situation. In particular, the digital camera is to be conceived not as an inert, neutral and complete technological tool distinct from its human operator, but rather as an element in a mobile collective arrangement or assemblage which expresses what can be done and which, in the context of Deleuze's concerns about the mutations of power, both controls and offers certain potential for resistance: 'The concept of assemblage shows us how institutions, organizations, bodies, practices and habits make and unmake each other, intersecting and transforming: creating territories and then unmaking them, de-territorializing, opening lines of flight as a possibility of any assemblage, but also shutting them down' (Macgregor Wise 2005: 86). To engage in photography education could be, under the auspices of the rhizome, to hack into and re-invent the machinic assemblages of which we are components. The notion of exploiting lines of flight emerging immanently within machinic assemblages can feed into the Student as Producer strategy and contribute to a culture of genuine creation as opposed to the communication of pre-digested information.

An academic commons

In 2009, in a book chapter called 'Student as Producer', Mike Neary and Joss Winn offered a historical overview of the development of the modern university and more recent attempts in the US and UK to work against the growing disjuncture between research and teaching. In the conclusion to that chapter, the authors specifically drew on the activities of the Free Culture movement as an exemplary model for how the disconnect between research and teaching, and the work of academics and students, might be overcome and reorganized around a different conception of *work* and *property*, ideas central to the meaning of 'openness' or, rather, an 'academic commons'.

Our approach to institutional openness at Lincoln has been to recover and develop the connection between the values of openness and the values of academic life. As such, there is no policy or ongoing discussion concerning openness, but rather we have seen Student as Producer as a vehicle for demonstrating how the values and practices of openness are historically grounded in the work of universities and the academic life, which Student as Producer seeks to promote, challenge and develop in a radical way.

In 2008, the CERD established the Learning Lab, an autonomously run virtual space for experimenting with and evaluating open source software that may be of value to research, teaching and learning at the university. One of the applications we first trialled on the Learning Lab server was the Open Journal Systems software, which was installed to help a group of students and staff develop an open access journal of Occasional Working Papers. While relatively short-lived due to staff and students leaving, we were able to support those involved by making the technology easily available to them and promoting their work within the context of what was being called the Academic Commons. More recently, the platform has been adopted by postgraduate students who intend to relaunch the student journal, *Neo*.

Running on an open source server, the Learning Lab allowed for much experimentation with and the adoption of different types of open source software, including Mahara (e-Portfolios), MediaWiki, Webpa-OS (peer assessment), Xerte (learning materials), feed2js (RSS to Javascript conversion), OpenSim (virtual worlds) and, most significantly, the open source blogging software, WordPress Multi-User.

Although from one perspective WordPress is simply an open source publishing platform, we intentionally configured it so that it would be open for any student or member of staff to create a modern, content-managed website to communicate their work to the public. There is no gatekeeper policy, but rather a set of community guidelines, similar to other online community guidelines.

The university's own acceptable use policy was also revised around this time and explicitly promotes and encourages the use of web applications. Within a year, WordPress was regarded as a technologically sound piece of software and widely used by teachers, students, researchers and university departments. As such, it was formally adopted by the university and now hosts and manages over 1000 websites at http://blogs.lincoln.ac.uk

The freedom we have through running our own server(s) at the university, as well as a progressive academic environment in which to work, allowed colleagues in CERD and the Library to spend over a year experimenting with the WordPress open source software and use it as a platform for technological enquiry and innovation, rather than simply a blogging tool. This began a bottom-up approach to innovation through openness, which was upheld and concurrently developed both theoretically in our published writing and strategically in the development of Student as Producer as the newly emerging teaching and learning strategy. In essence, as the university was developing a more progressive teaching and learning strategy which promoted the idea of openness, collaboration and that both teachers and students have much to learn from each other, a more progressive use of technology to support research, teaching and learning was also being developed through the use of open source software, the principles of open access, the promotion of open educational resources and, most recently, the release of open data. Each tactic supported and enabled the other.

Using Student as Producer as the overarching framework, CERD, the Library and ICT Services worked on a series of funded projects that had students and openness as their central theme:

- JISCPress (2009–10) allowed us to employ a second-year undergraduate student in computer science, to help develop an open source platform for publishing and discussing documents in detail.
- With ChemistryFM (2009–10), an Open Educational Resources project, we provided bursaries to two students to work with academic staff to develop and release an entire module of open educational resources (OER) for a Level One course in Chemistry for Forensic Scientists.
- For the Total Recal project (2010–11), two students working part-time in central ICT services worked on a rapid innovation project to develop a 'space-time' calendaring service at the university, resulting in open source code and the creation of a large data store which became the basis for our institutional open data project, http://data.lincoln.ac.uk.

The provision of these student posts in ICT was largely the result of the growing interest in Student as Producer at the university, reaching across not only academic departments but also the central service departments, too. The Head of ICT took on board the values of openness and collaboration between staff and students that Student as Producer promotes by employing students to act as 'critical friends' to the department and work with existing staff on the development of new online services. These students were encouraged to use the WordPress platform to blog about their experience in ICT. This intentionally disruptive influence of students working alongside staff began to change the culture of the ICT department and led to the development and adoption of a number of online services which promote a more open and transparent environment at the university as well as the introduction of new technologies and a much greater willingness and freedom to engage in research and development projects.

With students in trusted positions in ICT, collaborating with staff in CERD and the Library, we were able to develop our ideas beyond the original Learning Lab environment and further our experiments with technology at the university. This led to Jerome, a summer 'un-project' of 2010, where we explored new ways of exposing, searching and using Library information to create a better way of using Library services. Jerome was later funded by Joint Information Systems Committee (JISC) as our third 'rapid innovation' project in just over a year and, like Total Recal, made a huge contribution to our experience and understanding of new technologies such as MongoDB, the open source NoSQL database software, and data-driven development of Application Programming Interfaces (APIs).

Both Jerome and Total Recal contributed large amounts of data to what has become http://data.lincoln.ac.uk and the development of this service also led to the development of a new access and identity management (AIM) system at the university, created by students. These students, Alex Bilbie and Nick Jackson, also developed the university's new Common Web Design, a modern framework for new university websites, now widely used across our services. By working together on the research and development of components of university infrastructure, we have developed an open source 'toolkit' for both staff and student developers, including data storage, authentication and a presentation layer, allowing us to rapidly prototype and implement new services.

This successful working relationship between CERD, the Library and ICT Services, three key departments in the university, has been fundamental to building an academic commons, in which staff and students work together on open technologies to enable and support university life. It has been supported by senior management such as the Dean of Teaching and Learning, the Head of ICT and the university librarian, but driven by enthusiastic staff and students who are given access to open source tools and open data. That openness can also be conceived as a 'public good' is recognized and valued by all involved, but is not the primary underlying motivation. Rather, the progressive and well developed pedagogical project of Student as Producer has provided us with a framework with which to involve students, situate distinctive projects when writing funding bids and receive recognition *within* the institution for the recognition we have attracted *outside* the institution for our approach.

This recognition has more recently led to the university's committees approving the formation of LNCD (http://lncd.lincoln.ac.uk/), a new inclusive group which succeeds the Learning Lab and is informed by the progressive ideas of Student as Producer so as to engender critical, digitally literate staff and students. Core principles of the group are that we recognize students and staff have much to learn from each other and that students can be agents of change in the use of technology for education. LNCD consolidates and furthers ongoing collaborative work between the CERD, the Library and ICT Services and extends an open invitation to staff and students from across the university to contribute to the group.

A graduate intern post ensures that the student perspective remains core to the group's outlook. We also continue to employ students and recent graduates as core members of LNCD. In its first year, LNCD has a budget of £20,000, much of which is dispersed to students and staff who submit proposals for projects around the theme of 'technology for education'. These are available on a competitive basis in the form of grants and bursaries providing an incentive to staff and students to get involved in the development, support and critique of how technology is used in higher education. Examples of funded projects include: a tool that supports anonymous Q&A in class, encouraging less confident students to participate; a project to build a 3D printer and investigate the uses of this new technology across different subject disciplines; another project is assessing the use of WordPress as an ePortfolio tool for health and social care students; and another is building a robot for Open Day demonstrations. Each of these small projects is a genuinely collaborative undertaking between students and teachers. Furthermore, we invite third-year students from the School of Computing to propose dissertation projects based around the use of our toolkit and data.lincoln.ac.uk, allowing us to mentor students as they develop our work further. This is very gratifying and one of these students has recently been employed by the university, recognizing the contribution he can make to the development of new online tools for the university community.

In the setting up of the LNCD group, we have tried to ensure that openness remains a distinct theme throughout our work, both in the tools we use and the way we organize ourselves as a distributed, collegial group: 'LNCD is Not a Central Development group!'

Hacking the university

Work on Student as Producer remains very much at the heart of what we do. It is both an institutional strategy and a three-year project funded by the Higher Education Academy, now in its second year. It has been very well received across the university and the sector, and is being embedded into the curriculum design process and teacher education programmes we run.

Although internally consistent as a pedagogical theory, Student as Producer is being interpreted and adopted by staff and students at the University of Lincoln in different ways. Some, like Dean and his colleagues, recognize its basis in revolutionary praxis (drawing on the work of luminaries such as Walter

Benjamin and other avant-garde Marxist writers, and the philosophy of Deleuze and others), while other colleagues, working in professional services, see it as a way to engage students in the critique and redevelopment of institution-wide services. All academics, however, recognize Student as Producer as a framework by which teaching and learning, including curriculum development, can become a much more collaborative effort.

In the case of LNCD and the core contributors of the group from CERD, the Library and ICT Services, we have framed Student as Producer in both our advocacy of the tools and methods by which the Free Culture movement operates and in a re-examination of the role of students as developers or 'hackers' in the university.

We see our work as fundamentally a form of hacking the academy, using and writing open source software and producing open data with which to 'hack the university' and create useful services and effect positive technological interventions in the research, teaching and learning environment of the university. From the perspective of a rhizomatic pedagogy, also, projects can be conceived as hacking exploits, a means to effect a revolutionary becoming for which revolution (as for Deleuze) is never actual, but always virtual, a matter of unfolding new potential, multiplying points of entry to, and spontaneously surfing the propensities of, a situation.

Just as we recognized in our original book chapter that the Free Culture movement owes much to its academic origins, we also recognized that 'an exemplar alternative organizing principle is already proliferating in universities in the form of open, networked collaborative initiatives' (Neary and Winn 2009). The LNCD group is an attempt to develop that and, as such, understands that the origins of much of its work to date is in the hacking culture that grew out of MIT, Carnegie Mellon University and University of California, Berkeley in the 1970 and 1980s, the academic culture that developed much of the key technology of today's Internet.

When understood from this point of view, LNCD, as a Student as Producer initiative, is attempting to develop a culture for staff and students based on the key academic values that motivated the early academic hacker culture: autonomy, the sharing of knowledge and creative output, transparency through peer-review, and peer-recognition based on merit. We are mindful that this contributes towards a greater strategic priority of reconfiguring the nature of teaching and learning in higher education and encouraging students to become part of the academic project of the university and collaborators with academics in the production of knowledge and meaning.

This approach is grounded in the intellectual history and tradition of the modern university and visible in our understanding of and approach to openness at the University of Lincoln. However, for us, it is not the case that we are consciously working towards openness, but rather we work towards defending and maintaining the core academic values that recent notions of openness are largely derived from.

References

Bradwell, P. (2009) *The Edgeless University*. DEMOS. Online. Available at http://www. demos.co.uk/publications/the-edgeless-university (accessed 15 July 2012).

Cormier, D. (2008) 'Rhizomatic education: Community as curriculum', *Innovate*, 4 (5). Online. Available at http://www.innovateonline.info/index.php?view=articleandid=550 (accessed 15 July 2012).

Deleuze, G. (1995) 'Control and becoming', in *Negotiations*, trans. Martin Joughin, New York: Columbia University Press.

Deleuze, G. and Guattari, F. (2004) *A Thousand Plateaus*, London: Continuum.

Freire, P. (2000) *Pedagogy of the Oppressed*, London: Continuum.

Macgregor Wise, J. (2005) 'Assemblage', in C.J. Stivale (ed.) *Gilles Deleuze: Key concepts*, Chesham: Acumen.

Neary, M. (2008) 'Student as producer – risk, responsibility and rich learning environments in higher education. Social purpose and creativity – integrating learning in the real world', in J. Barlow, G. Louw and M. Price (eds) *Proceedings of Learning and Teaching Conference 2008*, Brighton: University of Brighton Press.

Neary, M. (2010) 'Student as Producer: A pedagogy for the avant-garde', *Learning Exchange*, 1 (1).

Neary, M. and Hagyard, A. (2010) 'Pedagogy of excess: An alternative political economy of student life', in M. Molesworth, R. Scullion and E. Nixon (eds) *The Marketisation of Higher Education and the Student as Consumer*, Routledge: Abingdon.

Neary, M. and Saunders, G. (2011) 'Leadership and learning landscapes: the struggle for the idea of the university', *Higher Education Quarterly*, 65 (4): 333–52.

Neary, M. and Winn, J. (2009) 'The student as producer: reinventing the student experience in higher education' in L. Bell, H. Stevenson and M. Neary (eds) *The Future of Higher Education: Policy, pedagogy and the student experience*, London: Continuum.

Powell, A. (2009) 'The role of universities in a Web 2.0 world?', *eFoundations*, Online posting. 14 May 2009. http://efoundations.typepad.com/efoundations/2009/05/the-role-of-universities-in-a-web–20-world.html

Student as Producer (2012) Student as Producer Project Report, End of second year (2011–12). Online. http://studentasproducer.lincoln.ac.uk/2012/07/06/project-report-end-of-second-year–2011–2012/ (accessed 15 July 2012).

University of Lincoln (2010) 'Student as Producer User's Guide 2010–2011', Online. http://studentasproducer.lincoln.ac.uk/files/2010/11/user-guide.pdf (accessed 15 July 2012).

Chapter 15

The LAMS Community
Building Communities of Designers

James Dalziel

EDITORS' INTRODUCTION

The chapter begins with the history of LAMS (Learning Activity Management System) as a new kind of e-learning design tool, going on to discuss the principles used for the design of the LAMS Community, and how they differ from those which inform traditional approaches for learning object repositories. Within the LAMS Community the focus has been on creating a community space in which barriers to exploiting Learning Designs are removed and sharing among teachers is fostered. Based on careful observations of the community in action over the previous six years, the author discusses what has been learned about how teachers use and reuse Learning Designs. As well as creating easy ways to preview, search, tag, rate, license and discuss designs held within the LAMS Community, the author finds that teachers value advice on versioning generic templates for their discipline and the opportunity to share designs within a closed community of close colleagues. Dalziel's concluding reflections complement Masterman's (Chapter 4) reports on interviews with teachers talking about how they prepare and share designs with trusted colleagues within their discipline. It can be seen how the sharing and reuse of Learning Designs could be facilitated by supporting teachers to combine generic designs with methods and content that meet the needs of their specific discipline communities.

Overview

As at February 2012, the LAMS Community (www.lamscommunity.org) was the largest online community for sharing Learning Designs. It has 7,300 registered members from over 90 countries, approximately 900 shared Learning Designs downloaded/previewed 34,000 times, and 7,300 discussion forum postings. These membership and forum posting figures are modest compared to those of the e-learning community formed around the Moodle virtual learning environment (VLE); and the number of shared objects and downloads are modest compared to those of Learning Object Repositories (LORs) such as MERLOT and ARIADNE. However, the LAMS Community provides an illustration of the potential for building communities explicitly focused on sharing Learning Designs. The fundamental driver for the development of LAMS, and subsequently of the LAMS Community, was my belief that if educators from around the world could freely share and adapt 'runnable' good practice then the education sector would be transformed by improved educational quality combined with reduced preparation workloads. This belief runs through much of the work on sharing e-learning materials (although often implicitly), but despite hundreds of millions of dollars in public and private investment, it is clear that the dream is in trouble – not many educators use repositories of educational content, and very few share back improved versions (see also Pegler, Chapter 9). For me, there are two fundamental problems: (1) education is more than just content, so any attempt to share good practice requires e-learning systems capable of replicating the pedagogy of a typical classroom – that is, a structured flow of content and collaborative tasks; and (2) the sharing of good practice requires a community of educators to discuss ideas and practice – a searchable 'content dump' is not sufficient. LAMS and the LAMS Community are an attempt to address these problems, because, despite the difficulties to date, the dream still seems worth believing in.

Frustration I

I have been involved in e-learning since the mid-1990s when the Internet and the World Wide Web became household terms. During that time, I saw the rise of the early Virtual Learning Environments (VLEs; now also called Learning Management Systems and perhaps, most aptly, Course Management Systems) such as FirstClass, TopClass and WebCT. In the late 1990s I marvelled at the rapid adoption of VLEs by universities around the world and, like many, had high hopes for how these platforms could transform pedagogy through innovative online tools.

By 2001 I had become concerned about the state of pedagogical innovation in VLEs. After the promising years of the late 1990s, the pace of innovation seemed to stall, and the same cluster of educational tools (forum, chat, document sharing, quiz, assignment dropbox, etc.) kept appearing with little real difference across a range of VLEs. Much of the focus of using VLEs was on content development and, while this might be an important part of e-learning, it lacked any collaborative dimension – the online analogues of classroom debate, small group discussion, teamwork, Socratic dialogue, etc. It was as if e-learning had become synonymous with the library (a repository of content), rather than the classroom (a collaborative learning experience of rich, structured interaction). While a few innovative educators used discussion forums (and very rarely, chat) to foster collaboration, VLE use seemed to be driven by content delivery (course information, lecture notes, past exam papers, etc.) and 'e-administration' (calendars, student email, assignment dropboxes, etc.). While useful, this was not the pedagogical transformation that many of us had hoped for.

My concern ran deeper than the way in which VLEs were used: it seemed that some fundamental dimension was missing – the 'process' of education. At the heart of most successful classroom experiences, whether they are K–12 school lessons or university tutorials, is some careful planning by the teacher/lecturer to structure the flow of tasks. This involves structuring the delivery of content as well as interleaving appropriate student activities, such as discussion, debate, small group work, etc. Whether explicit or implicit, the educational process usually involves a flow of content and collaborative tasks over time, and it was this 'flow' that seemed absent from VLEs. If the only educational aspect of universities was lectures, this might have been understandable, but tutorials and seminars have been integral to university education for many years: most K–12 school classes illustrate the importance of a flow of content and collaboration on a daily basis. My concern was not just at the absence of what would later be called an 'education workflow engine'. It was that until educators could easily capture the process and content of education together, there would be no way of sharing the heart of the teaching process, no way of building on good practice and adapting it in the way that schoolteachers develop and share (paper-based) lesson plans. Why didn't technology facilitate both the sharing and running of these activity structures?

I discussed the need for this dimension of education with senior members of several VLEs and similar initiatives. Some literally could not understand what I was saying; others indicated that this kind of feature was a 'pedagogical nice to have', but did not really matter to the bulk of their users, or, for that matter, to the managers who actually paid the VLE licence fee. For a while I thought the problem was that I had not explained the importance of this concept in a sufficiently persuasive way, but over time I came to recognize that no amount of persuasion was going to break this impasse soon. So I decided that if I believed as passionately as I did in this dimension of education, and its importance to the dream of sharing and improving good practice, then I would have to find a way to create a system that was based on the structured flow of content and collaborative tasks. And I would need to ensure that these 'flows' of tasks would be shareable, exportable, adaptable and re-usable.

The Learning Activity Management System

The Learning Activity Management System was a direct response to the frustrations outlined above. From its inception, it set out to provide educators with an easy-to-use authoring environment for creating structured flows of content and collaborative tasks (called 'sequences'). One pivotal aspect of this environment was a simple 'drag-and-drop' interface, which allowed educators to choose and connect a set of generic activity tools such as chat, forum, Q&A, voting, resources, and then configure each tool to suit their particular subject area (see Figure 15.1). While some of these tools would be familiar to VLE users, others had new features that emphasized the collaborative dimension. For example, the

Q&A tool allowed students to type in an answer, and LAMS then collated the answers from all the students in the group, so that they could also reflect on the ideas of others. However, it was the structured flow of collaborative tasks (and content) that set LAMS apart from VLEs.

Once an educator has saved a sequence, it can be run for a designated group of students, and students can access the sequence of activities from a learner area. As students progress through the sequence, the educator can monitor both group and individual activity, and a record of all activities is kept to allow students (and the educator) to see how they are progressing.

To share a sequence, the educator can export a simple file that can be emailed to colleagues or placed on a website or in a repository. The LAMS software also provides internal areas for sharing among educators who use the same LAMS server. Once another educator has received a sequence, it can be run with their students, or opened in the authoring area to be reviewed and modified. LAMS was 'inspired' by the ideas of IMS Learning Design, but extended it in a number of ways, particularly the close integration of activity tools. For a more detailed discussion of the development of LAMS see Dalziel (2003). But LAMS itself was not built to provide an environment for community discussion and sharing of sequences – it merely made the creation of sequences possible. The second part of the vision meant addressing a second set of frustrations – the difficulty of developing an LOR that appealed to educators (not just LOR builders).

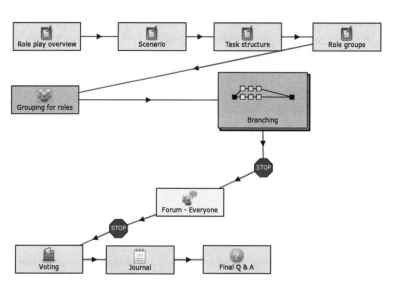

Figure 15.1 LAMS (Version 2) Authoring showing a sample sequence based on a role-play template

Source: www.practicaleteachingstrategies.com

Frustration 2

Traditional LORs are online facilities for collecting Learning Objects so that they can be searched for and obtained by educators. Some, but not all, allow for the submission of Learning Objects by typical educators – rather than specialist developers – and some allow for easy adaptation and resubmission by fellow educators. So some, but not all, LORs support the dream of sharing and improving good practice outlined at the beginning of this chapter.

Whether a Learning Design is called a Learning Object or not is less important than the recognition that a Learning Design as a sequence of collaborative activities is a radically different thing from an aggregation of content. In theory, Learning Designs could have been included in LORs; in practice, almost all LORs are content-centric – they contain individual content resources, or aggregations of content, or both.

In addition to the absence of Learning Designs, I was frustrated by a different set of concerns about how LORs were set up and managed. In September 2005, when I first presented the idea of the LAMS Community, I summarized the nine principles of its design as a response to these concerns (Dalziel 2005).

1 Learning Designs/Activities focus, rather than content

As discussed above, the sharing of good educational practice requires more than content, it requires the description of structured flows of collaborative activities (as well as content). An LOR that only shares content demonstrates a quite limited concept of what constitutes education. The challenging prior condition to the creation of the LAMS Community was the development of a new category of e-learning technology to support structured activity flows (Learning Designs).

2 Community focus, rather than repository focus

Most LORs are simply a searchable 'dump' of content – they lack the explicit voice of educators about how the materials have been used, what did and did not work, and how and why educators have adapted resources to suit their requirements. In many cases, the truth is that few educators have used the content from the LOR, so there is little community to build on. However, even if there is a large community of users, the technical design of most LORs focuses heavily on the management of content, with little, if any, support for community discussion around it.

For the LAMS Community, we started with an open source software system built for supporting online communities (.LRN – based on OpenACS), and then added repository functionality to this system. This allowed the LAMS Community to inherit all the mature community features of .LRN, such as the ability to have sub-communities, discussion forums for each community, delegation of sub-community management and many other community-centric features. The repository functionality was then added so that each sub-community could have its own area for sharing Learning Designs. This approach allowed sub-communities to build different kinds of collections, complemented by different kinds of discussion.

3 Search based on free-text, not metadata

Within the LOR field, an appalling amount of time has been spent fighting over descriptive metadata to aid searching. This might be defensible if educators used metadata regularly to find useful resources, but in reality most educators are satisfied with free-text searching in the style of Google. Even in other fields where extensive metadata is available (such as library catalogues), I understand from private discussions with library colleagues that very few search queries are based on metadata or other advanced search options (usually less than 5 per cent). A related problem is the cost of creating good metadata, which most LORs fail to factor into their operation (Currier 2004). Educators are often expected to create extensive metadata records themselves, which they generally refuse to do (due to lack of time), or do poorly (due to lack of expertise). In either case, the outcome is such that even if metadata searching was a natural habit of educators, in practice it would be of little value due to the absence or poor quality of the metadata. There is a strong case to be made that educational metadata would benefit from more cost–benefit analysis prior to implementation.

In the LAMS Community, based on lessons learned from the COLIS project (especially Goodacre and Rowlands 2005) we decided to provide a simple, Google-style search interface with as few metadata fields as possible to encourage easy submission (see point 9 'easy to share' below). The main field used was 'Description' for entering narrative text about the sequence, along with a number of optional explanatory items (Keywords, Subject, Audience, Run time, Delivery Mode, Resources, and Outline of Activities). By including these as plain text within the Description field, we supported free-text searching that included this information, without making these mandatory metadata fields for submission. Having watched the lengthy fights over terminology for other LORs, and given the principles outlined, we decided not to define any of these terms formally, nor provide particular vocabularies – instead, we left it to the community to evolve this terminology through practice.

4 Automated usage tracking/rating systems

One simple way of building a community around a repository is tracking usage and ratings, such as the number of views/downloads of a resource, and simple scoring of resource quality. These kinds of community features have become widely adopted with the rise of 'Web 2.0' approaches such as photo sharing at Flickr, or video sharing at YouTube. Some LORs have implemented complex quality control approaches, such as formal peer review processes. While these 'heavy-weight' community processes are often cited as desirable, they can have the significant downside of slowing the rate of publication of resources, which in a web context can be fatal to widespread use (as illustrated by the history of Wikipedia, which only grew rapidly once prior peer review of materials was discontinued).

For the LAMS Community, we adopted the simple community measures of counting the number of downloads, and allowing any registered community member to rate a sequence on a scale of 1 to 5. Rating data are collected automatically, and the averaged score is presented. While not supporting any formal peer review process, an asynchronous forum is added to each individual sequence to allow for community discussion.

5 Small set of simple licences

Few LORs are explicit about the rights of users in relation to resources, and their silence on usage rights leaves educators unclear whether resources can be freely used or modified, and what restrictions may exist. In some cases, LORs have attempted to encode usage rights into technical languages, but as almost none of the software that 'plays' resources is able to act on this information, it is of little value – and the encoding can only be understood by technical specialists. In other cases, complex special purpose licences have been developed to cover the appropriate usage of objects, but these licences are so long and difficult to understand that educators either fail to read them, or ignore the LOR itself.

The LAMS Community decided to use the now widely adopted Creative Commons licensing scheme (www.creativecommons.org) as a recommended approach for explaining usage rights for sequences. One of the most attractive features of Creative Commons is the use of 'human readable' rights descriptions – that is, simple summaries of the main usage conditions of a licence that do not require legal expertise to understand. After discussion with potential LAMS Community users of their expectations of appropriate usage rights, the 'attribution, non-commercial use only, share alike' licence was selected as the default licence (see http://creativecommons.org/licenses/by-nc-sa/2.5/). While educators are free to choose other Creative Commons licences (or even to enter the text of an alternative licence), a default licence was provided to encourage consistency in the sharing of sequences.

6 Learning software and learning content are free

If educators themselves need to pay a fee to access either learning software or learning content, then this is likely to greatly diminish its rate of adoption, particularly given the quantity of no-cost software and content already available on the web as an alternative. Going further, many educators have concerns about the commercialization of educational software and content, and this can act as a barrier to adoption and use. Going one step further again, the principles of free software ("'free" as in "free speech," not as in "free beer"', Free Software Foundation 2004) and open source software require that software can always be modified, and the modifications freely distributed, and this requirement may undercut some traditional commercial models.

The decision to provide both the LAMS software itself and the LAMS Community without cost was made for both philosophical and practical reasons. Practically it was a way to encourage widespread adoption and use; philosophically it ensured that benefits that may arise from the LAMS approach were not confined only to those who could pay a software or content licensing fee. While a part of the wider LAMS initiative is the commercial services and support company 'LAMS International', which offers fee-based technical support and content, there is no requirement on anyone to use these fee-based services – the software and the community are open to all who have the determination and skills to use them.

7 Resources can be easily adapted by others

One of the great failures of some LORs is that they provide packaged content that cannot be modified or localized by educators: either the package itself cannot be disaggregated to allow for modification, or, if it can, the nature of the content is beyond the technical abilities of most educators to modify. This is a significant failing, as the opportunity for modification/localization is highly valued both practically – real-world teaching situations may differ from the one for which the object was originally designed – and philosophically – not all educators may actually modify resources, but they want to know that they can if they choose. In the field of content aggregations, there are important techniques for externalizing key 'properties' such as simulation variables, instructional text, quiz items, etc., from aggregated objects to make these properties easy to edit independently (e.g. Dolphin and Miller 2002). Sadly, many expensive Learning Objects created in recent years have failed to implement this approach, and hence the objects are little better than web-viewable versions of the multimedia courseware of the mid-1990s.

The easy adaptation principle informed the original development of the LAMS software – particularly the emphasis given to the drag and drop authoring interface, and its necessary simplification of the concepts of Learning Design into easily understood activity tools. The LAMS Community, in this case, acts as the conduit for easy sharing and modifying of complex objects (structured flows of content and collaborative activities) via the existing features of the LAMS software.

8 Close integration of learning platform and the community for sharing

Many educators would prefer information about LOR materials delivered directly into their main online education workspace (typically their VLE), rather than treating the two as separate systems. In many cases, however, LORs have been quite separate from the software used to deliver learning experiences, which makes it difficult for educators to find and integrate relevant content, as well as causing problems for students (for example, requiring multiple log-ins and passwords). While some integration work has been conducted between LOR products and VLEs, LORs which arise from a single institution or government initiative have generally been poor at this. It should be noted that even when LORs conform correctly to appropriate technical standards (such as IMS Content Package or Shareable Courseware Object Reference Model –SCORM), some VLEs have not implemented these standards correctly, and hence packages acquired from a LOR may not 'run' in the VLE. This problem has been more prevalent with school and university VLEs and the use of IMS Content Package, whereas corporate e-learning use of SCORM and its predecessor AICC specification has been less problematic due to more rigorous certification of SCORM players in relevant VLEs as well as certification of SCORM content.

To support close integration with the LAMS Community, the various versions of LAMS have supported close connections to the LAMS Community (in version 1, this included a display of LAMS Community information within the LAMS account; in version 2, it included features for direct searching and downloading of LAMS Community sequences directly into LAMS accounts).

9 Easy to share

For LORs with the goal of sharing good practice among educators, a key barrier to the sharing of creations/modifications is a lengthy and complex repository submission process. The LAMS Community used a minimalist metadata scheme (see 3 above) to encourage rapid and easy sharing of resources, complemented by automated fields including author (based on login information) and date of submission, and 'secondary usage metadata' collected automatically such as downloads, ratings and asynchronous forum comments.

In summary, these nine principles represent the basis on which the LAMS Community website was designed and launched in September 2005. Most principles are relevant to any LOR, regardless of whether they focus on content or Learning Designs; a few are specific to the dream of sharing and improving good educational practice, which requires not only content but also structured flows of activities. While not all LOR designers would accept all of these principles, they represent a considered response to the failure of the first generation of LORs to achieve significant uptake. Given the amount of money spent in this field, a critical reappraisal of fundamental assumptions and the exploration of alternative approaches are surely justified.

The LAMS Community – six years on

In the six years since the creation of the LAMS Community, it has achieved the basic goals of the principles described above, including the creation of a community of educators sharing designs in the form of LAMS sequences. In subsequent years the features of the LAMS Community have been extended to match the evolving interests and requirements of users, in particular, the development of the 'embed' feature (see below).

In terms of sharing and adapting designs, there is now a body of around 900 community-shared sequences that have been downloaded or previewed more than 34,000 times. As noted, these figures are modest by comparison to other larger communities (such as Moodle and MERLOT), but they do represent an example of the ideas behind LAMS and the LAMS Community in practice.

In terms of the nine principles, these have been noticeably unproblematic within the community, and this is perhaps unsurprising given the massive adoption of Web 2.0 approaches generally since around the time of the launch of the LAMS Community. For example, almost every sequence has been licensed using the default licence (Creative Commons BY-NC-SA), and there has been no real debate about licensing within the community. Similarly, the approach to metadata has been accepted without significant debate, and the few comments I have received (privately) are from users who wish there were even fewer fields to complete when sharing a sequence. In both cases, my sense is that community members have taken the pragmatic approach of just 'getting on' with using the website, rather than debating its principles. The one area of moderate concern has been the 'ratings' feature – while download counts are popular, ratings have received a more mixed response – in part due to concerns about being rated on work that is considered 'in progress', and also due to concerns that these ratings might imply a higher level of quality assurance than they actually represent. Nonetheless, even these issues appear to be relatively minor factors in the practical use of the site.

It remains worth noting that not all LAMS users make use of the LAMS Community – indeed, many users of the software are not even aware of its existence, as the software itself provides an area for sharing sequences among those with accounts on that particular server. In one of the few quantitative studies of this issue, a study of LAMS users in UK schools (Russell *et al.* 2005) found that of a total of 565 sequences created by teachers during the project, 106 were adaptations of an existing sequence by the same teacher, and 36 of these were reuse of an existing sequence by a different teacher. This early finding suggested that teachers may be more prepared to share and reuse sequences created by people they can readily identify as colleagues. Masterman (Chapter 4) found that teachers also value anecdotal accounts of practice from those within a trusted, discipline-specific community. In more recent years, this finding of greater sharing among known colleagues has often been supported by informal discussions with LAMS users in various contexts – especially among schoolteachers.

Direct adaptation of sequences, and subsequent sharing back of the adapted design, remains relatively rare, but recent work on designing templates that provide a generic teaching strategy (such as role-play, problem-based learning, Predict – Observe – Explain) with advice to educators on how to add specific discipline content to these templates appears promising as an alternative approach to fostering reuse and adaptation. For an example of this approach, see www.practicaleteachingstrategies.com and Dalziel (2010). Related work on sharing of templates within teacher training courses has also supported the idea of sharing via templates – with an important finding being that those considering a novel teaching strategy like to see a discipline-specific example of the template as well as the template itself (Dalziel and Dalziel 2011).

Another recent project on reuse and adaptation from a medical context illustrated how educators may adopt a general strategy such as problem-based learning (PBL), but this does not mean they will directly use and adapt a PBL LAMS template when it is provided. Instead, educators tended to build their own sequences 'from scratch', and, following further investigation, they indicated that their own sequences had been inspired by the PBL template, but that they had not needed to use the template itself to build their own sequence (Dalziel and Dalziel 2011). It is possible that the ease of use of LAMS Authoring plays a role in this phenomenon. In another hypothetical Learning Design system where only technical specialists could build sequences, this may lead to more reuse of an existing template by educators (as they would not have had the technical skills to build their own from scratch).

The level of discussion within the LAMS Community forums has been frequent for the technical sub-communities, but less frequent for the educational sub-communities. As noted previously, this behaviour is unsurprising – software developers and system administrators are familiar with the use of online communities for discussion and support, whereas this remains less common for educators. Other e-learning development communities have observed high levels of activity in technical forums: for example, an analysis of the Sakai VLE mailing lists indicated that over 70 per cent of all discussion arose from the Developer list, whereas the Pedagogy list generated less than 2 per cent.

There is an ongoing sense that, among those familiar with LAMS, it provides a shared language about the educational process. My own experience of pedagogical discussions has been that almost no communication occurs between educators about what really happens in classrooms (this can easily be tested by asking one teacher to conduct a lesson based on the narrative descriptions of another). This may be due to the lack of a shared descriptive framework for the component parts of the educational process. The LAMS Community, building on the visual representations of the LAMS software, provides a forum where educators do have a shared language, at least inasmuch as it relates to things that LAMS can represent.

The major area of ongoing development of the LAMS Community relates to features for previewing and sharing sequences. In the first year of the site it was not possible to preview a sequence directly within the LAMS Community (rather, educators had to follow a cumbersome process of downloading a sequence first, uploading it to their LAMS account, and then previewing it). However, once a 'one click' preview feature was added in year 2, this feature became widely used, to the point now that there are more previews than downloads overall. In subsequent years, new features were added to LAMS Version 2 to allow for direct searching and downloading of sequences from the LAMS Community directly into an educator's account.

The most recent feature development towards fostering sharing is the creation of an 'embed' feature for LAMS sequences. This feature follows the style of other Web 2.0 embed functions, such as the YouTube feature of being able to directly embed a video into another webpage. In the case of LAMS, it is possible to embed a LAMS sequence into any other webpage, such as a blog (Galley *et al.* 2010). The embed feature shows a picture of the design (based on its layout in LAMS Authoring), and this allows for easier discussion of ideas as 'visualized' in the design. In conjunction with the embed feature, a new website (www. lessonlams.com) has been created as a 'cloud' version of LAMS in which educators can explore LAMS and use it with a class of up to 30 students without cost or any software setup – this is a further attempt to remove barriers to educators exploring Learning Designs. Sequences viewed using the embed feature can be opened into LessonLAMS directly, and easily edited or run with students. This feature has been used to support the sharing of templates (such as www.practicalteachingstrategies.com noted above), as well as discipline-specific examples, such as the English as a Second Language sequences in Figure 15.2, which

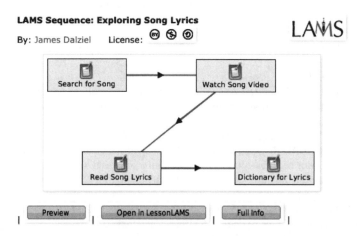

Figure 15.2 Example of the 'embed' feature for an English as a Second Language sequence, including link to LessonLAMS

illustrates the embed features of 'Preview' (Learner view of sequence), 'Open in LessonLAMS' (open a copy of this sequence in a LessonLAMS account for viewing/editing or running with students) and 'More Info' (link to sequence details in the LAMS Community).

The future

Recent work on the LAMS Community illustrates new methods of sharing Learning Designs, both in terms of functionality (e.g. embed) and in educational practice (e.g. teaching strategy templates). My sense is that a crucial next challenge for Learning Design is to connect generic pedagogical approaches with rich discipline content, and to make this combination easily adopted by educators within their disciplines of expertise. This will involve a shift from a collection of generic pedagogical designs to myriad varied implementations of generic designs according to different needs of specific discipline content. An important challenge in this evolution will be to ensure that the tension between generic methods and discipline-specific implementation results in outcomes that are useful to educators as well as expert designers.

Acknowledgements

I'm deeply indebted to Ernie Ghiglione for an extraordinary effort to develop, maintain and extend the LAMS Community website. I would also like to thank Helen Beetham for her extensive feedback on a draft of this chapter.

References

Currier, S. (2004) Metadata Quality in e-Learning: Garbage In – Garbage Out? Cetis Forum. Online post 2 April 2004. Online. http://zope.cetis.ac.uk/content2/20040402013222 (accessed 27 March 2012).

Dalziel, J. (2003) 'Implementing Learning Design: The Learning Activity Management System (LAMS)' in G. Crisp, D. Thiele, I. Scholten, S. Barker and J. Baron (eds) *Interact, Integrate, Impact: Proceedings of the 20th Annual Conference of the Australasian Society for Computers in Learning in Tertiary Education.* ASCILITE. Online. Available at http://www.ascilite.org.au/conferences/adelaide03/docs/pdf/593.pdf (accessed 27 March 2012).

Dalziel, J. (2005) Sharing Learning Designs: Building the LAMS Community Website. Presentation for EDUCAUSE 2005, Orlando, Florida. Online. Available at: http://lamscommunity.org/dot/rn/clubs/educationalcommunity/lamsresearchdevelopment/forums/attach/go-to-attachment?object_id=581118attachment_id=58113 (accessed 16 February 2013).

Dalziel, J. (2010) *Practical eTeaching Strategies: Predict-Observe-Explain, Problem Based Learning and Role Plays.* Sydney: LAMS International.

Dalziel, J. and Dalziel, B. (2011) 'Adoption of Learning Designs in teacher training and medical education: Templates versus embedded content', in L. Cameron and J. Dalziel (eds) *Proceedings of the 6th International LAMS and Learning Design Conference 2011: Learning design for a changing world*, Sydney: LAMS Foundation. Online. Available at http://lamsfoundation.org/lams2011sydney/papers.htm (accessed 27 February 2012).

Dolphin, I. and Miller, P. (2002) 'Learning objects and the information environment', *Ariadne*, 32. Online. Available at http://www.ariadne.ac.uk/issue32/iconex/ (accessed 27 March 2012).

Free Software Foundation (2004) 'The Free Software Definition'. Online. Available at http://www.gnu.org/philosophy/free-sw.html (accessed 27 March 2012).

Galley, R., Conole, G., Dalziel, J. and Ghiglione, E. (2010) 'Cloudworks as a "pedagogical wrapper" for LAMS sequences: Supporting the sharing of ideas across professional boundaries and facilitating collaborative design, evaluation and critical reflection', *Teaching English with Technology – Special Issue on LAMS and Learning Design*, 11 (1): 35–47.

Goodacre, C. and Rowlands, D. (2005) 'Real world metadata management for resource discovery: Proof of concept across education and library sectors in Tasmania', in J. Dalziel, R. Philip and J. Clare (eds) The COLIS Project: Collaborative online learning and information services, p. 139–62, Sydeny: Macquarie University.

Russell, T., Varga-Atkins, T. and Roberts, D. (2005) *Learning Activity Management System Specialist Schools Trust Pilot. A Review for Becta and the Specialist Schools and Academies Trust.* BECTA. Online. Available at http://www.bee-it.co.uk/Guidance%20Docs/Becta%20Files/Reports%20and%20publications/92%20LAMS%20Specialist%20Schools%20Trust%20pilot%20review.pdf (accessed 27 March 2012).

Chapter 16

Design Principles for Mobile Learning

Agnes Kukulska-Hulme and John Traxler

EDITORS' INTRODUCTION

In this chapter the context for design is unashamedly the technological context, that is designing for learners 'equipped with mobile technologies'. Part of the challenge is that the mobile technologies that learners are equipped with are most often their own personal technologies. These are technologies that have already been appropriated for social and informal activities, which may or may not be educational. Designing for mobile learning then provides a glimpse of what designing for the future could be – where education is no longer 'designed and delivered' to a group of learners situated in an expected, defined context, but where each individual engages in their own learning, through their own devices, from their own setting and on their own terms. This chapter lays out how our design principles need to evolve to support us to design content, activities, communications and spaces for such a context.

Introduction

Mobile learning, or *learning with mobile devices*, to adopt a more inclusive term, is an expanding field of research and practice, increasingly shaped by rapid technological and socio-cultural change that is at odds with the more leisurely pace of evolving pedagogy, especially the formal pedagogy within colleges and universities. In one sense, mobility has long been part of learning, in that learning usually takes place in more than one location. However, *mobile learning* has gradually become imbued with multiple meanings, some emphasizing the physical mobility of learners; some focusing on the affordances of mobile technology; some emphasizing connections between contexts or settings; and some noting the primacy of access to digital resources. Other meanings favour more holistic, sociological or ecological interpretations of a phenomenon ill-suited to be contained within the spatial, institutional and cultural boundaries that were largely respected by previous generations of educational technology – and indeed by other branches of the current generation of educational technology (Traxler 2009). It is our aim to simplify this increasing complexity by crystallizing some principles that educators can turn to when faced with the challenge of designing for learners equipped with mobile technologies who want more adaptable or personally engaging ways of learning.

We do believe, however, that design for mobile learning is at a cross-roads. In this chapter, we explore the proposition that the foundations of design as currently understood are shifting rapidly and that the process of design must be reviewed and reconsidered. In fact, it could be argued that, in practice, the place of design in developing learning with technology has long been problematic. Education has always been parasitic on technology, with educational institutions appropriating commercial and corporate hardware and software technologies and these have shaped how learning activities could be designed. One reason to review the process of design is the fact that educational institutions must now appropriate personal technologies – the mobile phone, as well as social networks, immersive worlds and micro-blogging – partly due to student demand for mobile access and partly because these tools facilitate interactions that can support educational ends. In the context of design, this is not just a change in focus. Selwyn (2007) has argued that the design of education technologies is almost wholly dependent on commercial interests; if he is right, we can assume that the technologies embody a commercial or corporate ideology. Educational institutions, when they appropriate these technologies, may attempt to overwrite the ideology designed into them. Now, in attempting to appropriate personal technologies for teaching and learning, they must also address the more complex ways in which different individuals and their communities adopt and adapt these personal technologies. The space available for educational design becomes much more complex and fragmentary.

Much thinking over the past two or three years has focused on the impact and significance of social and cultural change on the nature of learning with mobile devices (e.g. Pachler *et al.* 2010; Rasul 2011; Potter 2011). It has focused, more specifically, on the impact and significance of social and cultural changes associated with widespread ownership of powerful connected personal devices, on the ethics issues, the evaluation methodologies and the institutional policies relating to mobile learning. This has in part been a reaction, or an antidote, to the hegemony of the psychology, education and computer science that are the foundational disciplines of much mobile learning research and to the dominance of the e-learning legacy in framing the agenda for the mobile learning research community.

We believe that it is now time to review and reconsider design for mobile learning. There are several reasons for this, but fundamentally, we are at a tipping point in the relations between education and society, as the ownership and use of digital technologies become universal, social, ubiquitous and pervasive – conspicuous occasionally by their absence where not so long ago they might have been conspicuous by their presence. Mobile technologies are at the heart of these changing relations. Policy makers and practitioners, and their managers, as well as learners and the wider public, are now familiar with mobile technologies, and perhaps think they are familiar with the possibilities for learning with these technologies. Furthermore, the technology is more robust, cheaper, more scalable, commonplace and no longer the prerogative of institutions. So the idea that expensive researchers are necessary to develop imaginative and innovative propositions for mobile learning becomes increasingly difficult to sustain.

In recent years, Apple's iTunes and other similar services have proved incredibly successful in building the *apps economy*, a business model based on selling high volumes of inexpensive educational applications direct to learners. This was the birth of a mobile learning that could sustainably deliver learning to the long tail, resulting in the ultimate mass customization of mobile learning, but one where the impetus behind design is commercial rather than educational. It now seems reasonable to argue that the direction of mobile learning will no longer be guided exclusively by research. In reality, it seems that a combination of commercial sense, research, and pedagogical design expertise will be necessary.

These reflections have led us to examine the nature of design for mobile learning and how it might be reconceived. At the heart of this chapter is the relationship between design for learning that plays to the strengths of mobile technologies, and the design of aspects of learning such as content, activities and communication in the context of technology that has become universal. We also consider how design should take account of both physical space layout and the networking capabilities of mobile technologies. Taken together, these considerations lead to a set of design principles that we summarize.

Design 'for' learning

This section focuses on the ways in which design *for* learning (as defined by Beetham and Sharpe, Introduction) can exploit the affordances or characteristics of mobile technologies. These technologies offer unique possibilities to design for learning that are unlike any afforded by other e-learning technologies. They also offer unique possibilities to support designs for learning where access, inclusion, opportunity and participation are priorities, although like many technologies they also have the potential to exclude some people, which must be weighed up in the process of planning and design.

Mobile technologies support learning that is personalized, situated and authentic. This is currently the domain of informal and practice-based settings, often characterized by unpredictability and ad hoc problem solving. Mobile technologies support digital learning and interaction across a range of settings, but this challenges the notion that design must be intentional and systematic, planned in advance and represented explicitly (see also Kukulska-Hulme 2008). It is more difficult to design intentionally for learning that will be spontaneous and informal, indeed it is perhaps paradoxical; however mobile technologies do have affordances that support these types of learning. For example, mobile devices are by their nature private and personal, and so suited to spontaneous reflection and self-evaluation; these could be elements in an e-portfolio shared only with a tutor. In this example, a formal structure is used (an e-portfolio) but it is anticipated that this could be accessed on a mobile device at any time, which may change the nature of what is captured and how the learner wants it stored and shared.

By *personalized learning*, we mean learning that recognizes diversity, difference and individuality in the ways that learning is developed, delivered and supported. Personalized learning defined in this way includes learning that recognizes different learning preferences and approaches, and social, cognitive and physical difference and diversity (e.g. autistic people, see Rodríguez-Fórtiz *et al.* 2011).

Learning designed for mobile technologies offers a perspective that differs dramatically from personalized e-learning designed for networked desktop computers. It supports learning that can potentially recognize the context and history of each individual learner (and perhaps their relationships to other learners) and delivers learning to each learner when and where they want it. Prototypes exist for learning designed on the basis of knowing where the learner is, how long they have been there, where they were before, who else was learning nearby, their likely schedule and itinerary, their social networks and communities, their progress and preferences as learners (see Yau 2011). Furthermore, the design of the learning delivered by the system can evolve with the learner and their learning.

By *situated learning*, we mean learning that takes place in the course of activity, in appropriate and meaningful contexts (Lave and Wenger 1991; see also Mayes and de Freitas, Chapter 1). The idea grew up by looking at people learning in communities as apprentices by a process of increased participation. It can, however, be extended to learning in the field, in the hospital ward, or in the workshop (see Ellaway, Chapter 12). Mobile learning can be designed to support this context-specific and immediate *situated* learning (e.g. Kneebone and Brenton 2005; Wishart *et al.* 2005; Seppala and Alamaki 2003; Kenny *et al.* 2009). Key design considerations are access to situation-relevant content, situated support, and planning how learners will capture and share their experience either in situ or afterwards.

By *authentic learning*, we mean learning that involves real-world problems and projects that are relevant and interesting to the learner. It means that learning should be based on authentic tasks, that students should be engaged in exploration and inquiry, that students should have opportunities for social discourse, and that ample resources should be available to them as they pursue meaningful problems. Mobile learning enables these conditions for authentic learning to be met, allowing learning tasks designed around content creation, data capture, location-awareness and collaborative working in real-world settings (e.g. Hine *et al.* 2004).

Informal learning occurs spontaneously and independently of formal education – but in mobile learning the term is frequently used to describe forms of learning where the technology supports a specific activity that has been designed in advance with a particular user group in mind. For example, Corlett and Sharples (2004) describe the use of tablet PCs with software designed to support informal collaboration among engineering students. Various informal learning experiences have been trialled in art galleries and museums (Tselios *et al.* 2008; Vavoula *et al.* 2009); these are often experimental projects that are imaginative in terms of their epistemological and pedagogical approaches as much as in the technology that is used.

Much of the potential became apparent as technological and pedagogical expertise built up. Case studies in Kukulska-Hulme and Traxler (2005) made it clear that progress in design for learning with mobile technologies was often hampered by the state of the technologies and by the diversity of educational objectives. Both aspects remain a challenge to the development of mobile learning. The technologies are both easier to use in terms of intuitive interface designs and more complex in terms of multi-functionality and ever-smarter features; reliable and cheap connectivity is still a challenge in many environments. Educational objectives become clearer through classroom experimentation and pilot projects, yet at the same time they become more diverse as technological and social innovations add new layers of complexity.

Mobile technologies can also deliver learning specifically designed for learners' wider social and economic contexts. In particular, the widespread acceptance and ownership of sophisticated mobile phones allows educators to design learning that encourages participation in e-learning among groups often under-represented in formal learning, because mobile devices are perceived by these groups (for example, disengaged learners, or learners who have limited access to desktop computers) as a more motivating or convenient way to take part in learning (Attewell and Savill-Smith 2003; Unterfrauner *et al.* 2010).

Students in formal learning in the UK are under a range of growing pressures, those of time, money, resources and conflicting/competing roles. Learning designed around mobile technologies can allow these students to exploit small amounts of time and space for learning, to work with other students on projects and discussions, and to maximize contact with and support from tutors (Sharples *et al.* 2005; Traxler and Riordan 2004; Yau and Joy 2009).

Finally, mobile technologies also allow unique opportunities to design learning for students who might have difficulty fulfilling their potential with other e-learning technologies; one example is learners with dyslexia who may benefit from self-organization features, handy access to reference tools, being able to hear a speech rendition of a printed document (e.g. by using the phone's camera), and voice-based command interaction (Rainger 2005; Taylor *et al.* 2010).

Design 'of' learning

Now that we have some sense of how the design of learning with mobiles is constrained in various ways, we can consider design itself. In our view, there are three key designs to consider, namely, design of content, of activities and of communication. This is however an arbitrary distinction, since, for example, learners may design content (for each other) as an educational activity. Also these categories are not comparable or equivalent – within the kinds of constraints we discuss, designers are in control of the outcome of designing content but not in control of activities or communications. Learning with mobiles is very different from e-learning with computers in these respects.

Design of content

In terms of the ability to absorb and interact with educational content, including academic texts and interactive media, the use of small devices may initially seem unpromising when compared to desktop computers. This is increasingly less true. Not only does the technology continue to improve but more importantly so does the acceptance and appropriation of it. By looking at how the technologies are changing our approach to content, however, we can come to a better understanding of what will be appropriate on mobile devices. Our focus here is not on the content itself, but rather on ways of thinking about content. The following aspects are important to consider:

- *Learner-created content*: if students are expected to construct some of the content as part of their learning, this can be done in various locations and mobile devices can facilitate it. It is personal and specific to context, and usually to time and place.
- *Personalized content*: learners can receive, assemble, share and carry around personally useful and appropriate resources.
- *Updated content*: updates may be more easily delivered to mobile devices when learners are highly mobile and would not regularly access a desktop computer.
- *Timed or scheduled content*: learners can engage with content frequently, repetitively or periodically using a mobile device without overhead or inconvenience.
- *Prioritized content*: some content can be made available on mobile devices in such a way as to prioritize or reinforce it over other content; this may be a useful deliberate teaching strategy.
- *Aural content*: if listening is important, delivering audio via a personal mobile device can be engaging and convenient.
- *Flexible content*: learners may appreciate having the option of mobile access to learning materials and resources, as an alternative to desktop content.

Design of activities

The second area to consider is the design of learning activities. According to Naismith *et al.* (2004), mobile technologies can be used in the design of six different types of learning, or categories of activity:

- *Behaviourist learning*, where quick feedback or reinforcement can be facilitated by mobile devices because they are always to hand.
- *Constructivist learning*, where learners build new concepts perhaps through engaging with their physical and social environment.
- *Situated learning*, where learners take a mobile device into an educationally relevant real-world location and learn from that setting.
- *Collaborative learning*, where mobile devices are an essential means of communication and electronic information sharing for learners in groups outside their educational institution.
- *Informal and lifelong learning*, possibly unstructured or opportunistic, driven by personal curiosity, chance encounters and the stimulus of the environment. Mobile devices accompany users and become a convenient source of information or means of communication that assists with learning, or records learning experiences for future consultation and review.
- *Supported learning*, where mobile devices monitor progress, check schedules and dates, review and manage progress, receive errata.

At a more detailed level, there are particular tasks that are well suited to mobile learning, for example activities that involve data collection, testing, consolidation of learning, personal reflection and skills acquisition. There is always scope to develop learning activities that combine the use of mobile devices with other learning resources; for example, this can be done by providing a commentary accessed on a personal device as a means of orientation within a set of learning materials on another medium. Mobile devices can also be used as a way to facilitate remote, *on the move* participation in online activities that might be continued or completed at a desktop computer.

Mobile technologies are highly suited to learning that has variously been described as informal, opportunistic, spontaneous (Bull *et al.* 2004; Colley and Stead 2003) – but also as disruptive (Sharples 2003). This is however a major challenge for the design of formal learning since opportunistic learning and formal learning might seem difficult to reconcile, being very different in nature and intent (see also Beetham, Chapter 2). Furthermore these characterizations of mobile learning are implicitly making a comparison backwards towards conventional e-learning, seeing mobile learning as e-learning but mobile. This characterization previously defined the mobile learning design agenda. Now, in a society permeated by mobile technologies, mobile learning becomes instead the education that characterizes a mobile society and the design agenda may change focus accordingly. This is merely a different formulation of our opening remarks. Learning with mobile devices is not a new variant of e-learning, enlivening and extending an otherwise stable curriculum and pedagogy. Mobile devices are involved in the wider, social transformation of how people, not just learners, acquire and distribute information, images, ideas and opinions, and of how learning is redefined (Traxler 2009).

Design of communication

This is an exciting but problematic aspect of design, partly due to worries about the extent and reliability of coverage and the costs of connectivity that might be incurred by learners, and partly due to the contested nature of agency and control. Communication is at the intersection of the educational uses of mobile devices as determined by lecturers and teachers and the recreational, personal and social uses as determined by learners themselves. Within these constraints, mobile devices can support:

- spontaneous communication and collaboration, e.g. one-to-one or one-to-many by SMS; by sending a message to a forum or blog while travelling; by micro-blogging (e.g. Twitter);
- beaming of stored information and images from device to device (e.g. via Bluetooth);
- portable sound-recording, voice-recording, photos and video clips that are used in communication.

Many phones support voice, SMS, email, micro-blogging, instant messaging, social networks and web-based conferencing. Experience of *m-moderating* (moderating of mobile conferences) is still very limited (JISC 2008; Traxler and Leach 2006) but could in principle follow the same trajectory as e-moderating, moving from administrative support and reacting to individual queries, to pastoral support and proactive support for new forms of learning (Salmon 2011). Mobile learning communities are rapidly growing and diversifying. There is considerable anecdotal evidence of micro-blogging with Twitter forming the basis for unmoderated *personal learning networks*, self-help groups for academics, and increasing use of social networks, usually Facebook (Minocha 2009), within formal learning, in turn accessed via the mobile web or mobile apps. These are by their nature transient and difficult to document but a search of Twitter reveals hash-tags from archaeology through mathematics to zoology, with a similar range of dedicated groups on Facebook, predominantly accessed via mobile devices (Sengupta 2012).

Space design

Physical learning spaces, in other words buildings and their surroundings, must also be designed for learning and fit for purpose (Brown and Long 2006;

Oblinger 2005). In UK colleges and universities, this is enormously problematic since much of their estate is ageing and over-crowded. There is a need for greater exploration and recognition of the relationships between the location and layout of learning and the nature and success of learning, and a need to integrate virtual learning spaces, that is the design and practice of e-learning, more closely, with the physical learning spaces (JISC 2006; Jamieson *et al.* 2000). Much work on this topic is, however, still rooted in learning with desktop computers, as opposed to learning with mobile devices, and is also driven by other forces from outside education (Temple 2007). Mobile learning technologies are increasingly important in these relationships but this is an intrinsically more challenging problem: *BYOD, bring-your-own-device,* strategies introduce dramatically increased technical diversity into the situation, and research into the relationships between space, movement and interaction is still emerging and not yet specifically applied to learners (for example, Mizobuchi *et al.* 2005; Pasco *et al.* 2000; Perry and Hourcade 2008). There are a number of points at which these intersect and there is a tension between the (re)design of spaces for learning and the design of learning for these spaces.

First, there are some specialist classrooms designed to support collaborative learning based on wireless connectivity, handheld computers and interactive whiteboards (for example, Chang *et al.* 2004). These are developed experimentally or sold commercially as integrated off-the-shelf packages and can require high investment in dedicated and purpose-built rooms in new buildings or dramatically refurbished old ones. They also require a substantial commitment in staff development and curriculum design. Highly specialized learning is designed for these spaces but the emergence of more financially sustainable BYOD strategies is likely to forestall future activity.

Second, we can also see increasing opportunities for location-specific, immersive world and augmented reality learning being designed into the physical learning spaces of formal learning rather than designed into them subsequently – but these opportunities are not being systematically identified and exploited (Frohberg 2006). This runs parallel to the design of informal learning in heritage, cultural and landscape spaces using similar technologies, but both these trends are only sustainable if based on BYOD.

Third, laptops for general academic work are widely available for loan to students and for issue to staff, and many purchase their own. These laptops have the potential to free up substantial amounts of estate currently dedicated to ranks of networked desktop computers, to change the working lives of academic staff and thus change the demands these staff make on their accommodation (Vila *et al.* 2010). A related strategy, known as *learner devices* (Traxler 2010) or BYOD (CoSN 2012), as mentioned earlier, assumes the institutional default shifts to learners choosing and providing the technology for learning and is a financially attractive solution to resource problems. There are however, practical and technical challenges, such as network security, equality of access and quality assurance, and more profound issues about the shift in the locus of agency, authority and control when learners not teachers control and understand the technologies (Traxler 2010). In the current context, however, there is a paradigm shift from designing education activities and artefacts for stable institutional platforms to designing for the diverse and unpredictable devices that learners choose.

Fourth, in a wider sense, universities and colleges are public agencies, indirectly and sometimes directly funded to deliver the current government's education agenda and policy objectives (Shattock 2006). These have recently included community education, lifelong learning and widened participation, and have now moved on to internationalization and the student experience. The interaction of mobile learning design and physical learning space design has the potential to carry these issues forward since both challenge the arbitrary division between academic institutions, their markets and their catchment areas. Mobile learning development has the potential to carry education into communities including their most marginal and disaffected members, while physical learning space design has the potential to entice and welcome communities into academic institutions. This, too, introduces another dimension into the design of mobile learning, and again undermines expectations about a stable and consistent learner community.

Design principles

In this chapter, we have outlined key considerations in order to clarify how mobile learning designs differ from current practice in design for e-learning. To design for mobile learning, first of all we need to be clear about the unique characteristics and nature of mobile learning. Next, a rationale must be constructed around how the learning will be more personal, situated, authentic or informal than would be possible by other available means. Content, activities and communication should then be aligned with the proposed rationale. Third, we need to recognize the extent of popular, that is non-institutional, familiarity with using mobile devices to not only consume the elements of learning, that is, information, images, ideas and opinions, but also to produce and share them. This takes us beyond the increasing adoption of user-centred design practices in educational design and into the co-creation of education itself. It also challenges the primacy, authority and boundaries of formal education as the locus of educational design.

We believe that design principles for mobile learning should be based on two key observations. First, that mobile technologies are ubiquitous, diverse, personal, social and changeable, not uniform, consistent, or institutional. Second, that learners' expectations about educational uses of mobile technologies may be coming from outside formal or institutional education, as part of experiences driven by curiosity, personal enquiry and individual recreation.

On this basis we propose the following principles:

1   Start with learners – recognize their diversity, agency and habits, including patterns of mobility and ubiquitous social interaction.

2   Design to meet learners on their terms, with their devices, in their spaces.
3   Work with learners – seek opportunities for prototyping, participation and feedback.
4   Look for added value, e.g. opportunities for contingent learning, situated learning, authentic learning, context-aware learning.
5   Design for inclusion, enabling accessibility and greater access than may be possible using desktop computers.
6   Recognize that learning activities designed by you are liable to be played out differently as learners engage with them outside the classroom.
7   Be prepared to trial and discard activities more frequently as technologies evolve.
8   Wait for the novelty to wear off before evaluating, and take account of life-style and environmental factors that may impact on mobile learning.

Conclusions

The increasing power and diversity of mobile devices supports ever more powerful and diverse learning designs. As we argued earlier, mobile learning research has historically had a narrow base, drawing mainly on psychology, computer science and education, and it has developed its agenda as a continuation of, or reaction to, the perceived triumphs and limitations of e-learning. This made sense in the 1990s when the expense and expertise required for e-learning and then m-learning needed the resource base of educational institutions. It led to an acceptance of institutions, their authority, their agency and their practices as the preferred focus for the design, deployment and delivery of mobile learning. As mobile devices become widespread and popular, and as access to free web services, social networks and shared resources begins to shape learning practices, this makes less and less sense. The design principles we have put forward recognize the centrality of learners with their personal technologies and preferences, alongside the unique nature and added value of mobile learning, and the idea that mobile learning is synonymous with unpredictability and constant change.

References

Attewell, J. and Savill-Smith, C. (2003) 'Mobile learning and social inclusion: focusing on learners and learning', paper presented at mLearn 2003: 2nd World Conference on mLearning, London, May 2003.
Brown, M. and Long, P. (2006) 'Trends in learning space design', in D. Oblinger (ed.) *Learning Spaces*, Boulder, Colorado: Educause. Online. Available at http://www.educause.edu/learningspaces (accessed 15 July 2012).
Bull, S., Bridgefoot, L., Corlett, D., Kiddie, P., Marianczak, T., Mistry, C., Sandle, N., Sharples, M. and Williams, D. (2004) 'Interactive Logbook: the development of an application to enhance and facilitate collaborative working within groups in higher education', paper presented at mLearn 2004 – Mobile learning anytime everywhere, Bracciano, Italy, July 2004.

Chang, S.-B., Wang, H.-Y., Liang, J.-K., Liu, T.-C. and Chan, T.-W. (2004) 'A contest event in the connected classroom using wireless handheld devices', paper presented at the 2nd IEEE International Workshop on Wireless and Mobile Technologies in Education (WMTE'04), Jung-Li, Taiwan, March 2004.

Colley, J. and Stead, G. (2003) 'Take a bite: producing accessible learning materials for mobile devices', paper presented at mLearn 2003: 2nd World Conference on mLearning, London, May 2003.

Corlett, D. and Sharples, M. (2004) 'Tablet technology for informal collaboration in higher education', paper presented at mLearn 2004 – Mobile learning anytime everywhere, Bracciano, Italy, July 2004.

CoSN (2012) *Making Progress: Rethinking state and school district policies concerning mobile technologies and social media*, Washington: Consortium for School Networking.

Frohberg, D. (2006) 'Mobile learning is coming of age – What we have and what we still miss', paper presented at DeLFI, Darmstadt, Germany, September 2006.

Hine, N., Rentoul, R. and Specht, M. (2004) 'Collaboration and roles in remote field trips', paper presented at mLearn 2003: 2nd World Conference on mLearning, London, May 2003.

Jamieson, P., Taylor, P.G., Fisher, K.A.C.F., Trevitt, A.C.F. and Gilding, T. (2000) 'Place and space in the design of new learning environments', *Higher Education Research and Development*, 19 (2): 221–36.

JISC (2006) *Designing Spaces for Effective Learning: A guide to 21st century learning space design*, Bristol: Joint Information Services Committee.

JISC (2008) *MELaS – Mobiles Enabling Learning and Support: Final Report*, Bristol: Joint Information Services Committee.

Kenny, R.F., Park, C.L., Van Neste-Kenny, J.M.C., Burton, P.A. and Meiers, P.A. (2009) 'Using mobile learning to enhance the quality of nursing practice education', in M. Ally (ed.) *Mobile Learning: Transforming the delivery of education and training*, Athabasca, AB: Athabasca University Press.

Kneebone, R. and Brenton, H. (2005) 'Training perioperative specialist practitioners', in A. Kukulska-Hulme and J. Traxler (eds) *Mobile Learning: A handbook for educators and trainers*, London: Routledge.

Kukulska-Hulme, A. (2008) 'What should we do with Jack-in-the-box? Anticipating surprises in mobile learning', in M. Allegra, G. Fulantelli, M. Gentile and D. Taibi (eds) *Emerging Educational Technologies and Practices*, Palermo: Consiglio Nazionale delle Ricerche, Instituto per le Tecnologie Didattiche.

Kukulska-Hulme, A. and Traxler, J. (eds) (2005) *Mobile Learning: A handbook for educators and trainers*, London: Routledge

Lave, J. and Wenger, E. (1991) *Situated Learning: Legitimate peripheral participation*, Cambridge, UK: Cambridge University Press.

Minocha, S. (2009) 'Role of social software tools in education: A literature review', *Education and Training*, 51 (5/6): 353–69.

Mizobuchi, S., Chignell, M. and Newton, D. (2005) 'Mobile text entry: relationship between walking speed and text input task difficulty', in *Proc. MobileHCI 2005*: ACM Press.

Naismith, L., Lonsdale, P., Vavoula, G. and Sharples, M. (2004) Literature Review in Mobile Technologies and Learning, Report 11 for Futurelab. Online. Available at https://ra.le.ac.uk/jspui/bitstream/2381/8132/4/[08]mobile_review[1].pdf (accessed 18 March 2012).

Oblinger, D. (2005) 'Leading the transitions from classrooms to learning spaces', *Educause Quarterly*, 28 (1): 14–18.

Pachler, N., Bachmair, B., Cook, J., Kress, G. (eds) (2010) *Mobile Learning: Structures, agency, practices*. New York: Springer.

Pascoe, J., Ryan, N. and Morse, D. (2000) 'Using while moving: HCI issues in fieldwork environments', *ACM Trans. Computer-Human Interaction*, 7 (3): 417–37.

Perry, K.B. and Hourcade, J.P. (2008) 'Evaluating one handed thumb tapping on mobile touchscreen devices', in *Proceedings of Graphics Interface*, Ontario, Canada: Canadian Information Processing Society

Potter, J. (2011) 'Creation and curatorship in new media', in K. Rummler, J. Seipold, E. Lübcke, N. Pachler and G. Attwell (eds) *Mobile Learning: Crossing boundaries in convergent environments. Book of Abstracts*. London Mobile Learning Group.

Rainger, P. (2005) 'Accessibility and mobile learning', in A. Kukulska-Hulme and J. Traxler (eds) *Mobile Learning: A handbook for educators and trainers*, London: Routledge.

Rasul, A.A. (2011) 'Cultural factors in a mobile phone adoption and usage model: A case of UUM Postgraduate Students', unpublished master's thesis, Universiti Utara Malaysia.

Rodríguez-Fórtiz, M.J., Fernández-López, A. and Rodríguez, M.L. (2011) 'Mobile communication and learning applications for autistic people', in T. Williams (ed.) *Autism Spectrum Disorders – From Genes to Environment*. InTech: Open Access Publishing.

Salmon, G. (2011) *E-Moderating: The key to online teaching and learning* (3rd edn), London: Routledge.

Selwyn, N. (2007) 'The use of computer technology in university teaching and learning: a critical perspective', *Journal of Computer Assisted Learning*, 23: 83–94.

Sengupta, S. (2012) 'Facebook's prospects may rest on trove of data', *New York Times*, May 14.

Seppala, P. and H. Alamaki (2003) 'Mobile learning in teacher training', *Journal of Computer Assisted Learning*, 19 (3): 330–5.

Sharples, M. (2003) 'Disruptive devices: mobile technology for conversational learning', *International Journal of Continuing Engineering Education and Lifelong Learning*, 12 (5/6): 504–20.

Sharples, M., Corlett, D., Bull, S., Chan, T. and Rudman, P. (2005) 'The student learning organiser', in A. Kukulska-Hulme and J. Traxler (eds) *Mobile Learning: A handbook for educators and trainers*, London: Routledge.

Shattock, M. (2006) 'Policy drivers in UK higher education in historical perspective: "Inside Out", "Outside In" and the contribution of research', *Higher Education Quarterly*, 60: 130–40.

Taylor, J.D., Dearnley, C.A., Laxton, J.C., Coates, C.A., Treasure-Jones, T., Campbell, R. and Hall, I. (2010) 'Developing a mobile learning solution for health and social care practice', *Distance Education*, 31 (2): 175–92.

Temple, P. (2007) *Learning Spaces for the 21st Century: A review of the literature*, York: Higher Education Academy.

Traxler, J. (2009) 'Learning in a mobile age', *International Journal of Mobile and Blended Learning*, 1 (1): 1–12.

Traxler, J. (2010) 'Students and mobile devices', *Research in Learning Technology*, 18 (2): 149–60.

Traxler, J. and Leach, J., (2006) 'Innovative and sustainable mobile learning in Africa', paper presented at WMUTE (IEEE), Athens, Greece, November 2006.

Traxler, J. and Riordan, B. (2004) *Using Personal Digital Assistants (PDAs) to support students*, Belfast: Higher Education Academy Resources. Online. Available at http://www.ics.heacademy.ac.uk/Events/conf2003/John%20Traxler.pdf (accessed 25 March 2012).

Tselios, N., Papadimitriou, I., Raptis, D., Yiannoutsou, N., Komis, V. and Avouris, N. (2008) 'Mobile learning in museums: Design and evaluation challenges', in Lumsden, J. (ed.) *Handbook of Research on User Interface Design and Evaluation for Mobile Technology*, Hershey, PA: IDEA Publishing.

Unterfrauner, E., Marschalek, I. and Fabian, C. (2010) 'Mobile learning with marginalized young people', in I. Arnedillo Sánchez and P. Isaias (eds) *Proceedings of the IADIS International Conference Mobile Learning 2010*. Lisbon: IADIS.

Vavoula, G., Sharples, M., Rudman, P., Meek, J. and Lonsdale, P. (2009) 'Myartspace: Design and evaluation of support for learning with multimedia phones between classrooms and museums', *Computers and Education*, 53 (2): 286–99.

Vila, M.C., Gálvez, A.P. and Campos, J.C. (2010) 'Mobile services in the Rector Gabriel Ferraté Library – Technical University of Catalonia', *Reference Services Review*, 38 (2): 321–34.

Wishart, J., McFarlane, A. and Ramsden, A. (2005) 'Using personal digital assistants (PDAs) with internet access to support initial teacher training in the UK', paper presented at mLearn 2005 – The future of learning in your hands, Cape Town, October 2005.

Yau, J.Y.-K. (2011) 'A mobile context-aware learning schedule framework with Java learning objects', unpublished PhD thesis, University of Warwick.

Yau, J.Y.-K. and Joy, M. (2009) 'A mobile context-aware framework for managing learning schedules: data analysis from an interview study', *International Journal of Mobile and Blended Learning*, 1 (4): 29–55.

Chapter 17

Designing for Learning in an Uncertain Future

Helen Beetham with contributions from Gráinne Conole, Sara de Freitas, Rachel Helen Ellaway, Chris Jones, Liz Masterman, Christopher R. Pegler, Rhona Sharpe and John Traxler

EDITORS' INTRODUCTION

This chapter deals with the uncertainty of the future for which we are designing today. Rather than attempting to summarize the implications of the previous chapters, or worse, to predict a particular educational future, this chapter discusses the range of issues that designers of learning will need to engage with in the coming five to ten years. It examines a number of current trends and considers how design processes might need to evolve in response. The chapter was produced in an original way: a public version of the chapter was authored by open contribution, while a closed version was collaboratively written over 24 hours by many of the book's authors, working together in a live setting or remotely. The version produced here was written by the main author, drawing on the contributions of others without whom the chapter could not have been written.

Introduction

The future is uncertain. In an important sense, designs for learning always bear the mark of this uncertainty as they aim to help learners thrive in contexts that cannot be fully foreseen, sometimes far removed in time and space from the learning situation. In this chapter we attempt to sketch some possible futures for pedagogic design, restricting our view to the next ten years or so and to those contexts we recognize today as post-compulsory. We acknowledge that the contributors to this chapter are rooted in a particular time, place (largely the UK) and educational culture, from where the future can only be imagined in a partial way. Possible futures will look different from the standpoint of those nations that are emerging onto the global educational stage – those, such as China, India, Russia and Brazil, with the biggest populations of potential graduates to serve and the highest aspirations for them – and from the standpoint of nations with less international capital or specific indigenous needs whose education systems may be most under threat from a globalized market.

In our projections we make some important assumptions. First, we assume that educators will continue to design learning opportunities, although their roles, responsibilities and relationships with specific institutions may well change. We assume that learners will participate in those learning opportunities and will learn in ways that they would not have done if educators – with the specific intention of supporting their learning – were not involved. It follows that we see teachers as continuing to have a central role, and that digital technology is not going to be in loco docentis. We also assume that learners will continue to want or need to take up educational opportunities after their compulsory schooling is over and that these opportunities will differ from those available in school. In other words, while our imaginations have embraced some radically different futures, they have not allowed us to suppose that design for learning, in the sense explored by this book, becomes unnecessary or irrelevant. Nor do we see 'the future' as a radically different space: we see it as continuous with the present and as continually shaped by decisions we make in the here and how. Radical change/disruption/turbulence has long been the stock in trade of learning technology thinking (see, for example, Naughton 2012), but cultures of making and sharing meanings prove surprisingly resistant. Instead of the death of the book, we have the proliferation of e-book devices.

In the first edition of this book, we were interested in how digital technologies were being incorporated into learning activities and in the decisions teachers and designers of learning make in a technologically rich learning environment. In this second edition we have shifted focus to consider design at the level of programmes and curricula, and to note that design processes are themselves changing under the influence of digital technologies. This chapter broadens our focus again to ask how educators can help learners to thrive in a world that is profoundly changed and changing – a world that is locally rich with digital tools and data, and globally interconnected. We set out some critical uncertainties that we detect in this world and consider how educators might respond through the design of learning activities, opportunities, programmes of study, or educational environments. We ask what possible futures might emerge from crises in the economy, the climate, university funding and the legitimacy of higher education as a public institution, and from changes in technologies and socio-technical practices. We are not in the business of speculation about likely futures or desirable futures, but we have tried to delineate the space in which educators will be making decisions that impact on learners' futures, and helping learners to meet their learning goals.

Technological uncertainties

Digital tools for learning

Technology futures are notoriously hard to foresee, not least because change in this area is driven by a vast and accelerating global market. Technologies are taken up and appropriated in ways unforeseen by their original designers: texting is one commonly cited example of this. The Internet itself and many of the online services that we now take for granted were originally designed to support small-scale research communities. Today, researchers are adopting mass public technologies to build their own virtual research environments.

The NMC Horizon Report (NMC Horizon Project 2012) identifies six emerging technologies that are considered likely to have a major impact on learning: mobile apps, tablets, gesture-based computing, learning analytics, the Internet of Things, and game-based learning. Some of these have been covered in this second edition (see Kukulska-Hulme and Traxler on mobile devices, de Freitas on gaming, Jones on learning analytics, all this volume) and it would be interesting to speculate which might make it to a third edition. What Kukulska-Hulme and Traxler have demonstrated is that mobile technologies require a rethinking of design practice because they are *personal* technologies. Tablets and gestural interfaces similarly extend the intimacy of the computing experience: they are part of a well-established trend towards intuitive interfaces, small-scale devices for carrying or wearing, and frictionless adoption. The design space has changed as corporate systems – learning environments, assessment technologies, reliable networks and services – have become taken for granted and the focus has moved to understanding how learners relate to and value the technologies they have to hand, and how best to recruit those resources for learning. Design becomes, as a consequence, a much more contingent activity.

Mobile devices, platforms and apps are both local/personal and universal. They allow learners to generate, regenerate, valorize and transmit ideas and to communicate identities local to who they are and where they are, but in ways that leave a global footprint. They are widely accessible to learners who lack other forms of connectivity. However, services on mobile devices are tightly controlled by the mobile companies, unlike (currently at least) web services accessed through a browser. The limited storage capacity of mobile devices also means that users are dependent on storage in the cloud, which also raises issues over access to and ownership of personal data. In celebrating the potential of mobile technologies to support learning, teachers and designers will need to develop their own and their learners' awareness of these issues.

Similarly with learning analytics, what is technically possible may matter less than what learners and educators find useful and acceptable. Learners will need to understand how data about their learning interactions can be stored and analysed, and make decisions that weigh the potential benefits of close monitoring against the risks. As Simon Buckingham Shum (2011) has argued, it makes a big difference whether analytics are to become 'tools to study learners, or tools to place in their hands'. There are already signs that learners are preferring public technologies and third-party apps to institutional systems for many educational activities and, again, they need to understand the implications for their personal and educational data, to become more reflective in and conscious of the traces they leave rather than more dependent on what the system can tell them about themselves.

As the commercial gaming industry becomes ever more sophisticated, it seems likely that the potential to design environments for educational play – and to intersect those environments in more complex ways with real-world activities – will also advance (Arnab *et al.* 2011). Gaming environments have a number of advantages that are relevant in post-compulsory settings. Learning activities emerge dynamically from learner interactions; there is scope for learners to make different attempts at the same task; the environment can be calibrated for different levels of challenge; and learners can 'play' with who they are and what they can do. These choices are highly visible, allowing learners to reflect on subtle aspects of learning such as roles, identities and power relations. It is interesting to note the counterpoint between more sophisticated virtual environments and the Internet of Things. On the one hand, learners are immersed in a fully designed environment which presents controlled situations and reacts to inputs in predictable ways. On the other hand, learners engage in real-world situations in which locations, people and entities are enriched with data. Arguably, as more interactions take place in virtual spaces, and as the 'real' environment is overlaid with more information and entry points to virtual networks, the real and virtual are becoming co-extensive. Virtual or hybrid spaces may no longer be 'sandpits' for learning in the real world, but may be the very spaces where learners' personal, social, academic and professional life will be played out. On the other hand, the materiality of the real continues to assert itself in a time of increased scarcity and environmental degradation.

Implications for design

Of these six technologies and others we have considered, such as cloud computing, only learning analytics and game-based learning are specifically designed for educational purposes. Learners will continue to use personal technologies and extend their techno-social practices to support their studies; teachers will choose generic and public over institutional technologies where they are more accessible and easier to use. Key decisions will need to be taken about setting. The very ubiquity of virtual environments may lend new value to encounters in the real world. This world will be enriched in multiple ways with data, and capable of being enriched further by capture devices, to the extent that learners will be able to carry with them detailed memories of their learning as it has evolved. Whether they can make good use of these records to reflect, plan and present their achievements will be critical to how they thrive. Designing well in the future will, more than ever, mean seeing the creative potential of new technologies, articulating what technologies can bring to the unique contexts of post-compulsory learning, and giving learners the space and support to experiment for themselves. It may also mean placing special value on entities and experiences that do not have a virtual counterpart, recognizing that learners increasingly fail to consider these as useful to their learning unless guided otherwise (Masterman 2012).

Digital media and web 2.0

In the past decade we have witnessed a significant shift away from traditional forms of mass communication and editorial control towards user-generated content. Cook *et al.* (2011) have described how not only the content, but also the context of digital communication are augmented by users to suit the needs of the individual or the conversational community. So while the ease with which digital media are recorded, edited, repurposed and redistributed has blurred the boundaries between consumption and production, digital services are allowing individuals to personalize their media use as never before. These ongoing structural transformations are characterized by the following:

- personal processes of media selection, aggregation and archiving, often alongside more traditional editorial processes;
- 'push' media individually targeted (mass customization) based on information gathered and stored about personal interactions online;
- media and messages crossing platforms freely;
- more-or-less ubiquitous access to digital media on personal devices such as laptops, mobile phones, tablets and e-book readers;
- convergence of digital media with web 2.0 tools, leading to:
  - new media platforms such as YouTube, Flickr, Vimeo, SlideShare and MySpace, which are simultaneously social networks, distribution platforms and media archives;
  - users generating their own contents and contexts for sharing;
  - ongoing disputes over intellectual and creative copyright.

These structural changes represent important shifts in the relationship between individuals, their media/messages, and the people with whom they share their media experiences. For example, the mass experience of radio and television broadcasts has been in decline as the BBC and other providers have relinquished control of the timetable to individual choice. However, new synchronous, shared experiences have emerged as Twitter users follow and comment on broadcasts, or contribute to live chats, and these media are being reintegrated into the original broadcast in ways that seem likely to reverse their decline. Participants in newsworthy events are more likely to upload a video directly to YouTube than to contact a news agency, and news agencies make increasing use of citizen journalists in their editorial policies. Both these media platforms – Twitter and YouTube – also allow teachers and learners to build powerful communities and to intersect those communities with wider currents of exchange, whether social, academic or professional.

Implications for design

Designers will no doubt focus on these new opportunities:

• Learners can be actively engaged in aggregating, editing and producing knowledge in virtual spaces, focusing on read-write rather than read-only access to the World Wide Web.
• Learning outcomes can be made public in spaces where they can become part of a wider discourse, demonstrating that learners' perspectives are of value – though this must be done with care and full consent.
• Learners can participate in online knowledge communities, following, aggregating, commenting, tagging and contributing alongside people who are significant in their subject or profession.
• Learners can use social data and mass data in research or exploration/investigation tasks: learners can generate their own social data (asking questions on Twitter, using web analytics).
• Learners can use different media to communicate academic ideas, including, for example, generating original data visualizations and infographics, creating animations, videoing live activities and performances.
• Learners, researchers and teachers together can reflect on how digital media and web 2.0 services are changing practice in their subject, and in some cases changing the meaning of that subject.

Personal and social technologies

Explicitly or implicitly, institutions increasingly expect staff and students to use their personal technologies for academic work. 'Bring your own device' (BYOD), closely followed by 'bring your own service', began as an aspiration to support learner choice and to help learners to access course materials in ways that were familiar and convenient. However, it is increasingly becoming an expectation as surveys showed consistently high levels of laptop and smartphone ownership among student populations. The positive side of this development is that learners are assumed to have agency in respect of technology use, and their choices are recognized as aspects of their identities. Assuming personal access to digital communication and information media also allows classroom time to be focused on what can be achieved face-to-face. However, students without digital capital are increasingly disadvantaged by the assumption of BYOD (Hargittai 2010).

Implications for design

At the present time, the trend in personal and social technologies is towards the use of apps delivered via a mobile platform, backed up by web services with data and software increasingly stored in the cloud. Mobile devices offer an integrated hardware–software platform that limits or even excludes the control of the educator and the educational institution. The learner's primary relationship is with the platform provider, who determines what is available, how it is displayed, and how data is (or is not) shared. This may seriously attenuate the design and process cues that can be reliably communicated to the learner. Collaborative learning – and collaborative design – may become harder as learners buy into different platforms. Global standards such as IMS LD (http://www.imsglobal. org/learningdesign/) and SCORM (http://www.adlnet.gov/capabilities/scorm), which have been critical to the development of shared design processes and outcomes, need to be simple and robust enough to survive the transfer to app platforms. It may be some time before design for learning finds its voice in this new media environment.

It is possible that the move towards apps and browser-based services will make it more challenging for learners to acquire complex, technology-supported practices and the integrated systems associated with them. Examples would be data analysis software, reference management systems, editing and design tools, even basic productivity and Office-type applications. We already see instances of students shunning these systems in favour of mobile apps with much lower levels of functionality. Is this a welcome move away from system monopolies towards a 'build your own' approach, or are there real risks when the learning curve of complex systems seems too steep?

Designers at every level – programme, module, institutional portfolio, learning environment – need to be aware that differences in personal owner-ship and use will create new inequalities in learning. Expectations must be clear and all learners must have opportunities to acquire the necessary equipment (e.g. through loaned institutional devices), access relevant services, and become proficient in their use.

Economic and political uncertainties

Economic crisis and financial constraint

It is unclear what the long-term effects will be of the global restructuring that has followed the financial crisis of 2008, but some of the dimensions of the crisis are clear. The advanced industrial countries have embarked on large programmes of austerity which often redraw the boundaries between education provided by the state and that supplied by the for-profit and not-for-profit sectors, and to push much of the cost of post-compulsory learning back onto learners themselves. Unevenness in the world economy suggests that these constraints may not affect the newly emergent economies in the same way. Educational technology has been and will continue to be key, both to mediating new kinds of relation-ship between institutions and their students, and to allowing new providers to enter the educational marketplace. These include digital publishers, corporate providers of institutional infrastructure (e.g. proprietary learning management systems), accrediting bodies and professional associations, and in the future perhaps new institutions recruiting students to study for open qualifications or to be accredited for their work with open educational resources (see the section on open education below).

Even within institutions, financial constraints and the organizational restructuring consequent on these constraints are likely to affect the ways design takes place and the elements of educational provision that are open to design by institutional staff. Elements of infrastructure are likely to be outsourced, for example, and access to paid-for content may be severely restricted. Design for learning may well be focused on efficiencies rather than innovation, with the use of standardized design templates and restricted palettes of learning activity or learning resource that educators can use. The pressure in these circumstances will be to increase numbers of students per programme of study and to decrease the staff time devoted to student support, individualized guidance and feedback. Designs that can achieve this efficiently and without high levels of student dropout will be prized. Furthermore, efforts that have previously been put into widening access and participation may be reversed, as there are constraints on the flow of international students, and as education becomes more obviously a personal good than a public entitlement.

The use of learning analytics alongside cost-benefit analysis may lead to a much more managerial approach to learning design. Successful designs are likely to be judged on factors that matter to funders – both the public purse and paying students – whether these are employability, immediate learner satisfaction, or levels of drop out. As employability and economic recovery become key goals, there is likely to be still further differentiation in the educational system. Some subject areas, for example STEM (science, technology, engineering and mathematics) subjects in the UK, seem likely to receive a higher level of public subsidy, leaving humanities and social sciences the preserve of those who can afford an education for education's sake. Similarly, some approaches to learning such as face-to-face tutorials may become even more desirable as signs of an elite education, while technology may become associated with mass customization, adaptive systems, and automated assessments that can be delivered cheaply at scale.

Implications for design

While there is no clear picture of what kinds of economic instability lie ahead, it is clear designers will need to take into consideration new assumptions about student motivation, and the likely retreat of the idea of the public university. More value may be placed on personalized/individualized learning over participation in a cohort, reversing some of the trends associated with digital technology in recent years. Employability has already become critical to universities as they reframe their core mission around 'graduate attributes' and the value added to a degree qualification by certain kinds of post-compulsory experience. But learners continue to see education as an investment in their personal development and interests, and to be motivated by activities not directly related to work, and designers will engage learners more successfully if they remember this. In addition, 'employability' itself may be reframed in terms of resilience and the capacity to create social value from personal capability, rather than simply making oneself attractive to graduate recruiters (see section on New workplaces below). Learning designs will need to focus on repertoire and agility, as well as on a sound grounding in subject basics.

Digital reputation is likely to make an important contribution to the life experience and earning potential of graduates, and so learners may expect to see public evidence of their progress, personal qualities and achievements alongside the private asset of a 'good degree'.

Globalization

The project of post-industrial economic development and the process of globalization that has accompanied it, has undoubtedly been accelerated by digital communications and the Internet. The interconnectedness of national economies and – arguably – the dependence of the global financial system on digital transactions have left the entire economy more vulnerable to shocks, as dealt with in the previous section. Per Bak (for example, 1996) has argued that self-organized complex systems are inherently vulnerable to collapses at scale, and the global education system will certainly not escape such vulnerability.

Middle class jobs are being outsourced from the developed economies, just when the middle class are being encouraged to pay for their children's education. Going abroad to study is an increasingly attractive option. At the same time, the cachet of higher education in developed nations is leading to a large influx of students from other parts of the globe, who are increasingly able to pay. In pursuit of their own 'borderless' development, universities are using distance learning options to woo foreign learners, franchising course delivery to local colleges in other countries, and forming international partnerships. There are clear benefits to students from an intercultural experience, as it prepares them to live and work in the global businesses and the highly mobile social groups that are emerging. But there are also controversies. The 'global education' model being pursued by most institutions is a mercantile one rather than one based on inter-cultural exchange: nations with less developed higher education systems are being seen as a source of bright, fee-paying students. The potential for cultural imperialism as elite universities in the Western world export learning designs – in the form of reusable learning objects, open educational resources, open courseware and freely available podcasts – has been contentious (e.g. Rossini 2007; Larson and Murray 2008). As higher education becomes international and – in its business models and systems at least – more corporate, there will continue to be threats to fragile marginal cultures faced with a choice between preserving their indigenous ways of learning and knowing and losing out in the global knowledge regime. An example is the imposition of Western models of science in teaching in the Canadian First

Nation community (Kim 2011). Collaborative work with aboriginal peoples in the same region (see Ellaway, Chapter 12) has shown how design for learning can be revived in cross-cultural contexts, not simply by 'translating' designs into culturally appropriate forms but by engaging in partnership and dialogue with other ways of learning. Where this happens, designers may need to rethink their foundational ideas, for example about authority and the ownership of knowledge.

Implications for design

The challenge for educators and for learning designers is to build resilience into curriculum systems, while bringing forward curricula that also help learners to develop their own resilient responses. This is likely to mean designing for learner-centredness, cross-curricular and cross-cultural experiences, the application of interdisciplinary approaches to real-world problems, and the fostering of creativity and innovation. Typical designs will involve students in the co-creation of knowledge and the collaborative resolution of problems. New pedagogies will be required, and intercultural partnerships between educators will be one way to extend the repertoire of pedagogic approaches, so helping to promote resilience in the system. Designs will, of course, need to be sensitive to cultural differences, languages and identities, but – beyond this – they will need to draw on students' own cultural resources and place responsibility on students to negotiate cultural difference as an aspect of learning. The emphasis will be on learning across boundaries, and designers will need to establish supportive settings where groups with different assumptions about learning goals, methods and outcomes can work productively together.

New workplaces

In line with our remarks about economic crisis and globalization, it seems certain that graduates will be competing with a larger pool of highly qualified workers for a decreasing number of jobs in 'traditional' graduate workplaces. It remains uncertain what new forms of work will emerge. More graduates may be self-employed. Others will be combining careers, switching jobs often, mixing work with other responsibilities, or selling their labour in new and entrepreneurial ways. More middle class workers are likely to be flexibly employed on uncertain contracts and, as a consequence, they are likely to have a much weaker affiliation with their workplace or broader profession (Robson 2009).

During much of the last decade, the 'knowledge economy' has been hailed as the route to job satisfaction for the majority of graduates, and as the means of recovery for post-industrial nations. Even before the present financial crisis, though, evidence was emerging that for every 'learning organisation' (Senge 1990) with devolved decision making and corporate play rooms there were many more with a small core of executive decision makers and a large body of insecurely employed desk- and screen-bound workers (Lauder *et al.* 2008). Knowledge work does not necessarily offer more agency or autonomy, more job security or healthful working conditions, or indeed a sound basis for economic recovery.

There continues to be great uncertainty about the distribution of knowledge work around the globe. Who will be doing this work and where? Where will the knowledge businesses be located and what roles, rewards and divisions of labour will pertain in them? We can say with certainty, though, that global businesses require graduates who are comfortable building relationships across national boundaries, and maintaining them through virtual means. Some graduates will certainly gain employment through a high degree of specialization, but in a very rapidly changing and more crisis-prone economy this may be a risky strategy. High value workers are likely to be those who are multi-skilled and flexible, and can function in an interdisciplinary environment. At present, though, the funding and professional rewards in higher education tend to favour a strongly disciplinary approach to teaching. So how will post-compulsory education help learners to understand different approaches to knowledge building and problem solving?

Implications for design

Designs for learning will need to foster a project- or problem-based approach and the ability to work in multi-role teams. Demonstrating employability through public expression of achievements may be built in to designs across the learning experience, but particularly in the later stages of a degree programme. Self-awareness and self-diagnosis tools – increasingly used by the recruitment industry – may well find their way into learning designs. The results may be supportive of reflection and goal setting, or they may encourage learners to see themselves as examples of a particular 'type' and to avoid challenges that do not conform to that self-perception.

Environmental shocks

In addition to economic uncertainty, the past decade has seen a number of environmental shocks and crises in the supply of essential commodities, including oil and drinking water. Human-generated climate change and rising energy costs mean that major infrastructures are more likely to fail. These risks are, of course, linked to globalization, but attempts to alleviate them may lead to more local solutions such as local data hubs and micro-generation of electricity, or at least to multi-level solutions in which redundancy can be built in. The currents of globalization discussed previously may be met by a countervailing current of localization as communities build alternatives to national and international infrastructures and as travel becomes less affordable. Virtual transactions – both social and economic – may become more prevalent.

Implications for design

Already some universities require all programmes of study to include sustainability awareness (Dawe 2012), and there may be interesting cross-currents with digital capability. A critical digital literacy should encompass an awareness of all the impacts of technology use, and a capacity to question both the resources involved and the larger purposes for which technologies offer themselves as the means. This could cover issues as diverse as who owns data, where and how it is warehoused, or how digital devices are made, transported and marketed to users. Designs for learning which foster this kind of critical awareness will be relevant to both sustainability and digital literacy as core graduate attributes. Learning activities can also be designed to support the 'think global act local' ethos of the environmental movement.

'Green computing' is likely to become a mainstream concern: choices about digital technology in learning will be dictated by its environmental impact (Thomas 2009). This may be another reason for favouring small-scale, ready-to-hand technologies. Already, devices developed for use in countries with very little digital or energy infrastructure are being adopted in developed countries for their low environmental impact.

Status and legitimacy of post-compulsory education

Straddling this section and the next, we consider how economic and political uncertainties imply a changing contract between education and society, whether the relevant society is an international elite or a local community. There is a strong tendency in both developed and developing economies to position education as a driver of economic recovery rather than an aspect of public life or social and cultural entitlement. This has led to a focus in learning design on employability as the primary goal, rather than, say, widening access to opportunity, building shared resources and solutions, or supporting particular values. New funding arrangements have also fostered a belief in learning as a personal rather than a public good. These trends have an impact on what is possible in design, most significantly by adjusting the kind and degree of challenge that learners are willing to accept from their educational experience.

The rise of digital technology in education has played a role in two other trends. At a basic level it has allowed institutions to deliver learning beyond their immediate local reach, enhancing the stratification of institutions by brand and reputation. The global standards community, which has emerged to support the interoperability of learning systems, has had many positive effects on learner mobility but, by creating an international market in educational opportunity, it has unquestionably enhanced stratification. And the standards community is populated not only by leading universities but also by suppliers of proprietary systems, publishers, the military and technology industries. As a direct result of this work, universities as places where cohorts of students work alongside one another towards locally accredited qualifications will soon be overtaken by cheaper ways of getting a degree. There will also be ways of gaining graduate-level knowledge without studying for a degree at all, such as through the World Wide Web and its growing archive of high-quality learning resources, through membership of knowledgeable communities of various kinds, and by building digital reputation in a self-directed way. Open accreditation systems are already emerging, both proprietary (Mozilla's open badges: https://wiki.mozilla.org/Badges) and public (the OERu model: http://wikieducator.org/OER_university/Home).

All this means that universities are no longer the only gateways to high value work, and nor are they any longer the only guardians of intellectual capital. Publishing houses, news agencies, digital archives, citizen groups, research funders and private companies all have legitimate claims, and the Internet makes their claims stronger and their capital more visible.

Implications for design

One route for design is to emphasize the continuity between formal study and other kinds of learning – informal, Internet-based, work-based, at home. This may be attractive to learners who are trying to fit study into a busy life, and may involve highly situated forms of learning that use experience as material, along with accessible bite-sized resources. This approach might well be 'open as standard' and designed to be delivered at scale.

Another route will be to assert the special value of extended study in a time and place set aside for that purpose. All the evidence is that, given a choice, learners continue to place a high value on this kind of learning experience. This would lead to designs that focus on the 'teachable moment' in the classroom, lab, field, or research context, and deploy technology to enhance these high value encounters. This 'walled garden' approach to learning would be exclusive in the sense that designs would foster intensive work in a given setting, with a given teacher and taught cohort, but it might also be exclusive in the social sense that it would be beyond the reach of many learners.

Whether open or closed, designs for learning will have to more obviously meet learners' aspirations, and institutions may have to consider how they market their own designs through branding, kite-marking, reputation management, and opportunities to 'try before you buy'. It is interesting to speculate whether design for learning – as a shared practice based on agreed principles – could offer some form of lightweight accountability for organizations and individuals in terms of mandating the quality, variety, relevance, etc. of their offer.

Educational futures

Learning as connectivity

A fundamental characteristic of digital technologies is that they are connected, forming a global network of information, dialogue and exchange. There have been claims that this makes possible new kinds of learning, for example through distributed cognition (Salomon 1993), which sees learning as taking place in the system itself, or through the collective 'power of the crowd' described persuasively by (among others) Stephen Downes (2012). It is beyond doubt that networked computers generate new kinds of social data, and offer new means to communicate and collaborate, but it may be more significant that these opportunities have fostered new social meanings and cultural habits. So most learners expect knowledge – at least non-academic knowledge – to exist in a state of constant circulation, always available for comment, reframing, re-editing and re-contextualization. To an important extent, their connections *are* their knowledge resources.

To date, academic knowledge has moved only slowly into this state of 'constant beta'. Academic blogs and tweets tend to explore known themes and keep established debates in circulation. Research communities may sometimes share work in progress, or collaboratively author papers, but this tends to happen on a small scale. In global academic networks, the dominant mode is still research–review–publish. Among learners too, there are preferences for 'traditional' models of learning and teaching with networked contacts and resources used for augmentation).

Below are some considerations for learning in an environment where global connectivity and constant social participation are the norm.

The experience of massive open online courses (MOOCs) gives us some insight into the implications of learning in a global, connected environment. Participants can contribute in a range of ways from leading discussions and providing resources to tuning in on a very occasional basis, and although there

Table 17.1 Some implications of learning in a connected environment (devised by Conole, adapted by Beetham)

Opportunities	Risks
Global reach	Loss of local identities
Multiple forms of representation and participation	Disintegrating identities, fragmentary communications
Speed	Superficiality
Flat structures, rhizomatic organization	Loss of stability, order, established routes and markers
Ubiquitous connectivity	Breakdown of public/private boundaries; poor work/life balance
Viral distribution	Popular memes quickly dominate
Multiple interconnecting discourses	Danger of convergent memes dominating
Rich opportunities to capture learning	Surveillance and micro-management
Cultural exchange	Danger of cultural hegemony
Diversity of offerings, mass customization	Fragmentation of experience

is typically a collaborative environment at the heart of the programme, learners are encouraged to amplify the learning across their own networks, blogs, and Twitter feeds. Tagging allows resources relevant to the programme to be tracked across the Internet. Proponents argue that this is an emancipatory or 'rhizomatic' style of learning, enabling each individual to follow personal goals and create a personal context for learning (see Winn and Lockwood, Chapter 14; Cormier 2008, 2011).

Evaluation of participants' experience of these courses is mixed. The scale, ambiguity and heterogeneity of the learning 'environment' is confusing to those without highly evolved skills in managing their connectivity, while the lack of structure can mean that contribution is dominated by a core of individuals who already know one another's work. The number of learners who sign up for these courses is impressive, sometimes in the thousands, but the numbers who remain committed are much smaller. MOOCs are essentially no different from other online communities brought together around a particular local interest or worldview, the World of Warcraft and citizen journalism being others. In face of overwhelming connectivity, the response of almost all these groups is to limit their scope and active membership, and in the worst cases to perpetuate a single worldview among a group of self-selected cognoscenti.

Implications for design

Learners can hardly avoid knowing that the world is interconnected: learning designs can introduce the ways in which *academic* knowledge specifically is circulated and the changes under way in academic practices of communication. Educators will have a role to play in communicating and helping learners to manage the risks associated with a connected environment. Designs can provide structured activities or can model academic ways of working that help learners understand the risks of fragmentation, superficiality, convergence and cultural hegemony. Learners will need different kinds of preparation to engage meaningfully in connected communities. Sometimes this will involve building on existing social habits, and sometimes it will involve demonstrating that academic/professional ways of making and maintaining contacts are different.

Designers of learning will have to be constantly and modestly aware that learners will come into contact with other ideas and with other ways of approaching the same topic. Learners will use their connections to discuss and assess the learning opportunities they are being offered. If this seems to learners to be 'forbidden' then it will be hard for them to develop these habits of connectivity into good habits of learning.

Open educational practice

Engaging in open practices in research, teaching and innovation (as defined in Pegler, Chapter 9) draws individuals and educational institutions into new practices and suggests new teaching and business models. However, open access offers challenges as well as opportunities.

The first and most obvious driver for openness is the emergence of new open forms of educational product and service, previously only available through the gatekeeping of fee-charging institutions and commercial publishers. As with other forms of valued content, such as news and music, educational content has been pushed towards open licensing by the simple fact of its ease of reproduction and distribution. Unlike these other sectors, however, higher education has often been driving the technologies of open access, since content has never been the only or most significant good provided by educational institutions, and since they have always been at best ambivalent about monetizing of their product. However, at a time when the costs of post-compulsory education to individuals are rising and the benefits are looking more doubtful, there is the risk that, in releasing open content, universities have been building an attractive alternative to their own offer.

The second driver is to maximize value for money from public sector spending, which in the US has led to legislation in favour of free public use of educational content, and in the UK has led to open licensing requirements on many publicly funded projects. The same argument has also been made by research councils and in relation to research that is of overwhelming public interest – such as genomics – that receives both public and private funding. Governments might respond to resource constraints by enforcing forms of openness that result in reduced costs to the system overall.

The third driver for openness is the aspiration to improve educational access, particularly for less-advantaged groups, extending conventional 'open learning' to a potentially global scale. An example of this driver is the setting of targets by global organizations such as the World Bank and UNESCO's Education for All group, along with the World Economic Forum and USAID. In general these organizations see digital – especially mobile – technologies revitalizing and reforming existing systems: textbooks, curricula, teaching practices and existing providers are all to have a wider reach and deliver economies of scale. On the other hand, these organizations sometimes seem to foresee and even to hope that existing systems will be swept aside, to be replaced by a radically disaggregated and diversified educational marketplace with, for example, open content and open accreditation separately available to self-organized learners and learning groups.

The question is not only how revolutionary open access might prove to be, but what kind of revolution might be at hand? Is openness a drive to scale, leading to globalized mass production, the threat of cultural imperialism as more powerful digital cultures propagate their educational offerings, and less participative or learner-centred design? Or is it a revolution in the means of educational production, leading to mass participation in scholarly production and new forms of public pedagogy? A clear danger of the first option – globalized, scaled and cost-effective content availability – is the threat to less dominant epistemological communities in different parts of the world. As western European viruses wiped out many indigenous people, so occidental educational cultures might do the same for the learning traditions of the San or the Turkana people, or in Europe perhaps the Basque, Occitan and the Roma. The process of design would struggle not to be complicit with this process, willingly or otherwise.

Even if open content were to entirely replace 'closed' content on a like-for-like basis, the shift would be in business models rather than in the forms of learning taking place. In Chapter 9, Chris Pegler explored open participation as a more radical shift, with learning becoming an exercise in public generation of ideas, for example through MOOCs and virtual research communities. As with open content, however, while the rhetoric may emphasize democratization of access and the 'bottom of the pyramid', all the evidence from other ways in which the educational marketplace has been opened up is that the main beneficiaries will be those who already enjoy good access to learning.

Implications for design

The emphasis in funding and research to date has been on innovation projects rather than sustained services. In design, the challenge will be to introduce a *sustainable* full-service open education (activities, assessment, support, pathways as well as content) where not only access but also participation continue to be supported. For qualification-led open learning the lead time for learners to complete is likely to be longer than within conventional systems, and progress less certain. In emphasizing access to the broader base of the pyramid we might expect to see a proliferation of opportunities addressing the same entry-level requirements, with little variety beyond this point. Designing for massive cohorts of students where the level of support required, the nature of student pathways and the relevance of accreditation varies, is not yet well understood. Designers will need to consider the requirements of students from highly diverse backgrounds. Students will also need a high level of digital literacy and self-direction, or personalized guidance, which will be challenging to maintain.

Learner-defined contexts

The capacity of individuals to personalize aspects of their online experience has been covered in previous sections in relation to digital media and web-based services. As also discussed earlier in this volume (see Beetham, Chapter 2), aspirations to make education more 'learner-centred' seem to dovetail well with these capabilities. Digital environments are inherently more adaptive and open to multiple experiences than their offline counterparts. Also, digital technologies can allow learners to be in touch with educational resources and conversations while immersed in non-educational settings, whether at work, in the field, on placement, or at home.

Traditional educational design aims to define rather carefully the milieu within which learning takes place, including the tools and resources, and more subtle aspects of learning such as the layout of the classroom environment, how learners are grouped, their roles and rules of interaction. These features of context are intended to support specific educational goals, typically defined by the educator. When learners are asked to define their own contexts for learning, many of these ways that design can structure a learning experience are thrown out (see Winn and Lockwood, Chapter 14). It seems likely that the value to learners of defining their own learning contexts will remain contentious, and this may in fact be one way that different kinds of learning are identified.

Learner-centred design takes two main forms. One is drawn from ideas of participatory culture and stresses the value to learners of working collaboratively – with more or less guidance – to negotiate their own learning goals, outcomes, resources, and ways of proceeding. The second emphasizes the individual learner as having free choice within a broadly defined programme. Both forms can provide features of learner empowerment without troubling the power relationships between learners, teachers and institutions too deeply, but the latter in particular has been described as 'mass customization'. Learners are offered choice about how they access opportunity while being denied many of the contextualizing features – cohort identity, personal support, coherent progression – that might make the experience transformative. As with the liberalization of other markets, the rhetoric of free choice can be used against consumers, in the case of education, for example, making learners responsible for their own success or failure. Individual choice within a designed environment can actually make control strategies less visible than when they are being enacted in a traditional classroom.

Implications for design

Against the mass customization model, conceptions of learning design may be shared more explicitly with learners, giving them better insight into how particular activities, tools, resources and interactions support their own learning. Designers may exploit the capacity to 'make explicit' in virtual environments by framing learning activities with a negotiation over roles, rules and divisions of labour. The same capacities may be used by radical educators to 'make explicit' how power comes into play, not just in educational interactions but in other settings.

Learners will increasingly expect to use their own digital devices, networks, services and resources to support their study, and designers will need to be flexible in response. For some learners this will make educational opportunity more available, both pragmatically and psychologically. Others may choose a more bounded and supported context where this is an option. It will be challenging to bring forward designs that accommodate both preferences.

Learning in diverse settings

There is a significant potential for the use of social media and mobile devices in professional and work-based learning, and in other non-campus settings where learning can take place. However, a critical review of the way technologies are being used for work-based learning (Kraiger 2008) found that most approaches are based on an idea of direct instruction in a formal manner, for example, transferring lectures and seminars to computer-mediated environments or making expositional content available on a mobile platform. Recent work has begun to explore approaches that use social media and mobile devices in more innovative ways, particularly to amplify informal workplace practices. This is an area that is currently under-researched but will surely receive growing attention as more learners choose to study alongside paid work or in other non-formal contexts.

Professional education has proved a fertile ground for learning design approaches. Professional educators work with common vocabularies and common understanding, and this makes professional learning both accessible and accountable: relevant scholarship is meaningful across different contexts. This has allowed for more improvisation and hybridization of different designs and a better understanding of the power of context. However, professional learning can generate normative and reductionist approaches as whole sectors focus on what is agreed by stakeholders (often employers) to represent 'best practice'. Ironically, it may be that standard-delivery modes of education are in some ways better able to respond to changes in professions and workplaces, because educators are freer to reframe work-like learning environments than workplaces are free to reinvent themselves. Work-based learning practices are therefore only one aspect of how post-compulsory education will respond to new trends in work.

As people increasingly conduct aspects of their personal, social and working life online, and as information about those activities is captured and archived, individuals are gathering around themselves a digital memory which can be used as a resource for non-formal learning. At the same time, offline activities are increasingly capable of being enriched with learning opportunities. We can imagine a time when it will be natural to undertake brief episodes of learning as an enhancement to everyday activities, whether this takes the form of accessing guidance, being prompted to reflect and enrich a personal archive, connecting with other people who share an interest, or studying relevant materials. An important aspect of formal learning will be to instil in people the interest and motivation to engage in these opportunities and to make the best use of them.

Implications for design

So how can designers respond to the blurring of boundaries between on- and off-campus learning, and more generally between formal and informal settings? How can designs be made flexible enough to support learning in the wide range of locations in which they may be encountered?

One possible approach is for design to focus on complex, ill-defined problems in which learners organize the resources of their setting – co-located or virtual – to define and address the issues. Social participation of various kinds would be explicitly woven through the learning experience. Although design will continue to depend on the demands of disciplines and their practices, this will be with an awareness that not many graduates will have lives and jobs that are deeply rooted in one discipline's ways of thinking.

Employers and alumni could play a role in defining authentic learning tasks, stakeholders could define real-world needs that groups of learners could address, always bearing in mind that real-world needs may be research- or theory-based and addressed through scholarly approaches.

Learners will have opportunities to rehearse and present themselves in public digital spaces – to build their digital identities and reputation as they learn. There may be conflict here if learners who are financially supported by their employers are encouraged to rethink themselves into new roles and identities.

An important aspect of off-campus delivery, touched on previously, is the need to deliver an equivalent pedagogic experience to students who may be studying in different institutions, perhaps in different countries, coming from very different cultures and studying in situations with very different resources.

Conclusions

Although we perceive design for learning to be an ongoing aspect of educational practice, there are growing questions about who will do the designing, how the process of design will be represented and realized in specific programmes of study, and how design will respond to changed circumstances. We also need to ask: is 'design' a useful term for what we are doing as educators at all? We adopted it in the first edition of this volume as a way of valorizing the practices of teachers, their skilful, conscious realization of an intention towards the learning of others, both a counterpoint to the overvaluing of 'learning' in educational discourse and a way of aligning education with what seemed an exemplary discipline of the 21st century academic canon. But perhaps, in the intervening years, we have arrived at a time of such uncertainty over educational values and outcomes that the very idea of 'designing' for learning can no longer be taken seriously: perhaps it is either ridiculously hubristic or sinisterly managerial.

We believe there is still a value in the discourse of design as a way of making educators' practices more socially and professionally transparent, and of ensuring that, in our excitement about the possibilities of technology, we remain rooted in pedagogic theory and the ethos of developing learners. By making design more explicit, educators are better able to share their insights and learners are better able to understand and assimilate educational opportunities to their own aspirations. This points to a number of requirements that are continuous with our conclusions to the first edition:

- Design for learning is a skilled practice, rooted in the culture of different subject areas, which involves the capacity to translate educational principles into practical learning tasks, and the confidence to be creative with digital technologies.
- Teachers and learners need access to good examples of design practice, with the appropriate contextual information to appraise and repurpose them.
- Designers need to engage in dialogue – with learners and other designers – about the educational principles that underpin their practice and how best to translate these principles into learning opportunities.
- Educators need a degree of autonomy to design for specific cohorts of learners and to experiment and innovate in their practice.
- The expertise involved in teaching, whether deployed in the design process or in supporting learners to encounter existing designs, must be rewarded and recognized if the profession is to meet the changing needs of learners.

Gordon Graham observes that new technologies change what we value by changing the balance of what is possible (1999). Concepts of economies of presence (Mitchell 2000) and attention economies (Lanham 2006) suggest that the dynamics of the education system will shift to promote new values and new forms of transaction, partly in direct response to the affordances of new tools, and partly in response to new social and cultural practices that evolve in close relationship with them. Depending on one's perspective, design for learning can be seen as democratizing education, subverting the educational establishment, or collapsing the richness of human practice down to algorithms and design patterns. Design as it is practised by educators does not stand apart from the other social, educational and technical trends we have described, but co-constructs and is constructed with them.

The chapters in this book have represented design for learning at (at least) three levels: activities, principles or methods, and environments or systems. These levels seem distinct in terms of what is designed and how underlying philosophies are manifested in the design process – in task rules and resources, in programme level outcomes, and in features of learning environments. They also suggest different ways in which learners' and teachers' agency can be exercised. Flexible learning experiences require learners to be self-directed and resourceful. Flexible design practices, supported by institutions that invest a degree of trust in curriculum teams, require teachers to be innovative and responsive to change. Flexible learning environments provide structures for learners to aggregate contacts and resources, to share and collaboratively build know-how, and to record their learning from various contexts, without undue constraint.

At all three levels of design – activities, programmes and environments – design assumes some clarity of purpose. But for learners, at least, this clarity may not emerge until much later in the learning process. How useful are our outcomes-based designs for learners who are living and learning simultaneously in a rich variety of contexts, who are performing different identities in different milieu? The Open Courseware experiment clearly demonstrated (as MIT perhaps intended) that content, the fungible stuff of education, is a thin reflection of the embodied, presenceful and exclusive institutional experience. Attempts fully to represent the process of design for learning has similar limits. Learning is an emergent phenomenon, and the meaning-making of learners will always exceed any attempt at representation either before or after the event.

Against the idea of designs as adequate representations of learning, at any level, it might be interesting to view design for learning as developing a repertoire. Learners gain expertise through a variety of tasks in increasingly complex or uncertain settings. Educators understand more about what works for learners by trying a variety of approaches. Different disciplines can be seen as contributing different aspects of design thinking and method – information design, visual design, rhetorical design, research design, design of learning spaces and virtual environments – to the educational enterprise.

In facing the uncertainties of the near and more distant future, we can be sure that learners are better off – more resilient – if they have a broad repertoire of capabilities at their fingertips, those closely aligned with academic expertise and professional practice and those they have evolved from their digital experiences, along with hybrids of the two. Learners will be well served by tasks, programmes and environments that generate uncertainty, and foster a repertoire of resourceful responses. Educators, too, will have to become more resilient, more adaptive and multi-competent in the various niches that the new education system will open up. In the words of Douglas Rushkoff's (2010) best-selling title *Program or Be Programmed*: this is not a game one can opt out of. Either we are designers of our own futures, or we are having the future designed for us. As educators we must unequivocally place ourselves on the side of self-determination.

References

Arnab, S., Petridis, P., Dunwell, I. and de Freitas, S. (2011) 'Enhancing learning in distributed virtual worlds through touch: A browser-based architecture for haptic interaction', in M. Ma *et al.* (eds) *Serious Games and Edutainment Applications*, London: Springer Verlag.

Bak, P. (1996) *How Nature Works: The science of self-organized criticality*, New York: Copernicus.

Buckingham Shum, S. (2011) *Learning Analytics: Dream, nightmare, or fairydust?* Keynote to ASCILITE 11 Conference, Hobart, Australia, 5 December 2011. Online. Available at http://people.kmi.open.ac.uk/sbs/2011/12/learning-analytics-ascilite2011-keynote/ (accessed 15 August 2012).

Cook, J., Pachler, N. and Bachmair, B. (2011), 'Ubiquitous mobility with mobile phones: A cultural ecology for mobile learning', *E-Learning and Digital Media: Special Issue on Media: Digital, Ecological and Epistemological*, 8 (3): 181–95.

Cormier, D. (2008) 'Rhizomatic education: Community as curriculum'. Blog post. Online. Available at http://davecormier.com/edblog/2008/06/03/rhizomatic-education-community-as-curriculum/ (accessed 31 July 2012).

Cormier, D. (2011) 'Rhizomatic learning – why we teach?' Blog post. Online. Available at http://davecormier.com/edblog/2011/11/05/rhizomatic-learning-why-learn/ (accessed 31 July 2012).

Dawe, H. (2012) 'Education for sustainable development at Oxford Brookes University', *Brookes eJournal of Learning and Teaching*, 4 (1). Online. Available at http://bejlt.brookes.ac.uk/engaging_with_graduate_attributes/ (accessed 14 August 2012).

Downes, S. (2012) 'The Cloud and Collaboration', in S. Downes (ed.) *Connectivism and Connective Knowledge: Essays on meaning and learning networks*. Online. Available at http://www.downes.ca/files/Connective_Knowledge–19May2012.pdf (accessed 15 August 2012)

Graham, G. (1999) *The Internet://a philosophical inquiry*, London: Routledge.

Hargittai, E. (2010) 'Digital na(t)ives? Variation in Internet skills and uses among members of the "Net Generation"', *Sociological Inquiry*, 80 (1): 92–113.

Kim, E.-J.A. (2011) 'Cross-cultural learning in intermediate and secondary science class: integration of traditional ecological knowledge in Canadian science curriculum', paper presented at Canada International Conference on Education, Toronto, April 2011.

Kraiger, K. (2008) 'Third-generation instructional models: more about guiding development and design than selecting training methods', *Industrial and Organizational Psychology*, 1 (4): 501–7.

Lanham, R. (2006) *The Economics of Attention: Style and substance in the age of information*, Chicago: University of Chicago Press.

Larson, R.C. and Murray, M.E. (2008) 'Open Educational Resources for Blended Learning in High Schools: Overcoming impediments in developing countries', *Journal of Asynchronous Learning Networks*, 12 (1): 2–19.

Lauder, H., Brown, P. and Brown, C. (2008) *The consequences of global expansion for knowledge, creativity and communication: an analysis and scenario*. Beyond Current Horizons. Online. Available at http://www.beyondcurrenthorizons.org.uk/the-consequences-of-global-expansion-for-knowledge-creativity-and-communication-an-analysis-and-scenario/ (accessed 15 August 2012).

Masterman, L. (2012) 'Final chapter: Rethinking Pedagogy #2'. Personal email referencing results from the Digital Experience (DIGE) project, University of Oxford. 20 June 2012.

Mitchell, W. J. (2000) *e-topia: 'Urban Life, Jim – But Not As We Know It'*, Cambridge MA: MIT Press.

Naughton, J. (2012) *From Gutenberg to Zuckerberg: What you really need to know about the Internet*, London: Quercus.

NMC Horizon Project (2012) *The NMC Horizon Report 2012: Higher Education Edition*. Online. Available at http://www.nmc.org/horizon-project/horizon-reports/horizon-report-higher-ed-edition (accessed 15 August 2012).

Robson, P. (2009) *The Future of Work and Implications for Education*, Beyond Current Horizons. Online. Available http://www.beyondcurrenthorizons.org.uk/summative-report-the-future-of-work-and-implications-for-education/.

Rossini, C.A.A. (2007) *The Open Access Movement: Opportunities and challenges for developing countries*. Diplo Foundation – Intellectual Property Research Group.

Rushkoff, D. (2010) *Program or Be Programmed: Ten commands for a digital age*, Berkeley, CA: Soft Skull Press.

Salomon, G. (ed.) (1993) *Distributed Cognitions: Psychological and educational considerations*, Cambridge: Cambridge University Press.

Senge, P. (1990) *The Fifth Discipline: The art and practice of the learning organization*, New York: Doubleday.

Thomas, K. (2009) *Green ICT: Managing sustainable ICT in education and research*, Bristol: JISC.

Part III

Resources

Three (and a Half) Approaches to Understanding How People Learn

This appendix illustrates key features of the three theoretical approaches outlined in Chapter 1, and can be used as a starting point or retrospectively to help evaluate a particular approach to designing for learning (see Beetham, Chapter 2).

	Associative	Constructive (individual)	Constructive (social)	Situative
Learning is understood as:	building concepts or competences step-by-step	achieving understanding through active discovery	achieving understanding through dialogue and collaboration	developing practice in a particular community
The theory	People learn by association, initially through basic stimulus–response conditioning, later by associating concepts in a chain of reasoning, or associating steps in a chain of activity to build a composite skill. Associativity leads to accuracy of reproduction: for example when safety-critical skills are learned, or factual material is committed to memory. Mnemonics are essentially associative devices. Associative theories are not concerned with how concepts or skills are represented internally, but in how they are manifested in external behaviours, and how different training/instruction regimes manifest themselves in observable learning. However, all formal learning relies to some extent on external evidence (behaviour) as an index of what has been learned.	People learn by actively exploring the world around them, receiving feedback on their actions, and drawing conclusions. Constructivity leads to integration of concepts and skills into the learner's existing conceptual or competency structures. Learning can be applied to new contexts and expressed in new ways. Experimentation or experiential learning (Kolb's cycle), are typical constructive approaches. Constructive theories are more concerned with how knowledges and skills are internalized than how they are manifest in external behaviour. As in associative approaches, attention will be paid to how learning opportunities are presented so as to allow progressive discovery of relevant concepts/skills.	Individual discovery of principles is heavily scaffolded by the social environment. Peer learners and teachers play a key role in development by engaging in dialogue with the learner, developing a shared understanding of the task, and providing feedback on the learner's activities and representations. Collaborative work is typical of social constructive approaches. Social constructive theories are concerned with how emerging concepts and skills are supported by others, enabling learners to reach beyond what they are individually capable of (learning in the 'zone of proximal development'). Attention is paid to learners' roles in collaborative activities, as well as the nature of the tasks they undertake.	People learn by participating in communities of practice, progressing from novice to expert through observation, reflection, mentorship, and 'legitimate peripheral participation' in community activities. Like social constructivism, situativity emphasizes the social context of learning, but this context is likely to be close – or identical – to the situation in which the learner will eventually practise. Work-based learning, continuing professional development, and apprenticeships are typical examples of situated learning. The authenticity of the environment is at least as significant as the support it provides: much less attention is paid to formal learning activities.
Key theorists	Skinner Gagné (Instructivism and Instructional Design)	Piaget Papert Kolb Biggs	Vygotsky (Social Development) Laurillard and Pask (Conversation Theory)	Lave and Wenger (Communities of Practice) Cole, Engstrom and Wertsch (Activity Theory)

more formally structured learning tasks | more authentic contexts for learning

	Associative	Constructive (individual)	Constructive (social)	Situative
Implications for learning	• Routines of organized activity • Progression through component concepts or skills • Clear goals and feedback • Individualized pathways matched to performance	• Active construction and integration of concepts • Ill-structured problems • Opportunities for reflection • Ownership of the task	• Conceptual development through collaborative activity • Ill-structured problems • Opportunities for discussion and reflection • Shared ownership of the task	• Participation in social practices of enquiry and learning • Acquiring habits, attitudes, values and skills in context • Developing identities • Developing learning and professional relationships
Implications for teaching	• Analysis into component units • Progressive sequences of component-to-composite skills or concepts • Clear instructional approach for each unit • Highly focused objectives	• Interactive environments and appropriate challenges • Encourage experimentation and the discovery of principles • Adapt teaching to existing concepts/skills • Coach and model meta-cognitive skills e.g. reflection	• Collaborative environments and appropriate challenges • Encourage experimentation, and shared discovery • Draw on existing concepts/skills • Coach and model skills, including social skills	• Create safe environments for participation • Support development of identities • Facilitate learning dialogues and relationships • Elaborate authentic opportunities for learning

	Associative	Constructive (individual)	Constructive (social)	Situative
Implications for assessment	• Accurate reproduction of knowledge or skill • Component performance • Clear criteria: rapid reliable feedback	• Conceptual understanding (applied knowledge and skills) • Extended performance • Processes as well as outcomes • Credit varieties of excellence • Develop self-evaluation and autonomy in learning	• Conceptual understanding (applied knowledge and skills) • Extended performance • Process and participation as well as outcomes • Credit varieties of excellence • Develop peer-evaluation and shared responsibility	• Credit participation • Extended performance, including variety of contexts • Authenticity of practice (values, beliefs, competencies) • Involve peers
Example pedagogic approaches	• Guided instruction • Drill and practice • Instructional design • Socratic dialogue	• Cognitive scaffolding • Experiential learning (based on Kolb's learning cycle) • Experimental learning • Constructivist learning environments • Problem-based learning • Research-based learning	• Reciprocal teaching • Conversational model • (Computer-supported) collaborative learning	• (Cognitive) apprenticeship • Situated learning • (Legitimate peripheral) participation • (Continuing) professional development • Work-based learning

A Taxonomy of Digital and Information Literacy Linked to Bloom's Taxonomy of Educational Objectives

A taxonomy of digital and information literacy linked to Bloom's taxonomy of educational objectives, which can be used to support the writing of meaningful outcomes that encompass digital approaches and capabilities (see Beetham, Chapter 2).

Bloom's (revised) taxonomy	Example learning tasks with a digital literacy component	Relevant digital tools, applications and services (examples only)
Creating	Develop teaching/revision materials on a topic	Web design/authoring software Animation building apps and tools Presentation tools e.g. PowerPoint, keynotes, prezi e-publishing, e-book building sites Wiki – including Wikipedia (go on, write!) Online quiz generator or institutional question & test software
	Design an artefact using dedicated design software	Computer-aided design software e.g. Google SketchUp Graphic design software e.g. Adobe systems
	Design a research project and outline how technology can support the different phases	Project management tools/services e.g. basecamp Reference management tools/services e.g. Mendeley Open and public data sets
	Write an app or develop some code relevant to your topic	App building websites/services Code and scripting tools e.g. for editing html, perl, PHP, SQL …
	Make a film/podcast/presentation about your topic	Digital video camera Audio capture device Video and/or audio editing software Screen capture software e.g. camtasia, jing, screencast
	Start up an online community or take an existing community into a new area – invite others to contribute	Community building sites e.g. ning, elgg Social networks and media sharing sites Online conferences including MOOCs
	Explore a new way of using digital technology to support your research or studies, and demonstrate this to others	Any
	Develop an online profile or produce a digital story of your learning journey	Professional networking sites e.g. academia.edu, LinkedIn, GooglePlus Digital video camera or audio recording device and relevant editing software Website and web-authoring software Personal blog

Bloom's (revised) taxonomy	Example learning tasks with a digital literacy component	Relevant digital tools, applications and services (examples only)
Evaluating	Share solutions to a problem online: review and comment on other people's contributions	Commenting function in Google Docs (private) Review or comment function in social media sites (private) Annotation of pdfs
	Explore the implications of using a particular technology, or using digital technology to address a particular research, study or professional issue	Any
	Evaluate a range of online resources and produce a summary of the topic with links to validated sources	Google, Google Scholar and other search engines Scholarly databases and catalogues with search facilities Open repositories and data archives with search facilities Wiki post or other digital medium for reporting findings
	Moderate a discussion	Text-based conferencing Video conferencing Collaboration environment e.g. collaborate
	Draw conclusions linked to evidence	Blog post or wiki page with links (internal or external) Spreadsheet or database application with graphical outputs used as evidence
	Edit a presentation/article from a range of contributions	Wikispaces or wiki site Presentation software Collaborative authoring software e.g. Google Docs, buzzword Storify Social referencing tool e.g. Mendeley or shared bookmarking e.g. delicious
	Describe and apply a method for reaching a decision, including criteria used	Decision-analysis software Mapping software
Analysing	Identify patterns in data/evidence	Dedicated data analysis software with features such as sort, filter, formula and equations Visualization apps e.g. wordle Geotagging and mapping Open and public data sets

Bloom's (revised) taxonomy	Example learning tasks with a digital literacy component	Relevant digital tools, applications and services (examples only)
Analysing *continued*	Argue, defend, with links to evidence	Blog post or wiki page with links (internal or external) Spreadsheet or database application with graphical outputs used as evidence Open and public data
	Collect and analyse questionnaire data	Googleforms, SurveyMonkey Statistical analysis software e.g. SPSS
	Collect and analyse interview data	Video camera Audio capture device Qualitative data analysis software e.g. nVivo, HyperRESEARCH
	Predict and explain what happens in a simulation or virtual world	Simulation Game-based environment Virtual world/virtual reality environment
	Produce a map of a given topic or problem space	Reference management software Mind mapping software Process analytics Geotagging and geomapping
Applying	Demonstrate a complex method, practice or technique	Any discipline-specific device Audio or screen capture technology e.g. Camtasia, screencast, Audacity Digital video to capture a performance Illustration software e.g. Adobe suite Presentation software e.g. PowerPoint, Prezi Virtual world
	Explore a case study or situation through a simulation	Simulation Game-based environment Virtual world e.g. secondlife Open simulations/representations e.g. virtual human project, Google Earth, worldofmolecules etc
	Carry out a procedure or apply a method using dedicated hardware or software	Any subject-profession-specific hardware/software

Bloom's (revised) taxonomy	Example learning tasks with a digital literacy component	Relevant digital tools, applications and services (examples only)
Applying continued	Aggregate, curate or organize materials	Storify Social bookmark systems e.g. delicious Aggregation services e.g. Pearltrees, Tumblr, Pinterest Digital writing e.g. word processing, wiki post, blog post
	Reuse, repurpose materials	Editing software Digital writing e.g. word processing, wiki post, blog post
Understanding	Mind map a topic	Mindmapping software e.g. Cmap, Mindjet, Mindmeister, XMind Graphical features of presentation and writing software e.g. Prezi Aggregation services e.g. Pearltrees, Tumblr, Pinterest
	Reproduce ideas from one medium in another	Any digital production medium e.g. video, audio, photographs, drawing, animation, or multimedia e.g. web, blog post
	Select search terms to locate relevant materials	Google, Google Scholar and other search engines Scholarly databases and catalogues with search facilities Hashtags e.g. across Twitter, blogs, online discussions Open repositories e.g. of learning resources
	Organize relevant materials through tagging, filtering or categorizing	Keyword tagging in media sharing sites e.g. YouTube, SlideShare Tagging on blogs and wikis Online file management sites e.g. Evernote, Dropbox, Scrapbook
	Take a quiz or poll to test understanding	Electronic voting devices (with suitable questions and feedback) Online quiz generated by e.g. institutional question and test software or online quiz generator such as Hot Potatoes
	Practise writing in an academic style/voice for different media – Twitter, blog, web page, briefing, voice-over	Any *You may want to give guidance on writing for the web or other specific media as well as criteria for academic writing.*
	Gather examples or illustrations of a concept	Wiki page with links Bookmarking site e.g. delicious, reddit, Digg, StumbleUpon Archive building application e.g. Omeka Twitterfeed Subscription sites/aggregators e.g. RSS feeds, bloglines, blogger, Firefox extensions

Bloom's (revised) taxonomy	Example learning tasks with a digital literacy component	Relevant digital tools, applications and services (examples only)
Understanding continued	Explore pathways through a topic	Interactive learning resource or virtual tutorial Open learning resource or repository of resources Mindmap or graphical presentation (read mode)
Remembering	Label a diagram	Online whiteboard, collaborative writing/drawing apps *Diagrams to be labelled can be created in e.g. Adobe Flash, xerte, Hot Potatoes, some question and test software*
	Make a recording, upload and tag it	Digital audio device Digital video or stills camera Media sharing site e.g. Flickr, Vimeo Media repository
	Take a quiz or poll to answer factual questions	Electronic voting devices (with suitable questions and feedback) Online quiz generated by e.g. institutional question and test software or online quiz generator
	Identify and download a video, podcast, online tutorial or lecture relevant to your topic – remembering to take notes!	Open learning repository e.g. OCW, OpenSpires, OpenLearn iTunesU institutional VLE with podcasts/lecturecasts available
	Locate online resources using given terms/criteria or from a known source	Google, Google Scholar and other search engines Scholarly databases and catalogues Open repositories e.g. of learning resources
	Practise a basic skill or process in a simulated environment, e.g. to prepare using it in the field, lab or workplace	Simulation Virtual world Games-based environment Haptic environment

A Taxonomy of Digital and Information Literacies Linked to SCONUL's Seven Pillars

The following taxonomy has been developed at Oxford Brookes University (Benfield and Francis 2008). It is based on this adaptation of the SCONUL Seven Pillars of Information Literacy: Core Model for Higher Education (2011). It has been used by programme teams in order to articulate the 'digital and information literacy' graduate attribute. Once defined, the local articulations of the university graduate attributes have been published in programme specifications and module descriptions.

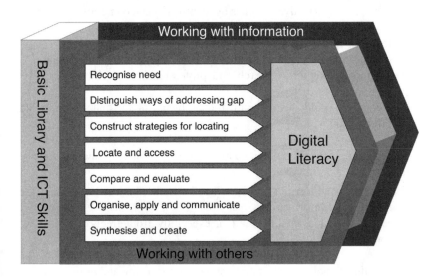

1 Being confident, agile adopters of a range of technologies for personal, academic and professional use:

- have the ability to apply general software interface principles to independently explore new software;

- selecting and using appropriate authoring technologies from a range (e.g., email, wikis, blogs, word processing, presentation, computer-aided design (CAD), html authoring);
- selecting and using a range of technologies for personal knowledge building;
- ability to securely and responsibly manage one's own and other people's data and online identities.

2   Confidently and competently analysing personal, academic, or professional information needs:

- identifying research needs by establishing gaps in one's knowledge;
- investigating likely sources of appropriate information available;
- making informed decisions about the type and level of information needed;
- recognizing the need to use varied and good-quality information.

3   Devising effective strategies and choosing appropriate tools for locating information:

- understanding how different types of search tools work (e.g. library catalogue, specialist databases, web search engines);
- searching systematically across a range of resources;
- constructing effective searches by identifying and combining appropriate keywords;
- learning how to use specific search tools (e.g. by reading help pages, manuals or search guides) and consulting appropriate professionals;
- supporting ongoing research and professional needs by using current awareness services;
- recognizing and dealing with the problems of too much or too little information.

4   Evaluating information obtained and assessing its appropriateness for one's needs:

- comparing and critically assessing the authority, currency, detail and relevancy of information;
- recognizing bias in information, especially from freely available web sources.

5   Using digital tools to reflect upon and record learning and professional and personal development:

- knowing and observing appropriate conventions on authoring in a variety of media and in a variety of professional and academic contexts (*note*: we see this as an academic literacy rather than specifically digital);
- ability to search, aggregate and organize digital information from a variety of sources for personal use;

- ability to represent oneself online in a suitable way for academic and professional purposes;
- selecting and using appropriate technology for recording and representing academic, professional and personal development.

6   Engaging productively in relevant online communities:

- selecting and using appropriate communication technologies for group work;
- knowing when and how to maintain appropriate levels of privacy in drafting and publishing to individuals and groups;
- effectively managing group interactions using multiple technologies;
- selecting and using technologies to represent and synthesize individual and group knowledge/learning;
- communicating effectively online;
- developing fluency and command of 'voice' in online authoring and publishing.

7   Integrating information obtained into one's own personal, academic or professional understanding, managing and communicating it effectively and ethically:

- taking appropriate notes, summarizing and adapting information for a new audience;
- synthesizing information from different sources to present a reasoned argument;
- creating new information through integrating one's own knowledge and understanding with prior reading and research;
- understanding academic and professional ethics (e.g. appropriate acknowledgement of sources, correct citation practices, and avoidance of plagiarism);
- continuing one's professional development by keeping up to date, sharing and debating information through appropriate communication tools.

References

Benfield, G. and Francis, R. (2008) *A Mapping of Graduate Attributes for a Digital Age at Brookes*. Online. Available at: https://mw.brookes.ac.uk/download/attachments/6750456/A%2BMapping%2Bof%2BGraduate%2BAttributes%2Bfor%2Ba%2BDigital%2BAge%2Bat%2BBrookes.doc (accessed 2 February 2009).

SCONUL (2011) *The SCONUL Seven Pillars of Information Literacy: Core Model for Higher Education*. Online. Available at: http://www.sconul.ac.uk/groups/information_literacy/publications/coremodel.pdf (accessed 11 May 2011).

Learner Differences and their Implications for Design

One of the challenges involved in taking a learner-centred approach is to know which, among the many ways learners can vary from one another, are significant to the learning at hand. As discussed in Chapter 2, in any given context of designing for learning, only a few of these differences are likely to be relevant. For relevant differences, it may be necessary only to know the range of variance a learning design should accommodate, or it may be important to discover individual learner differences in order to support them effectively. The latter approach will have implications for the resources of teaching and support staff.

This checklist can be used to support staff to check their knowledge of their own students' ICT use, and to prompt thinking about how this knowledge will inform their learning designs. It is available under a Creative Commons licence from the JISC Design Studio http://bit.ly/jiscdiglit

A   *About access and ownership*

1   What proportion of students have easy access to networked computers from home?

2   What proportion of students have easy access to a computer that can play video and audio files?

3   What proportion of students regularly bring a laptop, tablet, or notebook computer to their place of learning?

4   What support do students have for using personal technologies at their place of learning?

5   What proportion of students use assistive technology (e.g. to help with dyslexia or visual impairment)?

B   *About ICT skills and attitudes*

1   What proportion of learners can use their mobile/smartphone to access content?

2   What proportion of learners can personalize the technologies and services they use?

3   What proportion of learners describe themselves as proficient or expert users of ICT?
4   What do students think about the use of technology in their programmes of study?
5   What do learners think about their lecturers' ICT skills?

C   *About study habits and strategies*

1   Where do students prefer to study?
2   How do students like to access course information?
3   How do students manage study tasks and deadlines?
4   How often do students miss class? Why do you they do this?
5   How much time do students spend in paid employment?

D   *About information strategies*

1   What proportion of students rely on having their course materials (e.g. lecture notes) online?
2   What other sources of information do students use?
3   How do students manage references, bookmarks, etc?
4   How well do students judge the quality of information for academic purposes?
5   Who is most likely to have introduced students to wikis and blogs?

E   *About communication strategies*

1   What technologies do students use to keep in touch with each other?
2   How do students prefer to contact/be contacted by their tutors or course team?
3   What do students know about etiquette and safety online e.g. using Facebook, Flickr, YouTube, email, online communities?
4   What media do students use to present their ideas, for example in class presentations, and in assignments?

What other questions would you like to ask students about their digital access, ownership, use, and skills? How could you go about finding out more?

Learning Activity Design: A Checklist

This appendix summarizes the design considerations from Chapter 2 and over-arching design principles discussed in Chapter 10. It may be used to support staff through the learning activity design process.

Learning outcomes: considerations for design

1   What is the purpose of this learning session or opportunity?
2   What new knowledge, skills, capabilities and/or attitudes do learners need to gain? Are new digital capabilities made explicit in learning outcomes or not?
3   How open or closed are the learning outcome(s) in respect of how learners will actually engage with the task (context, resources, form/medium, technologies used)?
4   How will learners know when they have achieved the outcome(s), and how well they are doing?
5   How will they finally be assessed? Are the assessment criteria clear and relevant?
6   How could the learning process be captured (e.g. using digital devices) to support progression and reflection?

Learner differences: considerations for design

1   Is there a range of activities (especially remedial activities and extension activities) to meet the needs of learners with different capabilities?
2   Do learners have choices about how they carry out a task? About how they participate with others?
3   Are learners' differences valued, e.g. by setting collaborative tasks, by rewarding innovation as well as accuracy?
4   How are support and feedback adapted to individual learners' needs?
5   How are learners being involved in the design process? (Consider not only individual choices within the learning situation, but how learners can be involved collectively and also how learner feedback is acted upon in future iterations.)
6   How are differences in learners' digital confidence, capability and access addressed?

Digital resources, tools and services: considerations for design

1   What resources will learners have access to? What resources do you expect them to discover for themselves?
2   What information literacies will learners require and develop in accessing and using these resources? How are these supported?
3   How do you expect learners to manage, share and make use of digital resources? Is this explicit?
4   What devices and services (e.g. mobile or web-based) will learners have available for use? What devices and services of their own could they use?
5   How will you address issues of differential access to devices and services (if relevant)?
6   How will you use learners' digital access and know-how as a collective resource e.g. through groupwork, informal mentoring?
7   What support will you and your learners need (e.g. IT support, specialist librarian, other professional service) to make best use of these technologies?

Learning dialogues: considerations for design

1   What is the role of the course tutor(s) in this activity or course? How will tutor–learner communication be initiated and maintained?
2   How will learners interact with one another? What are the opportunities for peer learning and collaboration?
3   Are there opportunities to bring other people into the learning situation, e.g. 'public' audience, students at other colleges?
4   How are dialogues structured, guided and supported? How are the rules of academic or professional communication made clear?
5   How can computer-supported communication e.g. Skype, discussion lists, forums, blogs, be used to support ongoing dialogues?
6   Who will give feedback to learners on their progress and how will this be communicated? Have you considered how digital technologies could be used to support peer assessment and review?

General theoretical considerations for design

People learn more effectively when:

1   *They are actively engaged.* Base learning around tasks with the emphasis on learning outcomes, rather than around content to be covered.
2   *They are motivated.* Communicate desired outcomes clearly and relate these to learners' long-term goals. Where appropriate, allow choice over elements of the learning activity and link topics to personal experiences or interests of learners.

3   *Their existing capabilities are brought into play.* Revisit prior knowledge and skills at the start. Recognize and exploit learners' existing capabilities e.g. through collaborative work, shared knowledge-building.

4   *They are appropriately challenged.* Provide support and scaffolding for new activities. Offer more challenging extension activities as an option. Give options for learners with different capabilities and preferences.

5   *They have opportunities for dialogue.* Establish opportunities for dialogue with tutors, mentors and peers during the task. Recognize and reward collaboration as well as autonomy. Consider how dialogue can be maintained between face-to-face sessions, even if this is informally.

6   *They receive feedback.* Ensure tutor feedback at timely points, e.g. after first assignment, after a key session, during revision. Design tasks to give intrinsic feedback if possible. Consider peer feedback as an alternative to tutor feedback. Foster skills of self-evaluation. Ensure learners have examples of successful student work to compare against their own efforts.

7   *They have opportunities for consolidation and integration.* Encourage further practice of key capabilities. Record the processes of learning, so learners can see how they perform. Promote skills of reflection and planning, e.g. through portfolios, action planning.

Some Fundamental Decisions about the Student Experience of Learning

The questions below are edited extracts from materials used by Oxford Brookes University in their Course Design Intensives, to support curriculum design by practitioners working with digital technologies (see Chapter 10, Sharpe and Oliver).

Rationale

From the student point of view and in just a few sentences or bullet points, set out the rationale (or strapline if you want to think of it like that) for this course:

Choosing course texts

1   Agree three or four key textbooks that capture the essential content/syllabus students. You might want to designate some as core and others as optional.

Author	Title	Core/Optional

2   What do you want to be the paramount unit of organization for the student experience: the module or the programme? Locate your programme on the following line:

Modules are the
basis of student
experience

Programme is the
basis of student
experience

3   Circle the underpinning approach to understanding how students learn in this programme (refer to Appendix 1, Three (and a half) approaches to understanding how people learn)?

	Associative	Constructivist (individual)	Constructivist (social)	Situative
Learning is understood as	Building concepts or competences step-by-step	Achieving understanding through active discovery	Achieving understanding through dialogue and collaboration	Developing practice in a particular community

Programme Learning Outcomes

Referring to your course rationale or strapline, list the intended learning outcomes of your course. If possible list programme outcomes for each year of your course. This will enable you to design a coherent assessment strategy for each year of the course. Be sure to include important graduate attributes as well as subject knowledge.

When the list is complete, evaluate your final year LOs against your rationale/ strapline. Do they match?

Blue Skies Planning Checklist

This checklist is used by Oxford Brookes University in their Course Design Intensives (see Chapter 10, Sharpe and Oliver).

The aim of this exercise is to describe the broad scope of your course: why it exists, why it is special, how students and teachers will experience it.

The checklist below is designed to help teachers structure their thinking on the way to producing a programme level storyboard. This builds on decisions made in Appendix 6 'Some fundamental decisions about the student experience'.

Course title and level:
Purpose or main aims of course:
Learning outcomes:
Main strengths of current course, which you would not like to lose:
Main weaknesses of the course which need to be addressed:
Number of students: Number of staff:

Main characteristics of the students as they affect teaching and learning methods: (e.g. you may describe two or three students who describe a range of types that may be on your course, or you may just describe a range in each of several characteristics, like prior learning, diversity, their expectations, their likely access to technology)

Teaching and learning methods (e.g. online lectures, discussion, individualized self-paced learning, small group work, projects, problems, presentations, portfolios)

Assessment methods (both formative, e.g. quizzes, assignments, exercises, problems, seminars, presentations and summative, e.g. exam, coursework, portfolio)

Technology requirements (any special technologies that staff need to develop this course, or students/staff need to study/teach it)

Resources (other than those noted in technology above, e.g. textbooks, printed materials)

Administration (roles, responsibilities, tasks)

Support (how will students be supported on this course?)

Critics' Checklist

This checklist is used by Oxford Brookes University in their Course Design Intensives (see Chapter 10, Sharpe and Oliver).

The aim of this checklist is to guide and structure peer review of each design team's storyboard. Questions on the checklist are used to prompt discussions between course designers, to draw out advantages and potential difficulties of their proposals, and to help them think of alternative solutions.

A suggested structure for your conversations with designers ...

Remember that this process is planned as a useful experience for the course designer(s). Try to use your questioning to draw out of them advantages and potential difficulties of their plan that might not have occurred to them. Give them time to answer questions fully, to think about new solutions, and to take notes of their emerging ideas if they want to.

1   *Student experience*: Ask how a typical student might experience their progress through the learning activity, from start to finish.
2   *Activity design*: Find out which aspects of this activity design are particularly novel and interesting (give each other a chance to showcase the work before you start being too critical!) Are there aspects of this activity that could be done more efficiently or in a more interesting way?
3   *Student support*: Clarify how students will be supported in their learning. What aspects of the teaching, learning and assessment process might be new to them? How has support for this built into the activity? If you see holes in the student support issues, point them out.
4   *Assessment and feedback*: What opportunities are there for feedback to students on their progress before the summative assessment? What opportunities are there to make use of feedback in the production of students' work? How are students being engaged in understanding how the work will be assessed? How will the activity be integrated into the assessment of the course? How is this activity/task linked to learning in other parts of the course?

5   *Outcome audit*: Ask the designer(s) to take one learning outcome and follow through how students will become familiar with it and its related content, have opportunities to practise their developing skills, gain feedback on their learning, and finally, demonstrate their learning related to that outcome in final assessment. Is there a clear link to programme-level learning outcomes?

6   *Diversity*: How have issues of accessibility been accommodated within the design and preparation of the materials? Are there any types of students or student characteristics that are not adequately catered for in the design of the course? How does the design proactively accommodate diversity in the student body?

7   *Staffing*: Who will teach/tutor on the activity? What additional skills/facilities might the staff need? What would make teaching on this course/activity intolerable to you?

8   *Technology*: How much of the technology incorporated in the plan is already available and accessible to you? What additional technological requirements does this activity have? How are students' digital literacies being developed through their engagement in this course/activity?

E-Learning Practice Evaluator

Reflecting on a Learning Activity in a Technology-rich Context

This evaluator was designed for the Joint Information Systems Committee (JISC) Effective Practice workshops and adapted with feedback from participants. It can be used to evaluate an e-learning activity once it has been carried out by learners.

Descriptive questions	Your description
If you have used the Effective Practice Planner, this page closely follows the decisions you took	
What did you ask learners to do (learning task)? Did they do what you expected? Did this help them achieve the learning outcomes? Were there alternatives for learners to choose, and did you notice any patterns in their choices?	
How did learners interact? What kinds of dialogue took place between yourself and the learners, among learners working collaboratively, and with other support staff?	
What resources did they use? Did these prove useful and relevant to learners? Were they accessible and available to all learners? Were there any interesting patterns of use/non- use?	
What technologies did they use? Were these accessible and available to all learners? Did learners have the skills to use them effectively? Were equipment and support adequate?	

Descriptive questions	Your description
What was the e-learning advantage? What advantages were there to using electronic resources or technologies? Consider: accessibility, inclusion, participation, personalization. Or: what challenges did this help you to meet?	
How did learners receive feedback on this activity? Did feedback come from learners (self or peer), from you, or was it intrinsic to the activity itself? Was the feedback part of a formal assessment?	
(Optional) How did this activity support your rationale? How did it express your preferred approach to teaching and learning (ideals, values, beliefs)?	

Reflective questions	Your reflection
What was the experience like for learners? Did they meet the learning outcomes? Did they enjoy the experience? Were they motivated and involved? Have there been any unexpected benefits? *Use any formal or informal feedback, e.g. conversations, feedback forms, observations, etc.*	
What was the experience like for you? Were there any costs to you of taking this approach? Were there any benefits? Did you enjoy it? Did it involve working with other staff, and how was this experience? *Use your own reflections and any evidence you have gathered.*	
What do you think has worked well?	
What would you have done differently?	
How did your approach meet the challenges presented?	
What advice would you give to another teacher working in a similar context to your own?	

Index